The Steel Bonnets

By the same author:

Flashman series
Quartered Safe Out Here
McAuslan Entire
The Pyrates
Black Ajax
Mr. American
The Candlemass Road
The Light's on at Signpost
The Reavers

The Steel Bonnets

The Story of the
Anglo-Scottish Border Reivers

George MacDonald Fraser

Skyhorse Publishing

In memory of
Corporal IKE BLAKENY
of the Border Regiment, killed
by a Japanese sniper at Kinde Wood,
Central Burma, 1945, and for
BOB GRAHAM and SLIM IRVINE,
wounded in the same action

Skyhorse Publishing books may be purchased in bulk at special discounts for sales promotion, corporate gifts, fund raising, or educational purposes. Special editions can also be created to specifications. For details, contact Special Sales Department, Skyhorse Publishing, 555 Eighth Avenue, Suite 903, New York, NY 10018 or info@skyhorsepublishing.com.

www.skyhorsepublishing.com

10 9 8 7 6 5 4 3 2

Library of Congress Cataloging-in-Publication Data

Fraser, George MacDonald, 1925–2008.
The steel bonnets : the story of the Anglo-Scottish border reivers / George MacDonald Fraser.
p. cm.
Originally published: London : Barrie and Jenkins, 1971.
Includes bibliographical references and index.
ISBN-13: 978-1-60239-265-6 (pbk. : alk. paper)
ISBN-10: 1-60239-265-X (pbk. : alk. paper)
1. Scottish Borders (England and Scotland)—History. 2. Border reivers.
3. Cattle stealing—Scottish Borders (England and Scotland)—History.
4. Scotland—History—1057–1603. I. Title.
DA880.B72F7 2008
364.1'0660941—dc22
2008009536

Printed in Canada

Acknowledgements

For their help I am deeply grateful to the Librarians and library staff at Trinity College, Dublin; at Glasgow University; at Carlisle Public Library, and at the Mitchell Library, Glasgow. I am especially grateful to Mr E. F. Ladds, Librarian at Douglas, Isle of Man, for his assistance and kindness, not least in making available to me the excellent collection of Border material contained in the Talbot Library.

I wish also to thank Professor J. D. Mackie of Glasgow, H.M. Historiographer in Scotland, for reading the manuscript and making many helpful suggestions and comments.

And most of all I am indebted to my wife, for the immense work she did in combing through great quantities of State and Border papers and letters; for her advice, suggestions and encouragement at every stage of the book—and for the way she remained faultlessly impartial throughout, despite the fact that she is a Hetherington of the English West March. Without her it would never have been done.

G.M.F.

CONTENTS

The Steel Bonnets

The Border Marches of England and Scotland in the Sixteenth Century

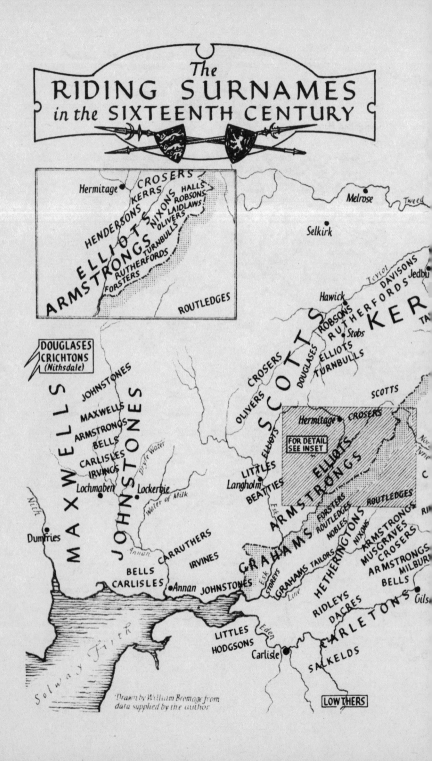

The RIDING SURNAMES in the SIXTEENTH CENTURY

Inset (upper):
Hermitage • CROSERS
KERRS
HENDERSONS
ELLIOTS
ARMSTRONGS
NIXONS HALLS ROBSONS
LAIDLAWS
OLIVERS
TURNBULLS
RUTHERFORDS
FORSTERS
ROUTLEDGES

Main map:
Melrose • Tweed
Selkirk •

Teviot
DAVISONS
Jedbu
Hawick •
SCOTTS ROBSONS RUTHERFORDS KER
CROSERS DOUGLASES Stobs • TA
OLIVERS ELLIOTS
TURNBULLS
SCOTTS

DOUGLASES
CRICHTONS
(Nithsdale)

JOHNSTONES
MAXWELLS
ARMSTRONGS
BELLS
CARLISLES
IRVINGS
Lochmaben • Lockerbie •

Dryfe Water

CROSERS
Hermitage • CROSERS
FOR DETAIL
SEE INSET
ELLIOTS
ARMSTRONGS

MAXWELLS
JOHNSTONES

Water of Milk

Langholm •
LITTLES
BEATTIES

ELLIOTS
ARMSTRONGS

North Tyne
C

FORSTERS
ROUTLEDGES
NOBLES
GRAHAMS
TAILORS
NIXONS
HETHERINGTONS
ARMSTRONGS
MUSGRAVES
CROSERS
ARMSTRONGS
MILBUR
BELLS
RI

Nith
Dumfries •

CARRUTHERS
IRVINES
BELLS
CARLISLES
• Annan
JOHNSTONES

Annan
Esk
Line
Eden

RIDLEYS
DACRES
CARLETONS
Gils

LITTLES
HODGSONS
Carlisle •
SALKELDS

Solway Firth

Drawn by William Bromage from
data supplied by the author

LOWTHERS

"Family" maps which show the country neatly parcelled out with exact boundaries can be misleading, since clans and tribes rarely occupied exact areas. Some surnames, like Forster, might be found widely scattered; others, like Graham and Hume, were more firmly localised. This map is designed to show where various surnames were concentrated or had particular influence, but the limits of such occupation and influence were vague, and there was much overspill. There was a tendency for "pockets" to form—thus Bells can be placed on Gilsland, Elliots on Stobs, Carnabys on Hexham, and Rutherfords near Jedburgh, although their surnames were also to be found elsewhere. On the other hand, the Tynedale and Liddesdale families can only be placed somewhere in the fairly wide areas of their respective dales.

Duns

The Merse
DIXONS
Berwick-on-Tweed

MES
TROTTERS
Tweed
SELBYS
GRAYS
HERONS

Kelso

FORSTERS

ROBSONS
Reede

COLLINGWOODS
Aln
Alnwick

Coquet

HALLS
MILBURNS
POTTS
DUNNES
HEDLEYS STOREYS
READES Otterburn
BSONS
MILBURNS
DOODS YARROWS
HERONS
SHAFTOES
OGLES

FENWICKS
Chipchase
WOODRINGTONS
FORSTERS
FENWICKS

Newcastle-on-Tyne

ltwhistle
YS South Tyne
CARNABYS
Hexham
Tyne

English-Scottish
Boundary

Miles
0   5   10   15

"If Jesus Christ were emongest
them, they would deceave him,
if he woulde heere, trust and
followe theire wicked councells!"

Richard Fenwick 1597

INTRODUCTION

The Border Reivers

At one moment when President Richard Nixon was taking part in his inauguration ceremony, he appeared flanked by Lyndon Johnson and Billy Graham. To anyone familiar with Border history it was one of those historical coincidences which send a little shudder through the mind: in that moment, thousands of miles and centuries in time away from the Debateable Land, the threads came together again; the descendants of three notable Anglo-Scottish Border tribes—families who lived and fought within a few miles of each other on the West Marches in Queen Elizabeth's time—were standing side by side, and it took very little effort of the imagination to replace the custom-made suits with leather jacks or backs-and-breasts. Only a political commentator would be tactless enough to pursue the resemblance to Border reivers beyond the physical, but there the similarity is strong.

Lyndon Johnson's is a face and figure that everyone in Dumfriesshire knows; the lined, leathery Northern head and rangy, rather loose-jointed frame belong to one of the commonest Border types. The only mystery is when the "t" which distinguishes Border Johnstones from the others of the name was dropped from his surname. Billy Graham has frequently advertised his Scottishness, perhaps a little thoughtlessly, since there are more Grahams on the southern side of the line than on the northern, but again, the face is familiar.

Richard Nixon, however, is the perfect example. The blunt, heavy features, the dark complexion, the burly body, and the whole air of dour hardness are as typical of the Anglo-Scottish frontier as the Roman Wall. Take thirty years off his age and you could put him straight into the front row of the Hawick scrum and hope to keep out of his way. It is difficult to think of any face that would fit better under a steel bonnet.

None of this, possibly, is capable of definite proof, but one can at least say that the names go with the faces, and that Johnson and Nixon especially are excellent specimens of two distinct but common Border types.

It seems reasonable to suppose that the people of the Border country have not changed a great deal, physically or characteristically, in four centuries. Although the frontier line still lies between Scot and Englishman, they are now considerably mixed in the racial sense, particularly on the English side. A good half of the people of Carlisle are at least partly Scottish; there are as many Armstrongs and Johnstones as there are Forsters and Hetheringtons. But the racial composition of the Borderland generally has not altered so very much; the Elliots and Fenwicks, Bells and Nixons, Littles and Scotts, Maxwells and Kerrs (and Carrs) are still where they were in the sixteenth century, and although the Border is in many ways an even greater mental barrier than it once was, one can say that both sides together form a distinct and separate cultural and social bloc which is apart from the rest of the British people.

It is always dangerous to generalise, and one hesitates to state too dogmatically what the difference is between the Borderers[1] and the rest. They are not, to put it as tactfully as possible, the most immediately lovable folk in the United Kingdom. Incomers may find them difficult to know; there is a tendency among them to be suspicious and taciturn, and the harsh Border voice, whether the accent is Scots or English, lends itself readily to derision and complaint. No doubt there are Cumbrians who are gay, frivolous folk, and Roxburghshire probably has its quota of fawning, polished sophisticates: they are in a minority, that is all.

This is perhaps a personal point of view; it is, nevertheless, being expressed by one who is a Borderer born and raised in spite of his name. And it can always be disputed. On the credit side, there is a Border virtue which in the human scale should outweigh all the rest, and it is simply the ability to endure, unchanging. Perhaps the highest compliment that one can pay to the people of the Anglo-Scottish frontier is to remark that, in spite of everything, they are still there.

---

1. Borderers—inhabitants of Northumberland, Berwickshire, Roxburghshire, Cumberland, and Dumfriesshire. Add Selkirk and Westmorland to taste.

For if there are qualities in the Border people which are less than amiable, it must be understood that they were shaped by the kind of continuous ordeal that has passed most of Britain by. That ordeal reached its peak in the sixteenth century, when great numbers of the people inhabiting the frontier territory (the old Border Marches) lived by despoiling each other, when the great Border tribes, both English and Scottish, feuded continuously among themselves, when robbery and blackmail were everyday professions, when raiding, arson, kidnapping, murder and extortion were an important part of the social system.

This had very little to do with war between the two countries, who spent most of the century at peace with each other. It was a way of life pursued in peace-time, by people who accepted it as normal. It meant that no man who lived between the Scottish Southern Uplands and the Pennines could walk abroad unarmed in safety; no householder in all the Marches could go to sleep secure; no beast or cattle could be left unguarded. The seamen of the first Elizabeth might sweep the world's greatest fleet off the seas, but for all the protection she could give to her Northumbrian peasants they might as well have been in Africa. While young Shakespeare wrote his plays, and the monarchs of England and Scotland ruled the comparatively secure hearts of their kingdoms, the narrow hill land between was dominated by the lance and the sword. The tribal leaders from their towers, the broken men and outlaws of the mosses, the ordinary peasants of the valleys, in their own phrase, "shook loose the Border". They continued to shake it as long as it was a political reality, practising systematic robbery and destruction on each other. History has christened them the Border reivers.[2]

How this violent and incongruous social condition arose in the comparatively recent history of the British Isles is a strange, frequently misunderstood story.

The English-Scottish frontier is and was the dividing line between two of the most energetic, aggressive, talented and altogether formidable nations in human history. Any number of factors, including geography, race movement, and the Romans decided where the line should be, and once it was there, on the map, on the countryside, and in men's

---

2. Reiver, reaver—robber, raider, marauder, plunderer. The term is obsolete, but lingers on in words like *bereave*.

minds, the stage was set. Possibly English on one side and Scots on the other could have lived peaceably as national neighbours—indeed, for long periods they did; but it was not in the nature of either of the beasts to stay quiet for long. No doubt they ought to have done; successive English kings thought so, and did their utmost, by fair means and foul, to bring about the amity and unity which eventually prevailed At least, unity prevailed; amity is a more questionable commodity, especially north of the Border, even today.

But in the making of Britain, between England and Scotland, there was prolonged and terrible violence, and whoever gained in the end, the Border country suffered fearfully in the process. It was the ring in which the champions met; armies marched and counter-marched and fought and fled across it; it was wasted and burned and despoiled, its people harried and robbed and slaughtered, on both sides, by both sides. Whatever the rights and wrongs, the Borderers were the people who bore the brunt; for almost 300 years, from the late thirteenth century to the middle of the sixteenth, they lived on a battlefield that stretched from the Solway to the North Sea. War after war was fought on it, and this, to put it mildly, had an effect on the folk who lived there.

What this effect was will be examined more closely later; for the moment it is enough to say that constant strife, or the threat of it, bred up a race of hard people along the Border line. They lived in a jungle, and they had to live by jungle rules. This is not to excuse them, if that were necessary, but to explain. If a man cannot live, and ensure that his family lives, within the law, he has no alternative but to step outside it.[3] It was inevitable that the way of life which the Borderer had to follow in time of war should be carried over into what was nominally peace-

---

3. Satchells' lines on the reiver philosophy are often quoted:

> I would have none think that I call them thieves
>
> ★
>
> The freebooter ventures both life and limb
> Good wife, and bairn, and every other thing;
> He must do so, or else must starve and die,
> For all his livelihood comes of the enemie.

The one observation to be made is that "enemie" might mean anyone, either Scottish or English, outside the freebooter's own circle of kinship.

time; habits are hard to break, and here they became so deeply ingrained as to be almost instinctive.

By the sixteenth century robbery and blood feud had become virtually systematic, and that century saw the activities of the steel-bonneted Border riders—noble and simple, robber and lawman, soldier and farmer, outlaw and peasant—at their height.

In the story of Britain, the Border reiver is a unique figure. He was not part of a separate minority group in his area; he came from every social class. Some reivers lived in outlaw bands, but most of them were ordinary members of the community, and they were everywhere in the Marches. The reiver was a rustic, but in some ways a remarkably sophisticated one. In a modern charge sheet he would probably be described as an agricultural labourer, or a small-holder, or gentleman farmer, or even a peer of the realm; he was also a professional cattle-rustler. In addition he was a fighting man who, on the evidence, handled his weapons with superb skill; a guerrilla soldier of great resource to whom the arts of theft, raid, tracking and ambush were second nature.

But he was also often a gangster organised on highly professional lines, who had perfected the protection racket three centuries before Chicago was built. He gave the word "blackmail" to the English language. For many generations he and his people formed almost a lawless state within, or between, two countries, and in spite of all that was done for their suppression, and the complicated international arrangements that were made for their regulation, they flourished until England and Scotland came under one king.

Of course they were checked and stayed, fined and hanged, pursued and evicted, when authority had the time and the strength to exert itself, but this was no more than a staunching process; the hoof-beats had not died away before they were drumming again. From the late Middle Ages until the end of Elizabeth's reign the Marches of England and Scotland were a perpetual badman's territory, dominated by raiders and free-booters, plunderers and rustlers, Border lords and outlaw riders.

Because it was so localised, and is now so long ago, and because the Border ballads and legends have cast a gloss of romance over it, there is a tendency to regard the high midnight of the Border reiver as a stirring, gallant episode in British history. It was not like that; it was as cruel and horrible in its way as Biafra or Vietnam. And the most unusual feature of it was that this was not, at its zenith in the sixteenth century, a case of an innocent, defenceless community in the grip of a war, or of a small criminal element's reign of terror—the Border folk made the war and terror on themselves; it was as much a part of their lives as agriculture. It follows that they were unusual folk, and that the stamp of the old days is on them still. If the Borderer is closer and tougher and dourer than his fellow-countrymen, it is because he is the descendant of men and women who lived by and in the shadow of raid and theft and bloody murder.

How the frontier society was born and grew, how Border raiding became a systematic thing, how the two governments tried to deal with it, how it fitted into the politics and diplomacy of the two realms and into the social life of the area, and how, almost suddenly, it passed away, is the theme of this book. Some of the stories have been told before, not always accurately; immense scholarship has been applied to various aspects of the subject, and I don't wish simply to re-tell old tales, or to presume to improve on the researches of eminent historians. But it has seemed to me, knowing something of the Border and its literature, romantic and factual, that the reivers themselves have never been given a history, and that there are still points to be made, and stories to be told, perhaps in a rather different way.

There is a school of Border writers who may be called the romantics. The first of these is the greatest man the region ever produced, Sir Walter Scott. It is not too much to say that Scott made the legendary Border as most people vaguely understand it; a land of brave men and daring deeds, of gothic mystery and fairytale beauty, of gallant Scot and sturdy Saxon, of high ideals and sweet dreams clothed in ballads that are the very heart of a nation's poetry. All perfectly true, in its way, but not the whole story. Scott knew the other side as well, the blood and the terror and the cruelty and the crime. He, after all, understood the Borderland as probably no one else has ever done, and no other writer or scholar has done anything like as much to rescue its real history from the past. But he was a professional romantic; it was not his job to view his subject as it snarled at him over the business end of a Liddesdale lance; there were no Whartons or Scropes descending on Abbotsford by night to ransack and burn it.

One concludes that most of the romantic writers on the subject had never seen a sword or axe wielded in earnest, or seen a hanging, or a thatch burned in anger, or wakened in terror to the sound of hoof-beats. That was not their fault; but if they had known these things, a little of their enthusiasm for the glamorous side of the Border story might have been modified. Nor is patriotism, a common resort of the apologist, of much use in this context; patriotism was, as will be seen, frequently well down the scale of the Borderer's priorities.

So, while admitting that it is difficult not to see the romantic side, it is important to keep it in perspective.

At the other extreme from the romantics are the historical specialists, who have dealt with various parts of the Border question—international politics, administration, military history, genealogical research, and a host of much smaller topics which have been examined in minute detail. These matters have been exhaustively done, but, quite rightly, they have not usually been concerned with what is called human interest. The Scottish policy of Henry VIII is a fascinating thing, offering as rich a field to the psychiatrist as to the historian, but I am less concerned with the effect that it had on, say, Franco-Scottish relations than with the more immediate and dramatic impact which it had on the good wife of Kirkcudbright who, during a skirmish near her home, actually delivered her husband up to the enemy for safe-keeping. Obviously one must take account of the machinations of Walsingham and James VI and I, but the prime consideration for me is how Nebless Clem Croser went about his business of cattle-rustling, and how the Grahams came to dispossess the Storeys, and how old Sir John Forster's wife got the door shut in the nick of time as a band of reivers came up the stair.

It is necessary, I feel, to try to understand the Border reivers, and if not to excuse what they did, at least to see why they did it. And among all this, to try to see what it must have been like to be a wife or a mother making a home on the Marches.

At the beginning, it is as well to make one or two general points which are perhaps not commonly known. One should dispose immediately of the notion that Border raiding in peace, or even in war-time, was a straight case of England v. Scotland. It wasn't. Raiding went both up and down and sideways. It has been common to show the English as the cops and the Scots as the robbers, but this was not the case. At this time of day no one can say who stole most from where, or who wreaked the greatest havoc; one might take a daring stab and say that probably the southern Scottish counties suffered the greater devastation, on a wide scale, as a result of English activity, including war-time inroads which cannot be classed as reiving proper—although the reiver and the soldier were often indistinguishable in war. On the other hand, the number of regular reiving forays by smaller groups was certainly greater from Scotland into England than vice versa. The net result over the centuries was probably not very different.

The important point is that it was not a one-way traffic, or even a two-way one. Scot pillaged Scot and Englishman robbed Englishman just as readily as they both raided across the frontier; feuds were just as deadly between families on the same side of the Border as they were when the frontier lay between them; Scots helped English raiders to harry north of the line, and Englishmen aided and abetted Scottish inroads. The families themselves often belonged to both sides—there were English Grahams and Scottish Grahams, for example (and no family ever made better use of dual nationality). Add to this the fairly obvious fact that sex attraction is immeasurably stronger than national policy, and the picture becomes more complex still. In spite of official opinion and even prohibition, inter-marriage took place, at least in some areas, to such a degree that one English surveyor made a point of noting particularly those Scots who did *not* have English family ties.

Consider also the perpetual petty jealousies, the conflict of national, family, and personal interest, the great criss-cross of vendetta and alliance, of feudal loyalty and blood tie, the repeated changing of sides and allegiances, and the general confusion bordering on chaos, and one sees that the traditional Anglo-Scottish antipathy, while it was ever-present and mattered considerably, will simply not do as an inviolable rule when one looks closely into Border reiving. National difference was at the root of the business, but it was frequently lost among the running cattle and the fell-side skirmishing.

This was what made the failure of law and order inevitable, so long as Britain was divided into two separate states. While one country could be played off against the other, while the frontier could be used as the safety line in a massive game of Tom Tiddler's Ground, and while the line was crossed by all the tangled threads of blood kinship, marriage, and personal and professional alliance, the reiver system presented an insoluble problem. The international Border law, operated by the Wardens of the Marches and other Border officers, could and did sometimes work surprisingly well, but it was at best a finger in the dyke.

All in all, it is not a pretty story, but in its small way it is essential to what T. H. White called the matter of Britain. The British, and their kinsmen in America and the Commonwealth, count themselves civilised, and conceive of their savage ancestors as being buried in the remote past. The past is sometimes quite close; these ancestors of Presidents Nixon and Johnson, of Billy Graham and T. S. Eliot, of Sir Alec Douglas-Home and the first man on the moon, are not many generations away.

Lastly, I should explain the plan of the book. The story of the reivers is not one that can conveniently be told in strict chronological order, so I have split it into five parts.

Part I is a brief historical sketch up to 1500, to show how the sixteenth-century Borderland was created.

Part II describes what the Border was like in that century, what manner of people lived there, who were the leading robber families, how they lived and ate and dressed and built their homes, what games they played, what songs they sang, and so forth, so that the background of the story can be understood.

Part III describes the reivers and how they rode their raids, the skills and tactics they used, how they conducted their feuds, and how they practised such crimes as blackmail, kidnapping, and terrorism. It also explains how Border law operated under the March Wardens, how the two governments tried to fight the reivers, and what it was like for the ordinary folk living in the frontier country.

Part IV is a historical survey of the reiving century, from 1503 to 1603 (when James VI of Scotland came to the English throne). It shows how the reivers fitted into the history of their time, and what part they played in the long-drawn Anglo-Scottish struggle.

Part V tells how their story ended when England and Scotland came under one king, and the old Border ceased to be.

PART ONE

The Making
of a
Frontier

Hadrian draws the line

In the beginning was the Wall. It runs across the neck of England from Solway to Tyne, a grey stone ghost to remind tourists of the mighty empire that once ruled the world from the Caspian to where Carlisle Cricket Club's pavilion now stands. It is, by any standards, a tremendous monument, to the brilliant, witty Roman emperor who conceived it, to Aulus Platorius Nepos, legate, who supervised its building, and to the three legions who actually dug the complex of ditches and mounds, and raised the parapet and intervening fortresses. They were assisted by Roman sailors and auxiliary troops, and no doubt they received local help, if they called it that, in the fetching and carrying. In five years or thereabouts from 122 A.D. the great rampart, dotted with castles and garrisons, was stretched across the countryside, over meadow and moor, down into steep gullies and up over rocky outcrops, along cliff summits and fell sides, a living symbol of military strength and civil power.

"Verily I have seene the tract of it over the high pitches and steepe descents of hilles, wonderfully rising and falling", wrote the great Elizabethan antiquarian Camden. While the Wall existed, no one in the region could forget Rome, or what Rome stood for.

The natives have never forgotten. In their time they fought and died over the Wall, gaped at it, played on it, reviled it, admired it, and removed its stones to make houses, dry-stane dykes, and sheep folds. Lately the Ministry of Public Building and Works have been working splendidly to restore it and have filled the mortar spaces with a curious green cement. But in spite of what Sir Walter Scott called "the ravages continually made upon it for fourteen centuries", the Wall endures, and no doubt always will.

It is much more than a mere fortification; it is a dividing line between so many things. Between civilisation and barbarism, between safety and danger, between the tamed and the wild, between the settled country and the outland which was too hot to handle and not worth fighting over anyway, between "us" and "them"; we have seen, in our own time, how a wall across Berlin is a barrier of the spirit as much as of bricks and mortar. Hadrian's Wall has lasted immeasurably longer than the Berlin wall ever will, and in its way it lives in the minds of people who have never even heard of it or seen it, or if they have, think of it only as an interesting relic which stands at an inconvenient distance from their cars and coaches.

Although any Northern Englishman can answer in five words the question: why was it built? ("To keep the Scots out"), there is still learned dispute on the point. The suggestion that it was erected to keep the inhabitants of England *in* has been advanced, not altogether frivolously; so far as the Wall was there for effect, it certainly operated in both directions. The layman, looking at its imposing size—it was originally about twenty feet high and ten wide, and although no part of it today is as tall as this, it is still an awe-inspiring barrier—may be excused for thinking it was a defensible castle wall on a gigantic scale. In fact, it was not intended to be a Maginot Line. As Viscount Montgomery has pointed out, it was a deterrent rather than a defence, which could never have resisted a well-organised invasion, and indeed the wild men from the north overran it and its chain of castles and platoon strongpoints on at least three occasions.

But it was not an obstacle that any raider could take lightly; even if he succeeded in crossing it, and escaping the attention of Roman sentries who were never more than half a mile away, and usually no doubt a good deal closer, he still had the problem of returning with whatever he had lifted on the southern side. The Wall was, in effect, a glorified police beat seventy miles long, manned by hard men who must have detested it. Any soldier hates cold and rain; to some of the men who garrisoned the wall, and who came from the Mediterranean lands, the raw damp and biting northern winds must have been intolerable. One can feel sorry for a cavalryman named Victor of the First Ala Asturum, who was born in North Africa and is buried at South Shields; he must have felt a long way from home. When one looks north into the bleak distance from Housesteads, and considers the kind of enemy who lived there, one can see that the Wall cannot have been a popular posting.

But whatever it did to the morale of Roman soldiers, the Wall had a lasting effect on the minds of those who lived either side of it. The regions and the people might have different names from those they bear today; the frontier might shift, as it did; the Romans might go and be forgotten; new waves of people and cultures might come to the land, but the Wall stayed, a permanent reminder of division. Long before there were Englishmen and Scotsmen, long before they had chosen their own subjects of contention and violence, long before there were Elliots or Fenwicks or Armstrongs or Ridleys, the frontier had been made, the line drawn. Undoubtedly, if the wall had been maintained at the outpost line of Forth and Clyde, or if, by some queer turn of history, the boundary had been established from Mersey to Humber, it would have happened there instead, in a different, unimaginable way. Publius Aelius Hadrianus, with the eye of a sound soldier and administrator, caused his wall to be built across the shortest distance and on the best defensible line. It was not his fault that the country on either side might have been designed for brigandage and foray; nor was it his fault that the people who came after were what they were. Land, until it is highly civilised and urbanised, gets the kind of people who are suited to it, and the country of the Wall was no exception.

By Hadrian's work, however, the first tangible and lasting division was made. He did as much as anyone to ensure, quite unintentionally, that the people who live in Gretna speak with a different accent from those who inhabit Longtown, a few miles away. And the men who built the Wall in the rain, and defended it, and died beneath it, and begot their children to grow up beside it, and finally left it, probably looked back as it faded into the mist and thought what a waste of time it had all been. They were quite wrong.

II

The moving boundaries

After the Romans came the deluge. It was the time of the barbarians, whose frontiers moved with them. Once the Wall had been overrun, it ceased to matter for the time being, which was the best part of a thousand years. In that time the frontiers of middle Britain came and went as forgotten kingdoms were made and unmade. From the west came the Scots, into the long sea-lochs and mountains of Argyll; from the east the great tide of Angles, and the kingdom of Northumbria spread north across the Wall-line as far as the Forth; westward of it ran the land of Strathclyde of the Britons; in the highland north the Picts lived, and fought it out with the Scots until they were absorbed.

Norse and Danish rovers from the cold seas over Britain came to Orkney, Shetland, and the Western Isles, to the Northumbrian sea-board and Strathclyde; they were a strong strain whose names and faces endure across the Border country. And another influence arrived, but without force of arms; a turbulent, fearless Irish priest, Columba, and a Briton named Ninian brought the benefits of Christianity to Scotland, and south of the Wall the quiet Aidan and the shepherd, Cuthbert, spread the gospel in Northern England, not without controversy; before serious Anglo-Scottish political differences began, there was a north–south dispute over the manner in which priestly heads should be shaved.

Very gradually, out of the changing fortunes of races and kingdoms, a pattern began to emerge. English kings loosened the hold of the sea-rover people, and what may be seen as the prototype of an English-Scottish struggle took place when in the tenth century Athelstan of England fought a great and successful battle against a combined force of Scots, Norsemen, and Britons; the site of the battle is lost, but one theory is that it was fought by the flat-topped mountain called Birns-wark, over the Solway.

England was slowly emerging as a nation, and although the name was still uncoined, Scotland was being born north of the Cheviot Hills. The line was coming back to something not far away from the boundary that Hadrian had drawn, across the narrow waist of Britain. In the eleventh century the mould was beginning to set; Scotland had her first great king, that Malcolm Canmore who in Shakespeare's version has bored and bewildered generations of school children with his self-examination, but who in fact did kill Macbeth and established himself firmly on the Scottish throne.

Equally importantly, perhaps, he married, a princess of the English house of Alfred. She was a pious, thoroughly determined lady, and she seems to have inspired something like awe in the great rough fighting chief she married. In her influence on him, and on her adopted country, she was one of the most important women in Scottish history; through her, much that was English was imported, and remained with lasting effect on southern Scotland.

But the vital event of Malcolm's reign took place far outside Scotland: in 1066 William of Normandy conquered England. In settling his kingdom he dealt ruthlessly with its northern areas, making a scorched desert from York to Durham, and floods of refugees poured over into Scotland; among them was the Princess Margaret who Malcolm of Scotland married. William was a thorough king, and as hardy a ruffian as Canmore himself; when Malcolm gave asylum to the refugees, and took up arms on their behalf, the Conqueror marched into Scotland in 1072, confronted Malcolm, made peace with him, and obtained his submission.

The last three words demand some explanation. Scottish kings had reached agreements with English rulers before; submission had been made, homage paid, and forms of superiority acknowledged. After Birnswark, Constantine of Scotland had become the vassal of Athelstan. But exactly what such agreements implied we cannot say; it is doubtful if the consenting parties could have said, either. Forms might be agreed publicly, but private interpretations would obviously vary. In later years, when Scottish kings were also English titled land-owners, the matter of vassalage had a real meaning, at least so far as their English possessions were concerned, and if an English king chose to understand vassalage in a wider sense, he was simply exploiting the situation to his own advantage, but without good moral ground.

Out of the historic tangle, there certainly emerged among English kings a belief that they had, traditionally, some kind of superiority over the Scottish king, and no doubt a feeling that for the sake of political security and unity—one might say almost of tidiness—it would be better if Scotland were under English control, or at best, added to England. This attitude can be charitably seen as politically realistic, or at the other extreme, as megalomaniac; it is all in the point of view.

Canmore made his submission, then, for what it was worth, but before long he was harrying in England again. In his earlier inroads he had done fearful damage, and carried off so many prisoners that "for a long time after, scarce a little house in Scotland was to be found without English slaves", which no doubt helped the process of Anglicisation in southern Scotland. Now Malcolm was back again, but he came once too often, and was killed at Alnwick in 1093.

By then the Conqueror was dead, but his energetic successor, Rufus, was an equally powerful influence in the making of the Border. It was he who had finally taken Carlisle from the Scots in 1092, settled an English colony, and rebuilt the city which had long lain in ruins, adding to it the castle which was the parent of the present fortress, and which complemented the "New Castle" which his father had built on the eastern seaboard. In addition Rufus helped Edgar, Canmore's son, to recover the Scottish throne, which had been in dispute after Canmore's death.

And then peace broke out. It seems surprising, in view of what had been and what would one day follow, but there now began an era of tranquillity between England and Scotland, and consequently along the Border, which was to endure almost uninterrupted for nearly two hundred years. It began when, following Rufus, Henry I married Malcolm Canmore's daughter; the close blood tie between the rulers, England's preoccupation with the Continent, and the absence of any major Anglo-Scottish difference, all helped to keep the peace.

In this quiet time the independent state of Scotland was finally made. The three sons of Canmore and Margaret—Edgar, Alexander, and David—shaped it in the decisive half century from 1100 to 1150. They were friends of England's, and they helped to fashion their kingdom in England's likeness; at the same time, England was content to leave the Scots alone.

Like their mother, the three sons were godly folk, and under them the great religious houses rose and flourished, in the Borders as much as elsewhere. They saw that organised religion was a prime instrument of political stability, and used it; they also encouraged what has been called the Norman invasion of Scotland. By promoting Norman settlement, they introduced another civilising influence in the shape of the Norman gentleman-adventurer loyal to the monarch and capable of keeping order in the area he was given to rule. Gradually the feudal system was introduced into Scotland, but although Normans were settled extensively in the Border area, the new system never entirely displaced the old pattern of clanship and family chieftainship. This never died; Border, like Highland blood, was a lot thicker than charters, and the traditional tribal loyalties endured up to and beyond the union of the crowns. Its importance in the Border country cannot be over-rated.

Under the three kings there emerged a southern Scotland very like the England over the Border. The language was the same, as were the habits and customs and systems of government; the frontier was perhaps less of a barrier then than at any other time in British history. The day was dawning which later centuries were to look back on as Scotland's golden age. For the Borderers, on either side, it was a time when they began to forget the horrors that war had once unleashed on them from beyond the line; when the peasant in Teviotdale and Berwickshire, in Tynedale or among the Cumbrian fells, could go to sleep secure.

Not that the temple of Janus was permanently closed; on three notable occasions the armies were busy across the Marches, and there was blood and fire from the Solway to the Tyne. But three wars in a century and a half, between England and Scotland when they were still in a semi-civilised condition, is not bad going; it was tranquillity itself compared with what was to come.

These outbreaks stemmed mainly from the fact that since the Scottish kings were part-English, and had considerable stakes in England— David, for example, held land in half a dozen English counties and was an English nobleman—they took an active interest in the question of the English succession. At the same time, their political duty marched with expansionist interest, and the northern English counties, to which there was at least an arguable Scottish claim, might in the process of settling the English domestic problem be secured to the Scottish side of the frontier.

Thus the Borders suffered again. In the period 1136–38 David was over the frontier, seizing Carlisle and Newcastle and devastating

Northumberland, until, when he was in full cry southwards, he encountered under the shadow of the great holy standards of the saints at Northallerton, a phenomenon that was to astound and terrify all Europe. This was the English peasant with his bow; beaten by the arrow shower, David was stopped, but he still managed to retain control of the northern shires.

Forty years later another Scottish King, William, carried his new rampant lion standard south in the debate between Henry II and his sons; he failed to take Carlisle and Wark, but wasted the countryside; a truce followed, and another invasion, and this time William divided his army, like Custer, into three, the better to scour the countryside. It was a fatal mistake; the English caught him near Alnwick, and Henry II, fresh from doing penance for Becket, no doubt felt his penitence rewarded by the capture of the King of Scots. Becket's spirit, his religious advisers assured him, had obviously been at work on England's behalf.

William's ransom was submission to England, of a most comprehensive kind, hostages of rank, and various Scottish strongholds, including the Border castles of Berwick, Jedburgh, and Roxburgh. However, Richard the Lionheart, when he found himself pressed for money, sold most of these advantages back to Scotland.

Much worse than either of these wars, from the Border point of view, was the outbreak of 1215, when the young Scottish king, Alexander II, became involved in the English civil war of King John and the barons. Aiding the Northern English lords, Alexander provoked a terrible retaliation from John; the Eastern Marches on both sides of the frontier were ravaged; Morpeth, Alnwick, Roxburgh, Dunbar, Haddington, and Berwick were burned, and the inhabitants of the last brutally tortured by John's mercenaries; "the king himself disgracing majesty by setting fire, with his own hand, to the house in which he had lodged".[1]

The Scottish retaliatory sweep through the English Borders was equally barbarous. As in the English inroad, churches and monasteries suffered along with the rest, and one ancient chronicler noted with satisfaction that a great number of the despoilers of one Cumbrian abbey were drowned in the Eden, weighed down with their loot.

But in the end, all that Scotland achieved was the loss forever of the

---

1. Ridpath, *The Border History*, p. 85.

Northern English counties; the Border line was finally established more than 1000 years after Hadrian, from the Solway to Berwick. It made no great difference to the Border people, who might well have been thankful that despite David and William the Lion and Henry II and John, and the petty squabbling for the English throne, the Marches had, by and large, been left reasonably peaceful during the twelfth and thirteenth centuries. In that time, the Border as a separate entity came into being; divided and yet united by a strange chemistry far above international politics. Half-English, half-Scottish, the Border was to remain a thing in itself; there, as nowhere else, however much they might war and hate and destroy in centuries to come, Englishmen and Scotsmen understood each other.

III

England v. Scotland, 1286–1500

The golden age, of Scotland, of Anglo-Scottish harmony, and of the Border country, ended when King Alexander III of Scotland fell over a cliff in 1286. Few stumbles—if indeed His Majesty was not pushed— have been more important than that one.

Until then, as we have seen, the frontier had not been an unusually troubled place. It had suffered, but not too severely by medieval standards; the two countries had been growing up and finding their feet. The year 1286 was to see the opening of a new era. From then onward Scotland was to be of increasing importance to England. This was bound to happen as England developed as a nation state; inevitably, too, a new Anglo-Scottish relationship was born. The reasons why these things happened are simple enough, but they are fundamental to British history, and they changed the shape of the world. The new Anglo-Scottish attitudes which were assumed after 1286 have developed and been modified, but even today they bear the imprint of those decisive years in the late thirteenth century when the relationship between England and Scotland was so decisively altered.

It may not be out of place to leave the mainstream of history just for a moment, to look closer at what I have called Anglo-Scottish attitudes. In simple terms—one might call them historically colloquial —and with tremendous daring, one can try to look at the traditional English-Scottish relationship from what, one hopes, is as nearly impartial a British point of view as possible. (Practically every word of what follows will be denied, refuted, and laughed to scorn somewhere or other; I would only remark that the conclusions have been reached by a Scot born and bred in England, and accustomed to being regarded as a Scotsman south of the Border, and an Englishman north of it. Which in itself is probably significant of the attitudes on both sides.)

The Scot has, and one suspects always has had, something of an inferiority complex where his big, assertive, overpowering neighbour is concerned. It is no wonder. The English race are certainly the most dynamic in history since the Romans. Within a few hundred years they turned themselves from a little nation state on an off-shore European island into the most profound influence in the world: they spread themselves, their language, their products and above all, their ideas, over the face of the earth. There has never been anything quite like them. Admittedly, at their peak they had the Scots helping them, and only a national extremist would worry about whether the Scots' contribution, per capita, was above or below average. The point is that the English were by far the major share of the effort; as a national power-house, they were in a class by themselves.

Scotland has lived with and alongside this for several centuries, and that in itself is an achievement. If anything in their history demonstrates that the Scots are remarkable, it is that in spite of being physically attached to England, they have survived as a people, with their own culture, laws, institutions, and, like the English, their own ideas.

But it has not been easy, and the marks show. The Scots are an extraordinarily proud people, with reason, as they are quick to point out, and like most geniuses, highly sensitive. Where England is concerned, this sensitivity borders on neurosis. Buried deep in the Scottish national consciousness is the memory of a cliff-hanging struggle for independence, which lasted more than three centuries in the physical sense, and in the minds of some Scots continues today. They know, better than anyone, how easily England spread itself, often apparently without trying, and the fear of English domination by force has to some extent been replaced by a fear of English supremacy almost by default.

In fact, if the Scot would look, or could look, objectively at his history, he would see that the English menace was perhaps over-rated, not in physical terms, for there it was truly immense, but in what can only be called a spiritual sense. Scotland's vitality has always been strong enough, and to spare, to resist outside influence.

But a small country that survives in Scotland's situation, under the shadow of a reigning champion, becomes quite naturally suspicious, sensitive, and fiercely jealous in regard to its neighbour. It fears him, but cannot help imitating him and being drawn to him. England appreciates this situation completely; the canny Henry VII put it into words when he noted that the larger inevitably attracts the smaller. And from its position of superiority it is natural that England should tend to overlook its smaller neighbour, and take Scotland very much for granted. Indeed, to England, Scotland is an appendage, an extension of the English whole, and when Scotland, resenting this attitude, makes its indignation known, the English are well aware that to find the indignation trivial or amusing is the very way to drive the Scot to distraction.

It must not be thought from this that the English under-rate the Scots. Far from it; they may forget or ignore Scotland, and patronise manifestations of Scottishness, but for the Scots people, for the Scot as an individual when he comes to their attention, they reserve a higher respect than they show to anyone else. They recognise the Scots as formidable, and are secretly just a little frightened of them. In their case it may not be folk-memory, although Scotland in its time was a very real danger to England, simply by virtue of its existence on the same island; more probably it has its roots in the knowledge that a Scotsman on the make is a terrible thing.

The present state of Anglo-Scottish relations, if one can call them that, and the beginning of their peaceful relationship in the sixteenth century, are to be traced to the same root: England was a menace to Scotland because Scotland was, by its separate existence, a constant anxiety to England. In the sphere of medieval politics, and in the politics of a later day, Scotland was a key to England—a foreign and potentially hostile and dangerous state on her very border, offering a stepping-stone to England's enemies, and not infrequently joining in against England when the latter was busily engaged on the Continent. How great a menace this posed was seen even after the union of the crowns, when only two centuries ago the London government found itself within an ace of falling to northern invasion.

To successive English monarchs Scotland was an embarrassment; for the safety of the English realm a neutral if not amiable Scotland was a necessity, and the surest—indeed, some thought the only—way to that happy state was to have Scotland firmly under English control. A reasonable enough point of view, but an objective to be realised only by the most skilful management, great strength, and endless patience. It took almost 500 years, in the long run. The period from 1286 to 1500, with which we are now concerned, in which the condition of the people in the Border districts was so radically influenced, occupied about half that time.

*

One can take as a starting point the night in March 1286 on which the Scottish King, Alexander III, in haste to return to his beautiful wife, set off in the dark against his counsellors' advice, and broke his neck in falling from the path. Scotland was left, for once, in a reasonably quiet and prosperous condition, united and in a viable national state. But with the death of Alexander the throne passed from a good king, in the prime of life, to an infant, his grand-daughter Margaret, who was not even in the country.

Subsequently Edward I of England saw the possibilities of bringing Scotland under control. A marriage between his son and the infant queen seemed the logical step, but Margaret died in 1290, and Scotland was left with a most difficult question of succession. To cut a long story short, Edward used the situation to realise his own claim to overlordship of Scotland. Balliol, his puppet on the Scottish throne, so far forgot himself as to conclude an alliance with France, and Edward's highhandedness and interference in Scottish internal affairs was answered by Scottish inroads into Cumberland and Northumberland in 1296. "They wrought some mischief", and whatever the immediate damage done to the English Borderers, the consequences were dramatic.

The preliminaries to open war included, on Edward's side, the seizure of property held in England by dissident Scots, and the massacre by the Scots of English sailors at Berwick. Edward, at Newcastle with a considerable force, demanded Balliol's appearance in vain; while he was waiting he learned that the lord of the English castle of Wark had abandoned his charge and gone over to the Scots, "the violence of his passion for a Scotch lady . . . proving too strong for his bond of duty to his king". Edward sent reinforcements to Wark, but the fugitive English lord returned unexpectedly with a Scottish raiding party and cut the reinforcements to bits in the dark. (Not a major incident in the campaign, but a perfect example of how national and personal affairs crossed and countered each other on the Border, and how Anglo-Scottish attraction could be even more powerful than Anglo-Scottish distaste. Here was the Borderer, self-sufficient and apart, using the frontier for his own ends in despite of central authority.)

Edward is said to have thanked God that *he* hadn't started the war; he did not doubt his capacity to finish it. He waited at Wark with his army, which included some Scottish nobles, among them a rugged young knight named Robert Bruce.

Nor did he have to wait long. The Scots, arming on the Borders for the crunch which was obviously coming, struck first across the western march. They devastated the country north of Carlisle, burned the city's suburbs, and stormed the walls which were England's bastion on the north-west frontier. The city held, not for the first or last time, with its womenfolk lending assistance in hurling stones and hot water down on the besiegers, and the Scots retired over the Border again.

Edward ignored them. He had made his plan, and he carried it out with ruthless efficiency. He took Berwick, the Scots suffering dreadful loss. No one can be sure quite how extensive or callous the massacre was, yet it is of some importance, because certain historians fix on Berwick's fall as a turning-point in Anglo-Scottish relations. The general opinion is that 7000 to 8000 Scots were killed; it does appear that Edward deliberately killed every man capable of bearing arms. One version says that later the women—and presumably the children— were sent into Scotland.

On the other hand, it has been suggested that the English slaughtered everyone in the town, regardless of age or sex. "Indiscriminate butchery", says one historian,[1] and the total of dead has been placed as high as 17,000. It is certainly not impossible that Edward ordered a general massacre, *pour encourager les Ecossais;* he was perfectly capable of it. If he did, then there may be grounds for the contention that this, more than anything else, bred hatred of England north of the line. I would doubt it; at least, so far as its lasting effect is concerned, it seems

1. Hume Brown.

unlikely that Scottish reivers three centuries later were galloping south thinking "Remember Berwick". But even if its effect has been over-stated, the Berwick massacre was another strong link in the chain of Anglo-Scottish hostility.

Edward now addressed himself to bringing Scotland to heel. It was not difficult. He marched through eastern Scotland as far as Elgin, defeating the Scots at Dunbar en route, received submission on all sides, appropriated the Stone of Destiny, and so back to Berwick again. He had taken five months over the campaign, and only once had to spend a night under canvas.

But Edward, like many native Scottish kings, was to discover that it was easier to get control of Scotland than to keep it. His triumphal progress had been designed to show Scotland who was master; in the place of the abject Balliol he left only a governor, John de Warrenne, but with English garrisons in the castles, English justice, and English taxes. It was not enough for the task, as Edward should have realised. To subdue Scotland, he would have had to treat it as he had treated Berwick. Instead, he made his tour, left behind an elderly and in-competent governor, and hoped for peace. What he got was William Wallace.

The story of the Scottish revolt has been told so many times that one need not go into it again. Its political effects were enormous, not least along the Border. While first Wallace and later Bruce carried the torch, while Edward, probably the ablest soldier-king England ever had, came again and died, old and done, in the Cumberland marshes, while the battles were fought and the English gradually borne south-ward again, the Borders learned what it was to be a no man's land. After Wallace's victory at Stirling, where the Scots gave a foretaste of things to come by flaying the corpse of Edward's detested treasurer, Cressingham, Northern England had been invaded; Northumberland was subjected to systematic plunder and devastation; to the west, Car-lisle again held out, but Cumberland was laid waste as far as Cocker-mouth and the Lakes. The county struck back, and Clifford's Cum-brians harried Annandale, slaughtering and burning. So it went on, to and fro, and while Scotland and England settled the great issue, the Borderland was being created in a sense that neither set of national leaders would have understood. Edward and Wallace left a terrible legacy, and to the people of the Marches it hardly mattered who had started it all. One thing the war ensured; whatever treaties might be made and truces agreed at the top, however often a state of official peace existed, there was never again to be quiet along the frontier while England and Scotland remained politically separate countries.

Bannockburn was the high point in Scotland's fight for independence. Bruce, whatever reservations may be held about his character, was that rare combination of an inspiring leader, a good general, and a personally expert fighting man. Under his supervision, the finest army England had ever put into the field was destroyed in two days; the English chivalry broke its heart against the steel rings of the Scottish infantry, and by night on the second day England's king was in flight, the best of his country dead or captured, and his father's dream of a unified Britain had evaporated. Indeed, it had been easier to take a kingdom from the son than a yard of ground from his father.

It was a smashing victory, and the general dismay in England was especially strong in the north, with good cause. Scottish forces under Edward Bruce and James Douglas poured into the English East March; Northumberland was pillaged again, and Durham only escaped similar treatment by paying a mighty ransom. Yorkshire and Westmorland were less fortunate, being plundered of cattle and prisoners; Appleby was sacked and burned, along with other towns; Redesdale and Tynedale, favourite targets of later raids, were ravaged, and Cumberland was forced to disgorge tribute to the Scottish king.

Bruce had been humane to his beaten enemies at Bannockburn; it is interesting to note that the surviving invaders of Scotland probably received better treatment than the civilian inhabitants of the northern shires who had taken no part in the campaign. Not that this was inconsistent with the chivalric code; indeed, it seems to have been part of it.

A significant feature of this Scottish invasion was that it saw the levying of vast indemnities from the English Borderers; Bruce set the example, on a large scale, for those later generations of Border gangsters who made blackmail and protection racketeering systematic.

Without going into further detail of the great raids and counterraids of this period, it can be judged in what condition the War of Independence left the Borderland. It had been most brutally used; in addition to the ravages of the contending armies, there had been an unusually heavy rainfall in the year after Bannockburn; seed rotted, crops could not be got in, sheep and cattle were dying. When Edward II

again marched into Scotland in 1315 "bread could scarcely be found
for the sustenance of his family",[2] and the expedition was abandoned.
It was as bad on one side as on the other—so bad, that another Border
phenomenon emerged.

"Many of the English who dwelt nigh the Marches, wearied out
with their sufferings, and despairing of protection from their own king,
abandoned their country, and confederating with the Scots, became
companions and guides of their incursions into England, and sharers
with them of the spoils of their unhappy countrymen".[3]

The guide-lines were being drawn with a vengeance; in the struggle
for survival the Border was learning new rules. Before the war, raiding
and foraying across the frontier has been less than a local industry;
invasions and attacks there had certainly been, in time of war, but for
more than a century before Edward I began to practise his Scottish
policy, the Border had been at peace with itself. The years of Bruce
and Wallace and the two Edwards changed all that; a new order was
instituted, not by any positive attempt of policy, but by a gradual and
inevitable development. People who have suffered every hardship
and atrocity, and who have every reason to fear that they will suffer
them again, may submit tamely, or they may fight for survival. The
English and Scots of the frontier were not tame folk.

*

When the War of Independence began the Borders had been moving
forward towards civilisation; when they ended the people of the
Marches had returned to something like the cave ages. Centuries of
progress had been destroyed in a generation, and the natives, to quote
Scott, had been carried back in every art except those which concerned the destruction of each other.

Partly this arose from the type of war prescribed, says Fordun, by
Bruce for the defeat of the invading English.

> On foot should be all Scottish war
> By hill and moss themselves to wear;
> Let wood for walls be bow and spear.
> In strait places gar keep all store,
> And burn the plain land them before;
> Then shall they pass away in haste,
> When that they find naething but waste.

2. Ridpath, p. 173.   3. Ibid.

> With wiles and wakening on the night,
> And meikle noises made on height.

Che Guevara would have approved every word of it. The Scots, unable except on a few notable occasions to match the might of England in pitched battle, fought a campaign to which their people and country were particularly suited. They scorched the earth, destroyed their own homes and fields, took to the hills and the wilderness with their beasts and all they could move, and carried on the struggle by onfall, ambush, cutting supply lines, and constant harrying. It was a wasting, cruel war, and they carried it into England whenever they could, so that both sides of the Border suffered alike.

What resulted was not only guerrilla warfare, but guerrilla living. In times of war the ordinary Borderers, both English and Scottish, became almost nomadic; they learned to live on the move, to cut crop subsistence to a minimum and rely on the meat they could drive in front of them. They could build a house in a few hours and have no qualms about abandoning it; they could travel great distances at speed and rely on their skill and cunning to restock supplies by raiding. All these things they were forced to do while English and Scottish armies marched and burned and plundered what was left of their countryside. This was how they were to live whenever war broke out for the next two and a half centuries.

Unfortunately, to the ordinary people, war and peace were not very different. The trouble with all Anglo-Scottish wars was that no one ever won them; they were always liable to break out again. There was no future for the Borderer in trying to lead a settled existence, even in so-called peace-time. Why till crops when they might be burned before harvest? Why build a house well, when it might be a ruin next week? Why teach children the trades of peace when the society they grew up in depended for its existence on spoiling and raiding?

And of course there was national hatred, ever growing. The other country was always the author of all ills, and it was natural to take revenge.

So they had to live as best they could, and in the two centuries following the War of Independence the Border developed its system of existence, which was seen in full flower in the sixteenth century, between Flodden and the accession of a Scottish king to the throne of England. It was a system of armed plunder, from neighbours as well as from subjects of the opposite realm. The astonishing thing about it was that, while both governments officially deplored what must be called the reiver economy, they exploited it quite cynically for their own ends. The Borders were an ever-ready source of fighting men, a permanent mobile task force to be used when war broke out. If by some strange process of mass hypnosis, all the Elliots and Armstrongs and the like on one side, and all the Forsters and Musgraves on the other, had suddenly been induced to burn their weapons and become peaceful peasants, there would have been consternation in London and Edinburgh. The Border, in a sense, was a bloody buffer state which absorbed the principal horrors of war. With the benefit of hindsight, one could almost say that the social chaos of the frontier was a political necessity.

In fairness to the two central authorities, they did try to pacify as far as they could, and this not being very far, they too adapted to the special conditions. Rules were drawn up for governing, if that is the word, the turbulent Anglo-Scottish Border society. The Wardens, again both English and Scottish, who were to be the nominal overseers of the community, made their appearance at the time of the War of Independence, and their roles as defenders of their respective national frontiers and co-operating governors of the Marches, developed from there. But the laws that were made specially for the Borders were self-defeating; they were in themselves a recognition of abnormality, and at worst they even encouraged it.

So the reiving system developed. From the Bannockburn era onwards the tenor of Border life was geared to it, and no medieval political development was strong enough to alter it. In a medieval context, what happened on the Border does not stand out especially, because it blended into those violent times. But with the advance of civilisation, the gradual alteration of human values, the tendency—admittedly not all that noticeable sometimes—to prefer diplomacy to violence, the anachronism of Border life was seen in greater relief. In the sixteenth century, when England at least was beginning to look far beyond her own coasts, when the spirit of Western man was being reborn, when internal peace was a not uncommon occurrence, the men of the Border were still going their old ways, lifting and looting, settling their disputes largely by force, clinging to their old customs and their own peculiar ethical code. Theirs was a frontier on which only the fittest had survived; what emerged in the 1500s was a very hardy growth.

PART TWO

People of the Marches

IV

Border country

Ask a Scotsman where "the Borders" are and he will indicate the counties of Roxburgh, Selkirk, Peebles, and Berwick. This is actually about one quarter of the Borderland, and includes some areas which are not really Border country at all. To most Scots the country which used to be called the West March is not within "the Borders", a curious example of eastward orientation which has historical roots.

Ask an Englishman where "the Borders" are and he may well not know, but he will recognise the singular "Border". To him it means the frontier with Scotland and nothing else.

This has to be explained, because the adjective Border in the context of this book covers that much wider area occupied by the old Marches, three in each country, which stretched on the Scottish side from the River Cree to the North Sea coast, and on the English from the coast of Cumberland to that of Northumberland. In Scotland the depth of the Marches was bounded by the Lammermuir Hills and the Southern Uplands; in England they covered, to all intents, the counties of Cumberland, Westmorland, and Northumberland. (It is worth remembering that the frontier line does not run straight east and west between the two countries, but south-west to north-east, and that at some points Scotland is actually south of England.)

The whole region, the very heart of Britain, contains some of the loveliest and some of the bleakest country in the British Isles. Along the central part of the frontier line itself is the great tangled ridge of the Cheviots, a rough barrier of desolate treeless tops and moorland with little valleys and gulleys running every way, like a great rumpled quilt. They are not very high, although they were steep enough to frighten Defoe and make his horse "complain", but they are bleak and lonely beyond description, ridge after ridge of sward and rough grass stretching away forever, and an eternal breeze sweeping across the tufty slopes. One walks in them with head constantly turning to the long crests on either side, but seeing nobody. Like their relations, the Cumberland fells and the broken foothills of the Southern Uplands, they are melancholy mountains; probably only the Border people feel at home in them, but even the incomer will recognise them as the most romantic hills in the world .

To the north are the Scottish dales, the Scott country which has had all the adjectives lavished on it, and is indeed beautiful, with its bright rivers and tree-lined valleys and meadows, its fairytale hills and its air of timelessness. "The beautiful valleys full of savages", as someone called them. South of the Cheviots are the Northumberland valleys, less picturesque than their Scottish counterparts, and suffering by comparison with the splendid dales of Lakeland to the west.

At either end of the Cheviots there are coastal plains and good farmlands—they were good even in the sixteenth century—but for the most part the Border is mountain, for where the Cheviots stop the hills to north and south continue, fells and Pennines and Southern Uplands. It is the hills that people remember; "craggi and stoni montanes", as John Leland called them in the 1530s, and his contemporaries echoed him. "Lean, hungry and waste" was Camden's view. Even from a distance one can conjure up sinister pictures from the names of the Border hill country—Foulbogskye, Ninestanerig, Muckle Snab, Bloody Bush, Slitrig, Flodden, Blackcleuch, Wolf Rig, Hungry Hill, Crib Law, Foulplay Know, Oh Me Edge, Blackhaggs, and so on; it is obviously not a palm-fringed playground.

The Border country was divided for administrative purposes into six areas known as Marches, three on the Scottish side and three on the English. Each of the six Marches had a governing officer known as a Warden, appointed by their respective governments; a detailed description of their work is given in Chapter XVIII, but for the moment it will do to say that their duties were to defend the frontier against invasion from the opposite realm in war-time, and in peace to put down crime and co-operate with the Wardens across the Border for the maintenance of law and order. Unfortunately they often fell far short in this duty; some of them were actually among the worst raiders and feuders on the frontier. The extent of the Marches which they ruled in the sixteenth century is shown on the maps at the beginning of this book.

The English and Scottish East Marches were the smallest of the six, though by no means less important than the others. They fronted each other exactly along the Borderline from near Carham on the Tweed to a point just north of Berwick, and if any stretch of the frontier could claim to have comparatively law-abiding inhabitants, it was this. Left to themselves, they might have been quiet enough, but they were never left; the good farm lands towards the coast attracted severe raiding from the Middle Marches, and there were no natural mountain defences, but only "plain champian countrey"; the river Tweed was very easily fordable.

In war-time the East Marches suffered particularly badly, for through them came most of the English and Scottish armies, bringing ruin in their wake. It was the obvious route, for the coastal plain afforded the easiest passage and the best forage, and Edinburgh, Scotland's capital, lay on the east, as did the important English bases at Berwick, Newcastle, and Alnwick. And unlike the fiercer tribes of the Middle and West Marches, the men of the east were less likely to make the invader's passage uncomfortable.

Being small, the Eastern Marches were easier to control. On the Scottish side the Hume family reigned almost unchallenged, locally at least, and Hume Castle was an inland bastion against invasion. Around it lay the Merse, the fertile plain which was Scotland's storehouse and even supplied the English East March with food: the garrison at Berwick depended entirely on the Merse for their supplies in peacetime, and as one of their commanders, John Carey,[1] put it, if Hume stopped the Merse farmers selling to Berwick, "we need no other siege". It is significant that Carey, writing to Burghley[2] at a time when

---

1. Sir John Carey (1556?-1617), one of a notable family of Border officers, was at various times Governor of Berwick, chamberlain of the town, Warden of the English East March and Captain of Norham. His letters and reports throw important light on affairs of the eastern Border, and on the work of Wardens and other officers. He was much given to indignant complaint. He will be frequently quoted in this book, along with his father, Lord Hunsdon, and younger brother Robert, both prominent Border officials.

2. William Cecil, Lord Burghley (1520-98), principal adviser to Queen Elizabeth I, and the leading English statesman of the day.

other Border officials had little good to say of their national opposites, spoke of the Merse Scots as "our good neighbours, who supply our markets with beef, mutton, veal, pork, and all kinds of pullyn (poultry), without which we could not live".

His concern underlines the importance of Berwick to England. It was in effect the capital of the Borders, and this although in peace-time it stood only on the fringe of the action. It was England's strongest fortress town, and most of the correspondence of its officers is concerned not with Border matters, but with details of its defences, its stores, garrison, armament, and finances. In the critical year of 1587, Lord Hunsdon[3] was reporting at length on its condition—a garrison of 667 men ("these nombers are well to be lyked", Burghley noted)—with a minute description of the height of its battlement, the depth of its ditches, and the characters of its pensioners. "Robert Moore, a verie proper man, Thomas Jackson, a good tall fellow, John Shaftowe, a tall able man as anie is", and so on. Considering the number of times it had changed hands in the past, England's concern is understandable; Berwick was her eyes, ears and shield on the eastern seaboard. Although we read much of decay and repairs in the second half of the sixteenth century, the town's equipment in earlier years rivalled that of any stronghold in Europe.

Wark was another English fortress of importance in the early days, and changed hands frequently, the English once recapturing it by crawling along a sewer from the Tweed into the kitchen. In Elizabeth's time, however, it was gradually falling into ruin. Norham was the other principal hold of the English East March, but it too was allowed to decay, and in 1595 surveyors estimated that the necessary repairs would cost £1800, say £20,000 of our money. What they got was £2 14s 9d, to repair the powder store only, a nice example of Elizabeth's thrifty house-keeping.

The Middle Marches were something else. They fronted each other across the Cheviots, and the Scottish Middle March overlapped to

---

3. Henry Carey, Lord Hunsdon (1525–96), father of John and Robert Carey, was a Warden of the English East March (and briefly in the Middle March). A powerful figure in Border affairs, although latterly often absent from his post, he was probably a bastard of Henry VIII's. Tough, bluff, brave and blunt-spoken, Hunsdon's "custom of swearing and obscenity in speaking made him seem a worse Christian than he was."

touch the English East and West Marches as well. The Middle Marches saw by far the most numerous raids, for the broken country was ideal for reiving, and the same place names crop up again and again. On the English side Redesdale to the east and Tynedale farther west were prime targets, and in turn they were themselves great nests of reivers. Their names can be taken to cover much wider areas than the mere valleys of the Rede and Tyne; the old Franchise of Tyndale extended south from the Border in a tongue forty miles long by fifteen wide.

Alnwick, Harbottle, and Otterburn were the principal centres of law and order on the English side, although Harbottle Castle was pronounced in 1595 a prison unfit for felons and a house unfit for anyone.[4] The decay into which all but the principal English fortresses were allowed to fall indicates their declining importance as actual strongholds, but even in partial ruin they were often usable as headquarters for Border officials.

The Scottish Middle March contained as choice a collection of ruffians as ever was seen in one section; here were the Kerrs, both of Cessford and Ferniehurst, and the Scotts, and running across the March, parallel with the frontier and barely a dozen miles from it, was one of the most beautiful and dreaded valleys in Europe: Teviotdale. Hawick, Kelso, and Jedburgh were the principal towns, and the March was littered with those towers which were the homes of the robber families. The criminal traffic across the Middle March frontier was enormous; it was wide, and desolate, and criss-crossed by the secret ways of the raiders, through the mosses and bogs and twisting passes of Cheviot, the "high craggy hills" above Teviotdale, and the bleak Northumberland valleys. This was the hot trod[5] country, the scene of the Redeswire Raid and the massive forays when as many as three thousand lances came sweeping over the moorland to harry Coquetdale or to make a smoking waste from Teviothead to the Jed Water. No Wardens carried such a burden as those of the Middle Marches; it was, as one of them said, "an unchristened country".

Yet there was worse to the west, for this was the tough end of the

---

4. Considering that it was alive with thieves and ruffians, the Border country was surprisingly short of prisons. One later English Warden, Ralph Eure, found that Hexham jail was so unfit for habitation "that I am forced to pasture myne own house with such men as are of the better sort."

5. Hot trod—lawful pursuit of reivers.

frontier. Technically part of the Scottish Middle March, but linked by
geography and tradition with the Western Marches, was Liddesdale,
the cockpit of the Border and the home of its most predatory clans.
It had what amounted to a Warden of its own, known as the Keeper,
and from it were mounted the most devastating raids, usually into the
English Middle March. Its people and their misdeeds make up such a
considerable portion of this book that there is no need to say more
about them at present, but the valley itself is worth more than a
line.

Few people go to it, even today; Sir Walter Scott is supposed to have
taken the first wheeled vehicle into the dale less than two centuries ago.
To get the full flavour, it should be visited in autumn or winter, when
its stark bleakness is most apparent. It is empty, drear and hard; there
are never many cars on the road, which winds up to Newcastleton and
then turns westward into a little glen that manages to tell the traveller
more about the dark side of Border history in a glance than he can
learn by traversing all the rest of the Marches.

Through the bare branches he suddenly catches sight of the medieval
nightmare called Hermitage, a gaunt, grey Border castle standing in the
lee of the valley side, with a little river running under its walls. The
Hermitage, which took its name supposedly from a holy man who once
settled there, is not a big place, but in its way it is more impressive than
Caernarvon or Edinburgh or even the Tower of London. For it is mag-
nificently preserved, and one sees it as it was, the guard house of the
bloodiest valley in Britain. One is not surprised to learn that an early
owner was boiled alive by impatient neighbours; there is a menace
about the massive walls, about the rain-soaked hillside, about the
dreary gurgle of the river.

It was a Douglas place once, and then the Bothwells had it; Mary
Queen of Scots came there to her wounded lover after the Elliots had
taught him not to take liberties, Borderer though he was. In the latter
days of the reivers it had a Captain, who held it for the Keeper of Liddesdale, and tried to enforce the law on the unspeakable people who inhabited the valley. Their influence seems to hang over it still, and it is a
relief to take the Hawick road and leave Hermitage behind.

Westward of Liddesdale is a desolate moss called Tarras, where the
reivers and their families used to retreat when outraged authority came
in force to wreak vengeance on them, and beyond it lies the Scottish

West March proper, Eskdale, the Dumfriesshire plain, and the gorgeous valleys of the Annan and the Nith. The West March of Scotland, although its people probably did England rather less damage than the Middle March clans, was in a state of constant feud and turmoil, thanks largely to the lasting enmity of the Johnstones and Maxwells, and to English inroads. The castles of Caerlaverock, Lochmaben, Langholm, and Lochwood are repeatedly mentioned in the histories of the March, and Annan and Dumfries were the main centres, as they are today.

Much of the West March frontier is covered by the tract once known as the Debateable Land, a unique area of disputed territory with a special place in Border history which is described in Chapter XXXIII.

The English West March, consisting of Cumberland and Westmorland, would appear to have been living on the lip of a lion, with Liddesdale's robber hordes and the fierce clans of the Scottish West March all within easy riding distance. Yet Cumberland, as a whole, seems to have suffered rather less from regular foray than the English Middle Marches.[6] Its immediate frontier region, the eastern fells and the Bewcastle Waste which was a notable haunt of outlaws and was constantly traversed by the Liddesdale raiders, did indeed see its full share of foray and violence, but the rich pastures of the Eden valley and the western plain should have been a much more tempting target. They were far from immune, but they probably took less continuous hammering than Redesdale or Tynedale.

There were several reasons for this. The English West March was the strongest of the six, with its string of holds dotted eastward from the Solway—Rockcliffe, Burgh (where the fortified church is still to be seen), Scaleby, Askerton, Naworth, Bewcastle, and others. The broad Eden, like the treacherous Solway tides, was a genuine barrier, and farther south there were castles at Penrith, Cockermouth, and Greystoke, while the remains of the once-great Inglewood and Westward Forests were refuges for folk and cattle when invasion

---

6. The question which of the two English Marches, West or Middle, sustained the greater damage from raiding, is highly debatable. William Bowes once estimated the spoils in the West as being twice as great as those in the Middle and East combined, but the statistics as a whole are contradictory, and relate only to a comparatively short period of Border history. One thing seems likely, on the evidence, and that is that thè Cumbrian riders did more damage to Scotland than they suffered in return.

threatened. Most important of all, across the main route south and within an hour's easy ride of the frontier lay the fortress-city of Carlisle.

Second to Berwick in political importance, and in the strength of its defences, Carlisle was nevertheless the hub of the Borderland. It was the biggest community in all the Marches, and the only actual city; every Borderer, English and Scot, knew it well, with its great red castle, its ancient cathedral and grammar school and market, and its famous gallows on the Harraby Hill, where a new hotel now stands. Time and again, in the old wars when the frontier burst open, Carlisle held; siege and endurance were part of its life—indeed, they were what it was there for. By the sixteenth century it had been hit with everything that invasion could throw at it, and it had seen them all— Romans, Normans, sea-rovers, mercenaries from the ends of Europe, and British warriors of every variety. Even its bishops were fighting men, and in the battle its women helped to man its walls. There is little of those walls left now, but the turbulent history of the city is to be read in the stones of the tiny cathedral, where one style of architecture is piled on another, testimony to centuries of destruction and repair.

In spite of its richly romantic past, which takes in King Arthur, Mary of Scotland, Cromwell, Bonnie Prince Charlie, and a long list of famous monarchs, Carlisle is no more history-conscious than a New Town. Its corporation, with a tasteful delicacy worthy of their bandit ancestors, transformed the magnificent northern approach across the Eden by adding to the fine silhouette of castle and cathedral a stark modern atrocity in concrete. Even the name of its ancient Grammar School, one of the oldest in Britain, has been allowed to vanish. Still, the network of old lanes off the symbolically-named English and Scotch Streets has been reprieved, and recently the medieval tithe-barn was restored and reopened as a centre for cultural activities; old or new, a city is there to be used, and if there is one thing Carlisle has always been, it is well-used.

The sixteenth-century Borderers respected it, and the reivers tended to give it a wide berth. Although its official garrison was often inadequate—in 1595 it was discovered that the city's master gunner was a butcher living in Suffolk, and that there was no one in the town fit to fire a cannon—it was an effective police base, and the West March Warden and his officers, with their outposts near the frontier, were an ever-present danger to marauders.

V

"A martial kind of men"

It is impossible to say how many people lived in the sixteenth-century Borderland, but a rough idea may be given. D. L. W. Tough made an ingenious calculation based on the muster rolls of the English Marches in 1584;[1] these were supposed to include every man between 16 and 60, and by taking this age group to be a certain proportion of the whole, Tough was able to arrive at a figure of about 120,000 as the total population of the English Border. Checking against later census figures seemed to confirm his estimate, and for what it is worth it is interesting to make comparison with known populations in our own time.

In 1959 there were 45 million people in England and Wales; four centuries earlier, as nearly as can be estimated, there were about 4·5 million—a tenth of the modern figure. In 1959 there were 1,170,600 persons in Cumberland, Westmorland and Northumberland, and a tenth of that gives a 1559 population of 117,000, which is very close to Tough's figure. Of course, this is a questionable calculation, but it is probably the best we can do.

Scotland is more difficult, because information is even scarcer than for England. Tough got as close as he could by making comparison with early nineteenth-century figures, and assuming a total Scottish population in 1600 of 600,000, arrived at a figure for the Scottish Borders of almost 45,000.

If this figure is subjected to the 1959 comparison, as we have done for England, it does not appear to stand up. Here it is:

In 1959 the population of Scotland was 5 million; in 1559, by reasonable deduction, it was possibly about half a million—one-tenth, as in the case of England. But the Scottish Border population in 1959 was 192,836, and one-tenth of that gives only 19,000 people in 1559, which is less than half of the 45,000 Tough estimated for 1600.

There is a possible explanation, and it tends to confirm Tough's higher figure. Thanks to urban development in places like the Newcastle area, Carlisle, and the Cumbrian west coast, the population of the

---

1. *The Last Years of a Frontier*, pp. 26–8.

English Marches has probably kept pace over the centuries with the growth of England as a whole. But we may be sure that the Scottish Border has not kept pace with total Scottish growth; it has had no urban development like that of Northern England. So it is reasonable to assume that Scottish Border population has declined proportionately, and that the 1559 population figure would in fact be much higher than a straightforward comparison with 1959 suggests. Seen in this light Tough's 45,000 seems reasonable—indeed, he himself wondered if it was not too low.

If we take 120,000 English and 50,000 Scots as the sixteenth-century Border population we are probably not far off the mark. And while we lack accurate figures, there are some facts obtainable; a document of November 1596 states categorically that the English West and Middle Marches far outnumber their Scottish opposites. It adds that the English East March is smaller and weaker than either of the others by "two-thirds at least", and points out that the Scottish East and Middle Marches together contain 400 villages and steads, while the English East March has only 120. This loaded comparison indicates that the English East March felt itself very much the prey of the two Scottish Marches (see also Chapter XII).

But if there is doubt about the Borders' numerical population, there is none about what kind of people they were. Visiting contemporaries as well as local sources are emphatic. Barbarous, crafty, vengeful, crooked, quarrelsome, tough, perverse, active, deceitful—there is a harmony about the adjectives to be found in travellers' descriptions and official letters. In general it is conceded that the Borderers, English and Scottish, were much alike, that they made excellent soldiers if disciplined, but that the raw material was hard, wild, and ill to tame.

The younger Surrey,[2] the great English veteran who led the van at Flodden when England inflicted the heaviest defeat in Scottish history, was in no doubt about the Scottish Borderers. To him they were "the boldest men, and the hottest, that ever I saw any nation". Froissart, writing from an earlier period, but again out of a knowledge that was Border-based, thought both Scots and English "good men of war, for

2. Thomas Howard the younger (1474?–1554), Earl of Surrey and later Duke of Norfolk (1524). Fought in Spain, 1512; Lord High Admiral of England, 1513–25; Earl Marshal of England, 1533. An experienced Border fighter, he suppressed the Pilgrimage of Grace in 1536. Uncle of Anne Boleyn.

when they meet there is a hard fight without sparing: there is no 'Ho!' between them as long as spears, swords, axes, or daggers will endure, but lay on each upon other". How right he was; of course, he and Surrey were looking at the Borderers as soldiers, but on the frontier the line between civil and military was often ill-defined, even in peacetime.

Camden found the Borderers hard, like their country. "In the wastes . . . you may see as it were the ancient nomads, a martial kind of men who, from the month of April into August, lie out scattering and summering with their cattle, in little cottages here and there, which they call sheils and sheilings." He could not survey the Roman Wall as closely as he wished "for the rank robbers thereabout".

Camden knew the Scots West Marchmen as "infamous for robberies"; his view is balanced by the account of the English Middle March in 1549, from the Chorographia:

"The chief [dales] are Tynedale and Redesdale, a country that William the Conqueror did not subdue, retaining to this day the ancient laws and customs. These Highlanders are famous for thieving; they are all bred up and live by theft. They come down from these dales into the low countries, and carry away horses and cattle so cunningly, that it will be hard for any to get them or their cattle, except they be acquainted with some master thief, who for some money may help them to their stolen goods, or deceive them."

Probably the fullest contemporary description of sixteenth-century Border life is that given by Leslie, Bishop of Ross, who will be more fully quoted in the chapter on reiving technique. He was a close student of social matters, and for the Scottish side at least, his account is the best obtainable.

The Borderers, he writes, "assume to themselves the greatest habits of licence. . . . For as, in time of war, they are readily reduced to extreme poverty by the almost daily inroads of the enemy, so, on the restoration of peace, they entirely neglect to cultivate their lands, though fertile, from the fear of the fruits of their labour being immediately destroyed by a new war. Whence it happens that they seek their subsistence by robberies, or rather by plundering and rapine, for they are particularly averse to the shedding of blood; nor do they much concern themselves whether it be from Scots or English that they rob and plunder."

Leslie has a good deal to say of the characters of the Borderers, and it is not all bad. He is the main authority for the myth that they were reluctant to kill, except in feud; he also maintained "that having once pledged their faith, even to an enemy, they are very strict in observing it, insomuch that they think nothing can be more heinous than violated fidelity."

In theory, possibly, but this is one of those hallowed Border legends which requires close examination. There was certainly in the sixteenth century a Border code of honour, a kind of hangover from the days of Percy and Douglas, recognised and referred to and in some ways respected. Robert Carey[3] wrote to Cecil[4] of Scottish gentlemen who "will rather lose their lives and livings, than go back from their word, and break the custom of the Border". The last phrase is significant. One of Ralph Sadler's[5] English spies said the Scots had no scruples about stealing, "and yet they would not bewray any man that trust in them for all the gold in Scotland and France." According to Leslie, to be publicly reproached a proven faith-breaker was a greater punishment "even than an honourable death inflicted on the guilty person".

These are flat, general statements, and they obviously have some basis. But they do not accord with the written records of Border life, with their long catalogues of broken assurances, unredeemed pledges, and the like. If one studies the lives of, say, John Forster[6] and John

---

3. Sir Robert Carey (1560–1639), was at different times Warden of the English East and Middle Marches, and also served in a subordinate capacity in the West March. Clever, brave, and something of a *beau sabreur*, he is one of the few Borderers to have left memoirs of his activities.
4. Sir Robert Cecil (1563-1612), third son of Lord Burghley, was Queen Elizabeth's Secretary of State from 1596, although in effect he had been holding the post for some years before that. He worked hard to secure the succession of James VI of Scotland to the English throne. Created Earl of Salisbury, 1605.
5. Sir Ralph Sadler, English Ambassador to Scotland in the middle of the sixteenth century.
6. Sir John Forster (1501?–1602), an extraordinary English Borderer, held the Middle March Wardenship for almost thirty-five years, with only one brief break. He was over 100 when he died, having lived almost exactly through the sixteenth century, and seen every aspect of Border life. No one was more experienced or sunk in frontier affairs than Forster; unfortunately, although he was outstandingly brave, his honesty was seldom out of question.

Maxwell,[7] it may not be possible to prove either of them liars, but there can be no doubt that lies were being told by someone, profusely and persistently. Sir William Bowes[8] despaired of the Scots, "that both can and will say more for a falsehoode, than for my own part I can doe for the truth", and John Carey thought them "the most crafty and deceit-ful" on earth. Many of his fellow-officials agreed. The necessity of repeated Border legislation to deal with perjury does not speak for a truthful populace.

It is sometimes argued that Border law could not have been based on good faith and truth-telling if these had not been the norm. This is to miss the point. The law was so based because there was no alternative in a fairly primitive and unusual society. Good faith was an ideal, then as now, and it was recognised, but that doesn't mean it was universally observed. Study of the written facts suggests that the Borderers were no more truthful or reliable than other men; they had their own eccentric notions of honour, but stainless veracity was not essential to it in practice. Bishop Leslie no doubt had good reason for his opinion, but the records appear to contradict him. Still, there will always be those eager to accept his view of the Borderers; personally, I wouldn't have trusted them round the corner.

Breaking a promise is one thing; deliberate betrayal and treachery are rather different, and it is said that these were uncommon. It is diffi-cult to judge at this distance, but again a study of the records makes one cautious about accepting blanket statements. Hector of Harlaw, the Carleton brothers, Black Ormiston, and Richie Graham will be men-tioned later; their behaviour provides food for thought on the subject.

Leslie is interesting on Border morality as applied to property and theft. "They have a persuasion that all property is common by the law of nature, and is therefore liable to be appropriated by them in their

---

7. Sir John Maxwell (1512?–1583), later Lord Herries, had a highly chequered career, during which he held the Scottish West March Wardenship five times.
8. Sir William Bowes, a treasurer of Berwick and a commissioner for Border affairs in the 1590s. There was a large family of Boweses, of whom the most famous was the earlier Sir Robert Bowes, who was Warden of the English East and Middle Marches in the 1540s, "a most expert Borderer", and author of "Forme and Order of a Day of Truce". A later Robert Bowes was Elizabeth's ambassador to Scotland.

necessity." Later he adds: "Besides, they think the art of plundering so
very lawful, that they never say over their prayers more fervently, or
have more devout recurrence to their beads and their rosaries, than
when they have made an expedition."

Sometimes one gets the impression that the good bishop secretly
admired the Border reivers. At least he is careful to do them justice,
and there may be a clue to his attitude in that passage where he notes
approvingly: "Nor indeed have the Borderers, with such ready frenzy
as many others of the country, joined the heretical secession from the
common faith of the holy church." Rascals they might be, but Leslie
counted them among his flock. Possibly he had not heard the story of
the visitor to Liddesdale who, finding no churches, demanded: "Are
there no Christians here?" and received the reply, "Na, we's a' Elliots
and Armstrangs."

Apart from the spiritual side, we know some other things about the
old Border character. One has to remember, in quoting travellers'
stories, that most of those who visited Scotland, for example, wrote
of the country as a whole, and what they described may not hold good
for the Marches. But Pope Pius II, who visited the country in his earlier
years when he was Aeneas Sylvius Piccolomini, made observations
which are pertinent; he noted the generally poor condition of the
country, and that the men were small, bold and forward in temper,
while the women, "fair in complexion, comely and pleasing" were
"not distinguished for their chastity, giving their kisses more readily
than Italian women their hands".

This was in the fifteenth century; fifty years later Pedro de Ayala, a
Spaniard, found the women "courteous in the extreme . . . really
honest, though very bold". He thought they dressed better than English
women, and were in absolute control of their houses.

Several writers testify to a boastful tendency in the Scots, and
Sylvius noted that nothing pleased them more than to hear the English
abused. An English physician who lived in Scotland in the 1540s found
that it was not in nature for a Scot to love an Englishman, and we have
plenty of evidence of mutual loathing on either side. John Carey
thought the Scots "the most perverst and prowde nacion in the world",
and paid them a back-handed compliment: whoever found himself up
against them, the Scots were "such a people as will soon find what is
in him."

Eure,[9] an English Warden, said of his own Marchmen that they "envied the stranger"; outsiders were not welcomed on either side of the line, as many of the later English Wardens, who were not Borderers, found to their cost. But one learns to be cautious about accepting some of the English officials' strictures on the Borderers at their full face value; they were doubtless sincere, but they were under severe pressures in their office, and in writing to London they tended to give full vent to their feelings. One detects a fine rising note of hysteria in John Carey's correspondence, and in that of Eure, who never found his feet as a Warden. Henry Leigh, a lesser official, once observed, with feeling, that the Borderers "were no cripples of their tongues"; neither were their Wardens.

A marked characteristic of the Marchmen, seemingly at odds with Anglo-Scottish rivalry, was their peculiar sense of community which made the Borderland an entity. Over and above inter-marriage and blood kinship, there was a common heritage that seemed to unite English and Scot on the Border against the outside world; they understood each other and, to use a modern *cliché*, shared common problems. C. P. Snow touched in one of his novels on the phenomenon of two enemies who felt somehow closer to each other than to their own supporters, and this was true of the Border people. At its extreme this feeling manifested itself in one English invasion, when English and Scottish Borderers, on opposite sides as part of their national armies, were seen talking to each other "within less than a spear's length, but when aware that such intercourse was noticed, they commenced to run at each other, apparently with no desire to inflict serious injury."[10]

---

9. Ralph, 3rd Lord Eure (1558–1617) was English Middle March Warden from 1595–98, and had a hard time of it. Like some other Wardens, he failed to live up to the reputation of distinguished ancestors—in his case, his father, grandfather, and great-grandfather had been Wardens. The great-grandfather, Sir William Eure, 1st Lord, had the East March in the 1530s and 1540s; his son, Sir Ralph Eure, held the Middle March in the 1540s, was notorious for his cruel raids in Scotland, and was finally killed at Ancrum Moor (1545)—he was the father of the 2nd Lord Eure, who was Middle March Warden in the 1550s and died in 1594. Confusion occasionally arises because of the various ways of spelling the name, which also appears as Eurie, Ewerie, Ewer, and Evers. Whenever "Eure" is quoted in this book the person referred to is Ralph, 3rd Lord, unless otherwise stated.

10. Scott, quoting Patten's account of Somerset's expedition into Scotland.

Often to English Wardens it seemed that their subjects were more at home with Scottish Borderers than with other Englishmen—usually for profit. The bond, created by geography, by common social conditions, and by a shared spirit of lawless independence, was a paradox that intermarriage strengthened. It has never entirely disappeared.

The tribal system, sometimes called clanship, also helped to foster it. Family unity as much as anything made the Borders and set them apart. Despite the feudal system, tribal loyalty was paramount; Scott noted that no matter what the family's origin, Saxon, Norman, or Celtic, clanship persisted and was too strong for the government. "No Prince but a Percy" was a Northumberland saying, and on the English side the power of the local chieftain was a continuing matter of concern to London, especially when the Catholic North became a menace to the Reformed state. On both sides the chief of the tribe was the man who mattered; in England "the inhabitants acted less under the direction of their landlords than under that of the principal man of their name". In Scotland clanship was recognised by a government that could do nothing about it anyway; the chiefs were to find pledges for keeping good order by the clan, just as landlords had to take responsibility for their tenants.

There is a tendency to think of clanship as a peculiarly Scottish thing, but it is evident that on the Border the tie of tribal blood was no stronger among the Kerrs and Scotts and Armstrongs of Scotland than among the Forsters, Ogles, Fenwicks, Charltons, Halls, and Musgraves of England.

And if it was not easy to be a chief or a landlord over such people, it was even harder to be a central government whose claims to loyalty and obedience were feeble by comparison. What member of the Scott family needed Edinburgh's protection—or approval—when he had Buccleuch's?

No doubt the clan system contributed to the poverty and economic decline of the Borders, as well as to their backwardness. Greedy overlords were a cause of decay, and so was overpopulation of the dales, which drove men out to steal. Poverty has perhaps been over-emphasised as a root cause of Border reiving, but it was certainly a spur. The oft-quoted phenomenon of Tynedale, where a deceased's land must be divided equally among all his sons, "whereby beggars increase and service decays" was rightly a matter for reform in Eure's eyes.

VI

Food and shelter

The tribal system, and the eternal turbulence of the frontier, dictated the day-to-day living of the people. Camden spoke of nomads; as such, the Borderers tended to live on mobile beasts rather than on standing crops. They ate beef and broth in quantity, and some mutton: "they live chiefly on flesh, milk and boiled barley", says Leslie, while Sylvius gives a diet of fish and flesh, with bread only as a dainty. Pedro de Ayala mentions immense flocks of sheep[1] in the wilder parts, and the lack of crop cultivation.

Leslie noted that not only was use of bread very limited, but that the Borderers took very little beer[2] or wine. Indeed, they seem to have been abstemious enough, although according to a document giving the number of taverns in the English Border in 1571, the inhabitants of the Middle March must have had a pub for every 46 people or thereabouts, and Berwick the same proportion. But drunkenness is seldom mentioned in Border records, with such notable exceptions as the six Scots reivers whom John Carey captured drunk at an inn, and Sir John Forster's bastard son and deputy, "wan that is so given over to drunkennes, that if he cannot get companey, he will sit in a chayre in his chamber and drinke himself drunke before he reise!"

Leslie was talking about the rural Borderers when he mentioned the absence of bread, which was commoner in the cities, larger houses, and garrisons.[3] An English traveller who stayed in the home of a Border knight in 1598 (it may have been Branxholm, the hold of Buccleuch), observed that "they commonly eat hearth cakes of oats" (the cakes or cracknels of which Froissart talks), and although he was entertained "after their best manner" he found "no art of cookery or household

---

1. Sheep-raising in the sixteenth century was primarily for wool production, not for mutton, but Border wool was considered of poor quality. The demand for mutton increased gradually from Elizabeth's reign onwards.
2. The better classes in the towns brewed ale, which was their "usual drink".
3. The garrison of the fortress of Roxburgh laid in 1800 loaves among the winter's victuals in 1548.

stuff, but rude neglect of both". His account of a meal-time in the hold of a Border chieftain is so detailed that it is worth quoting at greater length:

"Many servants brought in the meat, with blue caps on their heads, the table being more than half furnished with great platters of porridge, each having a little sodden meat. When the table was served, the servants sat down with us; but the upper mess instead of porridge, had a pullet with some prunes in the broth. The Scots, living then in factions, used to keep many followers and so consumed their revenues in victuals, and were always in want of money."

However, he found them hospitable to strangers, the city folk entertaining "passengers on acquaintance".

The agricultural system of the Borderers, peaceful and lawless alike, followed a regular pattern. From autumn to spring, when the nights were long, was the season for raiding; the summer months were for husbandry, and although raiding occurred then also, it was less systematic. Tillage took place in spring and summer, and the crops were mainly oats, rye, and barley, but the main effort went into cattle and sheep raising. For this the rural Borderer had to be mobile, leaving his winter dwelling about April to move into the "hielands" where he lived in his sheiling for the next four or five months while the cattle pastured.

Although the sheiling communities were safer than the winter quarters, they were not immune from the reivers. Their inaccessibility cut both ways, for if it made raiding more difficult it also placed the herdsmen farther from the protection of the Warden forces. Eure wrote to Burghley at the start of the 1597 summering to complain that he could not defend the Middle March sheilings "without I have 100 foot from Berwick to lie during the summer with them for defence." In that season at least the Scots were hitting the sheilings harder than usual, so that Eure found his people were reluctant to venture out summering, "which is their chiefest profitt".

Following this system of transhumance was easier for people who were not accustomed to build houses for permanence, and who had learned from generations of warfare and raiding to live on the hoof. Even their winter quarters were often makeshift affairs that could be put up in a matter of hours. They were fashioned of clay, or of stones when they were available, and sometimes of turf sods, with roofs of thatch or turf. Most of the isolated holdings would be of this type, "huts and cottages" as Leslie says, "about the burning of which they are nowise concerned". It was easy enough to build another, and Sir Robert Bowes described in 1546 how "if such cottages or cabins where they dwell in be bront of one day they will the next day maik other and not remove from the ground".

In the larger villages there was more effort at permanence, with sturdy stone houses and walls, and in Tynedale and on the Scottish side there were some "very stronge houses" constructed of massive baulks of oak bound hard together and "so thycke mortressed that yt wilbe very harde, without greatt force and lasoure, to break or caste [them] downe". By lining the walls and roofs thickly with turf the builders went some way towards fire-proofing these block-houses; Ill Will Armstrong's house in the Scottish West March was "buylded after siche a maner that it couth not be brynt ne distroyed, unto it was cut downe with axes".

The next stage up from the wooden block-house was the peel tower, many of which can still be seen all over the Border. An excellent example is Smailholm, near Kelso, or Hollows Tower on the Esk, which are rather de luxe models, but show exactly the purpose which the peel tower served.

The peel was built of stone, with walls of massive thickness, and ideally was three or four storeys high. The only entrance was through a double door at ground level, one of the doors being an outer iron grating, and the other of oak reinforced with iron. The bottom storey was used as a store room, and the floors above were reached by a narrow curving stair, called a turnpike, usually going up clockwise so that a defender retreating up the flight had his unguarded left side to the wall, and his sword arm to the outside; his attacker, coming up, was at the disadvantage of having his sword arm to the wall. Tradition has it that the Kerrs, who were notoriously left-handed,[4] built their stairs anti-clockwise.

The upper floors were the living quarters, and at the very top there would usually be a beacon, to summon help in attack or give warning of an impending foray.

---

4. A left-handed person is still called ker-handed, car-handed, or corry-fisted in the Scottish Borderland.

The peel was normally a chief's house, and no matter how rich or powerful a Border leader might become he needed a tower at least for his personal safety and to provide a rallying point and defensive centre for his dependants. Their great virtue was their simplicity and strength; they were impervious to fire from the outside, or indeed to anything short of artillery or a sustained siege. Once inside, with the doors shut, the defenders could hold out against a greatly superior force, firing from the arrow-slits and shot-holes, and hurling down interesting objects from the roof. Even when the doors were forced, determined men could fight from floor to floor.

The situation of the towers varied. Sometimes a dwelling house was attached, and normally the chief's immediate family and dependants, sometimes in large numbers, would live in and around the fortress. The peel might be surrounded by a large wall, known as a barmekin or barnekin; by statute of 1535 Scottish leaders on the Border were obliged to build them to regulation size, over two feet thick and between seven and eight feet high. The barnekin offered a refuge for people and cattle, and a defensible perimeter against minor attacks.

Even when he had to abandon his peel in the face of a large invasion, and retire to the wastes or mosses with his folk and goods, the Borderer had an ingenious way of preventing its destruction in his absence. The interior of the peel would be stuffed tight with smouldering peat, which would burn for days, and made it impossible for gunpowder charges to be laid, or for the attackers to get inside and set to work with crowbars and axes. When the Borderer found it safe to return he would have to renew and repair his woodwork, but the framework of his tower would be little the worse for wear.

There were methods of capturing a peel tower, one of which is described in detail by a reiver in Chapter XV. The Bold Buccleuch's[5]

---

5. There were many Walter Scotts of Branxholm and Buccleuch, the principal ones being that Walter Scott who fought at Flodden and Ancrum, was briefly Middle March Warden, and was murdered by the Kerrs in 1552; and his grandson, the "Bold Buccleuch" (1565–1611), a noted reiver who was also Keeper of Liddesdale from 1594–1603, and who is famous for his rescue of Kinmont Willie Armstrong from Carlisle in 1596. When Buccleuch is mentioned in this text it means the grandson, unless otherwise stated.

method, described by young Scrope,[6] of "fyre to the door" whereby
the defenders were smoked out, was probably common practice,
especially when attackers had succeeded in capturing the ground floor
and driving the defenders upstairs. Another ingenious method was
used by Robert Carey in attacking a Graham peel: "we set presently at
worke to get up to the top of the tower and to uncover the roofe, and
then some 20 of [the besiegers] to fall down together, and by that
means to win the tower".

Carey was fairly new to the frontier at that time, and since the redoubtable Thomas Carleton, an officer of great experience, was at his
elbow throughout the operation, we can guess whose bright idea it was
to remove the roof.

The towers and block-houses were no doubt comparatively com-
fortable places, and decently if crudely furnished, although there was a
total absence of such refinements as carpets or decorations, but the
peasant huts and sheilings were primitive in the extreme. Heat was by
peat fire, probably in the centre of the floor; the clothing, like the furniture, was of the simplest. "The husbandmen in Scotland, the servants, and almost all the country wore coarse cloth made at home of
grey or sky colour, and flat blue caps very broad," says our English
traveller.[7] The heads of tribes and leading landowners on both sides
might use satin, silk, damask, lace, and taffeta, but among the poorer
folk leather and buckskin for the men, and broadcloth, linen and
woollens for both sexes were the common dress materials.

---

6. Henry and Thomas Scrope (or Scroop) were respectively 9th and 10th
Lords Scrope of Bolton. Henry (1534–1592) was English West March
Warden from 1563 until his death; his son, Thomas (1567?–1609) held the
office from 1592 to 1603. Henry was an able Warden, Thomas much less so
(he was the unlucky victim of the Kinmont raid). To avoid confusion, they
are referred to in the text as old Scrope and young Scrope where necessary.
7. He also noted that Scottish gentlemen wore little extra adornment by
way of lace, and tended to follow French fashion as to cut. Married gentle-
women wore "close upper bodices after the German fashion with large
whalebone sleeves after the French; short cloaks like the Germans, French
hoods and large falling bands about their necks. The unmarried of all sorts
go bare-headed and wear short cloaks like the virgins of Germany. The
lower sort of citizens' wives and the women of the country wore cloaks
made of a coarse stuff of two or three colours in checker work vulgarly
called pladden".

We get some idea of clothing and household goods among the Borderers from the lists of goods stolen in raids. These vary from the
sumptuous apparel lifted from Robert Kerr of Ancrum, including fine
hats and dresses, feather beds and plate, to the crude kitchen utensils of
the peasants. An inventory of goods stolen from a servant of John
Forster's in 1590 is an interesting guide to the possessions of a "middle
class" Borderer. It includes two doublets, two pairs of breeches, a cloak,
a jerkin, a woman's kirtle and pair of sleeves, nine kerchiefs, seven
rails (shifts), five pairs of linen sheets, two coverlets, two linen shirts,
a purse containing six shillings, another purse, two silk ribbons, a
winding cloth, a feather bed, three shirts, a cauldron, and so on. Not a
badly furnished establishment; Forster's servant could obviously
afford to spend money on his wife's appearance—which is mentioned
elsewhere as a common Border trait.[8]

Within the towns conditions were somewhat different; Carlisle and
Berwick were sophisticated by the standards of the rural communities,
and on paper differed from southern towns only in that they were
garrisoned and heavily defended. On the Scottish side, towns like Dumfries, Annan, Jedburgh, and Kelso were strong, organised communities, usually walled and fortified, run by their own councillors, and
often containing houses of some strength. They were sturdily independent folk, quick to resent interference by rural potentates; Jedburgh especially, which carried on a feud with the Kerrs of Ferniehurst, was noted for the toughness of its inhabitants.

The standard of living was generally higher in the towns, as one
would expect. A man in the Berwick garrison, in 1597, when times
were hard and inflation had increased rapidly,[9] got a daily ration of a
twelve-ounce loaf, three pints of beer, one-and-a-half pounds of beef,
three-quarters of a pound of cheese, and a quarter of a pound of butter
—this was a considerable reduction in what his ration had been some
years earlier.

What is interesting about the Berwick garrison's rations is that they
do not seem to have been markedly better off than the civilians—at
least they could not afford the strong beer which apparently found a

8. de Ayala, in 1498, thought Scotswomen had the handsomest head-
dresses in the world, but omitted to describe them.
9. Wheat had doubled in price, and meat and butter gone up by 30%.

ready civil market. Nor was their food always considered satisfactory;
John Carey bluntly told Burghley on one occasion that it was not fit
for a horse.

VII

The riding surnames

It is significant that in the sixteenth-century Borderland the words
"road" and "raid" were synonymous. So were "raiding" and "riding"
—when the Armstrongs, for example, were described as "ever riding",
it meant simply that they never ceased from foraying. So when one
speaks of the riding surnames, the phrase covers those families who
were the principal reivers.

Any list of them must be selective, and what follows is not a comprehensive roll, but a brief and general guide to the main riding tribes,
with some of the smaller surnames added because they are of particular
interest. It should be remembered that the names are not chosen for
national or political importance, but for their prominence in the
limited sphere of frontier reiving; thus the Douglases and Percies,
famous families who were active in the early days of Border warfare,
are omitted, because they were hardly riding families, while the Burns
and Storeys, comparatively unimportant in any national sense, are
included because they were active forayers.

Similarly, the personalities mentioned have been chosen only for
their Border interest—e.g. Richie of Brackenhill is not a shining light
in the roll of the whole Graham family, which includes people like
Montrose and Claverhouse, but he was a Borderer and they were
not.

In listing twenty-one tribes I have simply given their names, with
some of their alternative spellings where appropriate; then their main
areas of occupation (it will be noted that some of them lived on both
sides of the frontier) and principal Border branches; a short comment;

a selection of some noteworthy individuals, and a final line indicating the status and numbers of the family in the Border country today.

★

ARMSTRONG
(Armstrang)

Principally Scottish, but probably of Cumbrian origin. Liddesdale, DL[1], Eskdale, Annandale, EWM, SEM. Chief branches, Mangerton, Whithaugh, Calfhills, etc.

The name means literally what it says (cf. Fortinbras), and the Armstrongs were the most feared and dangerous riding clan on the whole frontier. As Satchells put it:

> On the Border was the Armstrongs, able men,
> Somewhat unruly, and very ill to tame.

In Johnnie Armstrong's day (c. 1528) they could put 3000 men into the saddle, and probably did more damage by foray than any other two families combined, both in England and Scotland. Frequently allied themselves with England.

Notables: Johnnie Armstrong, Kinmont Willie Armstrong, Sim the Laird (c. 1528), Ill Will Armstrong, Sandie (his son), Old Sim of Mangerton, the Laird's Jock (c. 1587), Dick of Dryhope, Jock of the Side (c. 1570), Lance of Whithaugh, et al., et al.

Still numerous in Cumberland.

★

BELL

English and Scottish. Gilsland, SWM, Annandale.

A "great surname" of the West March, active in raiding and feud, and particularly hostile to the Grahams. One theory about the name is that it originally signified good looks.

Notables: Willie Redcloak, Christopher Bell.

Very common today.

★

BURN
(Bourne)

Scottish. East Teviotdale.

A most predatory and vicious family of the Middle March, whose

---

1. The various Marches are indicated by initials—SWM for Scottish West March, EMM for English Middle March, and so on. DL is Debateable Land.

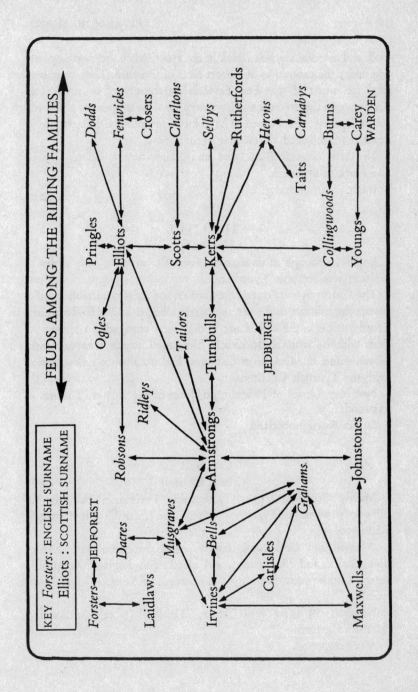

FEUDS AMONG THE RIDING FAMILIES

KEY *Forsters*: ENGLISH SURNAME
Elliots : SCOTTISH SURNAME

raids and murders reached a peak in the 1590s, when they were operating under the protection of Robert Kerr of Cessford. They were perhaps the worst of that East Teviotdale fraternity of whom Robert Carey wrote that to cross them was to provoke a sanguinary feud—for example, they are reckoned to have killed seventeen Collingwoods in revenge for the death of one man of their own.

Notables: Geordie Burn, Jock and Ralph of the Coate, Charlie and Mark of Elisheuch.

Fairly common today.

*

CHARLTON
(Carleton)

English, although in its alternate form the name appears in southwestern Scotland also. Tynedale.

The Charltons were one of the hardiest and most intractable families on the English side, and were alternately allied to and at feud with the Scottish tribes in the west. Latterly they were engaged in a bitter vendetta with the Scotts of Buccleuch. Although Carleton is another form of the name, the Cumbrian Carletons had no alliance or association with the Tynedale Charltons.

Notables: Lionel of Thornburgh, John of the Bower, Thomas of Hawcop.

Still in Northumberland.

*

CROSER
(Crosar, Crozier)

Mainly Scottish. Upper Liddesdale, Teviotdale, but also in Bewcastle where in 1592 they were "sore decaied". Chief branch, Riccarton.

A small but hard-riding family, often associated with Nixons and Elliots, and like them often allied with England. Frequently lumped under such descriptives as "theeves of Scotland" and "loose men".

Notables: Ill Wild Will Croser, "Nebless" (Noseless) Clemmie, Martin's Clemmie.

Much dispersed.

*

ELLIOT
(Elwood—see note)

Scottish, possibly of east coast origin. Liddesdale, Teviotdale, Ewesdale. Chief branches, Redheuch (whose chief was Keeper of Hermitage Castle), Lariston, Steile, Park, etc.

The second family of Liddesdale, and although less numerous than the Armstrongs, with whom they were frequently allied, they were as predatory as any clan on the frontier. Occasionally under English protection, they received a subsidy from Elizabeth during their feud with the Scotts.

Notables: Martin Elliot of Braidley ("a very wise and stout fellawe"), Little Jock of the Park, Robin of Redheuch, Archie "Fire the Braes", William of Lariston, Martin's Gibb.

[Note—A curiosity about the name Elliot is that there are more than seventy ways of spelling it, from Aylewood to Ilwand, and Dalliot to Ellot (which was the form most commonly used on the Border, along with Elwood). Any permutation of l's and t's is said to be permissible except Elliott, which for some reason the family affect to despise. The old rhyme says:

> The double L and single T
> Descend from Minto and Wolflee,
> The double T and single L
> Mark the old race in Stobs that dwell,
> The single L and single T
> The Eliots of St Germains be,
> But double T and double L
> Who they are, nobody can tell.]

Numerous today on the Scottish side.

*

FENWICK

English. EMM.

A powerful English family, described as "gentlemen", and often to be found among Border officials. They conducted many feuds, including a bitter one with the Liddesdale Elliots.

Notables: William of Wallington; William, Keeper of Tynedale; Richard Fenwick of Stanton.

Numerous in north-east England.

*

FORSTER
(Forrester, Foster)
Largely English. EEM, EWM (Line, Bewcastle), Liddesdale.

A large but not closely-knit family, the Forsters were to be found virtually everywhere on the English side. The Scottish Forsters intermarried with England, and the English Forsters were noted for their alliance with the Humes.

Notables: Sir John Forster, Red Rowy, Rowy's Will.

Widespread today.

*

GRAHAM
(Graeme)
Mostly English (so far as Border history goes), but notoriously ready to be on either side. Originally Scottish, and famous outside the Border area. EWM, SWM, DL.

Apart from the Armstrongs, the Grahams were probably the most troublesome family on the frontier. Their dual allegiances caused confusion, and they were cordially detested by their own English authorities. At one time the most numerous family in the West Border, with 500 riders in 13 towers in 1552, they were savagely persecuted in the reign of James VI and I.

Notables: Richie of Brackenhill, Jock of the Peartree, Young Hutcheon, Richie's Will, Will's Jock, *et al., et al.*

Highly numerous in Cumberland.

*

HALL
English and Scottish. Redesdale, Liddesdale, E. Teviotdale.

A large, widely-spread clan, at one time the most powerful in Redesdale, the Halls were well-hated and feared on both sides. (In the Redesdale hunting incident in 1598 the Scottish Halls and the Rutherfords were allegedly singled out by English officers as two surnames to whom no quarter should be given.) However, the Scottish Halls appear to have been much intermarried with English tribes.

Notables: Eddie Hall, "the famous thief", George of Burdupp (who had served with Philip Sidney in the Low Countries), Will of Heavyside, and two Jameses, father and son, both of Heavyside.

Numerous on both sides today.

*

HETHERINGTON
(Hetherton, Atherton)

English. Hethersgill, Line river, and EWM frontier.

A Norse family (Hetherings or Hoderings), they were "a disordered surname", although not active raiders. Frequently mentioned in connection with blackmail, both receiving and paying. Deeply involved in plot to murder Bishop of Carlisle, 1569.

Notables: Thomas "the Merchant", blackmailer; George of Walton. Still in North Cumberland.

*

HUME
(Home)

Scottish. SEM.

A great name in Scottish and Border history, the Humes achieved one extraordinary distinction as the only frontier family who would claim continuous domination in their own March. They usually held the Scottish East Wardenship, and although frequently in trouble with the Crown they never lost their eminence and influence.

Notables: Alexander, 3rd Lord Hume (c. Flodden); Alexander, 5th Lord; Alexander, 6th Lord; James Hume of Coldenknowes.

Still numerous.

*

IRVINE
(Irving, Urwen)

Scottish. SWM, Annandale, Lower Eskdale.

A very tough bunch indeed, the Irvines contributed much to the general disorder, despite their comparatively small numbers. Thoroughly involved in all the West March mischief.

Notables: Willie Kang, and his brothers Davy and Geordie. Widespread.

*

JOHNSTONE
(Johnston, Johnstoun)

Scottish, but possibly of English origin. SWM.

Second only to the Maxwells in their March, the Johnstones were powerful reivers and also frequent Wardens. Their feud with the

Maxwells was the longest and bloodiest in Border history. The "t" in their name sets them apart from other "sons of John", although even on the Border it was often dropped, and a famous grandson of the clan, Ben Jonson the poet, deliberately adopted his own spelling to avoid being confused with other Johnstons and Johnsons in London. (A very clan-conscious man, Ben walked all the way to Scotland to visit his ancestors' territory.)

Notables: James Johnstone, victor of Dryfe, and his father, John Johnstone.

Numerous and widespread.

*

KERR
(Ker, Carr, Carre)

Scottish, although there are many English Carrs nowadays. SMM, East Teviotdale, Liddesdale. Chief branches Cessford, Ferniehurst.

The Kerrs were, with the possible exception of the Scotts, the leading tribe of the Scottish Middle March, which they frequently ruled as Wardens. However, no family was more active in reiving. The Cessford and Ferniehurst branches were continual rivals.

Notables: Robert of Cessford (*c.* 1590), Thomas of Ferniehurst, Dand Kerr.

[Not the smallest controversy about the Kerrs concerns the pronunciation of their name. Modern Scots made it sound almost like "care", or the first syllable of "merry". To the northern English it is "cur", while the affected render it as "car", which, strangely enough, is how the ordinary Elizabethan Borderers pronounced it.]

Strongly represented today.

*

MAXWELL

Scottish. SWM, Annandale.

The strongest family in the Scottish West March, until the Johnstones reduced their power late in the sixteenth century. As often as not a Maxwell was Warden, and their name runs steadily through Border and Scottish history. Deeply involved with the English in the 1540s.

Notables: Johnny Maxwell (4th Lord Herries), John, 8th Lord Maxwell.

Strong in SWM today.

*

MUSGRAVE
English. EWM.

A powerful family of Cumberland who had a long record of service to the English Crown, both as soldiers and March officers. This did not inhibit their extra-legal activities, and one suspects that they often used their offices to cover their raiding. One of the two "greatest names" of the West Wardenry (the other was Salkeld) the Musgraves were constantly at feud on the Scottish side, and had a three-century vendetta with their fellow-Cumbrians, the Dacres.

Notables: Thomas Musgrave, Captain of Bewcastle, Richard Musgrave, Humphrey Musgrave, John Musgrave.

Comparatively rare.

*

NIXON
(Nicksoun)

Scottish and English. Upper Liddesdale, Bewcastle, Line rivers. Often described as having many "loose men". Chief branch, Steile.

The sons of Nick were a troublesome breed, and an important part of the Armstrong-Elliot-Nixon-Croser confederacy. Although a smaller and less compact family than the Armstrongs, they were important enough to have Thomsons, Glendennings, and Hunters living "under them", which is another way of saying associated with them.

Like other Liddesdales, they sometimes allied with England.

Notables: Fingerless Will Nixon, Archie of the Steile, Ill-drowned Geordie.

Common on West Marches.

*

ROBSON

Principally English. Tynedale, Liddesdale, West Teviotdale. Chief branches Middlesknowes and Owston.

The Robsons, "a wight riding sirname", were at one time the leading family of Tynedale, and highly troublesome. They formed a violent power bloc with the Charltons, and also with the Dodds and Milburns, the other two principal tribes of the dale, although the Milburns were also found in Redesdale and Gilsland.

Notables: Ralph of Middlesknowes, Rowe of Alanstead.

Still numerous on the Border, as are the Milburns and Dodds.

*

SCOTT

Scottish. West Teviotdale, Ewesdale, Liddesdale. Chief branch, Buccleuch (Branxholm).

One of the most powerful families in the whole Border, active both as reivers and officers. They are so much a part of frontier history, and their branches are so numerous, that it is unnecessary to go into detail here.

Notables: Walter Scott of Buccleuch (d. 1552); his grandson, also Walter Scott (known variously as "the Bold Buccleuch", "Flagellum Dei", "God's Curse", etc.); Walter Scott ("Auld Wat") of Harden.

Common throughout the Borders today.

*

STOREY
(Storie, Storye)

English. EWM, EMM, EEM, Eskdale.

A large but unfortunate clan who were forced out of the West by Lord Dacre in the 1520s for suspected treachery, and their land in Esk occupied by the Grahams. Latterly a surname of Northumberland and heavily involved in Middle March raiding and feud.

Notables: Jock of Awtenburn, Watt of the Hove End.

Common in English Border.

*

And finally, for the record, these are other Border tribes who, for reasons of space, have not been given more expanded notice.

EAST MARCH

Scotland—Trotter (listed as "gentlemen"), Dixon, Bromfield, Craw, Cranston.

England—Selby, Gray ("gentlemen"), Dunne.

MIDDLE MARCH

Scotland—East Teviotdale—Young, Pringle, Davison, Gilchrist, Tait. West Teviotdale—Oliver, Turnbull (Trumble), Rutherford. Liddesdale—Douglas, Laidlaw, Turner, Henderson.

England—Ogle, Heron, Witherington (Woodrington), Medford, Collingwood, Carnaby, Shaftoe, Ridley ("gentlemen"). Redesdale— Anderson, Potts, Read, Hedley. Tynedale—Dodd, Milburn, Yarrow, Stapleton. Also Stokoe, Stamper, Wilkinson, Hunter, Thomson, Jamieson.

WEST MARCH

Scotland—Carlisle, Beattie (also Baty, Batisoun), Little, Carruthers, Glendenning, Moffat.

England—Lowther, Curwen, Salkeld, Dacre, Harden, Hodgson, Routledge ("every man's prey"), Tailor, Noble.

VIII

Hands across the Border

> In auld times it was determinit...that there suld be
> na familiaritie betwix Scottis men and Inglis men,
> nor marriage to be contrakit betwix them, nor con-
> ventions on holydais at gammis and plays, nor mer-
> chandres to be maid amang them, nor Scottis men
> till enter on Inglis grond, nor Inglis men til enter on
> Scottis ground, witht out save conduct.... Bot thai
> statutis and artiklis are adnullit, for ther hes been grit
> familiaritie, and conventions, and makyng of
> merchandreis, on the boirdours, this lang tyme
> betwix Inglis men and Scottis men, baytht in pace
> and weir...
>
> — *The Complaynt of Scotland*

Of all the difficulties suffered by the Wardens, especially on the English side, none was more frustrating than the international character of the Borderers. This showed itself in several ways. Despite national rivalry, there was considerable fraternisation and co-operation between Scots and English along the frontier, socially, commercially and criminally. There was intermarriage on a large scale. There were "international" families like the Grahams, and communities of "our lawless people, that will be Scottishe when they will, and English at their pleasure", as Thomas Musgrave put it. As the century wore on, more and more Scots became settled on the English side of the frontier, to the distress of the English Wardens, who regarded them (rightly) as a dangerous fifth column. In short, the administrative advantages of a frontier system, whereby two sides are neatly divided and controlled *by* the frontier, were completely lost because the Borderers used the frontier as and when it suited them, and ignored it when they felt like it.

There were good reasons for this attitude. English and Scots Borderers had everything in common except nationality; as we have seen already, they belonged to the same small, self-contained unique world, lived by the same rules, and shared the same inheritance. They raided and killed each other by way of business, but their view of Anglo-Scottish relations was totally different from the views of London and Edinburgh. They had to live on and by the frontier, and traditional national hostility, while it was real enough, did not prevent personal understanding and even friendship. Englishmen and Scotsmen tend to like and respect each other, when they meet on equal terms; on the Border, at all social levels, they were perfectly ready—provided feud or professional differences were for the moment out of the way—to enjoy each other's company.

This was, of course, frowned on officially by governments who always had national security in mind.[1] "There is too great familiarity and intercourse between our English and Scottish borders," John Carey wrote primly to the Privy Council, "the gentlemen of both countries crossing into either at their pleasure, feasting and making merry with their friends, overthrowing the Wardens' authority and all Border law."

There spoke the born bureaucrat; the international race meetings, huntings and hawkings, football matches, and social exchanges, must have seemed unnatural and dangerous to him. Of course, he had some reason, for "in like manner, the common thieves and outlaws, English and Scots, devising murders and robberies with their fellows" were a very real threat to the common peace. The co-operation between the reivers of both sides, especially the fugitives and outlaws, was a menace beyond control, and all the more difficult to tackle because it often rested not only on a professional basis, but on a family one.

Intermarriage between Scots and English was, from authority's

---

1. Eure thought it politic "to draw some of the headsmen from friendship with the Scots" in 1597. He was particularly anxious about the Fenwicks, Erringtons, and Robsons.

point of view, a continual embarrassment and danger—"the same is the decaie of Her Majesty's service, and the greatest occasion of the spoils and robberies upon the Border," wrote Simon Musgrave in 1583. It was highly prevalent, especially in the West Marches, where the most troublesome tribes lived. Both governments did their best to prevent it by law—at its most extreme this imposed the death penalty on Scots who married Englishwomen without licence, or who even received English men or women; on the English side, it was March treason to marry a Scotswoman, or even to befriend her, without the Warden's permission.

Borderers were not the kind to ask leave for anything, and especially not to go courting. They married across the line with a fine disregard for the laws, which young Scrope in 1593 confessed were "too remissly executed"—so frequently, in fact, that when Thomas Musgrave drew up his celebrated list of Border riders, he made a special note of those Mangerton Armstrongs who were *not* married to English girls, and underlined his point by singling out the Elliots because few of them took English wives. The Armstrongs seem to have found the Graham and Forster girls particularly attractive, and vice versa.

The same thing happened all along the Border; one of the charges levelled against Sir John Forster, the English Middle March Warden, was that he tolerated inter-racial marriages—the Forsters with the Humes, the Selbys with the Rutherfords, the Collingwoods with the Halls of Teviotdale, the Reades with the Armstrongs, and so on. Forster, sunk deep as he was in Border politics, doubtless had his own private reasons for permitting these alliances, but these apart he was too old and worldly-wise to try to impose government's law on nature's.

These inter-racial marriages greatly complicated the Warden's work (to say nothing of the historian's) since they flatly contradicted the ancient working principle that Scot and English were mutually hostile. At worst, they provided an added incentive to English and Scottish marauders to combine in their depredations, and in their hostility to authority; at best they confused an already complicated social pattern. It was impossible for a Warden to rely on a man whose wife—and therefore father-in-law and brothers-in-law, to say nothing of uncles and cousins—belonged to the other side. A glance at Musgrave's list, with its massive succession of Anglo-Scots marriages, or at the Graham genealogy, over which poor Burghley spent so much weary annotation, will explain why young Scrope was driven to despair by subjects who had ties with both sides of the line, and exploited them shamelessly.

To a virtual outsider like Scrope it was a hopeless situation. One of his own principal Border officers, Thomas Carleton, a former constable of Carlisle Castle, was closely related by marriage to the great Scottish reiver, Kinmont Willie. His English Grahams were so intertwined with the robber families of Liddesdale that "no officer could move against evil-doers of England or Scotland, but the Grahams knew of it and prevented it." They were so strong by marriages on both sides that they were in a unique position to trouble the peace; apart from ordinary confederation with Scottish thieves, they were in the habit of importing their Scottish relatives to do their dirty work for them, and protesting their own innocence.

The Grahams were admittedly a special case. Scottish in origin, English by adoption, and ready to be either, they were settled within the limit of the English West March. The biggest family in the Western Border, they also had a fair claim to being the worst. In murder, blackmail, theft, extortion, and intrigue they were second to none—yet they held their English land on condition that they defend the Border against the Scots, watching the fords and being constantly "with gere and horses still reddye" to resist incursions. How well they did it was seen in the Kinmont raid when they actually assisted Buccleuch's foray to Carlisle Castle, having done much of the plotting groundwork as well.

"Many of them are linckede in marriage [with the Scots], and partakers with them, and some bringers in of the same." It was the understatement of the century, but manfully as Scrope tried to prove the Graham's treachery (which everyone knew, anyway), he was never able to do anything effective about them.

And of course with the passage of time the general situation became worse, with the international family ties growing ever stronger and more complex, until it must have seemed to harassed officials like Scrope that everyone in his March had relatives over the Border, and was therefore involved in their tangled and ever-changing feuds and alliances. It became increasingly hard to determine who precisely was who, much less who could be trusted.

But if intermarriage was a dangerous nuisance, thickening the plots of regular criminal conspiracy, it was no more alarming to the English Wardens than Scottish immigration. Illegal pasturing of cattle, and even raising of crops, in the opposite realm, was one thing, but the permanent settlement of thousands of Scots on the English side of the line was a threat to national security. Hunsdon in 1587 found "so many Scottes planted within Northumberland, especially on the very Borders, as no exploit or purpose can be secretly resolved uppon, but . . . the Scottes have straight warning." In some English towns there were more Scots than English; given authority, Hunsdon would get rid of two or three thousand of them.

This invasion was partly blamed on the fact that the English tenants had been driven out by Scottish raiders; it would have been fair to share the responsibility with oppressive English landlords. And it does not appear as though the ordinary English Marchman shared his superiors' concern at the presence of the incomers; large numbers of Scots found employment as servants on the English side.

Not all of them were so welcome. The English West March found itself "for Scottes roges . . . overlaide with thousands", and even in the largest English towns their presence constituted an insoluble problem. The Mayor of Berwick was complaining in 1592 of Scottish gentlemen banished from their own country for murder, who went armed about the city's streets; no Scots-born person, he thought, should be permitted there, in particular those Scottish merchants who provided embarrassing competition to local traders, and carried English money into Scotland.[2] But in spite of his complaint, there were still three or four hundred Scots in Berwick four years later (over 10% of the population), although those men of the garrison with Scottish wives had been dismissed, and all Scottish servants banished. Those who remained were "too many for safety", in John Carey's opinion—"Marye! the country is full of Scottes!"

Berwick, although it had provided a special Scottish market place outside the fortifications in 1587 (after all, it depended on Scottish food) and prohibited Scots from lodging in the town "or to walk up and down", was less successful with its unwanted immigrants than Carlisle.

---

2. This may have been a well-founded complaint, in spite of the debasement of English coinage throughout the century. It is worth noting that in 1545 the Scottish Privy Council had forbidden the import of the English groat, because they "ar nocht silver and are false".

"Scotch merchants" were avoiding tolls there in 1596, but as the largest city on the Borders, inured to guarding the worst stretch of the frontier, it seems to have been more tolerant of those from north of the line. Most of its guilds had regulations discriminating against Scots, and the city itself forbade "unchartered" Scots to live there, or to walk the streets after curfew without an English companion. However, it also distinguished between "outmen" (those having business in the city but living outside) and "foroners" (complete strangers), so the Scots were not alone in being specially classified.[3]

Enforcing the discriminatory rules in the cities, and resisting the mass immigration which Hunsdon deplored in the Middle March, depended on being able to tell who was Scottish and who English. This was not always easy. Names were not a reliable indication, since many Border families were represented on both sides of the line, and adopted nationality accordingly. Although the Armstrongs were predominantly Scots, there were plenty of English Armstrongs who had lived in Cumberland from time immemorial, and who felt no kinship whatever for their Liddesdale namesakes. The muster roll of Askerton in England in 1580–81 contains fourteen Armstrongs out of a total of forty-nine names. The Grahams have already been mentioned as the classic example of a divided family; the Nixons and Crosers, important names of Liddesdale, were also as much English as Scottish; the Forsters, Halls, Bells, Littles and many others were to be found on both sides (see Chapter VII).

This was not just a case of small groups having left the parent clan and drifted across the Border; it may have been quite the reverse. Many of the leading Scottish families were in fact English in origin—the Maxwells, Armstrongs, Carlisles, and possibly the Johnstones, among others.

One can pity the innocent "non-Borderer" Wardens, or the unfortunate Frenchman who once held the Scottish East March, when confronted with this kind of mixture. An Armstrong might be an Englishman of unimpeachable standing—but he might well have Scottish relatives, and anyway before he could be safely pigeon-holed

---

3. The Smiths' Guild of Carlisle went even further, specifically discriminating against "Francis forringers". Anyone speaking a foreign tongue was, to Carlisle, simply a Frenchman.

it would be necessary to find out if he was at feud with anyone, or to whom he was paying blackmail, or what professional alliances he might have. In the absence of computers, an "outsider" Warden could only call on God.

Birthplace and antecedents, when they could be established, provided a guide to a man's nationality, but were not infallible. A heated dispute broke out between James VI of Scotland and young Scrope over one Robert Graham, whom the king claimed as "a Scottisman, borne, bapteist, mariit and bruiking (holding) land in Scotland"— powerful qualifications. Possibly so, said Scrope, but he could prove otherwise; for one thing, he had Graham's admission that he was English. This, of course, was usually the decisive argument in doubtful cases: a man had to be accepted as what he said he was. Enterprising Borderers made the most of this; in 1550 Sandye Armstrong, ostensibly English and living in the Debateable Land, drove Lord Dacre to involved correspondence with London by threatening to become Scottish if the English Warden did not give him proper protection from his enemies.

These nationality cases baffled officialdom, who had no means of settling them. When Sir John Maxwell, Warden of the Scottish West March, laid before the Scottish Privy Council in 1564 a proposal that he should "admit George and Arthur Graham as Scottismen", the council played a master-stroke. "Efter the mater wes resonit, and all motives and perswasionis were considerit", Maxwell was told to use his own discretion.

In practice, there probably was one good test that could be applied to a Borderer whose nationality was in dispute, and whose antecedents were unknown: his accent. Even today, dialect has a habit of stopping dead at the Border line; to the native there is all the difference in the world between the harsh, resonant growl of the Cumbrian, the extraordinary guttural Northumbrian voice which makes "r" a drawn-out clearing of the throat, and the up-and-down cadences of the Scottish side. I suspect that on the Eastern Border a dialect expert would find that the accents have come closer together than they have in the West, where the social and cultural barrier between Scotland and England is today as solid as a wall, but in general the difference is strong and unmistakable. Too strong, at any rate, for any local person to confuse a Scots voice with an English one.

Yet there is a widely-held theory that in the sixteenth century there was a common Border accent, and that it was hard to tell Scotch from English. Possibly this belief has arisen because the vocabularies of the two sides are and were very close; the North-country Englishman says "ken" for "know", and "ower" for "over", and "cuddy" for "ass", just as the Scot does. But the pronunciations are quite different, although this may not be so evident to the outsider's ear.

The common-accent school cite as evidence the passage from a seventeenth-century London play in which a Northumbrian is mistaken for a Scot. "I was born in Redesdale," he says, "and come of a wight riding sirname, called the Robsons; gude honest men, and true, saving a little shiftynge for theyr living; God help them, silly poor men."

A woman answers: "Me thinke thou art a Scot by they tongue," and the Robson denies it hotly.

This does not demonstrate anything satisfactorily except that a Londoner had difficulty in telling the difference; one is inclined to prefer the contemporary evidence of the letters in which Borderers, with their eccentric spellings, set their accents on paper. Take the Laird Johnstone, a Scot, writing in 1597:

"I resavit your lordschipis lettre this Vodinsday at four efter nowne," he begins, and later continues ". . . and siclyk hes resavit ane lettre fra Thomis Senws (Senhouse?) desyring me to be in Cairlell this Vodinsday at iij, the quihilk lettre I gat nocht quhill fywe houris efter none."

Now there, as clear as a bell across four centuries, is a Border Scot writing as he talks, with a broad Scottish accent. Could anyone believe that Johnstone spoke with the same accent as a Northumbrian like John Forster, who can be heard muttering gruffly as he writes to Walsingham:[4]

"For we that inhabit Northumberland are not acquaynted with any lerned and rare frazes, but sure I am I have uttered my mynde truly and playnely . . . where as I am wonderfully charged with aboundance of catell fedinge and bredinge upon the Borders, as is aledged—I assure your honour I never solde non."

---

4. Sir Francis Walsingham (1530–90), secretary of state to Queen Elizabeth from 1573 to his death, and famous as chief of intelligence and counter-espionage.

The Northern English voice is unmistakeable—the last four words alone will clinch the matter for anyone who knows the Border voices.[5] Both letters fit precisely into modern Scots and Northumbrian speech, so it seems reasonable to assume that the modern difference in accents is no greater than it was four hundred years ago.

However, even if the outsider Wardens did learn eventually to tell Scot from English by listening to them, they can never have recovered entirely from the shock of discovering just how deep and strong were the links and ties of culture, marriage, outlook, and behaviour between the supposedly opposite sides. Perhaps there are lessons in race relations on the old Border which might be studied with profit by modern sociologists. It was all there—race discrimination, victimisation by law, illegal immigration, and inter-racial marriage—and Border experience seems to suggest that whatever laws may be passed about segregation and integration are fairly irrelevant unless the people closely involved want to go along with them.

---

5. One wonders if Shakespeare knew the Northumbrian accent—he could capture regional voices expertly, as he did in *Henry V* with Fluellen the Welshman and Jamy the Scot. Hotspur's lines in *Henry IV*, Part 1, go beautifully in Northumbrian, especially his "I remember when the fight was done" speech; it is remarkable just how many words and phrases designed to emphasise the Northumbrian vocal peculiarities are contained in this passage— "perfumed like a milliner", "guns and drums and wounds", "untaught knaves, unmannerly", and so on. The same is true for the whole of Hotspur's part; it is hard to believe that this was accidental. (There is, of course, a tradition that Hotspur had a speech impediment, and that Shakespeare knew this. But as one gentleman living in the Coquet Valley has suggested, this apparent impediment may have been no more than an ordinary Northumbrian accent).

IX

Bangtail and company

The Borderers were unusual in so many things that it is not surprising to find that they had their own peculiar customs in the matter of fore-names and nick-names, which fell into several categories.

The first, and most confusing of these, arose from the frequency with which men of the same clan and surname also bore the same Christian name—one index to the Calendar of Border Papers, for example, contains no fewer than twelve Hob Elliots, and there is an abundance of Jock Armstrongs, Walter Scotts, Richard Grahams, Andrew Forsters, and so on. It was necessary to distinguish them, and one method was to combine their Christian name with that of their father: thus Christie Armstrong the son of William Armstrong was Will's Christie, while Christie Armstrong the son of Simon Armstrong was Sim's Christie. This was sometimes carried on to a third generation, so that there were Gibb's Geordie's Francis, Dick's Davie's Davie, and Patie's Geordie's Johnnie. Occasionally the mother was cited, as in Bessie's Andrew and Peggie's Wattie.

A second method was to call a man by his place or land: Kinmont Willie, Lancie Whithaugh, Hob of the Leys, Jock of the Side, Jock of the Park, etc., or by his rank—Sim the Laird, for example. By a com-bination of the two methods we get Whithaugh's Andy, the Laird's Jock, Kinmont's Jock, Hob the clerk's brother, and the like.

All too often contemporary documents dispensed with surnames altogether, and since Armstrongs called the Laird's Jock or Rynion's Archie had a habit of cropping up generation after generation, the task of sorting them out becomes complicated. This happens well up the social scale, too, and it is sometimes difficult to distinguish the various Kerr family leaders, since they are almost invariably referred to not by their given names, but by their estates. One Cessford can look very like another, and the same is true of the great breed of Ferniehurst.

But the most interesting nick-names, and the ones in which the Borderers obviously took great pleasure, were those descriptive and often highly offensive appellations referring to personal appearance, habits, and behaviour. Thus we find Curst Eckie, Ill Will Armstrong, Fingerless Will Nixon, Nebless Clem Croser, the two Elliot brothers, Archie and George, who were familarly known as "Dog pyntle" and "Buggerback", and an Armstrong called "Skinabake". Names like these last three probably owe themselves to nothing more than the Borderers' delight in thinking up irrelevant and poetic obscenities to attach to each other; Border children still bandy them about with disarming fluency.

On the other hand, one can guess how David Armstrong came to be known as "Bangtail". Exploits of a sterner kind are commemorated in names like Ill-drowned Geordie, Archie Fire-the-Braes, Out-with-the-sword, Gav-yt-hem, Crack-spear, and Cleave-the-crune. These explain themselves, but one wonders how a reiver came to be known as Laird-give-me-little, or As-it-luiks, or Hen-harrow, or why the nickname Sweet-milk was so popular.[1]

Robert Bruce Armstrong, the Liddesdale historian, had a fine collection of these names, many of them given above, and one cannot do better than this representative selection:

Hob the king, Dand the man, Gib alangsyde, Hob-wait-about-him, Red Cloak, Unhappy Anthone, Sow-tail, Ower-the-moss, Lang Will, Red Rowan, Wantoun Sim, David-no-gude-priest, Evilwillit Sandie, Shag, Bull, Lamb, Mouse, Sore John and Wynking Will.

If we knew how they came to be awarded we would know more of the Borders than we can ever discover from conventional histories.

---

1. There is a striking resemblance between some of these names and those of Red Indians like Alligator-Stands-Up, Thunder-Rolling-over-the-Mountain, and Crazy Horse. Many of these meant the opposite of what they appeared to mean—e.g. Man-Afraid-of-his-Horses, far from being a term of contempt, meant literally a man so formidable that even the sound of his horses terrified his enemies. Probably some of the Border names above have the same kind of hidden meaning.

X

The game and the song

Like so many warlike people, the Borderers were sports enthusiasts, and still are. The little Scottish towns, with their small catchment areas, produce Rugby teams that compare with the biggest club sides anywhere; within living memory the wrestlers of Cumberland, farm boys and Saturday afternoon amateurs, could send out a team to meet the best in the world and beat them.

There was no Rugby in the sixteenth century, but there was "football", the father of Rugby, Soccer, and the American game. In its primitive form it lingers today in places like Jedburgh and Workington, where most of the young male population is supposed to take part, and the playing area covers the whole town. The old Borderers loved their football, and on the Scottish side even the nobility joined in, despite the laws against "futbawis, gouff, or uthir sic unproffitable sportis". Mary Queen of Scots once watched a two-hour match on the meadow beneath Carlisle Castle, and Francis, Earl Bothwell, the notorious "King Devil", played the game on the Esk with other "declairit traitours to his Majesty" in 1592. He occasionally played dirty too, if we can accept Robert Bowes' account of an earlier match in which "some quarrel happened betwixt Bothwell and the Master of Marishal upon a stroke given at football on Bothwell's leg by the Master, after that the Master had received a sore fall by Bothwell." Every football fan will recognise this sequence of events; obviously some things about the game have not changed. Following the incident Bothwell and the Master agreed to meet secretly next day to fight the matter out, and the king had to intervene.

Football incidents were not always so trivial, however. One match, the fore-runner of the Scotland *v.* England internationals, perhaps, resulted in slaughter. It happened in 1599, when six Armstrongs came to Bewcastle to play a match against six of the local English boys, and after the game there was "drynkyng hard at Bewcastle house". However, it happened that a Mr William Ridley, an Englishman, "knowing the continual haunt and receipt the great thieves and arch murderers of Scotland had with the captain of Bewcastle", determined to capture the Armstrong footballers while they were on English ground. No sportsman, he assembled his friends and lay in wait, but somehow the Armstrongs had been tipped off, and Mr Ridley's ambush party found themselves suddenly set on by more than 200 riders. Ridley and two of his friends were killed, thirty taken prisoner, "and many sore hurt, expecially John Whytfeild whose bowells came out, but are sowed up againe".

The result of the game is not recorded.

Even more popular was horse-racing, in which the Borderers excelled, especially in the West Marches. The prizes were usually bells, and the oldest, dating from the 1590s, is in Tullie House Museum, Carlisle. Like the football matches, race meetings were frowned on by the authorities because they attracted the dregs of society, and were commonly used as covers by plotters: the rescue of Kinmont Willie was planned, in its later stages, at a Scottish race meeting, and the murder of Sir John Carmichael, a Scottish Warden, by Armstrongs, was plotted at a football match.

However, Wardens and officers sometimes attended the races. Young Buccleuch was a race addict, Lord Willoughby[1] entered horses at Scottish meetings and won a bell, and young Scrope, who was a compulsive gambler, attended at least one meet where he conducted secret political business. The meetings appear to have been quietly run, considering the times, but there were occasional outbursts of violence, and at one meeting where a Graham and an Irvine quarrelled, the Irvine's horse was killed.

Racehorses were greatly prized, and although horse-trading between

---

1. Peregrine Bertie, 11th Lord Willoughby d'Eresby (1555–1601), Warden of the English East March and Governor of Berwick from 1598 till his death, is commemorated in the old ballad as

> ". . . the brave Lord Willoughby, who is both fierce and fell,
> He will not give one inch of ground for all the devils in hell."

A renowned military leader and splendid swordsman, Willoughby was slightly less of an aristocrat than his name and title suggest. He was the legitimate son of Baroness Willoughby and her gentleman-usher (whose father had been master-mason of Winchester Cathedral) and "could not brook the obsequiousness and assiduity of the court". In his own words, Willoughby was "none of the reptilia".

the realms was forbidden from time to time, leading Borderers as well as lesser men were willing to wink at the law where a good mount was concerned. It was not unknown even for a Warden officer to enter a horse for a race so that a prominent reiver from the other country might judge it with a view to buying—and this a reiver whom the officer had arrested in dramatic circumstances not long before (see p. 119, note 5).

Hawking, hunting and fishing were of course popular sports, and occasionally provided the excuse for Anglo-Scottish fraternisation, although one celebrated hunting resulted in bloodshed, and almost full-scale battle. Farther down the sporting scale cock-fighting was popular, and still takes place in Cumberland: during the war I saw a main organised by Border Regiment soldiers in Burma, and only a few years ago a Cumberland farmer ran for Parliament on a platform to legalise cock-fighting.[2]

All these sports lent themselves to gambling, which seems to have been quite heavy, and cards was also a popular way of losing money and stolen goods. Reivers commonly wagered their spoils; for example, William Taylor of Hethersgill, an Englishman who rode forays with the Armstrongs, "had fower nowte (cattle) about his house, stolen from Chalke, and plaied one of them away at cards". At the other end of the social scale King James IV of Scotland, visiting Dumfries in 1504, played cards against the English Warden, Lord Dacre, who took him for £2 6s 8d. Border papers and letters contain many references to cards, but dice is less frequently mentioned.

The more sophisticated entertainments were rare. London might be enjoying a theatrical boom late in Elizabeth's reign, but when a troupe of actors crossed the Border in 1599 it was such a phenomenon that John Carey wrote to Cecil about it: the Kirk had forbidden them to appear in Scotland, he reported, "and have preached against them with very vehement reprehensions". But to the great offence of the Church, King James VI, who was a theatre enthusiast, commanded that the players should perform and that no one should be prevented from seeing them.

But such entertainments, if they had ever reached the Borderland,

---

2. He was not elected, but attracted some enthusiastic supporters, who greeted his platform appearances with cries of "Git the spurs oot and let's git crackin' ".

would have seemed tame to people whose pastime it was to fashion their drama from their own lives. "They take great pleasure in their own music", wrote Leslie, "and in their rhythmical songs, which they compose upon the exploits of their own ancestors." When James IV came to the Borders, with a large following of minstrels and musicians, he also spent sums on local performers, who included a girl from Carlisle specially engaged to sing for him. Her fee was 28s. But although they might hold their own in music, it was in poetry that the Borderers excelled.

The Border ballads are world famous. They are earth poetry. That they have survived in such quantity is due largely to the industry and enthusiasm of Sir Walter Scott, who saved them from oblivion. He and others added ballads of their own, but both the original folk-poems and the imitations are in a literary class by themselves. It seems strange that such a crude, warlike folk should produce such a vital and lasting literature. Scott believed that the wilder the society the more violent the impulse received from poetry and music; the impulse in the Border was both violent and permanent.

They made their poems about their robber heroes, and as a result their characteristics are turbulence and melancholy. How much Scott amended and edited the oral traditions we shall never know exactly; he was never one to spoil a good thing for the want of a little adjustment. But the raw material was magnificent; listen to the opening lines of "Jock o' the Side", with its stark urgency and echo of hoofs on the tops:

> Now Liddesdale has ridden a raid
> But I wat they had better hae stayed at hame,
> For Michael of Winfield he is dead
> And Jock o' the Side is prisoner ta'en.

And compare the quiet, ominous words of the English reiver, Hobbie Noble,[3] planning his last foray:

---

3. Hobbie (Halbert) Noble figures in two of the best-known Border ballads. In one he is a rescuer of Jock of the Side from Newcastle prison; the second ballad describes Hobbie's own betrayal by one Simon Armstrong of the Mains to the English authorities. According to both ballads he was a Bewcastle man, outlawed for his crimes, and living with the Liddesdale Armstrongs. In fact there was a "Hobbe Noble" living in Bewcastle with others

> "But will ye stay till the day go down
> Until the night come o'er the ground,
> And I'll be a guide worth any twa
> That may in Liddesdale be found."
>
> But word is gane to the land sergeant,
> In Askerton where that he lay—
> "The deer that ye hae hunted sae lang
> Is seen into the Waste this day."

Or the saddest of all Border songs, "The Lament of the Border Widow", supposedly written of a reiver hanged at his own door in 1529:

> But think na ye my heart was sair
> When I laid the mould on his yellow hair?
> O think na ye my heart was wae
> When I turned about, away to gae?
>
> No living man I'll love again,
> Since that my lovely knight is slain,
> With ae lock of his yellow hair
> I'll chain my heart for evermair.

These are fragments; to read through Scott's "Minstrelsy" is to go into a new world whose echoes have sounded through the poetry and folk music of the English-speaking peoples.[4] For those who can take the ballads—and not everyone can—they provide a haunting impression of the Border spirit, captive and restless in a hostile world, sometimes breaking free in exhilarating imagination, but always returning to the resigned sadness of the North.

★

---

of his own surname and with the English Nixons in 1583 (Musgrave's list); he may be the famous reiver of the ballads, since he was contemporary with Jock Armstrong of the Side, and with several Simon Armstrongs. But there is no record of his being outlawed, or going to Scotland, although it is interesting to note that the Nobles, English in 1583, were being referred to by 1596 as "leige subjects of Scotland".

4. Among the modern poets who were touched by the spirit of the Border ballads, Kipling is foremost. And possibly a poetic gift may be inherited across the centuries—it is at least interesting that one of the greatest poets of the twentieth century was an Eliot.

This, then, was the background and culture of the Anglo-Scottish frontier society of the sixteenth century. We have seen how it arose, what influences shaped it, and how it had come to prey on itself for existence. The essence of the story is how the preying was done, who did it, and how authority tried to stop it.

PART THREE

"Shake Loose the the Border"

XI

Lance and steel bonnet

The Border robber was a specialist, and needed special equipment, the most important part of which was his horse. "They reckon it a great disgrace for anyone to make a journey on foot," wrote Leslie, and Froissart had noted two centuries earlier how the Scots at war "are all a-horseback . . . the common people on little hackneys and geldings." The Border horses, called hobblers or hobbys, were small and active, and trained to cross the most difficult and boggy country, "and to get over where our footmen could scarce dare to follow."

Such precious animals naturally attracted legislation, particularly in England, where horses were in short supply. In the late 1500s their export to Scotland was strictly banned; Hunsdon "condemde sundry" for this treason in 1587, and complained that English gentlemen were involved in the illicit trade. It was a well-broken law in both directions, for Scotland had banned horse export twenty years earlier, with no great success.

The Scots had long been noted horse-breeders, so much so that legislation was occasionally passed to restrain production. By statute of 1214 every Scot of property must own at least one horse, and in 1327 the country could put 20,000 cavalry into the field. Export to England at that time was highly profitable, and was carried on even by men of rank. The Stuart kings imported from Hungary, Poland, and Spain to improve the breed, and there emerged the small, swift unusually hardy mounts which in James IV's time were reputed to be able to cover as much as 150 miles in a day. They must have been short miles.

However, even allowing for exaggeration, such horses were ideal all-purpose mounts both for peace-time raiders and war-time light cavalry. They enabled the Border riders to muster and move men at high speed over remarkable distances. A leader like young Buccleuch could raise 2000 horse at short notice, able to strike faster and at far greater range than would have seemed credible to an ordinary cavalry commander; between sixty and eighty miles a day seems to have been within their capability.[1] In addition, the horses were cheap to buy and easy to maintain: there is evidence that they did not even need shoeing.

The Border rider, as he sat his hobbler, was a most workmanlike figure, far more streamlined than the ordinary cavalryman of his time. His appearance was "base and beggarly" by military standards, and this applied to the lords as well as to the lowly. "All clad a lyke in jackes cooverd with whyte leather, dooblettes of the same or of fustian, and most commonly all white hosen," Patten noted after Pinkie (1547). "Not one with either cheine, brooch, ryng or garment of silke that I coold see. . . . This vilnes of port was the caus that so many of their great men and gentlemen wear kyld and so fewe saved. The outwarde sheaw . . . whearby a stranger might discern a villain from a gentleman, was not amoong them to be seen."

On his head the rider wore the steel bonnet, which in the early part of the century was usually the salade hat, basically a metal bowl with or without a peak, or the burgonet, a rather more stylish helmet which, in its lightest form, was open and peaked. These head-pieces, many of which would be home-made by local smiths, were gradually replaced in Elizabethan times by the morion, with its curved brim, comb, and occasional ear pieces.

Over his shirt the rider might wear a mail coat, but the more normal garment was the jack, a quilted coat of stout leather sewn with plates of metal or horn for added protection. It was far lighter than armour,

---

1. Froissart says twenty to twenty-four leagues a day, which is around seventy miles. It has been suggested that this is an incredible distance for armed riders, and that for "leagues" one should read "miles". But Howard Pease has produced evidence to show that when Froissart said leagues he meant just that (i.e. three miles), and as we know that in 1603 Robert Carey rode close on 400 miles from London to Edinburgh in sixty hours (and took a nasty wound on the way, which reduced his speed) it seems safe to credit Froissart's estimate.

As to their mustering speed, there is abundant evidence, in Warden's correspondence and elsewhere, of the Borderers' ability to be armed and riding in force in a remarkably short time after an alarm; John Maxwell of Herries reckoned that 350 horsemen could be assembled in thirty minutes.

and almost as effective against cuts and thrusts; backs and breasts of steel might be worn by the wealthier Borderers, but for horsemen whose chief aim was to travel light they were a mixed blessing. The Scots Borderers were officially recognised by the Privy Council as "licht horsemen" who were not obliged to serve in heavy armour during war; the English Borderers, when employed on campaigns, were similarly used as scouts and "prickers".

Leather boots and breeches completed the clothing, which was without badges except in war-time, when the riders wore kerchiefs tied round their arms as signs of recognition, as well as the crosses of St George or St Andrew, according to their nationality—or their allegiance. Embroidered letters attached to their caps were also used for war-time identification. (There was a suspicion in the English Army in the 1540s that the English March riders used these identifying signs not only to be known to each other, but "that thei used them for collusion, and rather bycaus thei might be knowen to th'enemie, as the enemies are knowen to them, for thei have their markes too, and so in conflict either each to spare other, or gently each to take other. Indede men have beeen mooved the rather to thinke so, bycaus sum of their crosses—the English red cross—were so narrow, and so singly set on, that a puff of wynde might blowed them from their breastes.")[2]

This light and serviceable costume, so suitable for the cut-and-run activities of its wearer, reflected also the changing military patterns of the day. The sixteenth century saw a revolution in warfare; it was the bridge between the medieval knights and men-at-arms, with their heavy armour and weapons, and the age of firepower.

Gunpowder had come into its own, and when it was discovered that mail did not stop a bullet, the whole concept of protective equipment changed. Long leather boots took the place of greaves, plate gave way to the reinforced coat, and the knight's casque to the open helmet.

The great change, of course, was in missile weapons. For two centuries England's military thinking had been dominated by one of the most lethal hand weapons in the history of warfare: the six-foot long

---

2. The authority again is William Patten, a shrewd Londoner who accompanied Somerset's Scottish expedition in 1547. One of his army acquaintances was young William Cecil, later Lord Burghley; the two of them kept journals of the expedition, which Patten used when he published his account of the campaign.

bow with which the English peasant had mastered the powers of chivalry. Naturally, England was reluctant to change from this proven battle-winner, and in this as in most other military developments she lagged behind the Continent, even under such a war-conscious monarch as Henry VIII.

The hand-gun *v.* long bow controversy, which reached a climax in Elizabeth's reign, was a bitter one. The bow school, apart from their sentimental reasons, urged the efficiency of the archer who could despatch twelve shots a minute into a man-sized target at 200 paces (practice at shorter ranges was actually forbidden in Henry's time); against this the new arquebus could fire only ten to twelve shots *an hour* when Elizabeth came to the throne, although the rate had risen to thirty-five to forty by 1600. An arquebus was unsuitable in wet weather, it was cumbersome, and it cost 30s. (A bow cost about 6s 8d, with arrows). The Earl of Sussex, on the Border in 1569, demanded archers, not "ill-furnished harquebusiers", and local opinion seems to have supported him; the tenants of Home Cultram, as late as 1596, rejected calivers as too expensive.

But the fire-arms lobby, which included such influential figures as the veteran Sir Roger Williams, eventually got their way; in the 1560s the majority of English infantry carried the long bow, but by 1600 it was virtually obsolete in the country as a whole. On the Border, however, where a light, rapid-fire weapon was needed, the bow lived longer; in Leith Ward, Cumberland, in 1580, the muster roll showed over 800 bowmen to nine arquebusiers, and in the 1583 muster the English West March counted 2500 archers, with no mention of fire-arms. Hundreds of hand-guns with ammunition were sent to Berwick in 1592, but the powder was unreliable, and as for the guns, "when they were shot in, some of them brake, and hurte divers mennes hands." In the same year Richard Lowther asked only for bows for the defence of Carlisle.[3]

Like the local peasant infantry, the Border riders also used the bow, but there is increasing mention as the century progresses of their carrying arquebuses, the light pieces called calivers, and the dag, the heavy

---

3. Possibly the fact that one Scottish monarch, James II, had lost his life through a bursting cannon in 1460 helped to prejudice the Scots against fire-arms. Hertford noted in the 1540s that the "Scotishe borderers . . . love no gonnes, ne will abyde withyn the hearyng of the same".

hand-gun which was the rough equivalent of the modern large-calibre pistol.

The principal close-quarter weapons of the Border foot soldier were the bill, the long cleaver-cum-pike which had lasted through the Middle Ages, the spear, and a local arm called the Jedburgh axe, with a distinctive round cutting edge. Swords are seldom mentioned in the English muster rolls, but the March riders of both sides certainly carried them, occasionally with small shields.

However, in peace or war, the rider's favourite weapon was the lance. These were sometimes over thirteen feet long, but usually must have been shorter. They were used couched, for thrusting, and also for throwing. Camden describes the Borderers on horseback spearing salmon in the Solway; anyone who has tried to spear fish on foot will appreciate the expertise required to do it from the saddle.

Eure pronounced on this Border skill without qualification: he found the March riders better at handling lances on horseback than Yorkshiremen, and "better prickers in a chase as knowing the mosses, more nimble on foot."

This then was the Borderer's armoury, for war-time campaign or peace-time raid. So if one mounts the reiver on his hobbler, with steel cap, jack, lance, cutting-sword, dagger, and hand-gun,[4] he is fully equipped and ready to be pointed at the target—farm, village or grazing herd, peel tower or sheiling. This, quite literally, was his day's work.

---

4. Basically the reiver's equipment was not very different from that which the English Border light horseman was supposed to carry for government service, and which the Bishop of Durham defined as "a steele cap, a coate of plate, stockings and sleeves of plate, bootes and spurres, a Skottisch short sworde and a dagger, an horsemans staffe and a case of pistolls".

XII

How the reivers rode

The reivers themselves, as has already been mentioned, might be anything from peers to farm hands; some were full-time professional raiders, others divided their time fairly evenly between agriculture and stealing, and some made only occasional forays, when times were hard or they were offered a particularly tempting quarry. They commonly rode in family parties—Liddesdale raids were almost invariably made up of permutations of Elliots, Armstrongs, Crosers, and Nixons, just as the Redesdale and Tynedale incursions consisted largely of Charltons, Dodds, Milburns, and Robsons.

Obviously raiders got to know each other, and there is strong evidence of professional loyalty, the same men riding in each other's company again and again, whether or not they belonged to the same family. This professional tie often spanned the Border, and it was common for Englishmen to ride with Scottish bands, and vice versa. The outlaw operations, of course, were international; gangs like Sandy's Bairns, with whom Kinmont Willie rode latterly, would welcome recruits from anywhere.

Unfortunately there were no Pepyses among the reivers, to leave a day-to-day journal of their activities. So we can only guess how many raids were casual affairs, and how many were carefully plotted weeks in advance. We cannot know for sure if some raider's wife, aware that her larder was running short, ever did lay a dish of spurs before her husband as a hint to be busy. One can imagine an Armstrong, in his tower, finding time hanging heavy and whistling in his sons and cousins for a spur-of-the-moment foray to Redesdale or Gilsland; they would perhaps enlist a couple of Elliots on the way, or pick up a specialist in the shape of a rider who knew the target area particularly well. On the other hand, a leader like Buccleuch was, as we know, capable of the most meticulous planning and intelligence work before he mounted a foray.

Frequently raids began from what was called a "tryst", a prearranged meeting-place where the last-minute details were settled. These were usually well-known landmarks, and when a raid had set off without its full muster, a sign would be left to indicate the direction taken. According to Scott, one method was to cut the leader's name or signal in the turf, the arrangement of the letters indicating the path to be followed.

Everyone who writes about the reiver's technique invariably quotes Bishop Leslie, in one of his various translations. This is Camden's, quoted by Scott; it is worth remembering that it applies to both Scottish and English alike.

"They sally out of their own borders, in the night, in troops, through unfrequented by-ways, and many intricate windings. All the day time, they refresh themselves and their horses, in lurking holes they had pitched upon before, till they arrive in the dark at those places they have a design upon. As soon as they have seized upon the booty, they, in like manner, return home in the night, through blind ways, and fetching many a compass. The more skilful any captain is to pass through those wild deserts, crooked turnings, and deep precipices, in the thickest mists and darkness, his reputation is the greater, and he is looked upon as a man of an excellent head.

"And they are so very cunning, that they seldom have their booty taken from them . . . unless sometimes, when, by the help of bloodhounds following them exactly upon the tract, they may chance to fall into the hands of their adversaries. When being taken, they have so much persuasive eloquence, and so many smooth insinuating words at command, that if they do not move their judges, nay, and even their adversaries (notwithstanding the severity of their natures), to have mercy, yet they incite them to admiration and compassion."

His lordship the bishop writes with such feeling and descriptive skill that one wonders if he wasn't out with the Armstrongs himself on some occasion. He has the exact mood of the business, and everything he says is consistent with the voluminous records of raids left in Border documents. What he was describing was a long-distance foray, such as might be made by Liddesdale riders far into the English Middle March, with only a small number of men involved and the need for passing undetected of the first importance.

Raids varied in size. Bands of a dozen to fifty riders were normal, but there were one-man operations, and great forays in which upwards of two or three thousand reivers took part. The objectives also varied, from a single animal—as in the case of the black horse which helped to rekindle the Maxwell-Johnstone feud—to an entire town, or even several towns. Distance was no object for rustlers who were expert at covering their traces, or who ventured out in sufficient numbers to be able to defy pursuit. Border raids are recorded within three miles of Edinburgh, and as far south as Yorkshire. What is striking is that the thieves far more often than not got away with it, which suggests that Leslie's skilful captains and men of excellent heads were by no means uncommon.

Night-time was the popular hour for riding, although day forays of all sizes were frequent. There is some evidence that the reivers liked moonlight—"There'll be moonlight again" is a slogan long associated with the Scott family—but even more to suggest that they preferred complete darkness. The expert guides seem to have known their ground to an inch, and the kind of leader typified by Hobbie Noble, the legendary English fugitive, could pick his way through the wastes at night with ease.

The size of the foray naturally dictated the technique employed. While small bands depended heavily on stealth and secrecy, the great raids went much more openly; they had less to fear from a hot trod or the country's rising against them, since they were strong enough to fight off anything short of an army. Consequently, their leaders planned these forays like miniature military campaigns, often spending several days in enemy territory, or even longer, depending on the danger of the general situation.

A master of the large-scale foray technique was that old Walter Scott of Buccleuch who flourished in the first part of the sixteenth century, was an inveterate English-hater, spent several terms in confinement in Scotland for political and other reasons, and was eventually cut down by the Kerrs in the great Kerr–Scott feud. When he swept into the English Middle March in the winter of 1532 it was with 3000 lances, most of whom he held in reserve while smaller forays were detached at chosen targets. The main body thus served the double purpose of base camp, established on an English village, and ambush for any English trods which might pursue Buccleuch's smaller raiding bands.

The ambush was a common variation of the large and medium-sized raids, the reivers leaving a strong party posted on their proposed return route, so that pursuers chasing a raid frequently found themselves surrounded and beset by an unexpectedly large enemy force. This was a favourite stratagem of the Armstrongs, who practised it memorably against Lord Dacre in 1528 (see pp. 227-9).

The raiding season, although it was never closed in practice, was autumn to spring, when the cattle and their owners were in their permanent winter quarters in the valleys. As the summer waned, anxiety grew along the frontier; "the longer the nights growe, the worse they will be", wrote Robert Carey one late August, and young Scrope in November was lamenting: "The depe of winter and most unquiet season is come upon us." Carey made a study of this aspect of reiving, and pronounced the last months of the year as the worst, "for then are the nights longest, theyre horses at hard meat, and will ride best, cattel strong, and will drive farthest."

Of those closing months, the worst period was from Michaelmas (September 29) to Martinmas (November 11): "then are the fells good and drie and cattle strong to dryve". The dead of winter was comparatively less troublesome, because of foul weather and the weaker state of the cattle. This weakness had reached a peak by Candlemas (February 2), when with the nights growing shorter and oats dearer, the reivers' horses were less well fed and ready to be put to grass.

Thus Robert Carey, waxing technical on an admittedly technical subject: he even noticed that the thieves "will never lightly steal hard before Lammas (August 1), for fear of the assizes, but beeing once past, they returne to their former trade". In fact it was probably not the assizes, but the removal of the cattle to the high sheilings during the summer that restrained the robbers. But his observations show up some of the finer points of reiving, although judging by Border records the pattern of raiding was spread more generally over the year than his findings suggest.

As to any geographical pattern of raids, it is difficult to say more than that the general trend from Scotland was south-eastwards, the Western end of the frontier containing by far the most troublesome elements, while from England the Middle March raiders forayed in all directions. Edward Aglionby's report to Burghley of 1592 is quite definite that the English West and Middle Marches suffered most from Liddesdale, but that Teviotdale "doth never offend the West Border".

Lord Willoughby, at Berwick, was equally positive that all the spoils in the English East March were committed over the Tweed fords.

But it is dangerous to take these generalisations too much for granted, just as it is unwise to emphasise too strongly the importance of the so-called "reivers' roads" which cross the Border at various points. It is tempting for a geographer to pick on well-defined paths and passages, and suggest that these were used habitually by the rustlers. The last thing a Border reiver wanted was to follow a known route, especially on the way home. There were, by contemporary calculation, more than forty passages into the English Middle March,[1] but unless the Border character has changed considerably, they were probably often ignored in favour of going "over the tops". Men who know their business can take cattle over some unpromising country.

One thing is sure: the ground most often crossed by raiders was the Bewcastle Waste, a wild area of fell and moor lying south-east of Liddesdale on the English side. It was the very hub of the Middle and West Marches, and there is ample documentary confirmation of Lord Dacre's assertion in 1528, that "theye come thorow Bewcastelldale, and retirnes, for the moste parte, the same waye agayne".

But not invariably, according to Thomas Musgrave fifty years later. Writing to Burghley, he described two Liddesdale routes quite specifically; one, directed at the Coquet Valley, skirted Bewcastle to the east and ran "by the Perlfell without the Horse Head near Kelder, and so along abone Chepechase". The second, to Tyne Water, was by Kershopehead, skirting Gele Crage, and by Tarnbek, Bogells Gar, Spye Crag, and Lampert. Musgrave was an expert frontiersman, and his information can be relied on. But these were routes which would be fashionable for a time—as in the Elliot–Fenwick feud; for the most part, the reivers were liable to ride anywhere, at any time, in any numbers.

To understand how good their scouting and woodcraft was, we should see what they were up against, quite apart from the dark, the weather, and the rough country. On the English side the most expert of all Wardens, Lord Wharton, had established a formidable guard system in the 1550s, whereby the entire frontier, from Solway to Berwick, was under watch night and day, from October to mid-March; local gentlemen were made responsible for arming and horsing

1. The names attached to some of the Middle March riders' passages are highly evocative: Murders Rack, Hell Cauldron, Keilder Edge, Thrust Pick, etc.

their people, and setting and inspecting the watches, which were posted on hilltops, fords, valleys, and every conceivable passage over the Marches. Wharton, a hard man who believed in hanging first and asking questions later, reinforced his system with harsh penalties for neglect of duty; it was death not to resist raiders,[2] all intercourse with Scots was forbidden, and gentlemen were under the strictest instructions to see his rules enforced. He knew his Borderers, and was determined to stamp out any fifth column activities on the raiders' behalf.

Nor could the reivers count on watches always being in the same place; small mobile patrols were also used, and "plump" watches of unusual strength were liable to be set up as occasion demanded.

To man the frontier efficiently, about 1000 watchers were necessary; it follows that in spite of the regulations, there was some defaulting. Young Scrope found difficulty in maintaining plump watches of forty horse in the West, and at Morpeth in the winter of 1597 there was a flat refusal to stand watches, so that a plump watch had to be moved in. Possibly owing to shortage of men, day watches seem to have been indifferently kept in young Scrope's time.

Watches on the Scottish side seem to have been less organised, which may be significant, but here as in England there was a system of beacons on hilltops and the roofs of towers to give the alarm. Owners of towers were obliged to light their beacons on learning of any fray by night; the penalty for failure was a 3s 4d fine. In Liddesdale the approach of a raid in daylight was signalled by spreading a white sheet over a prominent bush on a hillside or crest, this being repeated all along the valley.

England had another line of defence, in the establishment of numbers of "slewdogges"[3] for the tracking down of raiders; money was raised

---

2. The penalty was eventually relaxed, and after 1570 watchers in the English West and Middle Marches who failed to raise a hue and cry against thieves were only held liable for goods stolen.

3. Also given as sloughdogs and sleuthdogs. Scott traces the name from the sloughs and mosses through which they followed the scent, but it seems more likely that it came from sleuth, meaning a track or trail. Trail hounds are common in Cumberland today, where they are used for long-distance racing. They travel at surprising speeds after scent, and it seems possible that the sleuthdogs of the sixteenth century were of this breed, rather than bloodhounds.

for their maintenance, and from the number of them stolen in raids it is obvious that they were highly prized. They could be worth as much as £10.

So, even allowing for those watchers who were in league with the reivers, or were too terrified to give them away, the business of raiding was fraught with hazards. From the moment the March limits were crossed, the marauders were riding in the shadow of the gallows; if some of their exploits were undoubtedly mean and cruel, they can hardly be called cowardly. Even when they were riding into a frightened countryside (which was often the case in the last decades of Elizabeth's reign), and were sufficiently expert to avoid or evade the guards, tracker dogs, and mobile patrols, to lift their plunder and shake off pursuit, there were some dangers which could not be anticipated. No band could ever be sure that they were the only ones out on the fells at night; half a dozen raids might cross each others' tracks in the dark, and although hi-jacking was not common, it did happen at least once, to an Elliot party who made a quick dawn foray into Bewcastle only to be jumped by a returning band of English night raiders, who lifted the Scots' booty of eighty head.

XIII

Nothing too hot or too heavy

It is this side of the reiver's work—the danger, the bravery, the almost sporting spirit in which he rode out—that has been emphasised by the romancers. It was there, no doubt of it, and it is easy to treat him as a hero figure because sometimes he was indeed heroic. People like to remember him at his best, as a jolly, daredevil Robin Hood, rough but generous, a product of his times who was no doubt full of mischief, but was decent at bottom, and had some peculiar patriotic aura glowing round him as he went about his work of pillage. It is not difficult, by a judicious selection of cases and evidence, to justify this view.

Isabell Routledge, a widow, owning a small herd and a house of her own in the English West March, saw him rather differently. On April 2

1581 she was visited by thirty Elliots, who ransacked her home, took her four oxen, her six cows, and her only horse, and made off with all her possessions. At that, she was luckier than another woman named Hetherington, who a few years later was raided, again by Elliots, who murdered her husband and another man, and stole her herd of forty head.

And both were more fortunate than Hecky Noble who, within a few nights of Mrs Hetherington's widowhood, was a victim of that gay desperado, Dickie Armstrong of Dryhope,[1] and his 100 jolly followers. Apart from reiving a herd of 200 head, and destroying nine houses, the raiders also burned alive Hecky's son John, and his daughter-in-law, who was pregnant.

For Dick of Dryhope this was part of the night's work. Two days earlier he had murdered a miller named Tailor and another man, burned the mill and twelve houses, and reived 100 beasts. Two months later, he and his friends were despoiling another woman, Margaret Forster, of Bewcastle, stealing her eighteen cattle and rifling her home.

These are not isolated cases. On the contrary, they are typical of Border raiding. The lists are endless of small herds lifted, of homes burned, of "insight" (household goods) removed, value a few pounds, of men wounded, or kidnapped, or occasionally killed. To give an idea of what this meant, one can only examine figures for certain areas and periods.

When the Elliots of Liddesdale were riding in the summer of 1581, they were moving in bands generally 100 strong. In June and July alone they stole in the West March of England 274 cattle and twelve horses, ransacked nine houses, "wounded and maimed" three men, and took one prisoner. Statistics are deceptive; if one tries to see it in the light of a modern newspaper report, it is easier to imagine the horror of thirty sturdy hooligans descending on a woman's house in the night, looting and smashing, and then riding off. This happened along the Marches day in, day out, year after year.

---

1. Dickie of Dryhope (or Driupp) is mentioned in the Ballad of Kinmont Willie as a principal in the raid on Carlisle Castle, and the slayer of "the fause Sakelde". He is not mentioned, however, in the detailed list of the Carlisle raiders sent by young Scrope to Burghley (April 14 1596), so there is no reason to suppose he was there at all. The last mention of him is on March 7 1594, when at a Warden meeting at Kershopefoot he was stated to be no longer living in Liddesdale.

It is instructive to consider the havoc wrought by only one of the Border raiding tribes, over a period. Figures are available for the forays run by the Elliots over a decade from the early 1580s; they are almost certainly conservative figures, since they take account only of actual raids complained of and recorded. And they include only raids in which the Elliots were in a majority; other forays in which the Elliots took a hand, but were not the ringleaders, have been excluded.

There were more than forty of these "exclusively Elliot" raids, and the total score, at the lowest estimate, was more than 3000 cattle stolen, over £1000 worth of insight taken, sixty-six buildings destroyed, fourteen men murdered, and 146 prisoners kidnapped. And this was done, not by the entire Elliot clan, but by only seventy-nine principal riders with their unnamed followers. Taking account of population, property values, the purchasing power of money, the size of the area involved, and the general social conditions, it is worth considering whether the Gennas in Chicago, or the Jameses in the Midwest, or the Gilzais of the North-west Frontier, were such an appalling continual menace as this one Scottish family of the Western Border.

The state of affairs looks even worse when regarded not from a family standpoint, but a geographical one. The Elliots were one of many robber families; Liddesdale was one of many robber's roosts, though admittedly the worst by far. According to a list of bills against Liddesdale, dated April 30 1590, the reivers of that valley alone were riding an average of a raid a week through the winter of 1589–90. In that time they carried off more than 850 beasts, took sixty prisoners, wounded ten men, killed one, took insight of £200, and burned five houses.

If one adds in the previous year, Liddesdale's total is swollen by another 600-odd beasts, four murders, twenty-four prisoners, and one town sacked.

It is quite a record, and from it and other lists of complaints—for it must be emphasised that the figures cited are not unusually high or out of the way—a different picture of the Border reiver emerges. He can be seen for what he very often was, not at all heroic, but a nasty, cruel, mean-spirited ruffian, who preferred the soft mark provided by small farmers, widows, and lonely steadings; who came in overwhelming force, destroyed wantonly, beat up and even killed if he was resisted, and literally stripped his victims of everything they had.

It is fair to quote from a detailed list of the goods taken by a band of thirty Crosers and Elliots in November 1589 from a home on the Middle March; apart from cattle and weapons, the robbers' haul also included a woman's kirtle and sleeves, kerchiefs, underclothes, sheets, a cauldron, a pan, shirts, and four "children's coates". A far cry from Sherwood and the legendary code of robbing the rich to give to the poor. Nor were such petty spoils the exclusive prey of the broken men and outlaws; this was the kind of work that such romantic champions as the Bold Buccleuch and Kinmont Willie were doing; the fact that they did it on a much greater scale lends them no dignity at all.

This is to look at reiving's blackest side, and it is fatally easy to make the mistake of judging by modern standards, and to forget that, so far as the actual pillaging was concerned, no one thought it a matter for shame. A great deal of nonsense has been talked and written about the Borderer's moral standards, and one is right to be sceptical of apologists; nevertheless, it is most important to appreciate the distinction, in the Border mind, between reiving, with its associated offences— blackmail, kidnapping, feud killing, and so on—on the one hand, and "ordinary" crime on the other. Robert Carey was one outsider who fully understood this distinction, and although he did not condone the reivers' behaviour, he did try to explain it. "So have they (the Scots) been used to rob and spoil, and think it their inheritance, scorning all opposition", he wrote, adding that "the English thief [is] as bad or worse than the Scot". Most of us do not think of ourselves as criminals, but possibly there are things in our daily lives which we regard as our "inheritance" which will move future generations to critical disgust.

Crime which had nothing to do with reiving, however, was regarded by the Borderers much as other communities have always regarded it. Interesting evidence of this appears in Carey's memoirs, when he mentions "2 gentlemen theeves that robbed and took purses from travellers in the highways *(a theft that was never heard of in these parts before)*". Carey "got them betrayed", and they were hanged at Newcastle.

This is not to argue, as some writers have done, that the reiver should be judged in a more sympathetic light than an ordinary criminal, but to point out that, if he is to be judged, his own standards of right and wrong should be taken into consideration. To assume that they were the same as those of even his fellow-Elizabethans would be a mistake.

Another common error about Border reiving is to suppose that one side was worse than the other. Most of the examples cited here are of Scottish raids against England; this is simply because the English records are far fuller, and provide more interesting details; if one reads through the colossal lists of raids contained in Elizabethan papers, without a proper background knowledge, one might conclude that poor in-offensive England was an unresisting prey of the predatory Scots. How untrue this would be is shown in the accounting prepared by young Scrope himself in September 1593, of the respective damages done by Scottish and English reivers in the Western Border.

Liddesdale, for once, had taken worse than it gave; for £3230 worth of damage done to England, it had suffered £8000 worth. The Scottish West March raiders had despoiled England to the tune of £6470, but in return had suffered £33,600 of loss. English maurauding had exceeded that of Scotland by the astounding total of almost £32,000 for that particular period.

But usually there was little to choose between the two, and it is more useful to consider the total damage listed by Scrope, which was over £50,000 worth—and this is for only one-third of the Border. Admittedly, the figure covers several years, but if one is extremely conservative and multiplies it only by ten to give an idea of what it means in modern values, we have a crime bill, for the Western Marches only, of half a million pounds.

Another estimate, made in 1596–7 by William Bowes, gives a figure, for all Scottish raids over a ten-year period, of £92,989 6s 1d, of which three-quarters was charged to Liddesdale and Teviotdale. A total, by our standards, of about a million pounds.

Reiving was a very big small business.

XIV

A parcel of rogues

The following are case-histories of three Border reivers, pieced together from the records of the time. They are incomplete, but they may be sufficient to give an idea of a typical raider's activities, and show the kind of factual basis on which so many legends rest.

*

William Armstrong of Kinmont

Kinmont Willie, perhaps the best-known of Border reivers, deserved his reputation. He raided on the big scale, striking not at single farms and villages, but at whole areas, at the head of bands 300 strong. He liked to ride by day, usually eastward from his tower at Morton Rigg, which was right on the Border not far north of Carlisle. His favourite target was Tynedale.

The first of his raids recorded was against the Milburns in that valley, in August 1583, when Armstrong was probably in his forties. Eight separate villages were attacked, several houses burned, 800 cattle stolen, £200 worth of goods taken, six men killed, eleven wounded, and thirty prisoners carried off.

The following year he and Nebless Clem Croser were back on another day foray with 300 riders, lifting 1300 cattle, sixty horses, and £2000 worth of goods, burning sixty houses, and killing ten men.

In 1585 Kinmont Willie was occupied with raiding in his own country; he accompanied the Earl of Angus's campaign against the Earl of Arran, and took the opportunity to pillage in Stirling. It was this raid that made his name, and turned it into a byword for violent crime. But his biggest raid of all occurred eight years later, when he was in Tynedale with 1000 men, carrying off more than 2000 beasts and £300 in spoil.

He seems to have been fairly quiet until 1596, when his famous capture and rescue from Carlisle Castle took place (see Chapter XLI), and after that some of the old fire died. Perhaps he was just getting old, but his raids thereafter were minor affairs. He took the Captain of Bewcastle and sixteen others prisoner in 1597, ransomed them, stole twenty-four horses, and committed some "slaughter"; the bill (charge) against him for this was fouled by confession—which means he pleaded guilty to it. At this time he was being raided himself, from the English West March, his house sacked twice and burned once, 300 of his beasts stolen, and two of his men killed. He fell into English hands again on one of these occasions, but was released.

By this time the former leader of the great day forays had declined to the joint command of an outlaw gang called Sandy's Bairns; in 1600 he attacked the village of Scotby with 140 riders, burning, taking prisoners and over 100 cattle, and with a last spark of his old bravado, riding on to Carlisle the same evening with some "English disobedients". They smashed in a few doors at the Rickergate, damaged the bridge chains, took some prisoners, and rode under the Castle wall roaring, "Upon them, upon them, a Dacre, a Dacre, a red bull, a red bull!" which caused some alarm; the citizens stood to arms and the beacon was lit, but presently the raiders retired, no doubt to sober up.

Next year the old ruffian was operating a protection racket at Scaleby, and doing a little in the way of illicit horse-trading and receiving stolen goods. In 1602 he rode his last foray, probably on Low and High Hesket, south of Carlisle. He was still alive two years later, and his four sons who had helped to get him out of Carlisle Castle in 1596, are frequently named in the later Border raids. But the old robber, full of years and dishonour, probably died in his bed.

*

Walter Scott of Harden

"Auld Wat" of Harden has been represented as the Falstaff of the Borders, a fierce, big-bellied humorous old rascal who is supposed to have passed a haystack on returning from a raid and muttered: "Aye, if ye had fower legs ye wouldnae stand there lang." A number of Border myths are connected with him, and possibly they have some truth, but the bare facts of his foraying are as follows.

He and a handful of Elliots stole two mares and a foal from the Gelt in July 1595, and sixty head of cattle from Triermain two months later. In the following year, with the same Elliots, he ran a day foray in Gilsland with 400 men, took 300 cattle, twenty horses, burned twenty houses, "taking and burning [sic] gold money apperrell worth £400" and "mutilating" several persons. Another raid yielded him 300 beasts and the spoil of two houses, worth £100.

He raided Bellingham in 1597 with more than 300 horse, killed three men, and carried off 400 head, the March being too weak to pursue him. "With shame and grief I speak it," wrote Eure, "the Scotts went away unfought withall."

Auld Wat was a principal in Kinmont Willie's rescue, and in his preliminary report young Scrope mistakenly credited him with being the actual ring-leader. Yet although he is referred to as Buccleuch's right-hand man, he does not appear to have been well known south of the frontier. Scrope refers to him as "one Wattie Harden", and Eure even gave his surname as Elliot. But he was important enough on the Scottish side to have been involved in the Raid of Falkland in 1592, in which the wild Earl of Bothwell tried to capture King James VI;[1] for his part in the attempt Scott had his tower at Harden destroyed.

The popular stories about Auld Wat include the tradition that at his marriage to a noted beauty, Mary Scott, his father-in-law agreed to keep him for a year and a day provided that Scott promised not to take forcible possession of the father-in-law's house at the end of that period. Another is that when his sixth son was slain by a rival band of Scotts, Auld Wat, refusing to let the rest of his hot-headed family take up the feud, locked them in his dungeon, rode to Edinburgh, obtained a grant of the murderers' lands by way of compensation, and then took possession, observing that the acquired territory was worth the loss of one of the family.

The facts of his life are rather less colourful than his legend, but he did make one unwitting contribution to romance: one of his descendants was Sir Walter Scott the novelist.

*

Geordie Burn

Geordie Burn, or Bourne, was a common thug, and would hardly merit special attention but for the fact that almost alone among Border reivers, he left something like a personal testament. He did it unconsciously, the night before they hanged him.

---

1. Francis Stewart, Earl of Bothwell (nephew of Queen Mary's Bothwell), was a notorious desperado, outlaw, reputed witch, and rebel, active on the frontier and in Scottish politics. He made a habit of raiding the king's residences, and on one occasion surprised his majesty in the most embarrassing stage of his toilet. Bothwell spent his last years on the Continent, casting horoscopes and doing conjuring tricks for a living. He died about 1612.

Geordie was a Middle March Scot, over-shadowed by his father and brother, both named Jock, who were prominent reivers. Indeed, when Geordie's name is first mentioned in connection with a raid, it is the last in a list of seven, mostly Youngs, who had lifted twenty cattle and £5 sterling in a foray on July 23 1588. They were a hard bunch, and when followed by hot trod they turned so successfully on their pursuers that they wounded five of them and captured ten horses.

After this his name does not occur again in the Border records for eight years, but in the meantime the Burns, and their associates, the Pringles, Youngs, and Davisons, were savagely at work on the Middle March, and Geordie probably did his share. When his brother Jock, raiding Sir Cuthbert Collingwood's neighbours, was killed by that gentleman on a hot trod, the Burns took a fearful revenge. Seventeen of Collingwood's people were killed in feud,[2] and he himself forced to leave the area.

Under the protection of Sir Robert Kerr of Cessford, the acting Scottish Warden, whose countenancing of the gangsters in his area was an open scandal, the Burns rode high and handsome in the early 1590s; fear of their hot-headed young protector and their own fatal readiness to feud prevented adequate reprisal from England. It was Geordie's bad luck that, on a September night in 1596, while driving stolen beasts back to Teviotdale, he should run into the one man on the Border who was not frightened of Kerr or anyone else—the adventurous young acting Warden of the English East March, Robert Carey, out with a mobile patrol of twenty riders.

There were only four of the Burns, but they put up a stalwart fight. Two were killed, Geordie's uncle being shot in the head, and one escaped, but Geordie laid about him, "bravely resisting", says Carey, "till he was sore hurt in the head". Even when taken "his pride was such, as he asked, who was it that durst avowe that night's work?" He was confident that his captors would be frightened to offend Kerr, and indeed Carey's advisers were conscious that while in Kerr's "great favourite" they held a powerful bargaining counter, they could expect considerable reprisal if he were executed.

---

2. According to Robert Bruce Armstrong, the total of Collingwoods killed in the feud was at least 35.

Carey wasted no time in having Geordie convicted of March treason, and condemned, but postponed the execution to await Kerr's reaction. In the meantime he did an unusual thing; disguising himself as a soldier of the garrison, he went with two of his servants to Geordie's cell. They had come, Carey told him, because they had heard he was a stout and valiant man, and true to his friends, and they were sorry that their master was determined to execute him.

How the aristocratic Carey passed himself off, to a Borderer, as a Northumbrian Marchman, is hard to imagine; however, Burn was willing to talk to them, and Carey took a careful note of what amounted to a reiver's confessional.

"He voluntarily of himself said, that hee had lived long enough to do so many villainies as hee had done; and withal told us, that he had layne with about 40 men's wives, what in England, what in Scotland, and that hee had killed seven Englishmen with his own hands, cruelly murthering them; that he had spent his whole time in whoreing, drinking, stealing, and taking deep revenge for slight offences. He seemed to be very penitent, and much desired a minister for the comfort of his soul."

How much one could have learned of the Borders, if only the modern tape recorder had been available for that hour when Geordie Burn reviewed his misspent life; as it was, he sketched his own character admirably. One suspects that Carey had a regard for him, as one adventurer for another, but he came out of the cell convinced that Geordie was too wicked and dangerous to live. Also, it seems likely, Carey was playing a deadly game of chicken against Robert Kerr.

"I should have offended God, my prince, and my country, if . . . I had suffrd so wicked a man to live," he wrote to Burghley; Burn's misdeeds had been so many that he had said himself he could not remember half of them. So he was hanged, and Carey was embarked on his duel with Robert Kerr, which is not appropriate at this point, but is set out in Chapter XL.

XV

Carleton's Raid

A Border raid might be a one-man affair directed against a solitary farmhouse, or a full-scale invasion for primarily political reasons, in which whole counties were devastated. But in either case, whether it was Dande Pringle lifting Thomas Dickson's horse at Wittoun, or the terrible two-week sweep in which the Earl of Hertford destroyed seven Scottish monasteries, sixteen castles, five market towns, and 243 villages, the principle was the same.

The raider calculated his time, his route, and his objective, was ready to fight or trick his way out as necessary, and had his various "drills" for whatever problems arose. For the men who rode the raids knew both worlds, that of the invading army in time of war when towns and castles were the target, and that of the stealthy foray through the dark fells to bring off the sleeping farmer's little herd. The object was always plunder, often with wanton destruction thrown in, and to get home with loot and skin intact.

An excellent example, which illustrates not only reiving technique at its best, but also the happy adaptability with which the Borderer was ready to combine public duty and private inclination, exists in the narrative of Sir Thomas Carleton, of Carleton Hall, Cumberland, one of the few reivers who ever bothered to describe a raid in writing. Carleton, one of that active family[1] who made life almost as difficult for their fellow-Englishmen as for the Scots, might stand as the arch-type of Border reiver on a large scale. Tough, clever, unscrupulous, self-assured, and with his own grim touch of humour, he was expert in every department of Border raiding, fighting, and politics. If one wanted a practised professional forayer, Carleton was the man.

His raid into Dumfriesshire in February 1547 may be seen historically as part of the policy of the lately-deceased Henry VIII, who demonstrated to Scotland the benefits of English association by doing his best to

---

1. As will be seen later, there were many Thomas Carletons, and Sir Thomas should not be confused with Thomas Carleton the younger, a notable Borderer in the 1580s and 1590s who was Constable of Carlisle.

obliterate the Lowland counties. As such, it was of minor importance, but in its details the raid contains many of those features which distinguish the Border foray.

In the first place, although Carleton was acting officially for the English Crown—he had been Captain of Caerlaverock Castle, and was lieutenant to Wharton, who commanded the English West March—his force was mixed Scottish and English. Like so many English raiders in war-time, he enlisted Armstrongs and other free lances, and crossed the Border in foul weather to descend on Teviotdale, where he "got a great booty of goods". The weather forced him to find shelter first in Canonby and then in Dumfries, where the citizens, who were old hands at being invaded and knew superior numbers when they saw them, did not hesitate to become English subjects for the moment.

Carleton was in the unusual and happy position of being master of more than the ground he stood on, for his force was strong enough to be quite secure against a confused and troubled countryside from which no organised resistance was to be expected—provided he did not linger too long. In the meantime he made a proclamation in the English king's name, demanding submission and getting it, and promising in return English protection.

For ten days Carleton lorded it in Dumfries, receiving pledges from lairds and others in Nithsdale and Galloway, but getting only defiance from the town of Kirkcudbright. Urged on by Wharton from Carlisle, he descended on it at dawn, and found its gates barred and its dykes manned. Carleton attacked, but made little headway, and had to withdraw when a Scottish force under one McLellan of Bombie arrived and had to be dealt with. There was slight loss on both sides, and in withdrawing, Carleton, who never lost sight of the main object, gathered up 2000 sheep, 200 cattle, and about fifty horses.

A curious incident took place during the fighting over the Kirkcudbright dykes, which illustrates the Border code of hostage and ransom. While the arrows were flying and the two sides struggling in the outer defences, a woman of the town "came to the ditch and called for one that would take her husband and save his life". Presumably she expected the besiegers to succeed and was insuring beforehand.

One of the attackers, Anthon Armstrong—probably one of Carleton's Scottish mercenaries—called out to her "Fetch him to me and I'll warrant his life." The woman ran back into the town, says Carleton, "fetched her husband, and brought him through the dyke, and de-livered him to the said Anthon, who brought him into England and ransomed him."

Even in the heat of the skirmish, both sides knew the rules; it was a straight commercial transaction, and Carleton relates it as a passing incident of interest, but nothing extraordinary.

With their plunder, the English raiders fell back towards Dumfries, and were preparing to cross the river at Forehead Ford when a force of "Galloway folk, from beyond the water of Dee" descended on them. Carleton was caught in one of the reiver's classic predicaments; in hostile country, with the locals counter-attacking, a river at his back, and a vast herd of stolen beasts to protect and bring off if he could.

He was too old a hand to panic. Thinking in the saddle, he saw, like Field-Marshal Montgomery, what had to be done. The slow-moving and unmanageable sheep were abandoned, and the cattle and horses hurried across the ford. "We put our worst horsemen before the nowte and nags," says Carleton, "and sent thirty of the best horsemen to preake at the Scots, if they should come over the water, and to abide with the standard in their relief."

The screen of thirty lances, daring the Scots to come over, and ready to engage them in one of those broken, running skirmishes in which the reivers specialised, while the main party escaped, were sufficient to the work. The Scots weighed up the odds and decided not to take them on, "so that we passed quietly that night to Dumfries, leaving the goods in safety with a good watch."

Setting aside the loss of the sheep, a reasonably profitable day's work, and no doubt Wharton in Carlisle, himself a reiver to his backbone, would think so too.

But Carleton was not out of the wood yet. Plunder can be an em-barrassment if the robber has to stay near the scene of the crime, and Carleton had political duties to keep him in Scotland when he would have been safer making for Cumberland with all speed. In the mean-time, he and his followers would divide the spoil; it was under guard a mile from the town, and there they went next day for the carve-up.

Carleton's description is illuminating of the kind of following he had; the King of England's representatives they might be in name, but they were first and foremost riders of the West Marches, with livings to make, and no doubt outlaws among them to make the mixture even more explosive. The discipline that had prevailed like clockwork at Forehead Ford was forgotten: "some claimed this cow, and some that nagg . . . one man (a Scot) came amongst the goods, and would needs take one cow, saying that he would be stopped by no man, insomuch that one Thomas Taylor, called Tom-with-the-Bow, being charged with the keeping of the goods, struck the said Scotsman on the head with his bow, so that the blood ran down over his shoulders."

With the thieves falling out, Carleton found himself in trouble. The injured party, true to form, ran roaring for help, and shortly returned with no less a person than John Maxwell, Scottish Warden of the West March, with a considerable force at his back. It has been asked what Maxwell, who of all men was supposed to protect Dumfriesshire from English inroads, had been doing during the previous fortnight, while Carleton had been looting and killing in his March, proclaiming the King of England, and generally acting like an occupying power. And now Carleton was caught, red-hand if ever a reiver was, in the moment of cutting up the spoils. The answer is simple: Maxwell was playing a very odd double game with the English authorities at this time; he had his own good reasons for letting Carleton alone, but now, having been brought face to face with him, he had at least to act like a Warden.

At any rate, he addressed Carleton "with an earnest countenance. 'Is this, think ye, well; both to take our goods, and thus to shed our blood?'" It was an extraordinary speech for a Warden catching a raider in the act.

Carleton was calculating rapidly. Maxwell's force outnumbered his by two to one, so he must fall back on the reiver's second line of defence, his tongue.

"I thought best to use him and the rest of the Scots with good words, and gentle and fair speeches, for they were determined, even there, to have given us an onset, and to have taken the goods from us, and made that their quarrel. So that I persuaded him and the rest to stay themselves."

But the only immediate restitution that Carleton offered was on behalf of the injured Scottish reiver—who was standing by bleeding and aggrieved—and this consisted of speaking "sharp words before them" to Tom-with-the-Bow. However, Carleton did offer "that the goods should all be stayed, and none dealt with till the next morrow, and then every man to come that had any claim, and upon proof, that it should be redressed: and thus willed every man quietly, for that time, to depart."

It was a considerable feat of oratory, precisely in the form described earlier by Bishop Leslie—"so much persuasive eloquence, and so many smooth and insinuating words." When he had to, Carleton the rugged Border fighter, could, in the saying of his own county, wheedle a duck off a tarn. But it was not just that; one can see the picture of the Englishman, showing a bold front but with his eyes weighing up his enemies, while his own reivers moved slowly closer in behind him, hands straying towards hilts and lances, ready at the word to turn the parley into a blood-bath in defence of their loot, and in the last resort to break for the tall timber with whatever they could carry. And on the other hand Maxwell, knowing he had the upper hand in strength, but reluctant to take on an enemy who might well be ready to fight to a finish, and who, if he could not hope to defeat the Scottish Warden's "great rout", could certainly maul it severely. And of course, Maxwell had his own personal good relations with England to think about. He had no wish to offend Wharton, with whom he was privately negotiating.

Apart from that, he must have wondered, too, what the harvest would be if word went back to Carlisle that Carleton's foray had been wiped out. Dumfriesshire in that decade had had its fill of invasion; Wharton had wasted them before, and the English victory of Solway Moss was a very near memory. Maxwell had no wish to provoke fresh violence. Whichever way his thoughts ran, as he looked from the stalwart Cumbrian and his tough following, to the bleeding plaintiff, and to his own riders, sitting on a hair-trigger, he decided eventually to let it go. Carleton's silver tongue offered an excuse, and he took it.

Carleton was under no illusions; he had won a respite, no more. No sooner was he back in Dumfries than he saddled his garrison, giving secret warning to every man to arm and put on his jack. As soon as opportunity served, he sent a detachment to drive off the stolen cattle to Lochmaben, himself riding with his followers for Canonby. The closer to England, the safer he felt. "And thus," he writes, "with wiles we beguiled the Scots."

Carleton had some grounds for considering himself safe at Canonby; so disordered was the Scottish West March at this time, and so strong the English influence that, by his own account, "all Annerdale, Liddesdale, and a great part both of Nidsdale and Galway (Galloway), were willing to serve the Kinge's Majesty of England." If Liddesdale was submissive, England must indeed have been in the ascendant. But Carleton, with an eye to English interest in the future, decided it would be advisable to take the opportunity of seizing and holding some strongpoint strategically placed on Scottish ground.

He seems to have consulted one of his Scottish followers, Sandie Armstrong,[2] a rider experienced in Border war and politics. Armstrong suggested Lochwood Tower, the chief fortress of the Johnstone clan; it was strong, would contain Carleton's entire force, and was temporarily under-garrisoned, as a result of Lord Johnstone's recent capture by the English. In fact, only a handful of men held it, and as many women.

And no doubt, in recommending its seizure, Sandie Armstrong was paying off a score of his own; there was long-standing bad blood between the Armstrongs and the Johnstones.

Carleton and his force set off for Lochwood, and here again his narrative provides an admirable example of reiver technique. They reached the tower an hour before dawn. It was a fine model of the Border fortress, having an encircling barnekin wall which enclosed a hall, kitchen, stables, and sleeping quarters, and the main keep. Isolated among the moss and massively strong, even with its depleted garrison it could only be taken by surprise.

Carleton's attack was thoroughly professional. His men slipped through the marsh in silence, and ringed the outer wall. Then a dozen of them climbed the wall, "stole close into the house within the barnekin, and took the wenches, and", adds Carleton discreetly, "kept them secure in the house till daylight."

There remained the tower, still fast and secure, and housing the unsuspecting men of the garrison. In fact, there proved to be only two of them, and one girl, but for all the chance a frontal assault would have stood, they might as well have been a hundred. The reivers waited in silence; at dawn one of the men in the tower appeared on the towerhead in his shirt, saw everything quiet, and ordered the girl to open the tower door and rouse the sleepers in the outer building.

There were two doors, an iron one within and then a wooden one,

---

2. Son of Ill Will Armstrong and father of Kinmont Willie.

and as she opened the second, the plan nearly misfired. "Our men within the barnekin brake a little too soon," says Carleton, the girl saw them, sprang back, and almost had the outer door closed when the leading reiver got to it. She must have been a strong girl, for Carleton's story suggests that she managed to hold them out for a moment, but then they were in, and Lochwood Tower was in English hands.

Carleton could be well pleased with himself; the castle proved to be well stocked with provisions; he had struck a valuable blow for his royal master. He left Sandie Armstrong to command the tower, and returned himself to Carlisle to report to Wharton. As a result Carleton was confirmed as Keeper of Lochwood and governor of Annandale. In that capacity he "rode daily and nightly upon the king's enemies", looting, burning, and taking prisoners, and generally combining business with pleasure. It was not often that the reiver had so much time and opportunity, and Carleton used both to the full.

Of course, as has been said, his foray in that winter was primarily political, and as such was of minor importance. What makes it of particular interest in the present context is his detailed description of how he raided, fought his rearguard action—a most necessary science to the reiver—talked his way out of trouble, and captured an enemy tower. It could serve as a little manual in the craft.

Apart from his professional skill and resource, Thomas Carleton must have been a man of some force of character. He had the authority of Wharton and the King behind him, certainly, but this counted for nothing when he was being pursued by Gallovidians, cornered by Maxwell, or lurking under the walls of Lochwood. The force he led, English, Scots, and broken men, would have been a tough handful for any commander, but he seems to have managed them on the whole with remarkable success. Not that even he could dominate them completely; there was no doubt what most of them were bent on, and it was not the political interest of little King Edward. Carleton writes ruefully of one raid during his command of Lochwood that winter, and how he "gave every man an oath to bring in all his winnings of the journey; wherein, truly, the men offended so much their own conscience, every man layning (hiding) things, which afterwards I speired out (investigated), that after that time my conscience would never suffer me to minister an oath for this, but that which should be speired or known to be brought, and every man to have share accordingly."

Whatever the Border romancers may say, there was no honour among thieves on the West Marches.

Carleton continued some time in Scotland, raiding as far north as Crawford on occasion, and taking a Douglas hold which was defended to the last man. But for the most part he was at Lochwood, lording it over the countryside, and by his own account, ruling it so well that the inhabitants looked to him for protection and redress, which he afforded with speed and efficiency. Who protected them against *him* is another matter. Dumfriesshire was being fast reduced to a desert, and its people starving, before the Scottish Regent Arran was persuaded to re-invade. But it was a half-hearted rescue; the West March of Scotland lay wide open to English power all through 1547; in the two years following the local leaders did indeed take arms against Wharton and his invaders, but it was not until the treaty of Norham in 1551 that peace was restored.

Carleton's men, at least, came well out of it, and the good wife of Kirkcudbright got her husband back.

XVI

Hot trod and red hand

Carleton, raiding in what was virtually war-time into a chaotic countryside, was able to foray methodically and at some leisure. But in peacetime, when law enforcement was working rather better, the smaller-scale Border reivers could not afford to waste time. With the house plundered and perhaps burned, the beasts rounded up, and possibly a prisoner or two tied over a horse, they made for home without delay. The despoiled farmer, powerless to resist on the spot, had now three choices open to him. If he was a weak or friendless man, his recourse would be a complaint to his Warden and a demand for justice under the international law of the Marches. If he was a man of his hands, and most were, he might decide to wait and plan for the day when he could raid the robbers in his turn, and get his revenge illegally with interest. Or he could decide on pursuit, across the frontier if necessary.

This was a strictly legal, almost a hallowed process, known by the descriptive name of "hot trod". Scott called it "the fatal privilege". It enshrined the right to recover one's property by force, and in practice to deal with the thieves out of hand. A trod might lawfully be made at any time within six days after the offence; if it was followed immediately it was a hot trod, otherwise it was known as a cold trod. In either case it was governed by strict rules; a careful line was drawn, under Border law, between a trod and a reprisal raid.

The man who followed the hot trod had several advantages on his side. His despoilers might well have twenty miles or more to travel, and they were cumbered with slow-moving cattle. If he was well situated, he might be able to raise a superior force from among his neighbours to pursue them. It did not take long, for to the Borderer the margin between being in bed asleep and in the saddle fully armed could be measured in moments. If it was daylight, it might be all the easier to muster a posse and get on to the raider's tail.

But the problems of pursuit were formidable. Even assuming that the foray had been run by a comparatively small band of less than a dozen, the pursuers were up against expert frontiersmen who knew every fold in the ground, and could lose themselves and their stolen herd with practised ease. On the other hand, the pursuers were no less skilful —in many cases they would be reivers themselves—thieves out to catch a thief.

So what followed might be a breakneck chase or a highly sophisticated guessing game played among the broken hills and gullies, with ambush, back-tracking, feints, and possum-playing thrown in, and if the pursuit was swift and clever enough, a murderous *mêlée* with lances, swords, pistols and knives ending with the raiders overcome or the posse driven off.

If the trod crossed the Border, there were well-established rules to ensure that it was seen for what it was, a legal pursuit, and to assist it. The 1563 agreement between England and Scotland speaks of "lawfull Trodd with Horn and Hound, with Hue and Cry and all other accustomed manner of fresh pursuit"; according to Scott, this obliged the pursuer to carry a lighted turf on his lance-point, as earnest of open and peaceful intentions. He was also bound to announce his trod to the first person he met across the Border,[1] or at the first village, and to seek assistance. There seems to have been an obligation to give this assistance when it was asked for; certainly impeding a trod was a grave offence, punishable at least by making the impeder liable for the goods stolen. In England in the 1550s failure to follow a trod was punishable by death; later this penalty was reduced to seven days' imprisonment, plus a fine of 3s 4d.[2]

Quite often, of course, a trod would be led by a Warden officer, and the despoiled countrymen would have the advantage of the Warden's men to help them. Even then, evidently, it was as well to organise the pursuit with some care, to ensure that all those taking part in it were genuinely ready to do their best against the raiders. It was not unknown for accomplices of the reivers to join a hot trod, as seems to have happened in a pursuit undertaken in November 1596 by an officer of Henry Leigh's in the English West March. This unlucky man was accompanied on a small trod into Scotland by ten Grahams and a bloodhound. They caught up with the raiders, who were two of that dangerous branch of Irvines known as Kangs, and the Grahams stood by while the Kangs cut the trod-leader down, stole his horse and dog, and then went their way with the loot.

If a trod was successful, and the robbers were overpowered, those who had survived were usually taken back as prisoners, either for ransom, or for delivery to the Warden's justice. On occasion they were cut down in cold blood or hanged on the spot; in the saying of the Border, which has passed into the language, they had been taken "redhand", which was "in the deede doinge", and the law was not likely to call a trod-follower to account if his rage got the better of him and he despatched a reiver out of hand.

How often lynchings or semi-official executions concluded a successful trod, we have no means of knowing. But there is ample evidence that they were often extremely lethal affairs when the reivers were numerous and determined, and the pursuers full of indignation and blood-lust. How bitter these onfalls could be is illustrated in a trod followed by Sir Cuthbert Collingwood in the winter of 1587.

---

1. Early statutes directed the pursuer actually to seek out some worthy person in the opposite realm, and require him to join the trod as a witness.
2. Englishmen assisting a trod were entitled to 1s in the £ for goods recovered on English soil, and 2s in the £ on Scottish ground.

This gentleman, an English Border official and a man of consequence, had made a raid on his own account into Teviotdale, without his own Warden's permission. In spite of the fact that he led a band more than 800 strong, Collingwood got nothing; the Scottish intelligence service had been efficient enough to allow the Teviotdale folk to clear out, with their property, and Collingwood found empty houses with open doors. He returned, having lost four men prisoner and achieved nothing except the prospect of a retaliatory raid from the Scottish side.

It was not long coming. Word reached him that Buccleuch, young Robert Kerr of Cessford, and more than 2000 riders from the Scots Middle March, were preparing to descend on the English East and Middle Marches within three days; accordingly the English Wardenries stood to arms and awaited the onslaught. The Middle March watchers saw nothing, however; young Kerr was out to get Collingwood, and his part of the foray was directed against Sir Cuthbert's house at Eslington and the township nearby. A band of riders descended on the town, taking four or five prisoners, and Collingwood promptly sallied out from his house with his two sons and half a dozen servants— not much of a garrison in the circumstances. It clashed with the raiders, but was outnumbered, and Collingwood had to retire hurriedly to his house again.

Some help was at hand, however, in the presence of Captain Bellas and a band of English infantry; Collingwood took up the pursuit again, but neglected to send out scouts and paid the obvious penalty. The raiders ambushed him, and again he had to fight his way back to his house. He got in at his orchard door, but his eldest son, riding full tilt for the gate, found it shut, and was captured. The other son got in, at the cost of a face wound, but Collingwood's other riders were all taken.

Captain Bellas was luckier, for the moment at least. The group of Scots which had raided the town was only a fragment of the full force, which had presumably been engaged in rounding up cattle. Now Bellas found himself so outnumbered that he and his foot soldiers, about twenty in all, had to fall back to a ruined house on a hill. Surrounded by a force of reivers several hundred strong, the English party's plight was desperate; they shot it out manfully, and tumbled two or three Scots from their saddles, but the besiegers came in on foot, and a bloody hand-to-hand tussle took place over the ruined walls. Twice Bellas was called on to surrender, and twice refused; once the Scots seemed ready to call it a day, but a rider called Watty Turnbull, whose brother had been killed, spurred them on to the onslaught.

It could only have one end: the ruin was over-run, and fifteen of the English died fighting in the shambles. Bellas was wounded and taken prisoner by Armstrong of Mangerton with the other survivors. With their loot and their prisoners Kerr's raiders made for home.

Bellas's gallant resistance—for which he was to be blamed by his own Warden, who thought he should have surrendered—had not been entirely in vain. In the time taken to overcome him, the country around had risen to "follow the fray", and unlucky Sir Cuthbert, who was nothing if not game, took up the trod a third time. The mounted Scots were too far ahead to overtake, but those on foot were surrounded, and after a skirmish in which half a dozen were killed, about 150 were taken prisoner.

There was no question of killing them as "red-hand" thieves; it would have been too dangerous. "Theis countrymen will not willingly kill any of them," wrote Hunsdon, the East March Warden, later. Besides, all the cattle except thirty of Collingwood's had been recovered. But what the countrymen were too cautious to do was not beyond the Warden himself: "by that tyme I have hangde 40 or 50 of the prysonars, whyche I will doo at the leste, I trust they shall have smale cawse too boste of that jorney," he told Burghley, grimly underlining the words with his pen.

So it was an expensive business for both sides, in lives lost. Whether Hunsdon kept his fatal promise or not, the Scots had the worst of it, although Hunsdon—who did not like Collingwood—insisted that the whole band of raiders could have been captured if the trod had been followed more energetically. Young Kerr had escaped, only to meet the wrath of King James, who clapped him into Edinburgh Castle for his disorderly conduct. His Majesty also commanded the return of young Collingwood and the redoubtable Bellas; from the fact that Bellas was drawing pay in the following February we must assume that he came home safely.

Even when a hot trod was well organised and on a large scale, the pursuers still had to be careful. The art of ambush was so well developed that even large, well-armed forces were not safe, as the Scott family discovered on a trod in 1580. A combined party of English and Scottish thieves had descended on Branxholm and removed a large herd, which they drove off towards England via Liddesdale. The route taken should have made the Scotts cautious, since no one took stolen cattle through that valley unless he had an arrangement with the inhabitants.

However, the Branxholm trod forged ahead, reinforcing themselves by enlisting the aid *en route* of Robin Elliot of Redheuch, Captain of Hermitage and deputy Keeper of the valley. They pursued the thieves into England, but lost them there, probably in the maze of Bewcastle Waste. The trod turned back empty-handed into Liddesdale, and were near the home of Armstrong of Whithaugh when they were ambushed by 300 Armstrongs, Elliots and Crosers. Many of the Scotts were taken prisoner, as was the Captain of Hermitage—the fact that the captors were his own tribesmen made no difference; a matter of business was obviously involved, and kinship for once took second place.

Experiences like Collingwood's and the Scotts' perhaps explain why following the trod was not an everyday occurrence. It was one thing to get on a reiver's tail, and quite another to capture him. But a trod could be pursued successfully into the very heart of hostile country if the pursuer was resolute enough, as Humphrey Musgrave, a deputy Warden[3] of the English West March, demonstrated on more than one occasion.

He seems to have been one of those lawmen who is frightened of nobody, and he had the added spur that the thieves against whom he was usually employed were folk with whom his family was at feud— Armstrongs, Grahams, and Irvines. When the notorious Dick of Dry-hope ran a dawn raid on Hethersgill in June 1584 and lifted forty head of cattle, Musgrave, accompanied by Henry Leigh and a party of soldiers, followed the reivers into Liddesdale, and refused to leave his trod in the face of "a great shouting and assembly" which ended in fighting. One reiver, named Howloose, was killed, and Musgrave came out of the hornet's nest with Dick of Dryhope, two other Armstrongs, and a renegade English outlaw as his prisoners.[4]

---

3. Following the trod was a specified duty of the deputy Warden of the English West March. It was his task, when any raid occurred, to follow or intercept the reivers with at least twenty men.

4. Unlike some other Armstrongs captured by another Musgrave (Christopher) the previous year, who were hanged at Carlisle—"all dying to theyre deservings"—Dick of Dryhope escaped the gallows, and continued to drive his reiver's trade.

Humphrey Musgrave made a point of braving the Armstrongs on their own ground. When the feud was at its height, and the Scottish riders were scouring the Bewcastle area, he and Leigh penetrated into Liddesdale again and captured Sim Armstrong of Mangerton, one of the leaders of the tribe, in his own tower, and brought him to Carlisle Castle. Mangerton, "the special evildoer and procurer of spoils", was a rare catch; "his taking is greatly wondered at here," wrote old Scrope enthusiastically, adding that it was unheard of for such a light of Liddesdale to be taken without the loss of a man.[5]

When a trod was undertaken successfully, the pursuers still knew that they could not afford to relax their vigilance. Raid was followed by trod was followed by counter-raid and so on *ad infinitum*, and the farmer who had pursued his stolen cattle and brought them safe home again knew better than to think the raiders would let him alone in future. He had won a round, that was all, and it might prove to be an expensive victory.

The village of Killam, in the English East March, discovered this on the morning of April 14 1597 when four Scottish reivers attacked a poor man's house in the small hours, broke in his door, and made off with his stock. The villagers were promptly on the trod, and in catching up with the thieves they badly wounded three of them and returned in triumph to their village, bringing back not only the stolen cattle but also the three injured robbers.

One reiver had escaped, and Killam soon had cause to regret it. At daybreak forty Scottish riders swept into the village, and only after a stiff fight was the reprisal beaten off, the villagers, "who behaved themselves very honestlye", taking two other prisoners. But there was more to come; the defeated Scots were back within two hours, with more than 100 Teviotdale riders and footmen to help them, and this proved too much for the sturdy villagers. One Killam man was slain, seven

---

5. In spite of feud and professional hostility, Armstrong of Mangerton and Humphrey Musgrave were apparently capable of something approaching friendship. This may be inferred from the fact that in 1585, little more than a year after Musgrave had captured the Laird in his own house, Musgrave entered his horse, Bay Sandforth, at a race meeting in Liddesdale, so that Mangerton might see if he liked the animal. Bay Sandforth won all three prizes, and Mangerton became its owner. An interesting example of reiver-Warden relations.

left for dead, many others were wounded, and the captive reivers were all rescued.

The villagers must have wondered if the hot trod was worth while. If they had taken the easy course, and let the poor man complain to his Warden, they might not have got his cattle back, but Killam would have been spared a disastrous raid. Yet if the incident proves anything, it was that neither side was accustomed to giving up easily; they were used to fighting their own battles.

To Robert Carey, acting Warden of the East March, the Killam raid called for only one kind of answer: he wanted to hit back, and he had not the men or means to do it. "I beseech you, either establish me as I ought to serve my prince and country," he told the Privy Council, "or else send down one more worthy. . . . I desire not to hold it to see these calamities unsufferable, without means to revenge it."

In the circumstances, with their own governments unable or too unconcerned to protect them, the Borderers had to fend for themselves, in theory by complaint and hot trod, in practice by reprisal in whatever way they could. It was a grim, deadly war which no one was going to win.

XVII

The ability to kill

Most of them . . . use the greatest possible precaution
not to shed the blood of those that oppose them.

BISHOP LESLIE

They abhorred and avoided the crime of unnecessary
homicide.

SIR WALTER SCOTT

In the light of the previous chapter, which gave a fair idea of the kind of slaughter involved in Border reiving, the two statements above must look remarkable. They are, in fact, the basis of one of the most persistent and hallowed Border myths: that the Marchmen, while they pillaged and burned and extorted and kidnapped, had an unusual reluctance, based on humanitarian feeling, to kill each other. It is a tale that has naturally been fostered by the more romantic Border writers.

And like most myths it is not totally unfounded. There is even some quite good-looking evidence for it, but it needs considerable qualification.

The Border reivers were aggressive, ruthless, violent people, notoriously quick on the draw, ready and occasionally eager to kill in action, when life or property or honour were at stake. They were a brave people, and risked their lives readily enough; when they had to die, they appear to have done so without undue dramatics or bogus defiance which would have been wasted anyway. They lived in a society where deadly family feud was common, and when they were engaged in feud they killed frequently and brutally, as we shall see.

When they were *not* engaged in feud, they certainly killed less readily. Their ordinary reiving did not, perhaps, entail quite as much bloodshed as one might expect in the violent circumstances. Bishop Leslie and Scott explain this by pointing out that the Borderers regarded reiving as legitimate (which is true), but that they held murder to be a crime, and consequently were reluctant to commit it—except in the heat of action or when covered by the virtual absolution of deadly feud. It is rather like saying that a heavy drinker, in his sober moments, is an abstemious man.

The fact remains that the records of Border reiving show a deplorably high killing rate, and not much evidence to suggest that the Borderers were, for robbers, unusually humanitarian. When Scott says that they abhorred and avoided the crime of unnecessary homicide, one can only comment that they seem to have found homicide necessary with appalling frequency. Yet the myth has grown, in spite of all the contrary evidence.

One of its roots, of course, is that quite frequently (especially late in the sixteenth century) the Borderers had pressing reasons for not killing each other, but these had nothing to do with humanity. A powerful inducement to spare the lives of captured reivers, and to avoid bloodshed in the pursuit of plunder, was that killing could easily provoke deadly feud. Some Borderers were obviously as ready to feud as to eat, and almost every male member of a riding clan was willing to pursue a feud once it had started, but most of them were understandably reluctant to provoke one wantonly. Again, quite apart from feud, the reiver

who killed during a raid could expect little mercy if he was taken by
pursuers, or when he himself was raided in return.

And, of course, a corpse had no ransom value.

There are other sources for the belief that the Borderers had an unusual delicacy about killing. As we have seen, good evidence exists
that in time of Anglo-Scottish war, Borderers on opposite sides would
sometimes be at pains to avoid injuring each other. But this, when it
did happen, was an isolated phenomenon, explained by the fact that
English and Scottish riders might be professional reiving allies, or even
kinsmen, and placed their personal good relations above mere national
interest (see Chapter VIII). And although national quarrel did sometimes paradoxically tend to strengthen the curious sense of Border community which spanned the frontier, the March rider in war-time was
usually just as ready to slaughter as the next man, whether the enemy
was fellow Borderer or outlander.

It has been necessary to go into this myth of the Borderers' supposed
reluctance to kill, if only to dispose of it, and at the same time to be as
fair to them as possible. With their curious society they did have a
curious morality, and their own sense of honour and even chivalry,
which is not always easy for us to understand. But having said as much,
no one should have any doubt that the Borderers of the riding families
were killers, and that the business they drove was often a highly lethal
one. The records of their activities, liberally sprinkled with murders
and slaughters, speak for themselves. And for people who supposedly
abhorred homicide, they were capable on occasion of truly cold-
blooded cruelty.

One may take the case of Sir John Kerr of Spielaw, who held some
unspecified grudge against one Nicholas Bolton of Mindrum, described
as an "honest yeoman". On a summer's day of 1596, Kerr rode up to
Bolton's house with a party of armed men, and asked his wife where
her husband was; the woman pointed him out at the plough, among
several other peasants working in the fields. Kerr went over to them,
and again inquired which one was Bolton. They told him, and this
careful gentleman then went up to Bolton and asked him his name.

"Whereupon the poore man in good manner put of his hatt, told
him his name was Boulton; presentlie Sir John verie valientlie drewe
owt his sword and cutt him three blowes upon the head, and left the
rest of his companie to cutt him all in peces."

It could hardly have been more deliberate or callous; there is a touch of Mafia-style liquidation about it. Ironically, we owe the detailed description of this killing to John Carey, who set it out in an attempt to justify an equally cold-blooded murder which he had just caused to be committed himself. And Carey, it should be remembered, was not a Border bandit, but an important frontier official who at this time held the deputy Governorship of Berwick.

In a letter of July 3 1596 to his father, Carey describes how he dealt with a reiver named Jock Dalgleish of Wideopen. Dalgleish, with his brothers Robin and John, and a fourth rustler named Tom Pringle, had stolen six horses from the bounds of Berwick, one of them being Carey's. The deputy Governor found out the names of the thieves who, possibly anxious not to offend such an important man, sent a message asking if Carey would take the horses back "without further trouble". Carey hesitated, apparently because he wanted the satisfaction of having the law on the robbers, but eventually consented to take the horses back, provided they were in as good condition as when they were stolen—"protesting to their friends, if I were not satisfied, I would have some of their lyves".

Apparently the horses were not returned, and Carey, in a rage, sent fifty riders across the frontier to Dalgleish's house. They broke open the door, "and cutt himself all in peces"—Carey's own words. He further explains that he had wished to take revenge on all four robbers, but because they lived separately he had settled on Dalgleish as being the ringleader.

There was no question here of March law; it was a straight murder in retaliation for a minor theft, committed openly by a high-ranking official. Queen Elizabeth herself was shocked, and described the act as "verie barbarous and seldom used emonge the Turckes". At this Carey was indignant, and cited John Kerr's murder of Bolton to show, presumably, that there were other cold-blooded killers on the Border. He also added details of Kerr's kidnapping two "protected" Scotsmen from England, one of whom he deliberately drowned on the way back to Scotland, where he hanged the other. And of how some of the Burns had come over to pillage John Selby's home in Tynedale, and had cut him down under his own roof; and of the "extreme bloddy hurting" of Mr Haggerton, Thomas Burrell and others "most cruelly mangled", and so on.

Against all this carnage, Carey suggested, the murder of one Scottish reiver was surely no great matter. But he reached his finest extenuating flight in a letter to Burghley the next month, when he wrote of the Dalgleish affair:

"And my good lord, for your honors better satisfaction, that it was not so barbarouslie nor butcherlie don as you thinck it to be, it should seeme your honor hath bene wrongfullie enformed, in sayinge he was cutt in manye peeces, after his deathe—for if he had bene cutt in many peces, he could not a lived till the next morninge, which themselves reported he did—which shewes he was not cutt in verie many peeces!"

Burghley may well have asked himself what kind of place the Border must be, that it had so warped the outlook of one who was, after all, a gentleman, a responsible officer, and a close relative of the Queen herself. He would hardly have regarded Carey's amazing letter as evidence that homicide was abhorred on the frontier. In the light of it, and the murder of Bolton, and Selby, and the "mangling" of Haggerton and Burrell, the slaughter of the two protected Scots, the shooting of an English scout under Berwick walls, the murder by Robert Kerr of Cessford and his riders of three "poor men" at Wooler, plus the killing of one Will Storey[1]—it is difficult to take the quotations at the beginning of this chapter seriously. For this was only the East March, over a period of some months. Murders as callous as those committed by Kerr and Carey may not have been everyday, but neither were they rarities. One has only to go back one year, to the summer of 1595, to discover the attitude to premeditated murder of young Walter Scott, the Bold Buccleuch, who has been generally held up as a mirror of Border chivalry.

In May of that year he came to Tynedale with 300 men, looking for Charltons, with whom he was at feud. He inquired at a Charlton widow's house, and finding no men at home, he burned the building down and destroyed the food in it. A week later he came back, caught and killed four Charltons, and rode off announcing that he would

---

1. This murder was quickly avenged by the Storeys, two of whom rode into Scotland and killed Robert Kerr's shepherd. The Storey-Kerr feud had originally arisen over the theft of sheep—"for one sheep hogg that was taken from Sesfordes shepherd, so highlie was Sesfordes honor toiched therein!" (John Carey).

come back soon and kill some more.[2] (At this same time his associate
Robert Kerr of Cessford was making invasion in the hope of mur-
dering Storeys.)

One could go on giving chapter and verse of atrocities, both Scottish
and English, but there is not the need. Obviously not all Borderers
delighted in killing, but there were enough ready slayers to give the lie
to the legend of frontier humanity. No murder rate figures are available, but Eure's general certificate of January 29 1596, showing "near
200 persons murdered, and no restitution of quick for dead, by March
law", is indication enough.[3]

For all the blood and thunder, one thing that is rarely mentioned in
Border records is torture. John Forster was accused of diabolical cruel-
ties to prisoners, but since making exaggerated charges against him was
almost a Middle March pastime it would be unwise to accept the allegation too readily. A shocking case did occur near Caldbeck in February 1593, when a man named Sowerby had his home broken into by
six unidentified thieves—"they sett him on his bare buttockes upon an
hot irone, and there they burned him and rubbed him with an hote
gridle about his bellie and sondry other partes of his body" to make him
reveal where his money (it was less than £4) was hidden. However,
this kind of atrocity was not common, and in reporting the Caldbeck
case a Border official referred to it as "a speciall outrage".

Before leaving the gory subject of death and capital punishment, it
should be added that the average reiver, even if he avoided being
killed in raid, trod, or feud, still stood a fair chance of dying with his
boots on. Judicial executions were frequently ordered by Warden
courts, Border officers were quite apt to hang captured raiders after

---

2. Ruffian and bully though he was, Buccleuch undoubtedly owed some of
his evil reputation to propagandists on the English side. He is charged with
many killings, some of which may well have been exaggerated—it is unlikely that on one raid he left 35 Tynedale men dead, as was suggested.
William Bowes estimated that Buccleuch was guilty of about twenty murders, "he present and chief actor, some said to be done with his own hand".
Robert Kerr of Cessford was held guilty of about sixteen of whom twelve
were queen's soldiers.

3. William Bowes wrote in November 1595: "Execrable murders are constantly committed." He cited four which had taken place in a few days, "and
three others this month in Athelstone moor."

summary trial, and on the Scottish side the government's great judicial raids against Border offenders were liable to conclude with mass executions. Official reprisal raids also produced their share of semi-official lynchings.

When judicial execution took place, the most common method was hanging. The Border is littered with Gallows or Gallow Hills, Hangman's Hills, Hangman's Closes, and the like. Probably the most celebrated of these was Harraby Hill, about a mile south of old Carlisle, and now well within the city limits close by the main road. But beheading also took place, and so did drowning, in a convenient pool or stream. This last is a subject on which historians have little to say, probably not so much for reasons of delicacy as because there is not much to be found out about it. Scott, with his eye for the sensational detail, writes at some length of drowning in special pits, or "murder holes", and suggests (quite incorrectly) that this explains the expression "pit and gallows".

Drowning seems to have been particularly popular on the Scottish side, especially in the Middle March. As many as a score of reivers were drowned in the Jed on one occasion, and at Hawick in July 1562 a batch of twenty-two were drowned in the Teviot. Mass hangings also took place, and in one of these no fewer than thirty-six Armstrongs were hanged together. However, one reason why drowning was popular was probably because it was cheaper. There is a grim reminder of the economics of capital punishment in the financial accounts of James IV's expedition to Dumfries in 1504:

"To the men hangit the thevis at Hullirbus, 13s; for ain raip to hang them in, 8d. To the men that hangit the theves in Canonbie, be the Kingis command, 13s."

XVIII

The Wardens of the Marches

TROUBLESHOOTERS

To keep the peace on such a frontier, to prevent internal crime and international incident, was virtually impossible. Strong central governments might have done it, given the time, the money, and the will, but these were only occasionally available. England certainly had a comparatively strong central power from Henry VII's reign, but the Border was a long way off, and to assert control from London was difficult. On the Scottish side the Border area was closer to the seat of central authority, but that authority was seldom strong enough to keep its southern bounds under proper control. One can be sorry for Scottish governments—to the north the notoriously intractable Highlands whose notion of law enforcement was three feet of steel independently wielded, and to the south the Border hills, with their equally war-hardened tribesmen whose respect, if any, was reserved exclusively for their own leaders and for the local enemy, whether Scot or English.

To attempt to apply normal law and government to the Border area was a waste of time, and both countries had long recognised this. Thus there grew up a body of local law and custom, often extremely complex, seldom consistent, and in practice all too rough and ready, by which the two governments attempted to keep their frontier subjects in order. It can probably be said to have worked moderately well, in that it prevented a decline into complete anarchy; it was at least practised by both sides with some co-operation. The wonder is that it worked at all.

The lynch-pins of Border law were the Wardens of the Marches. There were six of them, as a rule, three on either side of the frontier, governing their respective East, Middle, and West Marches, with a fourth official on the Scottish side who had special responsibility for Liddesdale. This was because Liddesdale was an extremely special place; as the cockpit of the Border it required a Keeper of its own.[1]

The Warden can be defined in two words as the monarch's man; he was the governor within his own area. But that is to say nothing: to be effective he had to be a mixture of soldier, judge, lawyer, fighting-man, diplomat, politician, rough-rider, detective, administrator, and intelligence agent. His duties varied from time to time and were not always consistent on both sides of the Border. Very briefly, they were officially: to guard the frontier, to confer with his opposite Warden regularly for the good government of their areas, to appoint subordinate Warden officials,[2] to supervise strongholds, suppress crime, give and obtain redress against offenders, pursue fugitives, hold domestic courts as well as international courts with the opposite Warden, muster the March for defence as required, and generally keep "good rule".

And of all these the most important in peace-time were to guard against raiders, to suppress and arrest reivers from his own March who had raided into the other country, and to co-operate with the opposite Warden in punishing the offender and compensating the victim. This last was the sphere in which co-operation was vital.

---

1. There was often resentment and rank-pulling over the position of the Keeper of Liddesdale. He was regarded in Scotland as having virtual Warden status; the English, however, were occasionally reluctant to recognise this, and the English ambassador told King James in 1596 that if the Keeper of Liddesdale was senior enough to hold March meetings with English Wardens, then Scottish Wardens must be prepared to do the like with the English Keepers of Tynedale and Redesdale, who were generally considered as being farther down the pecking order. These were fine points of precedence which it could be useful to exploit in a cold-war situation. Of course when the Keeper of Liddesdale was also Scottish West or Middle March Warden, as sometimes happened, the difficulty did not arise.

2. The appointment of a deputy was of great importance, since he had "in charge all particular service" either in defence or offence "as when any sudden rode, or secreat thift is made by any Scottes or Englishe borderers, to be readie upon the first shout or fray, with a score at least of the Warden's men, to follow to where the fray is, or to ride betwixt them and home." In other words, the deputy led the posses, and some of the most active Borderers held this office at one time or other. They quite frequently acted as full Wardens, without the official title. Other subordinate officers included the commanders of various strongholds (Bewcastle, Hermitage, and the like), captains, constables, and land sergeants (see Glossary).

In general, then, the Warden's task was to guard and govern his March in time of peace, and command it in time of war unless or until some more senior official from the central authority was sent to take over from him. His powers and responsibilities were enormous; his activities might range from the minute detail of determining how to divide the damages among the members of a band of convicted reivers to fighting a war with scratch forces against an invading army; from supervising the redecoration of a church to breaking into Carlisle Castle; from negotiating with a foreign monarch to fighting a running skirmish with outlaws in some wild corner of the mosses.

He was one of the most accomplished troubleshooters in history, and he was paid about £100 a year on the Scottish side, which could mean as little as £20 sterling.[3] This was by no means an absolute figure; at the tougher Western end of the Border the pay could be as high as £600, with the Keeper of Liddesdale receiving (and no doubt earning) as much as £1200. In addition there were perquisites in the form of the property of convicted criminals, the captured goods of fugitives, and such occasional indirect payments as land grants and minor revenues.

The English salaries varied between £300 and £1100 sterling, including perquisites. Like most Elizabethan officials, the Wardens suffered from Her Majesty's chronic stinginess. Viewed strictly from the point of view of salary, and considering the burdens of the office, it cannot be called a highly paid job on either side of the frontier.[4]

Still, there were other considerations which explain why (in Scotland particularly) Wardenship was a coveted office—again, Liddesdale must be excepted: it was not always easy to find anyone ready to take the office of Keeper—and the object of considerable rivalry among the leading families. A Warden had opportunities of enrichment and power; he was officially the master of his March, and could use his office to establish himself and his family and secure himself and his property against his enemies. His influence was vast, and in an atmosphere of constant feud and family rivalry the shadow of royal power

---

3. The pound Scots was worth about four English shillings. Not only were the Scots Wardens comparatively worse off, their salaries ended altogether in the 1580s.

4. As Sir John Forster pointed out indignantly to Walsingham in 1583, "it is not the fee of myne office that will maynteyne my howse."

obviously counted for a good deal. He was the law, and he could take the profit.

LOCALS AND OUTSIDERS

The office was not officially a hereditary one,[5] but on the Scottish side it tended to reside with the same families. In the East March the Warden was as often as not a Hume; in the Middle March the Kerrs frequently filled the office, and in the West March the Maxwells had a virtual monopoly until it was broken late in the sixteenth century by their arch-enemies, the Johnstones. On the English side there was less readiness latterly to entrust Wardenries to powerful local nobles, who might, at such a distance from London, prove embarrassing power-points in times of national crisis. London had suffered from Northern English risings, and was jealous of such powerful and potentially dangerous families as the Percies, especially if they were not over-enthusiastic for "the new religion"; it was safer to have as Wardens men who could be kept firmly under central control—in fact, no fewer than three of the later English Wardens were close relatives of Queen Elizabeth. Thus in the late sixteenth century there was a growing tendency to appoint non-Borderers and to curtail their powers, and Sir John Forster stands out as almost the only truly local Warden on the English side.[6]

The difference between the Scottish and English appointment policies was a vital one. The Scottish Wardens were usually local because the Scottish government really had little choice in the matter, and there were advantages to having Borderers in office: they knew the area and the people, and with men like the Maxwells and the Kerrs there was an element of setting a thief to catch a thief. If they could not keep order, who could? On the other hand, local men had the disadvantage of being embroiled from the start in local feuds, alliances, and

---

5. In the fifteenth century, at one time, the Wardenship of the Scottish West and Middle Marches was secured to the Douglases in perpetuity, but they rarely held office in the sixteenth century.

6. In the early days Englishmen of the first eminence were often appointed to the Wardenries—Warwick the Kingmaker, John of Gaunt, and Richard of Gloucester (later Richard III) were Wardens.

similar mischiefs,[7] and tended to have an enlarged contempt for central authority. In Scottish domestic upheavals, the Borders were a most important factor, and it was in the government's interest to keep them loyal; the office of Warden was supposedly an inducement in that direction. The Scottish government sometimes went to odd lengths to placate its Border officials—even past rebellion, treason and outlawry could be forgiven (as they were with the Maxwells) if the man involved was of the strength and influence which would make him a useful Warden.

And it was understood that Scottish Borderers did not take kindly to outside Wardens. The oustanding example was the unfortunate Frenchman, Anthony Darcy, the Sieur de la Bastie, who in 1516 was ill-advised enough to accept the Wardenry of all the Scottish Marches, with particular responsibility in the east. This was Hume country, and they regarded Darcy with "horrid resentment". He seems to have been a brave, honest and conscientious Warden, which no doubt rendered him all the more odious. The outcome was that the Humes finally caught up with him near Duns, cut off his head, and took it home in triumph, tied by its long locks to a saddle-bow.

English "outsider" Wardens might reasonably expect to be luckier than that, but their task was still far from an easy one. They often came to the work ignorant of the area, its people, and its ways, resented by the local English factions, and hampered by a central authority whose support was unpredictable. With such notable exceptions as Robert Carey few of them adapted to Border ways. The younger Scrope, son of a famous West March Warden, found himself resented by the powerful Lowther faction, one of whom had been acting Warden; he also quarrelled with his own officers, including the influential Carleton brothers, and with the Graham clan. He was convinced that both the Grahams and the Carletons were out to undermine his authority; he

---

7. They were also, in English eyes, liable to be biased and partial. "The opposite Wardens and officers being always borderers bred and dwelling there, also cherish favourites and strengthen themselves by the worst disposed, to support their factions." This was William Bowes's view, echoed by an English contemporary who found the Scottish Wardens "extraordinarylie addicted to partialities, favour of theire blood, tenantes and followers". But the charge, while frequently true, applied equally to English Borderer officers, particularly those in subordinate capacities.

was quite right, but his own lack of political intelligence had brought
much of the trouble on himself. He quarrelled with Eure, a fellow-
English Warden who had troubles of his own, having followed the
long-serving John Forster in the turbulent Middle March, and found
that Forster and other Northumbrians were unco-operative, to say the
least.

It was the same elsewhere. Lord Willoughby, a distinguished soldier
and something of an autocrat, was out of place as East March Warden;
Robert Carey's elder brother, John, was driven to distraction in the
same office. Yet reading through the correspondence of such Wardens,
with their never-ending complaints and protests as they tried to tackle
jobs that were beyond them, one concludes that the great disadvantage
under which they laboured was not so much that they were not local
men—English "Borderer" Wardens like Forster and William Dacre
were no great shakes—but that they seldom received the trust and
backing and finance from London that they needed. They were regarded as political instruments rather than as peace-keepers, and this,
from a Border view point, was quite wrong.

TROUBLEMAKERS

It was inevitable that, with national interests always in the background,
co-operation between English and Scottish Wardens should often be
very erratic indeed. They seldom trusted each other, and often they
were in a state of personal enmity.[8] Each regarded the other, rightly, as

---

8. Eure gives a fascinating account of inter-Warden relations as they stood
in midsummer of 1596. Scrope (English West) was on good terms with
Johnstone (Scottish West), but on bad terms with Buccleuch (Liddesdale).
Eure (English Middle) was on bad terms with Johnstone, but friendly with
Buccleuch, although he did not expect that amity to last long. Cessford
(Scottish Middle) was friendly to Eure, but was "displeased" with Robert
Carey (English East).

To complicate matters further, Wardens on the same side were sometimes
at variance. Only a few months after making the report condensed above,
Eure and Scrope were snarling at each other— "Lord Scrope [was] jelious
over me and withdrawne from me", complained Eure; he also alleged that
"gentlemen alied to the Caries procureth emulation and hartburning of ther

an agent of the traditional enemy, and they were fatally ready to cause trouble in each other's Marches. This was often national policy, of which more will be said later; for the moment it is enough to note that while justice and co-operation were possible when national and personal difference could be forgotten, and purely mutual Border interests placed first, this was a fairly rare occurrence.

This was the curse of the system. The Wardens in theory were there for the good of the Border and its inhabitants, to protect, govern, and administer in co-operation. In practice, their governments used them as agents to contain, embarrass, and spy on the other side, and provided these duties were carried out, and the national interest was served, the local interest of the Borderers could go to the devil. Other things being equal, Elizabeth and James no doubt wished their Border subjects well, or at least no harm, but they were perfectly ready to sacrifice them in the greater cause. They and their ministers paid lip service to the ideals of peace and prosperity along the frontier, and from time to time dealt summarily with law-breakers, but this did not stop them from pursuing national policies which meant disruption and destruction on the Border line.

An example: when Mary Queen of Scots wished to embarrass the Maxwells, for domestic political reasons, she was ready to intrigue with Dacre, an English Warden, so that he would encourage the English Grahams to raid in Maxwell territory. Elizabeth's Wardens repeatedly "kept the Scottish Borderers at home" so that they could not play a part in Scottish internal affairs which would have been contrary to English interest. In time of war, invading English Wardens habitually enlisted Scottish Border riders to help them to sack and ravage; the Scottish government was always ready to turn a blind eye to Scottish depredations on English soil when it suited.

One does not necessarily blame the governments for acting in this way. But neither can one take too seriously their repeatedly expressed

---

part against me". Eure plainly felt that nobody loved him, and he was probably right. On the Scottish side, Buccleuch and Cessford, relatives and old raiding companions though they were, also had their differences: their mutual correspondence contains allegations of intent to murder, such expressions as "I give you the lye" and "Use your behaviour as ye list", and the fine concluding flourish: "Your brother in na termes, Bucklugh."

pious horror at the "decaie" of the Borders, when they so cynically exploited and added to that decay for their own ends.

KEEPING THE BALANCE

This double standard made life hard for a Warden (to say nothing of the unfortunates he was supposed to govern). He had difficulties enough anyway, what with the imperfect administrative machinery at his disposal, and the deplorable people he had to deal with. Obviously, in spite of the powers vested in him as a justiciar charged with administering his March and punishing crime, as a military captain, and as an international negotiator, a Warden's efficiency depended largely on his own character and personality.

Officially, he could summon people to serve and assist him, and in theory he had the full support of the central government. In fact, he depended on winning the co-operation of the most powerful elements in his March, enlisting their assistance to apprehend criminals and keep order, and in judiciously mixing tact, shrewdness, and brute force as required.[9] It called for nice judgement; let a Warden be too tough or over-zealous, and he would rouse the resentment of clan chiefs and powerful land-owners; let him be too timid, and his March would become a jungle. Whatever he was *de jure*, it was necessary that *de facto* he should be the rather paternal supervisor of the turbulent power blocs of his March, an accepted leader rather than a military policeman.

In short, a Wardenship was properly a job for a man who knew his Borderland, who could win the respect if not the friendship of his fellows, terrorise evil-doers, play the politician and the wise judge, redress wrong, compose quarrels, and defend his country's interest; who could, ideally, be trusted to give a fair shake between Englishman and Scot or feuding clansmen, who could protect and comfort the people of his Wardenry, go bail for them and pledge his honour and

---

9. A blind eye was occasionally invaluable. Forster made no secret of condoning reprisals by those of his March subjects who could look after themselves, as he admitted to Walsingham in a letter of March 6 1587: "As for her Majesty's tenants in Tynedale and Redesdale, they spoil others as they are spoiled, and suffer little harm—any other tenants have had justice done as far as I can" (see also Chapter XXIII).

money on their behalf, and who, in the ultimate, would be ready to gather his lances at his back and challenge a crowned head on behalf of one man wronged.

It was not an ideal often realised. But even a Warden with all the virtues, and given the assistance of powerful allies, would have had difficulty in coping merely with the high crime rate in his March; add to this the possibility that he might be involved personally in blood feud,[10] that he might have to deal with an unco-operative Warden on the opposite side, that the central power which should have supported him was weak, slow, and unreliable, and that he might well lack the simple physical armed strength to deal with the troublesome folk in his region, and his task became well-nigh hopeless. The problems confronting Eure when he took over the English Middle March in 1595 were typical—". . . these difficulties—a strong enemy—a weak and distracted country—suspicion of privy practice to cross him—a year of scarcity—and a very unsafe place of abode, being on the high way of the worst disorders". In these circumstances a Warden could not hope to keep his March quiet; he could only hope to keep it from boiling over.

For the Scottish Wardens, who were expected to act more on their own initiative than their English counterparts, and were less frequently supplied with state troops,[11] life could be hard indeed. In particular crises they might find their responsibilities temporarily taken over by central officials, like the Border lieutenants, in which case the Warden was often expected to act in a subordinate capacity (sometimes with

10. It was patently impossible for a Warden to deal impartially in cases involving a family with which he was at feud. When a Maxwell was appointed Scottish West March Warden in 1529, it was stipulated that his deputy should handle any matter affecting the Johnstones, the Maxwells' bitter rivals.

11. Even the English Wardens, especially late in the century, were often chronically short of men. Hunsdon in 1587, with at most a few hundred horse and foot to defend Northumberland against an estimated 3000 to 4000 well-mounted reivers, asked for 1000 men for a month or six weeks, with which he believed he could "get full redress for all bypast spoils, and inriche her Majesties subjects to the valew of £10,000, and to beggar the opposite border." Hunsdon, it will be observed, was a realist. At other times old Scrope reported that Bewcastle was in danger of being overrun because he could not pay for a garrison there, Eure once found himself with only seventy-one light horse after a muster, and Robert Carey found "my 20 horse" insufficient.

disastrous results[12]). This happened also on the English side. But in the continuing rough-and-tumble along the frontier it was normally the Warden, with the deputies, assistants and others whom he appointed, plus whatever he could raise on the spot, who had to try to keep the peace of the Border-line.

The Scottish Wardens, with a weaker and less stable government behind them, and if anything a more turbulent domestic population to deal with, sometimes found their authority set entirely at naught. Generally, they had less control over the native inhabitants of their Marches than the English did, although it would not be fair to suggest that they were—with a few notable exceptions—less zealous and upright in performing their duties. Yet one feels, to use a North Country expression, that the English Wardens do seem to have been a better class of people, although they had a high failure rate too.

WARDEN/RAIDER

However, in judging characters at this distance one has to rely a good deal on the opinions passed by Wardens themselves on each other. Most of the evil they imputed to their opposites and fellow-officers was probably justified, but there was ample scope for exaggeration and misunderstanding. For example, quite apart from Warden foraying in war-time, when raiding had a legal cover, it was one of a Warden's occasional duties to conduct peace-time reprisals (Warden rodes) across the frontier, when normal process of law had failed—and sometimes just for the hell of it. In such cases it is often difficult to decide where a legitimate Warden rode ended and straight reiving began. What looked to Eure like a flagrant piece of banditry by Buccleuch could be justified—to Buccleuch's satisfaction anyway—by the

---

12. Lord Maxwell, Scottish West March Warden, was superseded by a royal favourite during a Border campaign, as a result of which the Scots were disastrously beaten at Solway Moss in 1542. Lord Hunsdon stated the case against outside commanders with characteristic vigour in 1587, when it was suggested he should serve under the Earl of Huntingdon—"one that never saw any servys, nor knowse yn any respecte what appertaynes too a capten . . . but I perceive yt ys a grete matter too be an Erle!" Hunsdon flatly refused—"I wyll ley yn pryson rather."

argument that he was making reprisal for some English offence. (It could doubtless be argued that every raid in Border history, except the first one, was a reprisal). And there is no doubt that the Cessfords and Buccleuchs played this kind of excuse for all it was worth; both made travesties of their offices. Buccleuch[13] probably did more damage than any other Border rider of his time, and young Kerr of Cessford, far from keeping the peace, was the "cheafest animator to evil", although the Englishman Forster must have run him a close second, in a less obvious way.

Even the normally well-behaved Wardens sometimes looked uncommonly like reivers; the *preux chevalier* Robert Carey took plunder on one occasion (it was admittedly from Scottish outlaws, with King James's approval), and young Scrope was named in several bills for raids committed by his direction. His is an interesting case, because it illustrates how close the activities of Warden and rank robber could be in practice.

Following the Kinmont Willie rescue at Carlisle in 1596, when Buccleuch had illegally enlarged that illegally imprisoned man, Scrope vented his rage and frustration on the opposite Wardenries. "By his special warrant" one of his officers, a veteran named Captain Carvell, raided in the Debateable Land with 2000 men, lifting 700 beasts and burning houses, and then turned on Liddesdale, where he stole over 3000 head, burned twenty-four buildings, and took prisoners whom, it was alleged, he tied in pairs, naked, and led back to England on leashes.

Even allowing for exaggeration, it was rough work for a Warden in peace-time. Scrope's explanation was that in view of previous Scottish outrages unredressed "I could not restrain her majesty's subjects from taking what amends they could get"; he did not mention why he failed to restrain his own officer. He was duly charged, the Scottish complainants adding atrocious details of how more than sixty women and children had been stripped and left "exposit to the injurie of wind and weather", as a result of which nine or ten infants died. Scrope had received the marauders "reid hand with the goods".

The Warden's defence was that his alleged 2000 raiders were in fact 100; as to children dying of exposure, the raid had taken place in

---

13. To be strictly accurate, young Buccleuch was never a Warden, but as Keeper of Liddesdale he, at least, enjoyed Warden status.

hot summer. The English commissioners who investigated the complaints then added an ingenious touch, that it was an ancient custom for a Warden to assist his opposite, and the Keeper of Liddesdale, to harry thieves on the Scottish side. In other words, Scrope had been helping the Scottish officials. Furthermore, Buccleuch was a scoundrel, in league with all the worst outlaws in his area, who had done untold damage in England, for which no redress could be obtained. Scrope's action had been "a pune, an auncient Border term, intending no other than a reprisal", and as such it had been expressly ordered by the Queen.

The defence concluded with words which are deeply significant of Border thinking: ". . . upon extremities . . . [a pune] is rightly termed and taken for armed justice, differing from peaceable justice only in forme, being in matter and substance one and the same".

In fairness to Scrope, he was only giving as good as he had got. Buccleuch was an impossible man to deal with legally, and there was no way of redress in his area but by force. Still, it might have looked better for Scrope if he had not taken particular pains to raid Kinmont Willie twice, burning his house, despoiling him, and killing two men— personal revenge rather than judicial reprisal seems to have been the motive there at least.[14]

If Scrope's case is defensible, that of old John Forster is surely not. Rivalry and jealousy certainly inspired some of the charges levelled against him as a Warden, but even so there can be no doubt that his own slackness and dishonesty helped to make his March a happy hunting ground for the worst Border elements. It was said that the felonies he had overlooked "woulde fill a large book"; in the space of ten years he had released "30 great Scottish thieves" who were ripe for the gallows, he had glossed over sixteen murders, and "none [were] so cherished as murderers, thieves, and March traitors".

It was openly alleged that he had protected Elliot marauders "les it

---

14. Although the English Commissioners defended him, Scrope was rebuked by Cecil for these raids—"Your lordship should not too suddenly use that kind of force . . . that course would be kept for the last extremity." He also warned Scrope against using any "undecent or violent terms" to King James—a timely warning, for Scrope, unlike other English Border officials, seemed to be blind to the fact that James was soon probably going to be his royal master, and his attitude was cavalier. Indeed, he even received a gentle warning from James himself.

shuld break the baund of kyndnes betwext hime" and them, and persecuted Englishmen who offended the Scottish thieves. His answer to all this was characteristic: "I am accomptted a necligent officer, an oppressor, a man enclyned to private gayne and lucre, a destroyer and not a maynteyner of the Borders, a bearer with Scottes and their actions, and a maynteyner of them ageynst my native countrith men. . . . God forbid that any one of them cowlde be proved ageynst me!"

Although he was once officially cleared, there is no doubt that Forster played a most peculiar double game in the frontier rackets; even a good Warden had to bend the rules sometimes, but old Sir John turned them inside out. His successor, Eure, was accused of misappropriating pay, among other things, and although cleared he resigned office.

Obviously it took all kinds to fill a Warden's boots and saddle. Against the brigands like Cessford and Buccleuch, and those who, like Forster, set their standards low and coasted along, must be counted those who never stopped trying—Robert Carey, and John Carmichael who paid for his integrity with his life; old Lord Scrope, and the often-forgotten Hume Wardens of the Scottish East March. The Humes were not all plaster-saints, but the English Wardens found little to complain against them in Elizabeth's time. The Scottish East March was admittedly a fairly quiet one, but one wonders if perhaps that was because the Humes made it so.

DANGERS OF OFFICE

It goes without saying that the Wardens were never short of enemies, on both sides of the Border. They carried their lives in their hands in a society where there was much popular support for the view that the best kind of lawman was a dead one—at least four Scottish Wardens were killed in office[15]—and indeed the one quality which all Wardens, English and Scottish, appear to have had in common was courage. The younger Scrope, as cordially detested as any man on the frontier, was warned of a plot by English assassins against his life, "but I fear he will be careless of himself," commented Robert Carey. Old John Forster,

---

15. They were Robert Kerr (1511) Darcy (1516), Lord Maxwell (1593), and Carmichael (1600). Special provision was made for the dependants of Wardens killed on duty.

retired and a centenarian, was being pursued by armed gangs almost to the end.[16] It was simply not an occupation for a man who was nervous of his skin.

Some died in battle, but one who was killed simply because he was a good Warden, and had incurred the hatred of his charges, was Sir John Carmichael of the Scottish West March. He was a great loss, and his quality as a Border officer may be judged from the fact that probably no Warden in history was at once so highly valued by his own government and so well liked by the other side. The Scropes, father and son, John Forster, and Lord Hunsdon, were united in their good opinion of Carmichael; the Bishop of Durham called him simply "the most expert Borderer". His popularity with the English, his willingness to oblige Elizabeth and her ministers, naturally did not win him many friends on the Scottish side, nor did the fact that he was such a favourite in Edinburgh that he was accorded more than normal powers in the West March.

But although Carmichael was unusually friendly to England, and certainly received payment from Walsingham, there is no evidence that he was anything but an honest and conscientious Warden. A good soldier and skilled captain of mercenaries, he learned his Border duties as Keeper of Liddesdale, where he was unusually efficient. Old Scrope noted that he always concurred in redress, and would even bring Scottish offenders to Carlisle Castle in person. So much virtue[17] would be suspicious if Carmichael's letters did not show the kind of man he was; they are blunt and business-like, and in them he did not hesitate to reprove even the irascible Hunsdon with tardiness—what is more, Hunsdon accepted it.

Being honest and efficient, he did not lack ill-willers. He was used to travelling armed; at least one leading Scottish Borderer had vowed to take his life, and on another occasion he was warned by old Scrope of a

---

16. In addition to attempts on his own life, Forster lost two brothers-in-law and one son-in-law, all murdered.

17. Possibly Carmichael shines by comparison with other Borderers, but he does seem to have been a most worthy man. When he was followed, after his first term as West March Warden, by Lord Maxwell, Carmichael described his successor, with a humility rare on the frontier, as "more worthy nor ewir I was or yit wilbe." He even tried to reconcile young Scrope and Buccleuch.

murder plot against him. It is surprising that he lived well into his fifties, and then the experts—the Armstrongs—caught up with him. It is supposed that some gentleman in Carmichael's service had insulted an Armstrong, and that the clan vowed revenge on the Warden. This may have served as a pretext, but the real reason was that Carmichael was a good Border officer.

On June 14 1600 Carmichael held a Warden meeting at Gretna with Richard Lowther, the English deputy. Meanwhile a band of Armstrongs and others were laying their plans at a football match; the ringleaders were Ringan's Tom Armstrong, Adam ("the Pecket") Scott, and Willie Kang Irvine, without whom no West March mischief could be complete. On the 16th, when Carmichael was riding from Annan to Langholm to hold a Warden court, they were waiting for him, fourteen Scots and two Englishmen. He rode for it, but they chased him and Ringan's Tom shot him down. Then they robbed the body, Willie Kang threw it over his crupper, and they carried it to Lochmaben.

"Now the thieves will ride," predicted Richard Lowther, adding in an almost Irish excitement: "This is the third warden they have killed and taken prisoner in Scotland."

Young Scrope was in no doubt why Carmichael had been murdered—"for his good service and agreeing with me to keep them in order: and thus they are broken loose".

And shortly afterwards the assassins were adding insult to injury by raiding Stanwix, under the very walls of Carlisle, stripping it of horses "while the lord Bishop was preching", and then sweeping on to Linstock, to lift all his lordship's cattle. They beat up and wounded his sister-in-law in the process. But justice caught up with Ringan's Tom and Adam "the Pecket"; they were captured and tried the following year, and both were hanged after their right hands had been cut off. Even as late as 1605 the other murderers were still being pursued for Carmichael's killing; Sandie Armstrong was hanged for it in that year and Willie Kang indicted.[18]

Carmichael would have been a loss at any time; dying when he did,

---

18. There is a tradition that one, of the Armstrongs condemned for the Carmichael murder composed one of the best-known Border poems shortly before he was hanged. Scott doubted if the words which have survived are the original ones, but it is worth quoting because, although rather senti-

only three years before James VI's accession in England and the pacification of the Border, he was denied the opportunity of tackling a work
for which he more than anyone was superbly fitted. If he had lived the
Marches might have been spared some of the misery of that pacification; perhaps the reivers who shot him down were their own worst
enemies.

DISFAVOUR AND DELAY

Most Wardens were luckier than Carmichael, but there were still
lesser hazards to face. One was the possibility of royal displeasure. On
the Scottish side the changing political and religious winds blew strongly
in the Borders, and it was sometimes hard for a Warden to stay in
favour; removals from office and even outlawry were not uncommon,
and there were instances of Wardens being in open rebellion against
the Crown. Sometimes Marches were without Wardens for a time,
and the frequency with which Scottish Wardens shuttled in and out of
office made it extremely difficult to get a continuity of policy and good
relations.[19] Only thirteen men all told held Warden offices on the
English side in Elizabeth's reign, and there were fourteen changes
made; on the Scottish side in the same period twenty-three men (as
nearly as can be ascertained) held Wardenships, but there were no
fewer than thirty-five changes, twenty-three of them in the West

---

mental, it could serve as an epitaph, not only for its author, but for all the
Border reivers. It is called "Armstrong's Goodnight".

> This night is my departing night,
> For here no longer must I stay;
> There's neither friend nor foe of mine
> But wishes me away.
>
> What I have done through lack of wit,
> I never, never can recall;
> I hope you're all my friends as yet;
> Good night. And joy be with you all.

19. "As they are often changed by the King for their misdemeanors, the new
man always refuses to answer for attempts (offences) before his time"
(William Bowes, 1595).

March, where Wardens came and went roughly once a year in the last decade of the century.

But perhaps the greatest frustration of all was the difficulty of carrying out the fundamental function of the office, and obtaining justice from the other side. Only a fraction of the crimes committed were redressed, and then sometimes only after months or years of delay—in 1584 the Scots complained that the elder Scrope had refused to keep meetings or make redress in the West March "be the space almaist of sevin yeirs by past"; in 1594 Forster was charging that "the opposite Warden has not met me for 12 months past, and besides refuses to answer for any but East Tevydale and his own servants". Such evasions and delays were common; in one seven-year period only a dozen meetings between opposite Wardens took place.

When all the drawbacks and dangers are considered, it is not surprising that Wardens who were eager enough to take on the post to begin with found themselves anxious to be rid of it. Hume, Scottish East March Warden, told the Privy Council in 1564 that his office was too "difficill and cummirsum", but seems to have stayed on. This was a fairly common form; when young Scrope found the Grahams too much for him in 1596, he "earnestly entreated" to be allowed to resign, and later swore to "leave this office . . . choosing rather to die honorablie, or leave my country, than to live in place where I must be subjected under the mallice of those whom once her majesty helde me worthie to governe". Eure, plagued by "malice and opposition" from his March subjects and "contempned" officers, asked Burghley "to think of some one more fit than myself" for the Wardenry; in the same letter his deputy also asked to be relieved. Robert Carey honestly admitted that "the government of the Middle March is too hard a task for me"; he could not govern it with credit, and wished to resign. His father, the veteran Lord Hunsdon, had once found himself "neyther in purse nor boddy able too indure ytt" in the East March; he was troubled with the stone, "havynge I think asmuche gravell withyn me as wyll gravell the way betwene Hakney and Wansted!"[20]

---

20. "Thys hellyshe dysease", as Hunsdon called it, may have run in his family. Poor John Carey in 1595 was bed-ridden at Berwick with "a great ache or payne, which the surgeons here have not yet determined whether it be a seatica (sciatica) or the stone—but so grievous it is that I can nether sett, goe nor stand, but continually lying. . . ."

But Hunsdon stayed on, like most of the others—even the fastidious Willoughby, who detested the northern weather. "Yf I were further from the tempestuousnes of Cheviot hills, and were once retired from this accursed contry, whence the sunn is so removed, I would not change my homlyest hermitage for the highest pallace ther", he told Cecil, and a few months later he was dead—"of a great cold."

ESPIONAGE

Gathering intelligence was an important part of the Wardens' work, and they ran extensive espionage networks. That of the Scots seems to have been highly efficient in local affairs, and little happened in the English Marches which was not quickly known in Scotland. On the other hand the English Wardens, particularly in the years when they were serving one of the greatest of all spy-masters, Francis Walsingham, gathered intelligence from all parts of Scotland and beyond, literally from the king's bedside, and even covering his foreign correspondence.

"I can have news out of Sckottland assone as any one man in Northumberland," boasted one of Walsingham's agents. "I have lyttell blewe cappe laddes that will tell me howe the world goeth." And it is evident from the Wardens' reports that nothing was too trivial to be sent back to London, even to the smallest scrap of gossip. John Carey found it worth while to report that the Brunswick and Danish ambassadors in Edinburgh were "everey daye allmoste drunke", for example.

It was following an apparently unimportant Border incident that Walsingham achieved one of the most important breakthroughs in the history of international spying. It happened in the summer of 1582, when three of Sir John Forster's men came on a man in "ane old graye cloke" in the wastes; he refused to give his name, and they arrested him. They took from him some luggage, including a set of dentist's instruments and a looking glass, but on his offering them a substantial bribe they let him go. Forster got to hear of the incident, the three men were examined and jailed, and the effects they had taken from the fugitive were left in Forster's possession.

He inspected the various articles, quite casually, and then "lookinge more circumspectlye unto the glas, by chaunce dyd espie paper within the said glasse. Whereupon I searched the said glas thorolie and openinge the same, dyd finde certen lettres so well compacted together and enclosed within the said glas, that it was verie hard to be espied or fownde owte."

They were written in code, and Forster guessed they were of importance. He bundled glass and all off to Walsingham, with an appeal that if the code, when "dissifured", contained any useful news about the Borders, he should be informed.

What the letters contained, Walsingham's code-crackers discovered, was a reference to something called the Enterprise of England. Walsingham went to work. From the inquiries that his agents made he was able, after several false starts and dead ends, to get on to Mary Stuart's secret pipeline to France. The rest is history, and without trying to depict old John Forster as an Elizabethan 007, it is possible that if he had not looked as "circumspectlye" as he did on the vagrant dentist's effects, the fateful few years of Fotheringay and the Spanish Armada might have run a different course.

An interesting example of a Warden conducting an intelligence operation is contained in letters from Hunsdon to Burghley and Walsingham in 1587. Hunsdon, through an intermediary, received an offer from a servant of Monsieur Courcelles, the French Ambassador in Scotland, to supply Hunsdon with all the ambassador's private correspondence. The servant, whose name was Browne, also offered to remove his master's jewels, but Hunsdon took up the offer of the correspondence only.

Browne's one requirement was a good horse, for his own getaway; this Hunsdon supplied, through the intermediary, with a garrison rider to act as escort for the fugitive. Browne then put his plan into operation. He served his master at dinner, "and presently after dynar, hys master beynge at chese, and hys bake towardes the wyndo, Browne browght the caskett of wrytynges under his cloke too the wyndo behynd hys master bake, wher he threw the caskett too the garryson man, who attended there for ytt, and presently went downe where theyre horsys stoode yn the subbarbes of Edenborgh, and so came theyr wayse, and so came hyther to me thys mornynge by x a clok."

They had had to break open the casket on the way, because it was too cumbersome, and had put the letters in a satchel, which Hunsdon received with satisfaction. "I hope herby", he wrote to Burghley, "hyr Majesti shall understande thys imbassytors hole negocyacyon yn

Skottland, for Browne doothe assure me he hathe nott left any one letter or wrytynge behynde hym. He wold a browght away all hys jeueles and apparell, but I forbad hym yn any case too meddell with anythynge, but the wrytynges."

In view of this last sentence, it is interesting to find Hunsdon writing again to Burghley the following day, to say he had just received a message from the French Ambassador in Scotland "too lett me understande that a servant of hys, a Skotshe boay, had robde hym of 6 or 700 crownes and apparell, praynge me that yf any suche came thys way, he myght be stayde; but spake no woorde of any wrytynges."

Which suggests either that the French Ambassador could not tell an English servant from a Scots one (Hunsdon is quite clear that Browne was English) or that Browne had obediently left the jewellery alone, only to have some other enterprising member of the embassy's domestic staff following in his wake scooping up the leavings. Hunsdon may have amused himself with the speculation, but if he did he was probably being unjust to Browne, for what Hunsdon almost certainly did not know was that Browne was in fact a Walsingham agent, who had only stolen the casket because the keys he had been supplied with by another top Walsingham operative, Robert Carvell, would not open it. Carvell therefore resolved to have Browne steal the casket; this he decided on in May, when he wrote to Walsingham asking for a date to be fixed. In the event they had to wait until October to do the job; Carvell had originally offered to go and fetch Browne and the casket out in person "but then I must come no more in Scotlande". It was presumably decided to keep him out of the final operation in order not to break his cover, and although not long after the theft was completed he was said to be in danger of his life in Scotland, he continued to operate there from time to time.

Altogether an interesting example of the Walsingham technique, and his sound observance of a first rule of espionage—not to let one agent (even a Warden) know what another one is doing.

In this context of espionage it is appropriate to mention the remarkable Henry Leigh, one-time deputy Warden of the English West March, absconding debtor, intimate of royalty, adventurer and eccentric. One could wish that more of his writing was extant, for he was a most entertaining gossip and snapper-up of detail; in a long memorandum to Cecil, for example, he describes at length his intimacy with

King James VI, and the numerous occasions on which the king would have "a cracke with him, as he called it". His observations throw a not unpleasant light on James's character. But while Leigh was a brave and occasionally active officer, he was not a success on the Border, as will be seen from subsequent references to him. And for a man who undoubtedly had a talent for ingratiating himself, he had an unhappy knack of offending royalty; Queen Elizabeth vented her rage against him, and we also read of him being excluded from King Jamess' presence because he had had the misfortune to contract "the French pocxe."

He spent a good deal of time in trouble, hoping for something to turn up, and while there is little doubt that he had some of the qualities of a first-class spy, his contemporaries often took him less than seriously. Young Scrope's last reference to him describes how Leigh was lurking in Lancashire in a false beard and putting it about that the Queen had appointed him a spy in state matters; however, Scrope's informant "suspecting that he lyed, learned covertly that he mostly abode in a petty little house in a forest destitut of all companie; and was promised for £200 to get him betrayed." Poor Henry was always on the run from someone.

*

This sketch of the Wardens has had to be restricted to generalisations with a few examples, because to treat them and their work in any detail would be to write the whole story of the Border from that particular point of view. Much more about them will be found in what follows, and in considering their role on the frontier two things ought to be borne in mind. One is that their job was near-impossible; the other, that even when one makes allowances for all its difficulties, it cannot be said that they did it well, although many of them tried manfully. Some were in the office for what they could get out of it, but others were motivated by the ideals of service, and probably most of them fell somewhere in between. The best of them had faults, and the worst many virtues, and between Scot and Englishman it would be pointless to try to choose. In their way they were a distinguished company, and if there was justice on the frontier it was because they made it.

XIX

Leges Marchiarum

The lawis of marchis, or bordour laws, betwixt the
realmis of Scotland and Ingland, in the time of peace,
are common and indifferent to the subjectis of baith
the realmis; the groundis and effect of the samin
lawis ather being contenit in the contractis and
treaties of peace past betwixt the Princes . . . or then
they are ancient and loveable custumis, ressavit and
standing in force as law, be lang use, and mutual
consent of the Wardanis and subjectis of baith the
realms.

BALFOUR, *Practicks*

From time immemorial, England and Scotland have had their separate
domestic legal systems, applying to their own subjects in their separate
realms. Along the frontier, where law-breaking was international, it was
necessary to agree on some form of international law, recognised and
operated by each country where the other was concerned, in a spirit of
co-operation. It was plainly not easy to devise such a system, between
two countries frequently at war with each other, and whose Border inhabitants could be relied on to use and abuse and twist legal arrangements
as it suited them, but a system was evolved, and officially subscribed
to.

The origin of this international Border law, the Law of the Marches
so-called, can be seen in the conference of November 16 1248, when
six English and six Scottish knights met by royal command "and cor-
rected, according to the ancient and approved custom of the March,
such matters as required to be redressed".

In the following year a similar meeting, this time with twelve knights
from each side, agreed on a written code of thirteen articles. This conference, although some of its notions, such as settling disputes by single
combat on the Border line, were fairly primitive, saw the necessity
of framing laws to cover crime committed by parties of one realm in
the other, and to prevent criminals escaping the justice of one country by

slipping across the frontier. The conference therefore provided for the return of fugitives, and for recovery of debts, and established an important procedure, which was the summoning of accused persons to answer at fixed places on the Border. Here was the origin of the day of truce, the international Warden meeting which was to play such an important part in Border life later on.

Over the next three centuries Border law was restated, amended, and embroidered at intervals, by treaties, by meetings of English and Scottish peace commissioners—the end of a war was obviously a good occasion for revising laws which were meant, after all, to apply to peace-time—and by local agreement.

It is not a body of law that can be easily defined. The expression "Laws of the Marches", as one expert remarked, is vague; he noted that the subject was so complicated that most historians had shirked it. One cannot blame them. The Bible of Border law, compiled by Bishop Nicolson of Carlisle in the early eighteenth century under the title "Leges Marchiarum", contains eight separate collections of laws, dating from 1249 to 1596; like any anthology of laws and human rights it is a grand vague statement of good intentions, but it is by no means complete. Two English Wardens of the sixteenth century, Sir Robert Bowes and Lord Wharton, compiled lists, as did Richard Bell, a Warden clerk of the English West March, and from these and other sources attempts have been made to compile a Border code.

No doubt a thoroughly researched code would be of great interest to a legal historian, although how far it would help to enlighten understanding of the law as it was viewed and operated at the time is another matter. People seldom understand their own laws exactly; they have a sound idea of what is right and wrong, and a fairly vague notion of what they may and may not do. A historian three centuries hence may give a learned exposition of the British breathalyser laws operating in the 1970s, but he will probably not understand the attitudes to them of the modern motorist or policeman.

In spite of the great attention which both kingdoms gave to the Border laws over several centuries, a manuscript of 1537 refers to the uncertainty of the March laws, and the lack of written records, and recommends that by Anglo-Scottish agreement "substaunciall knowyn lawez" should be codified under seal. This reflects a concern which

Border officials—and no doubt ordinary citizens—were never tired of expressing: that while it was easy to make law for the Border, it was quite another matter to make it work.

Indeed, the preamble to the agreement of 1563 refers to "the great disorders . . . of all the marches and frontiers" caused by the negligence of "some officers" and lack of law enforcement generally, but despite the efforts of the commissioners on that occasion, things do not appear to have improved much by 1596, when the last Border law code was published. The commissioners then bemoaned "the lamentable effects which the lawless and disobedient disposition of the most part of the inhabitants [of the Border], emboldened with long impunity and toleration of careless officers, hath wrought . . ."

In other words, the agreeing and passing of international laws was really a half-measure, since the administration and enforcement of that law depended on a co-operation and trust that were less than perfect. In its basic dependence on complaint made at a distance, Border law was at a disadvantage from the start.

The system, roughly, was that if a Scot robbed an Englishman, the Englishman complained to his Warden, who passed the complaint to the Scottish Warden concerned, who was in duty bound to investigate, and if the complaint seemed justified, to summon the offender to the next international Warden meeting to answer for his offence. And this applied, of course, to all manner of offences, the principal ones being robbery, theft, murder, arson, and assault. And since there was a jealously watched frontier involved, other offences assumed unusual importance, such as pasturing cattle in the opposite realm, or felling trees there, or hunting without permission, or ploughing and sowing beyond the Border—an offence which could hardly have arisen in the more warlike days, but was the subject of a special agreement in 1561, when official peace had come to stay.

Penalties for these various offences varied considerably,[1] and it must be remembered that to the Borderer punishment was often of less

---

1. By 1563 the commissioners were desperate enough to resort to a kind of "three-time loser" penalty. Item 18 of the 1563 agreement provides that "for three several offences and attempts" the penalty should be death. Offences and attempts covered virtually all crimes, but the commissioners took care to specify that the three offences must be consecutive and entirely separate.

importance than redress and compensation.[2] For example by the agreement of 1553, a fire-raiser was bound to pay the damages of his complainant, with a "double and sawfey"[3]; thereafter he was handed over to the opposite Warden to do six months' imprisonment.

For robbery the penalty varied from simple restitution (1367), to hanging (1384), deliverance of the thief to his victim "to slay or ransom at their liking" (1398), restitution by double and sawfey (1551), and death, but only for known thieves (1586). In the same year it was agreed that "masterful and violent" theft accompanied by bodily harm should be punished at the discretion of the opposite Warden.

Curiously enough, the early Border lawmakers seem to have been reluctant to state bluntly a penalty for murder, but by the middle of the sixteenth century execution was the official punishment. At this time it was agreed that a murderer's goods should be forfeit to the victim's family.

An early Border law, re-enacted with ever-increasing severity, dealt with fugitives and rebels crossing from one realm to the other, and with any who received or harboured them; indeed, at various times the latter were punished by death, or confiscation.

The penalty for taking prisoners unlawfully (i.e. kidnapping) was imprisonment and payment of restitution.

Since complaint was a necessary preliminary to most legal action, it followed that special provision had to be made for perjury and "over-swearing". Whether the Borderers were bigger liars than anyone else is beside the point; Anglo-Scottish prejudice and distrust no doubt tended to swell prevarication to heroic dimensions, especially in an area where one legal method of proving innocence was simply to swear it. Sworn statements were held in great importance, so there were obvious temptations where the oath was concerned, and the law took note of them.

The man who made false complaints, like alleging theft where none

---

2. In March 1597 Eure caught fifteen Liddesdale robbers red-hand in the looting of a house in Tynedale. He did not hang them immediately, but spared them to see if ransom should be forthcoming. If it was not, he informed Burghley, he intended that they should "suffer the severitie of the law."

3. "Double" meant simply paying twice the value of the damage; the "saw-fey" was an additional expense payment equivalent to the value.

had taken place, was imprisoned and fined at the Warden's discretion; those who exaggerated the value of goods stolen simply had their demands diminished by a special jury—over-swearing was obviously habitual, and young Scrope told Burghley in 1596 that it was "the practice of the Border . . . for one pound loss to make their bill of twentie".

Perjury was held to be more serious, however; at one time it was a capital offence, but latterly it was punished by imprisonment—branding in the face was suggested, but rejected, in 1553. Perhaps the greatest punishment for perjurers, however, was to be publicly declared liars before the Wardens, and proclaimed men in whom no trust could be placed.

Other March law offences included truce-breaking, attacking castles, impeding a Warden, importing wool, and a delightful local custom known as "bauchling and reproaching". This meant publicly vilifying and upbraiding someone, usually at a day of truce; such abuse might be directed at a man who had broken his word, or had neglected to honour a bond or pay a ransom. The "bauchler" (also known as brangler, bargler, etc.) sometimes made his reproof by carrying a glove on his lance-point, or displaying a picture of his enemy, and by crying out or sounding a horn-blast, indicating that his opponent was a false man and detestable.

This was taken as a mortal challenge, and could be answered by combat. Probably for this reason, "bauchling" was forbidden under Item 22 of the agreement of 1563; even where a combat did not take place, the hurling of abuse was contrary to the spirit of the day of truce, and liable to disturb the peace. But a complainant could make his public "bauchle" provided he got the Warden's permission, and first submitted his reproach in writing. [An echo of "bauchling" lingered on, it seemed to me, in Cumbrian rural police courts until a few years ago. Nowhere else, as a court reporter, have I heard so much abusive interruption and blasphemous invocation from the public benches during the hearing of cases. Cumbrian magistrates dealt with it most tolerantly.]

Other offences, which were not international, related specifically to the frontier. On the English side there was the blanket offence known as "March treason", punishable by death. It has never been discovered just how many crimes were covered by "March treason"; in some ways it was not unlike Section 40 of the British Army Act, and could be applied to almost anything.[4]

For example, John Carey writing in 1595 describes "tristing" between Englishmen and Scotsmen as March treason, and notes that it was as common as meeting in the market place. Plainly, the most serious kind of March treason was for an Englishman to assist Scottish depredations in England, or to do anything which might be construed as betrayal, even down to selling wood to Scotland for house-building, or paying blackmail (i.e. protection money).

*

This has been a very brief and selective treatment of March laws, designed to give some idea of the most common offences committed by the Borderers in peace-time, and the kind of penalties they incurred. It must be remembered that even over relatively short periods the laws changed, and the penalties with them. And throughout Border history there ran a strong element of "Jeddart" justice (summary execution) and lynch law, applicable according to chance and circumstance; forms of procedure were far from sacred, and even the law itself, by its provisions for hot and cold trod, encouraged rough-and-ready justice. Still, the Leges Marchiarum, however imperfect and erratic they might be in actual performance, did at least provide a series of working conventions to which both sides subscribed.

XX

Days of truce

As the basis of Border law was mutual co-operation, so its keystone in practice was the actual meeting of the law's representatives at the Border line. These meetings between Wardens of opposite Marches,

---

4. Geordie Burn, the "great thiefe" whose career has already been described, was convicted and hanged by Robert Carey for March treason, although from Carey's own account Burn's immediate offences were no more than normal cattle rustling and resisting arrest.

called days of truce or March, or diets, had their beginnings in the meetings of 1248 and 1249; their purpose was to hear and settle the complaints arising out of the endless raids, thefts, killings, burnings and kidnappings which went on, day in day out, between the two countries in the sixteenth century.

The days of truce were supposed to take place at least every month, but if a Warden did not want a meeting, for political or personal reasons, any excuse was good enough for a postponement—the weather, a breach of etiquette real or imagined, a legal technicality, or a simple implication of distrust or dislike.[1] The protocol governing a day of truce was formidable, and lent itself to hair-splitting and the kind of stalling which characterised the recent Vietnam peace talks in Paris, where so much time was wasted over deciding the actual shape of the conference table. A Warden who played by the rule-book—or what he contended was the rule-book, for opinions differed—could avoid meetings almost indefinitely.

To agree a date and place was simple enough. By custom, several spots on the frontier became recognised venues for days of truce—Norham ford on the Tweed; a number of sites like Wark, Carham, Reddenburn and Coldstream, at the north-west corner of the English East March; Cocklaw and Reideswire; Kershopefoot, and several places towards the Solway — Gretnakirk, the Lochmabonstane, and the English Rockliffe.

Date and place being agreed and announced, those who had complaints against men of the opposite nation were supposed to lodge their bills of complaint with their Warden, if they had not already done so, and the Wardens forwarded the complaints to each other. Of course some settling out of court took place, but where it did not, Wardens were bound to summon accused persons to the day of truce, and also to deliver any persons previously convicted to answer for their crimes.

On the day itself the two cavalcades, headed by the respective English and Scottish Wardens, converged on the meeting place. When they came in view they sat tight and watched each other for a space. Even for seasoned veterans like old John Forster it must always have been a

---

1. When Buccleuch was pressing for a meeting in 1598, young Scrope reported blandly to Cecil, "I answer with delays."

slightly nervous moment as he looked at the impressive band of horse-men across the burn or valley, recognising all the familiar faces of hos-tile friendly enemies, men with whom on occasion he had fought hand to hand in bloody mêlées—and with whom he had probably also drunk in the taverns of Kelso and Carlisle. He would reckon instinc-tively the number of lance-points, the bearing of the riders, the weight of their arms, and apply for the thousandth time that sixth sense by which the old soldier can feel trouble in the breeze.

In that brief pause both sides would remember that days of truce had been known to end in open battle;[2] they would pick out the noted trouble-makers on either side, and wonder. Then, according to ancient custom, the English Warden would give the word, and one or more of his leading riders would canter across to the Scottish side and ask that assurance of peace be given until the following sunrise. This was a vital provision, since it would enable everyone to reach home in safety before the truce had expired.[3] If there was a great deal of business to do, and the meeting was liable to take more than a day, a longer period of assurance would be demanded.

The Scottish Warden would give the required assurance, and then send riders of his own to ask similar assurance of the English Warden. When this was given, the two Wardens would hold up their hands in token of good faith, and remind their followers to keep the truce. Then and only then would the English Warden and his train advance into Scottish ground, and according to protocol, the Wardens em-braced each other. No doubt they sometimes actually did.

This then was the form, probably adhered to more often than not, although this would depend entirely on the Wardens' personal feelings. A stickler like Robert Carey might be prepared to insist on a mid-

---

2. Most notably at the Raid of Reidswire in 1575, and at Cocklaw in 1585, when Lord Russell was murdered. On that occasion the English made the mistake of taking assurance before they had come in view of the Scottish Warden's force, which they later claimed was unusually strong and drawn up in battle array (see Chapter XXXVIII).

3. Kinmont Willie was a notable exception, being captured in violation of truce in 1596, and one English Warden was actually returning from a day of truce when Scottish riders "hooved after him over Eden Bridge, and took eight of his company prisoners between it and Carlisle"—that is, within easy shot of the city walls.

stream meeting with his opposite number, rather than have it thought that an English Warden was under any obligation to go into Scotland; rough-and-ready old John Forster was more easy-going. He makes it clear in his writing on the subject that in his time meetings were held either side, according to convenience; on one occasion in 1586, when there was a heavy load of business to be done, he and the Scottish Warden drew lots, and the six days of the truce were divided between Alnwick and Kelso ("where I gott very good enterteignment at the opposite wardens handes, and greater justice than ever I did see in my lyfe in so short tyme"—no doubt he was mentally comparing another truce day ten years earlier when he had had to fight his way clear, only to be captured and carried into Scotland).

However the preliminary confrontation was conducted, the business of a Warden meeting normally took place on the Scottish side of the frontier. A note to Cecil of December 1599 says it was customary for the English Wardens to enter Scotland; the Scots seem latterly to have regarded this as an English duty, and it was their insistence on the point that provoked Robert Carey to demand a mid-stream encounter. Following this incident the whole subject was well aired, and Sir William Bowes, a Border official of experience, advised Cecil in a long memorandum that most ordinary meetings were held in Scotland, that the English normally asked assurance first, but that according to mutual arrangement the meetings sometimes took place in frontier towns. (Most sessions of Border commissioners, Bowes noted, were held in Carlisle or Berwick—no doubt because, like all diplomatic negotiators, they gave due priority to their creature comforts.)

One reason why the English normally took the initiative at Warden meetings, and crossed into Scotland, was according to Bowes a matter of Border tradition. "It is held . . . when a war between the realms ended, the Scots must first demand peace. During peace, at ordinary meetings, the English must first demand assurance." He also recalled an occasion when a Scottish Warden, Sir Robert Kerr,[4] had been murdered at a truce day on English ground—"they say the Scots swore they would never after come on English ground for justice".

The ceremony of meeting no doubt varied from the strict formality

4. Not to be confused with young Sir Robert Kerr of Cessford, reiver and Warden who flourished in the 1590s.

described above to the other extreme of a quick look, a nod, and a handshake between friendly Wardens, although the latter style was probably rare. Caution was necessary, for several reasons, among them the desire for physical self-protection. Where a strict procedure was followed, fatal misunderstandings were less likely to occur.

With the two sides mingled, the business was opened on a nice note of almost oriental subtlety; a jury of twelve was chosen, six Scots being picked by the English Warden, and six Englishmen by the Scottish Warden. The calculation that went into this, with personality, circumstance, and family relationship being weighed against the known business to be dealt with, must sometimes have been Macchiavellian. Only respectable men were supposed to be empanelled, "tratours, murderers, fugitives, betrayers" and other infamous persons being debarred, which must have reduced the selection somewhat. They were then sworn in.

The bills of complaint were now considered, taking the most recent offences first, and the accused were summoned to answer to them. Where a trial was necessary there were several forms by which it might be held; here again, the forms varied with the times, but in practice there may not have been much to choose between them. They were all fairly unsatisfactory.

One method of trial was by the jury, English bills being tried by the Scots jurors, and vice versa. This at least has a recognisable legal and practical basis in modern eyes, although its weaknesses are apparent. But the two other common methods of trial were even less secure: they consisted of trial on the Warden's honour—the Warden having to declare, out of his own knowledge and on his honour, whether a complaint against a subject of his March was valid or not, and to take responsibility for the offence if he happened to be mistaken—and trial by avower. An avower was simply a countryman of the accused's, acceptable as a referee to both plaintiff and defendant, who would swear to the truth of the case. On some occasions a defendant might clear himself simply by his own oath, apparently unsupported.[5]

---

5. The oath required the defendant to "swear by heaven above you, hell beneath you, by your part of Paradise, by all that God made in six days and seven nights, and by God himself, you are whart out sackless (innocent) of art, part, way, witting, ridd, kenning, having or resetting of any of the goods and cattels named in this bill, so help you God". The accuser's

In short, these were splendid methods in a world where everyone—Wardens, plaintiffs, defendants, and avowers—could be relied on to tell the truth. How often this perfection was realised, even in an age when an oath counted for something, we can guess. Eure summed up the situation:

"Without a commission from both their Majesties, [redress] will rarelie be had, for the two means of justice by March law are taken away, viz. a vower is food,[6] and none can be hadd of Scottishe, the Englishe are terryfied by these slaughters to avowe for the Scottes. Assyse is likewise taken awaie by the carless respecte of religione, honor the wardens will not be assented unto of the opposyte."

Modern policemen will sympathise with Eure. How to get justice by avower, when that supposedly impartial referee may be at feud? How to get honest testimony in a countryside where terrorism and extortion are rampant? Yet Eure was showing it at its worst; justice was obviously done, and seen to be done, much of the time, or the truce days would have fallen into complete discredit and disuse.

It does not do to generalise. On the one hand we must remember Forster's happy experience of justice done harmoniously at Kelso, and on the other hand Eure's despairing conclusion, and Robert Carey's warning to Cecil of the difficulty of getting Scottish vowers for English bills, because of the risk of deadly feud. The Scots, he added resentfully, got "Englishmen ynowe" to support Scottish complaints. But elsewhere Carey's brother John admits of his own countrymen that they "have too great a kindred to doe uprighte justes".[7]

Whatever the imperfections of justice at a day of truce, it was usually

---

oath was "You shall leile price make, and truth say, what your goods were worth at the time of their taking to have been bought and sold in a market taken all at one time, and that you knew no other recovery but this, so help you God" (Howard Pease, *The Lord Wardens of the Marches*, p. 109).

6. At feud.

7. And not only in Warden courts. Eure wrote to Burghley that if prisoners in domestic courts were allies, or servants or tenants of "any of great name, we found it most hard to arraign them, or get a verdict". There is much to be read into the Scottish Privy Council minute of 1597 which recommends that broken men and thieves should be tried before "speciall honest gentlemen, least suspect, maist neutrall".

done without disturbance, by the three methods mentioned. When a bill was found proved it was said to be "fyled", fouled or foul. "Cleared" or "cleane" meant innocent; "foule condicionally" meant that the accused had been summoned but had not appeared—an interesting assumption of guilt in the case of non-attenders.[8]

It is difficult to dissociate our own ideas of court procedure from what happened at a truce day, and to appreciate how different from our own were the attitudes to both prisoners and charges. Cattle theft was, officially, an offence, but among the Borderers it carried no stigma. The Graham or the Musgrave, the Nixon or the Armstrong facing a charge of rustling at a truce day, cut a very different figure from a modern prisoner in the dock. For one thing, he might be an outlaw or a powerful nobleman. He might well face his accusers and judges with his weapons on, and his horse near at hand—Forster seems to indicate this in a description of a March meeting. He could be sure that he was morally no guiltier than many of the onlookers; his accuser might well have a crime record as long as his own. Accused and judge might even have raided together on a previous occasion. All in all, there was nothing to be ashamed of, and if the outcome was that he had to pay, with his money or his life, well, that was how it went.

Nor could a trial be as clear-cut and precise in procedure as a modern court hearing. For one thing, it was held in the open air, at an assembly of perhaps several hundred men, in an atmosphere that must often have had some of the conviviality of a Rugby club supper, with the Wardens calling bills at one spot, and the generality either watching—and doubtless commenting—or talking in groups about the field. The accused in a case might well outnumber the witnesses; there were few trained legal minds present; the facts of the case might be months or even years old, and so on.

Take a Middle March bill of April 1590. Steven Pescood, with six

8. There were many classifications of "fyled" bills; for example, on February 19 1596, of the Scottish bills called in the East March, twenty were "fyled" by avower, twenty-one "fyled" for non-appearance, seven "fyled" by the English jury, ten were "fyled and agreed", and so on. On this occasion a total of 196 English bills were "fyled" and thirty-one were cleared; ninety-four Scottish bills were "fyled" and sixty-eight cleared. "Fourtene score bylles" remained uncalled; this fact was recorded with the pious observation "God send good redresse for them."

others, complained upon a group of accused consisting of five Elliots, two Nixons, a Croser, and a Simpson, the charge being that in the previous autumn they had come to Over Warden and stolen about fifty cattle and horses; that, on being pursued, they had captured four of their pursuers and subsequently ransomed them for a total of £23 1s 4d. They had also ransomed their horses, with the exception of one which they had kept.

Not an uncommon bill (it is from a list of more than fifty covering a two-year period), but with quick-witted defendants it could have been confused to a point where a modern jury would have thrown it out, or had it thrown out for them on technical grounds. In fact it was found "foule", by what process does not appear. Incidentally, the leading Elliot accused in the case appeared four times as a defendant in the list of bills.

In the same list appears another bill, whose details give some idea of the possible intricacies of a case tried by avower. Arche and Will Croser (known as Ill Wild Will) were accused by Sir John Forster of lifting eight head of cattle; according to the entry they were "quit (cleared) by their oaths", but the case was referred to their fellow-Scots, Robin and Martin Elliot. The accused were cleared by Martin's oath, "but Robin refused to swear, whereby the bill is fyled under the truce". It looks as though the reluctance of one witness has counted for more in the minds of the deputy Wardens who heard the bill than the three oaths combined.

Often a case went by default. A long list of Scottish West March bills presented at Carlisle in 1597 (the total value of goods involved was over £13,000) are mostly "foul for lack of answer", the accused not having appeared. One complaint, by Kinmont Willie Armstrong of all people, against Sym "Rydebefore" and Ranys Davy Grame, carried no verdict, but only the possibly significant note: "Rydebefore dead, Ranys Davy a fugitive."

Not all bills had to be proved; sometimes a reiver admitted his guilt and paid up, as in the case of Thomas Musgrave, Captain of Bewcastle, who was not only an English Border official of some consequence but one of the greatest ruffians in the West March (see Chapter XLII). Rynyon Armstrong's complaint against him in the Carlisle list shows Musgrave as a plunderer on the grand scale —over 1200 beasts taken and twenty houses ransacked. The bill was "foul" by confession of Captain Musgrave" and cost him £2000.

(He may later have wished he had been less ready to confess and pay up; the Armstrongs, after a period of "assurance" with the Musgraves, got tired of being good and raided Thomas Musgrave in style. But with unwonted courtesy, they prefaced their raid with a letter to the English Warden, stating their reasons for ending the assurance.)

Study of the bills presented at days of truce goes some way to explaining why such primitive means of trial as avowing and Warden's honour had to be used; the difficulty of presenting and weighing proper evidence was such that there were few alternatives to simple swearing and declaring to the facts. A good Warden could probably see justice fairly well done by using his common sense, and attending to the spirit of the law as much as to the letter.

When a bill was successfully "fyled", the amount of compensation had to be carefully calculated. Sir Robert Bowes in 1551 says the normal compensation scale was an ox at 13s 4d, a cow at 10s, an old sheep at 2s, and a hog or goat at 1s 4d, with horses and household goods to be valued on the oath of the complainant. Similarly, a complainant's oath determined the number of beasts, or the sum of money, allegedly stolen. (No wonder there were penalties for over-swearing.) But Bowes pointed out that even with double and sawfey, "the thieves had gaine and proffitte by their theft", as a good ox was actually worth more than the redress they had to pay for stealing it. The following year the Scottish Council noted that the traditional rates of restitution were in fact an encouragement to crime, and recommended the strict enforcement of the three-fold penalty of double and sawfey, but it was not until 1563 that the treaty-makers fixed a new scale, with an ox at 40s, a cow 30s, a young ox or cow 20s, and sheep and swine around the 6s mark.

We may guess that when this point in the proceedings was reached, the Wardens often turned from judges into arbitrating chairmen, helping accuser and accused to agree on the sum to be paid in restitution. Nothing illustrates better the Borderers' attitude to cattle theft, "the common usage taking away the natural abhorrence of the crime", as Scott put it, than this idea of the convicted offender agreeing the penalty. It is almost to turn a criminal charge into a civil action.

Of course this question of negotiation and compromise would depend entirely on the kind of people involved; between men of consequence, possibly clan chiefs or Border officials, with some kind of stake in stability, reasonable settlement would be easier than when one or both of the parties was a broken man or the kind of criminal saddle-tramp with no ties to respectability.

In dealing with individual complaints, the Wardens could never lose sight of the fact that it was important, wherever possible, to strike an even balance between Scot and English overall. This was recognised in practice, although the agreement of 1563 laid down (Item 3) that the Wardens must deal with *all* offences, and not make redress on a value-for-value, bill-for-bill basis. (Young Scrope pointed out, reasonably enough, that there was something to be said for the bill-for-bill system, when his Wardenry were paying up promptly but Liddesdale was not.) The balance was struck by ensuring that an equal number, or an equal value, of bills was presented by either side; this entailed some private bargaining by the Wardens beforehand, so that each side could arrive at a truce day knowing approximately what bills would be "fyled" against it, what their total cost would be, and that the total amount of bills "fyled" against the opposition would be roughly the same.

When one remembers that over even a comparatively short period the difference in depredations between two opposing Marches might amount to thousands of pounds, it is obvious that the balancing process must have resulted in large numbers of bills remaining unsettled, some-times for years. For example, it took William Fenwick of Wallington six years to get a bill of £30 "fyled" against three Robsons, and Robert Spragon's complaint against two Halls who had rustled 120 sheep waited five years for satisfaction.

In fact, for those whose bills were called, it may have been a satis-factory enough system, always assuming that the Wardens were able to collect full and prompt payment from defendants against whom bills had been "fyled". Not every convicted reiver was willing, or even able, to hand over the value of stolen goods, or compensate the wounded or widowed. When he did pay up, the process implied by the 1563 agreement was that the money should pass from Warden to Warden and finally to complainant. Knowing the time and the people, it seems unlikely that the payment would invariably arrive intact.

Of course, in a case where cattle had been stolen, and no physical damage done, redress should simply have been a matter of driving the cattle back to their rightful owner. But this, too, had its drawbacks, as we may judge from a letter of James VI in 1593, in which his majesty personally "fyles" an English complaint against Kinmont Willie and certain Elliots, and offers a gentleman as pledge for the bill's satisfaction, "which will be difficil inoughe to be gott done, consideringe the goods are fallen amonge the hands of such a multitude for the most parte vagabonds and unresponsal, dwelleinge in sundrie marches". And the goods apart, the culprits were "often disobedient".

Plainly, if the Wardens could strike a balance on paper between the two sides, the actual business of compensating individuals could be dealt with more privately, and a good Warden could probably keep complainants reasonably happy. The worst aspect of the balancing system was obviously the selection process, whereby certain bills would not be heard—in direct contravention of the 1563 agreement. Here the Warden had to use all his tact and diplomatic skill with his aggrieved subjects, and no doubt the weaker and less influential among them waited longest for satisfaction.

As Scott observes, with a splendid judicial understatement, "it seems probable the extremity of the legal satisfaction was seldom exacted or obtained". The Wardens might conclude their paperwork to their own satisfaction, and report their harmony to Burghley and King James, but the despoiled farmer whose bill had not been called would be no better off.

This official tendency to wipe the slate clean, to let bygones be bygones and take the view that unredressed offences often cancelled each other out, is understandable and not unreasonable. Wardens could justifiably have claimed that if they had pursued every complaint to a finish, the machinery of justice would inevitably have bogged down. But if this argument was nationally acceptable, it had less appeal to the man who had lost his cows.

For those dissatisfied, of course, there was only one obvious remedy, which was to swallow disappointment, wait for the next full moon, and take compensation the hard way. It was doubtless quicker than legal action, and much more satisfying.

And this, too, was often a balancing process. It is by no means uncommon to find a reiver appearing before the Wardens both as a plaintiff and a defendant. In a brief list of bills between the English West March and Liddesdale, 1582–87, "fyled" because of persistent nonappearance by the offenders, Sim Armstrong of Mangerton appears three times as a complainant (total alleged loss over 1200 beasts plus £1500 and himself once taken prisoner, the offenders being named as Musgrave, Forster, Hetherington *et al.*), and twice as a defendant (charged with murder, kidnapping, arson and spoiling to the extent of £400). This probably represented a deficit in the firm's working, by Armstrong standards.

The non-appearance of accused at days of truce was an insoluble problem. This was the Warden's responsibility, but in a country where prisons were few, where prisoners were regarded as an expensive nuisance, and where accused were too numerous, personally dangerous, and in many cases too influential or powerful to be lightly arrested, the Wardens in practice often trusted to defendants answering summonses, or obtained pledges from their leaders and relatives for the accused's appearance.

It follows that "leg-bail" was not uncommon; this simply meant seeking refuge in another March or in the opposite country.

Reference has been made to pledges, and these were of immense importance in Border life. A pledge was, in effect, a hostage. For example, when a bill was "fyled", an offender who could not pay might be handed over as a prisoner to the opposite side[9] until the money should be forthcoming. If the offender had not appeared, the Warden handed over some other willing person in his place; this might be one of the Warden's officers, and the extraordinary situation sometimes arose where a Warden handed over an officer as a pledge, and then "borrowed" him back again to carry out his duties. Sometimes a Warden surrendered himself to the opposition as a pledge. On occasion, too, a Warden finished up paying the bill, as when an accused died, and the Warden's only hope of recompense was that the dead man's heirs would honour his debt.

There seems no doubt that "professional" pledges existed who were ready to offer themselves in place of offenders. Dr Rae mentions the

9. The actual process of handing over offenders was sometimes a delicate one. Cases of prisoners breaking loose in the moment of transfer were apparently common enough for the matter to receive special attention in the 1563 agreement (Item 21), which prescribed the death penalty for escapers. If this seems harsh, it must be remembered that an attempted escape at a truce day would be almost certain to start a fight between the two sides, with consequent slaughter.

case of one, a Kerr, who was pledge to England for 102 bills.[10] It does not seem to have been difficult, for anyone who was reluctant to be handed over, to find a pledge to stand in, which is surprising, because pledges were often lodged in such "lothsome prisons" as Haddock's Hole in Berwick, where in 1602 two of the four pledges confined were "very sick and like to die". Pledges of the higher class might be kept in private homes—Robert Kerr was lodged at Robert Carey's house, for example—paying their own expenses. In the case of Buccleuch, when he was a pledge in England, this amounted to £10 a week. He was obviously a most important pledge, and a great embarrassment to his keeper, John Carey, who wrote begging that he should not have to take "so dangerous a prisoner", and vowing that "before I will take the chardge to kepe him here, I will desier to be put in pryson my self, and to have a keper of me!"

The business of pledging did not relate only to convicted offenders. Pledges were also entered with the authorities by families and communities to ensure the good behaviour of the tribe; the pledge might be the chief of the family, or a prominent man who would undertake to be answerable for his tenants or fellows. It was a highly complex system in practice, and could cost the pledge his life or his property;[11] Maxwell pledges were executed at Carlisle in the 1540s, and indeed according to the letter of the law pledges for offences could be executed if redress had not been made "before the yeare come owte".

A difficulty arose in the case of pledges for broken men, for whom no one was willing to be held answerable, and by the 1596 agreement Wardens were ordered to enter gentlemen as pledges on the broken

---

10. *The Administration of the Scottish Frontier, 1513–1603*, p. 58.
11. How complicated pledging could be is seen in an entry for November 15 1571 in the Register of the Scottish Privy Council. John Graham of Canonby attacked one Jardine of Applegirth, burned his corn, killed two of his men, stole eighty cattle, and kidnapped Jardine's brother. Graham's son had previously been entered as a pledge for the good behaviour of his father and his gang of broken men, but the Regent Moray, who had originally received the pledge, had passed young Graham on to Laurence, Lord Oliphant, who had released him (or passed him on in turn, it is not clear which) on "sufficient warrand". The Council now demanded the pledge, or the "sufficient warrand", on pain of the pledge-holder's forfeiture or outlawry, but as far as can be seen, they demanded in vain.

men's behalf. In the event that such a pledge died in custody, another pledge from among the broken men was to be entered in his place.

There were other forms of guarantee, akin to pledging, for keeping the peace. It was customary to exact promises or "bands" from tribes and communities and individuals. These were of various sorts: they might be simple promises to live quietly, they might specify abstention from feud, or involve undertakings to assist the Warden, apprehend fugitives, and so on. Without going too deeply into the question, it is reasonable to say that the authorities, by reason of the physical difficulty of maintaining order, were forced to rely on their subjects' promises to behave and co-operate and pay up; these promises might or might not be backed up by human hostages. When the assurances were broken, as they so frequently were, it became necessary for authority, if it could, to move in and deal with the situation.

How well this assurance system worked depended on the folk involved. Border officials themselves were divided in their opinions of whether human pledges were a good thing or not; they were certainly a deal of trouble. As in many other Border formalities, they often appear as convenient instruments whereby it could be pretended that justice was being done, and law and order maintained. They were certainly useful to the Wardens, especially at days of truce, and their delivery satisfied honour on both sides, and enabled business to be settled.

This, after all, was what a day of truce was all about. Wardens, like all governors and statesmen, learned early that there is seldom such a thing as settlement in human affairs; there is adjustment and compromise, and a semblance or promise of solution, but at best all that can be hoped is that life will go on without too much disturbance, and immediate crises be avoided. So they called their bills, and fyled or cleared them, balanced their books, delivered their pledges, and by a mixture of fixing, cajoling, bribing, threatening, and general politicking, sent their volatile subjects away reasonably content, they hoped. There is something in common between the open-air meetings at Kershope and Norham and the modern smoke-filled rooms.

Of course it was not satisfactory. The condition of the Border deteriorated steadily through the peaceful half-century up to the death of Elizabeth, and one reason was that the Warden administration was faulty, and that the justice administered at days of truce was simply not good enough. But it was the best they could or would do, and it was better than nothing.

Their business done, the Wardens made joint proclamation of what had been accomplished, and agreed on a date for the next day of truce which, theoretically, should have been within the next month. In the later years of Elizabeth's reign, however, the intervals between meetings increased; "shooting" (avoiding) meetings became more common, so that Forster was able to complain in 1594 that he had not seen his opposite number for a year.

With the next meeting arranged, the Wardens charged their followers to keep the peace until then, made their good-byes, and withdrew, still keeping a watchful eye on each other. The assurance was still in force, and was almost invariably kept, until next day's sunrise. It was not too much to expect that, for that one night at least, the people of the March might sleep undisturbed.

XXI

The unblessed hand

There is said to have been a tradition among the Borderers that when a male child was christened his right hand should be excluded from the ceremony, so that in time of feud he would be better equipped to strike "unhallowed" blows upon his family's enemies.

"Deadly feud", the vendetta between clan and clan, was the great cancer of the Borders. When a man was killed, it was common for his family to take up the quarrel not only against the slayer, but against his whole surname, and so by chain reaction the mischief grew into a bloody debate sometimes lasting over generations, causing countless deaths and unlimited destruction.

Burghley defined it as "deadly foed, the word of enmytie on the Borders, implacable without the blood and whole family destroyed".

Thomas Musgrave described how "they are grown soe to seeke blood, for they will make a quarrel for the death of there grandfather, and kill any of the name". He may have had in mind the feud between Scott of Buccleuch and the English Charltons, of which John Carey wrote:

"Mary! He makes another quarrel, that long synce in warr time, the Tynedale men (the Charltons) . . . tooke his grandfather and killed divers of his countrye, and that they took away his grandfathers shworde, and would never lett him have itt synce. This sayeth he is the quarrel."

It is difficult to reconcile the old fallacy that the Borderers were reluctant slayers, with the Chorographia's account, quoted by Scott, of feuding in Northumberland in 1549:

"The people of this countrey hath had one barbarous custom among them; if any two be displeased, they expect no lawe, but bang it out bravely, one and his kindred against the other and his; they will subject themselves to no justice, but in an inhumane and barbarous manner fight and kill one another. This fighting they call their feides, or deadly feides, a word so barbarous that I cannot express it in any other tongue."

Some of the feuds, such as that between the Maxwells and the Johnstones, amounted to civil war, and culminated in pitched battles like Dryfe Sands. Others were purely personal, and were settled in single combat. Sometimes Wardens found themselves at feud, and unable to discharge their office in consequence; sometimes a tribal leader was at feud with a whole township. National difference took second place; as often as not feuds were between Scot and Scot, or English and English, and frequently men and tribes found themselves involved in several feuds at once. It all added up to death and destruction on a savage scale.

Feud could break out over something less than a killing. Anyone who crossed one of the riding families was liable to have a deadly quarrel waged against him; it was alleged in 1597 that the Armstrongs had declared a vendetta against all the Gilsland Bells because two members of that clan had arrested an Armstrong for their Warden. But frequently feud followed on a raid in which a man was killed defending his goods, or a raider was cut down "red hand".[1] Traditionally, feud

---

1. Eure gives an excellent example: in June 1596 a dozen Teviotdale Scots were driving off stolen horses when they were overtaken by a posse under

seems to have been regarded as outside the law, and one can under-stand the reluctance of authority to intervene—and possibly get hurt—when it could hold aloof and watch two troublesome factions ruining each other and ridding the world of several bloodthirsty knaves.[2] The more the Scotts and Kerrs, or the Armstrongs and Robsons, or the Elliots and practically anybody, damaged and murdered each other, the less time they had for harming honest folk—so the Wardens might reason, at any rate.

Officially, of course, feud was meant to be suppressed, for at least one pressing practical reason. It was a weapon of terror; in a country-side where indiscriminate slaughter might follow from such a trivial matter as the theft of a single horse, or, as we have seen, the possession of a grandfather's sword, all but the strongest went in fear of provoking powerful reivers or clans into vendetta. Better to be raided and left alive, than to resist and perhaps have one's whole family wiped out; better to stomach loss than to take legal action (which might get no-where) and provoke the anger of the despoiler.

Fear of feud, in fact, was the principal reason why the Border slipped farther and farther into chaos in the closing decades of the sixteenth century. "The country dare not kill such thieves for fear of feud," wrote Robert Carey. "If they be but foot loons and men of no esteem . . . it may pass unavenged, but if he is of a surname, as a Davyson, a Young, a Burne, a Pringle or Hall . . . then he who killed or took him is sure himself, and all his friends (specially those of his name) is like, dearly to buy it, for they will have his life, or of 2 or 3 of his nearest kinsmen, in revenge."[3]

---

the constable of Alnwick, Thomas Percy, who "rescued them and shot one James Burn a chief man and great rider, quite through the back with a petronell, who is dead thereof . . . this act is imposed as a foode to [Percy] and his companie that then weare with him".

2. Wardens and governments were quite cynical about encouraging feuds when it suited them: Eure was writing to Cecil in August 1596 that "at a small charge to Her Majesty, the feud between Sir Robert Kerr and Buccleuch, whose reconciliation is not yet perfect, might be easily renewed, causing one of them to wreck the other".

3. Feud could also be with an office, as when the Burns and Youngs were at odds with Carey, in his capacity as Warden, and his officers, and also with the "officers, etc., of the Earl of Northumberland at Alnwick".

And the families Carey mentions were not the most fearsome. They carried nothing like the power of the Maxwells or the Armstrongs, or of such individuals as Buccleuch.

Again, there was the danger that a cross-Border feud might lead to a full-scale international incident involving the two powers. Officialdom could not always resist the temptation to join in on a countryman's behalf. When the Scottish Laidlaws killed Hobby Forster's son in 1585, and Forster gathered his kinsmen and friends to carry the feud into the Laidlaws' country, the English Captain of Bewcastle, Christopher Musgrave, led out thirty riders to the edge of the frontier, officially to prevent any violence spilling over into the English March. However, Foster's foray ran into trouble just across the Border where it was attacked by a superior force and was in danger of being overwhelmed; Musgrave, apparently, could not bear to stand by while his fellow-Englishmen were cut up, so he crossed the line illegally with his troop, rescued the Forsters, and defeated the Scots, taking about forty prisoners. Three or four Scots and one Englishman were killed, and several wounded.

Musgrave frankly admitted his fault, and pleaded "the safety of the country", but the English Warden was "greatly grieved" and reported as much to Walsingham. In the event, nothing came of it, probably because within the week a far more serious breach occurred with the murder of Lord Russell at a day of truce.

The tacit recognition of feud by authority is seen on a number of occasions,[4] such as the justice court held at Jedburgh in 1509, when those at feud were ordered to abstain from both old and new quarrels during the sitting of the court, and to carry no weapons except knives. When Liddesdale and Teviotdale families were at feud, the former were ordered to keep out of Hawick and Jedburgh, and thus could not even come near their Warden on legitimate business. Feud could even be licenced, as in the case of the two Cumbrians, Lancelot Carleton and Thomas Musgrave, both Crown officers, who were allowed to fight it out in 1602 after a generation of enmity. In the Collingwood v. Burn

---

4. A casual attitude to feud is shown in Sir John Forster's report of August 1593, when he notes that there were "no attempts by Liddesdale worth mention, but onlie the slaughter of two Dodds in Tynedale by William Elliot of Harscarth for feeds amongst them".

vendetta, already referred to, a fight to a finish by six men on either side was arranged, and only prevented at the eleventh hour by the intervention of King James, who jailed some of the Burns and sent word to England whereby Collingwood was intercepted by Sir John Forster. It was just as well; Collingwood was on his way to the scene of the meeting with 1200 followers, which suggests that the six-a-side encounter might have become more general. But the interesting point about the Burn–Collingwood affair is that it was only stopped because the fight had been arranged without permission of the respective Wardens; the implication being that if proper form had been observed it could have taken place.

In an effort to stamp out feuding, agreements were reached in the 1550s and 1560s that the killing of declared traitors and red-handed thieves should not be a cause of vendetta, but these were entirely ineffective, and it was not until 1597 that any proper attempt was made to deal with the problem. In that year the two countries agreed that a person at feud might be compelled by his Warden to renounce his quarrel in writing, or be handed over to the opposite Warden to be held until he had renounced it. But this again looked better on paper than in practice.

Although feuding was as common in England as in Scotland, there is some evidence that the Scots held their grudges longer. The Kerrs nursed one revenge for more than twenty-five years, and on another occasion carried a blood-hunt as far south as York. This was in 1511. Their leader, Sir Robert Kerr, was a Warden of the Middle March, and his justice was too uncompromising for many on both sides of the line. At one day of truce fighting broke out, and Kerr was murdered by an English trio named Lilburn, Starhead, and Heron the Bastard of Ford. Lilburn was successfully arrested, and Heron's legitimate brother was handed over for the Bastard's fault. Starhead, a follower of Heron's, fled to York, "and there lived in private and upon his guard", but two of Kerr's followers, named Tait, made their way south, sometimes apparently in disguise, murdered him in his home, and brought his head back for public display.

Sixty years later the Herons and the Kerrs were still at feud, and "would rather overthrow each other than the enemy".

Similarly, the Maxwells complained in 1593 of a thirty-year-old vendetta revived by the Irvines, one of whose kinsmen had once been delivered by a Maxwell to the English Warden and legally executed. The principals in the case were long dead, but the Irvines "caste up a feede" against a kinsman of the offending Maxwell, "and meetinge by accident . . . they most cruellie murdered and mangled him, hewing him to peeces with their swordes". In fairness to the Irvines, it should be pointed out that in the course of the thirty years they had suffered considerably at the hands of the Maxwells, so it is difficult to say whether they were paying off the original score or a later one.

No doubt the matter of feuding is a subject for learned study by sociologists and psychologists, to say nothing of anthropologists; it is an element of human existence. But here it needs to be seen only as an additional disruptive influence on Border life. It was inevitable in the conditions of the time, and so endemic that to tell the story of all the feuds would take a book in itself. It is best to look briefly at those vendettas which were most important, and one or two others of particular interest.

MAXWELLS *v.* JOHNSTONES

This was probably the bitterest and bloodiest family quarrel in British history—including even those of the Highlands. Curiously, it does not exist in folk-memory today; most Maxwells and Johnstones (unlike MacDonalds and Campbells, for instance), have no idea of how their ancestors warred with each other during much of the sixteenth century, Nor is it clear exactly when the feud began; it developed because the two families were rivals for supremacy in the Scottish Western Border, and there was no effective balance of power to prevent a head-on collision. The English encroachments of Henry VIII's time helped to feed the feud, and it flourished especially in the disturbed political climate of the 1580s. But whatever national, political, or religious interests they might be serving, the two tribes seem to have been chiefly motivated by mutual jealousy and dislike.

As early as 1528, Lord Dacre was reporting to Cardinal Wolsey that the Johnstone-Maxwell feud had turned the Debateable Land into a waste; twenty years later the sagacious Lord Wharton was busily keeping the feud going in England's interests, while trying to secure Dumfriesshire for the English Crown. Johnstone and Maxwell leaders were in and out of English prisons like clockwork at this time. But it was not until the second half of the century that the struggle for pre-potency in the Scottish West March turned into virtual warfare which, an English Warden reported, threatened to devastate the Scottish Borderland as far as Peebles.

An important counter in the contest was the March Wardenship. It changed hands so often between the two families (with the occasional outsider serving a turn) that it is still impossible to draw up a wholly reliable register of the various terms of office; never in Border history were there so many cases of Wardens outlawed, imprisoned, killed, or deposed. A short and necessarily simplified description of a few years in the course of the feud will give some idea of the chaos it wrought in the West March.

Beginning in 1580, one finds John, 8th Lord Maxwell, at an assembly of nobles in Edinburgh, "taking in hand to pacify the West March". Although not yet thirty, he had been twice Warden already, resigning once, being dismissed once, and spending time in custody in between. In 1580 the Wardenship was occupied by John Johnstone, like Maxwell a tough and adventurous man who had been outlawed in his time. The two were keen rivals, and although the Regent Morton had tried to patch up their differences, the feud was soon to be rekindled with a vengeance.

Johnstone's Wardenship ended abruptly when he was proclaimed a rebel in 1581, and Maxwell began his third term of office, but it ended in 1582 when he was dismissed for inactivity. He had been styling himself Earl of Morton at this time, but the increase in dignity had not prevented his being raided by outlaws who burned and spoiled his property at Langholm. When he was dismissed, Johnstone was rein-stated as Warden, and Maxwell promptly ordered his followers not to recognize Johnstone's authority. The new Warden, finding himself in some difficulty through this disobedience, obtained military rein-forcements from the king; he needed them, for the Johnstones at this time could put no more than 300 men in the saddle, and Maxwell, apart from his own powerful clan, had a following of the Armstrongs and other turbulent families: he was, according to old Scrope, the English Warden opposite, a chief countenancer of "loose Borderers".[5]

The next stage was that the Chancellor of Scotland, Arran, a

---

5. It has been suggested that the reason why the Armstrongs supported the Maxwells was that one John Johnstone had killed Meikle Sim Armstrong in

kinsman of Johnstone's, fell into dispute with Maxwell over some land. Out of spite, he tried to engineer the appointment of a Johnstone as Provost of Dumfries, which was traditionally a Maxwell office. Maxwell, with his armed men and Armstrongs behind him, barred Johnstone's entry to the town in July 1584, and Johnstone was still trying to get in in October. In the meantime he had been taking some unofficial action, egging on the English Grahams to burn Maxwell crops and barns, for which he was summoned to appear before the king. (Scrope described this as a most unusual thing—the summoning of a Warden on such a charge.)

It is not clear when Maxwell was outlawed, but early in 1585 the King was demanding his person[6] and the keys to his houses. Johnstone had been ordered to arrest him for his "rebellious partes", and Maxwell now gave further offence by contriving the escape from Johnstone's custody of two notorious reivers—one of them a son of Kinmont Willie's. Within the month he had dealt Johnstone an even more devastating blow; aided by his bastard brother Robert Maxwell, with 400 Armstrongs, Scotts, Beatties, and Littles, he had descended on the Johnstone castle of Lochwood, sacked it and surrounding houses, killed six Johnstones and taken twelve prisoners, and then burned the castle "that Lady Johnstone might have a light to put on her hood".

At this the King stripped Maxwell of his title of Earl of Morton, and a force was sent against him through the Middle March; Maxwell's response to this was to warn Teviotdale that if they sided with the King's troops he would pay them with burning for burning and spoil for spoil. Scrope, watching in apprehension from the English West March, wondered if Johnstone could hope to control the situation; Maxwell seemed to have every powerful tribe and outlaw leader in the West Border behind him, and with Dumfriesshire slipping towards chaos and Johnstone apparently powerless to stop it, lawlessness was spilling over into Scrope's charge. By the end of that fateful April of 1585, eighty Johnstone houses had been burned, and Scrope was expecting the hard-pressed Scottish Warden to ask for English help at any moment.

1527, which seems reasonable. The Johnstones also had faithful allies, such as the Irvines.

6. James was much displeased with Maxwell at his failure to support him when Mar and Angus made their abortive coup in the spring of 1583.

The Johnstones struck back with a raid on the Maxwell village of Duncow, and partly burned it before being driven off, but in return the Maxwells gutted two Johnstone villages, Robert Maxwell and his Armstrongs scoured the Dryfe valley of Johnstone cattle, and the town of Lockerbie was partly burned. Maxwell himself struck at Lockerbie again a week later, hanged four Johnstones at their doors, and returned with prisoners, burning and spoiling as he went. Still in May, he took 1700 lances to Moffat, foraying a circuit of sixteen miles of Johnstone territory, burning 300 houses and reiving over 3000 head. David Maxwell nearly took Lochmaben Castle, the Warden's principal hold, surprising a sleeping garrison, but a porter got the inner door shut just in time, and after some looting the Maxwells were repulsed. At Bonshaw, the strong tower held by the Johnstones' allies, the Irvines, another Maxwell siege was beaten off.

But there was worse to come for the Johnstones that summer. The Armstrongs forayed Crawford, killing the Warden's men, and by July Scrope reckoned that every major stronghold in the West March was in Maxwell hands, except Lochmaben; it soon followed. In August Johnstone himself was captured, and Maxwell erected a great gallows in Dumfries and promised to hang the Warden and his fellow-prisoners unless the castle surrendered. It did, and Maxwell demanded the submission of the Johnstone clan. That, too, followed, and Maxwell was undisputed master of the March.

But it was a near thing, even then. Intercepting a messenger, he discovered that his own brother, Robert the bastard, was plotting on the King's instructions to release Johnstone and take Maxwell himself. This filial treachery was rewarded with "harde handling" and prison, and Johnstone was confined more closely than ever.

Possibly this convinced King James that might was right in the West March; an expedition against Maxwell was called off, and he announced himself Warden. Winner took all in the Border in those days.

But even as convincing a winner as Maxwell was not secure. In 1586 his open Roman Catholicism brought him into disfavour, and he was imprisoned in Edinburgh. Johnstone, who had been released, took the opportunity to repay some of the damage he had sustained. He intercepted a foray being run by 100 of Maxwell's private army, and took most of them prisoner, a dozen men being killed in the encounter.

Johnstone then made abortive raids on Annan and Dumfries, burned a dozen Maxwell villages, stole 400 beasts, and sacked the estate of Applegarth, a Maxwell adherent. The Maxwells retaliated, burning three villages, and devastating along the Milk and Dryfe waters. Even when Johnstone himself was detained by the King, the feud raged on— a long catalogue of burning, spoiling, hangings, outlawry and the rest. The Maxwells generally continued to hold the upper hand, and in 1587 Johnstone died, a broken man.

Maxwell, meanwhile, was in exile, busying himself in encouraging Spain to undertake the enterprise of England, and in 1588 he was back in Scotland, seizing strongholds and levying men to act in concert with the Spanish Armada. He was captured by the King, imprisoned, and twenty-two of his kinsmen executed, but the remarkable Maxwell himself somehow talked his way out of trouble—possibly he was just too important and useful to be harshly dealt with—and in 1592 he was back in the Borders, his misdeeds forgotten, the Wardenship granted him for life, and his power apparently greater than ever. He could even take a patronising interest in the young Johnstone chief, James, who was married to a Maxwell—Sarah, the grand-daughter of our old friend Johnny Maxwell, Lord Herries—and there was talk that the feud might be composed for good.

And then one fine summer's day in 1592 a simple reiver named Willie Johnstone of Kirkhill lifted "ane blak horse" at Gretna from Willie Carmichael of Reidmyre. A very minor theft, whereof hundreds of men died, for with it the last act of the long and bloody Maxwell-Johnstone struggle began.

Willie Carmichael was a cousin to no less a person than Sir John Carmichael, Maxwell's immediate predecessor as Scottish West March Warden. Carmichael resigned the office on July 11, and probably his last official act was to write on July 10 to Lowther, acting Warden of the English West March, and to the Laird of Johnstone, asking their assistance in seeing that the black horse was returned. Apparently Johnstone ordered his clansman to restore the stolen beast, and nothing more might have come of it had not Willie Johnstone, deprived of his booty, looked elsewhere for a mount, and eventually stolen one belonging to the Crichtons.

A Johnstone historian contends that as a direct result of this the Crichtons and Johnstones skirmished, and fifteen Crichtons were killed. It is certainly true that the Johnstones were raiding in Nithsdale at this time, and that in one engagement about twenty men died.[7] The versions are not inconsistent; what matters is that Maxwell, as Warden, was under pressure to put the Johnstones in order.

It seems, because of the recent harmony that had been prevailing between the houses of Johnstone and Maxwell, that the Warden was reluctant to move. However, he did go the length of entering into an agreement with the Crichtons, Douglases, and others to combine against Johnstone, but it might well have remained just a paper agreement if a copy of it had not fallen into the hands of Johnstone of Cummertrees, who promptly gave it to his chief.

This put the fat in the fire. Maxwell had to set his reluctance aside and move officially against Johnstone late in 1593; he summoned him to surrender, received the inevitable refusal, and determined to settle the defiant chief and his tribe once and for all.

He raised a force 2000 strong, and issued an offer of £10 in land to anyone who brought him Johnstone's head or hand. His rival, being less affluent, made a counter-offer of a £5 land for Maxwell's extremities. Johnstone had his back to the wall, but with his own clansmen and a mixed band of Elliots, Scotts, Irvines, and English Grahams, he was ready to fight to a finish.

Against Maxwell's 2000, who were preparing to besiege Lochwood, Johnstone had about 400, but he was a crafty Border fighter, and lured Maxwell's vanguard into an ambush. The vanguard broke, and Johnstone's riders drove it headlong into Maxwell's main body on Dryfe Sands, near Lockerbie. The battle surged into the town itself, and the Johnstones, who knew they were fighting literally for their family's existence, cut the disordered Maxwell force to pieces.[8] Maxwell himself, burdened with heavy armour, was knocked out of the saddle, it is said by Johnstone himself; he stretched out a hand in surrender, but it

---

7. According to tradition, one of the Nithsdale raids was made by Willie Johnstone of Wamphray, known as "the Galliard", an uncle of Willie of Kirkhill. The Galliard is supposed to have been taken and hanged by the Crichtons, and avenged by his nephew with considerable slaughter.

8. The downward back-handed sword-cut delivered by a horseman at the head of a dismounted enemy, is said to have become known as "a Lockerbie lick".

was cut off, and he went down with many wounds—one version has it that the deathblow was delivered by a Johnstone who was the nephew of Willie of Kirkhill, the horse-stealer.

Dryfe Sands, fought on December 6 1593, was the last battle on the Borders, and one of the bloodiest family fights on British soil. The Maxwell dead were estimated at 700, including many of the chief's closest kinsmen. The Johnstones had paid off a long score; how desperately they had come to the fight may be judged from the presence among their riders of one Robert Johnstone of Raecleuch. He was eleven years old.

The Johnstones were, of course, outlawed after Dryfe; their losses, too, had been heavy, and Maxwell's cousin, who effectively succeeded as Warden, pursued them vigorously. However, after two and a half years in which the Warden office changed hands with bewildering speed, James Johnstone was appointed; he served two terms, and was the last Warden of the Scottish West March.

Despite efforts to compose the feud, it lingered on until 1608, when the then Lord Maxwell and James Johnstone met under the most solemn circumstances to effect a reconciliation. Every precaution was taken to ensure a friendly meeting, and during it Maxwell shot Johnstone twice in the back.

In this way the feud was finally settled, for Maxwell was eventually arrested (after betrayal by one of his own kinsmen) and executed. Four clan chiefs and countless of their followers had died in the vendetta; the spoil and burning had been incalculable.

GRAHAMS *v.* IRVINES AND OTHERS

Anything to do with the Grahams is complicated by the fact that they were an international family, part English, part Scots. But the feuds of the English Grahams are interesting in their variety.

In May 1582 old Scrope noted that the Grahams, "for revendge of one of their kinsmen latelie killed in feaid, have entred into Scotlande, and slayne two of the Belles, *and one also of their own name and kinsman, being a partaker with the Belles against them*". With Graham killing Graham as well as Bells, Scrope foresaw "the greatest feud ever on these Borders".

A month later he was describing the feud as being between the Grahams on one side, and the Bells, Carlisles, and Irvines on the other.

But a year later, while the Bell–Graham feud continued, the Grahams were also feuding with the Maxwells, and had apparently joined the Irvines *with whom they had just been feuding*, to assault the Musgraves; the Armstrongs also joined in against the Musgraves, and at the same time conducted their own private war against the Robsons and Taylors. (Meanwhile the Elliots were at feud with the Fenwicks, and the Forsters with Jedforest.)

It is confusing, to say the least, to discover that ten years later the ubiquitous Irvines, whom we have just seen as allies of the Bells and Carlisles against the Grahams, are noted as having been "longe in feid" with those same Bells and Carlisles.

The diagram on page 57, which is an incomplete list of Border feuds, shows how little the frontier line could mean where vendettas were concerned. Not all the feuds shown were simultaneous, but some of them were, and it was not unknown for a number of feuds to form a vicious circle (see the various enmities of the English Grahams, and of the Armstrongs and Elliots).

Apart from families shown in the diagram, the following surnames were also recorded, in July 1586, as being at feud with unspecified opponents:

England—Shaftoes, Hetheringtons, Halls, Milburns, and Witheringtons. Scotland—Nixons, Olivers.

In 1596, when a general agreement was entered into for the cessation of feuds (not, apparently, with any lasting effect), no fewer than twenty-five English families, and ten Scottish, were recorded as being then in a state of feud with another clan.

KERRS *v.* SCOTTS

With families of such size as the Kerrs and Scotts, one has to remember that feuds did not necessarily involve the entire surname.[9] The Kerrs,

9. In 1579 the Turbulls were at feud with the Debateable Land Armstrongs, but not with the Armstrongs of Liddesdale, who in turn were at feud with the Elliots of Ewesdale but not with the Liddesdale Elliots.

for example, apart from differences with other clans, were sometimes
at feud with each other; the branches of Cessford and Ferniehurst were
rivals for the Wardenship of the Scottish Middle March, and were in
and out of the office during the sixteenth century.[10] On occasion other
families, like the Rutherfords, were involved, aiding Ferniehurst
against Cessford, but at least once, when Ferniehurst was feuding with
Jedburgh, the Rutherfords were on the other side. Disentangling these
feuds is rather like trying to give a coherent account of playground
squabbles.

The "very bloody" feud between the Scotts and the Kerrs began in
1526, and was in fact started by an Elliot. The young James V, wishing
to escape the tutelage of the Earl of Angus, enlisted the assistance of
Scott of Buccleuch, who brought 600 lances of Liddesdale and Annandale to Melrose to intercept the King and his train, which included
Kerrs of both Cessford and Ferniehurst. The escape did not proceed as
planned, and the Scotts were driven off after a savage skirmish in
which they lost almost 100 dead. The Kerrs were in hot pursuit when
an Elliot, a rider in Buccleuch's service, turned on Cessford at the foot
of a path (the place is still called Turn Again) and ran him through with
a lance.

Officially the whole affair was patched up, but Cessford's death led
to a long and bitter struggle; various attempts were made to resolve it,
and in 1530 the widower Sir Walter Scott of Buccleuch married Janet
Kerr, daughter of Andrew Kerr of Ferniehurst, as a result of which the
two leaders were temporarily reconciled. But under the surface the
feud smouldered on,[11] and twenty-six years after it had begun the
Kerrs finally got their revenge.

Scott of Buccleuch was walking on the High Street of Edinburgh on
an autumn night of 1552 when he was waylaid by a band of Kerrs
and others who cut him down on the spot. John Hume of Coldenknowes ran the old chief through, shouting to one of the Kerrs,
"Strike! Ane straik for they father's sake!" They threw the body

---

10. The Scott family also feuded among themselves, as when the Buccleuchs
conducted their vendetta against the Scotts of Alanhauch, slaying one David
in revenge for the death of a Buccleuch servant.

11. In 1545 Robert Kerr of Ferniehurst was writing to Shrewsbury that
"Buccleuch's haill intent is four our destruction".

aside, and when it was later discovered that it was still alive, two of Hume's men stabbed it repeatedly until Scott was dead.

The murderers were outlawed, and the Kerrs suffered much from Scott retaliation, but thereafter the feud was mended by treaties, of which Scott gives details in his *Border Antiquities*, and by further marriages between the two sides.

This was in keeping with the general method of settling Scottish feuds, which were often resolved by assurances by both parties, followed by government inquiry into the causes, and eventually contracts of reconciliation. Sometimes tokens of redress were imposed—at one stage in the Kerr–Scott feud it was agreed that pilgrimages should be undertaken on behalf of those who had died in the original Melrose fight.

The Kerrs of Ferniehurst were engaged in a curious feud in the early 1570s with the town of Jedburgh. The unruly Sir Thomas Kerr, with a "rebel force" composed of his own riders, plus English loose men and a band of outlaws under one Alexander Trotter, was preparing to invade the town "with fyre and sword" in February 1572. He also had the assistance of Scott of Buccleuch, who like him was a supporter of the exiled Mary Queen of Scots, while Jedburgh was solidly on the side of little King James VI.

Between them Scott and Kerr posed a formidable threat to Jedburgh, but the townsmen, a sturdily independent community, were not easily intimidated; when a messenger brought them letters from the Queen they made him eat them, and when Ferniehurst's force advanced against the town they promptly stood to arms "weill bodin in feir of weir" with six days' victuals. Ferniehurst had 3000 men; Jedburgh's only hope of assistance lay in a small band of riders and musketeers who were being sent by the Edinburgh government, under Lord Ruthven. Ferniehurst tried to cut off Ruthven's line of march to Jedburgh, but the bold townsmen, having been joined by riders under Kerr of Cessford, who was always willing to try conclusions with Ferniehurst, came out to offer battle.

Ruthven arrived in the nick of time on Ferniehurst's rear, and caught between two fires the bandit army made off and dispersed, Ruthven capturing some of them at Hawick after a night march through the snow.

Ferniehurst did not confine his hostilities to Jedburgh alone; Roxburgh also suffered his "fyre, sword, and all kind of creweltie", and he seems to have been assisted by Robert Kerr of Ancrum, who entertained the Trotter gang "with great and sumptuous preparation", and did his bit against Jedburgh by waylaying certain Rutherfords from the town, and "kest them in the pit" at Ancrum.

Jedburgh and the Rutherfords got their own back in 1573. Robert Kerr was a wealthy man (no doubt the "pit" at Ancrum was a powerful persuasion in exacting ransom), and the Jedburgh men, under Provost Richard Rutherford, broke up his gates and doors and pillaged him; the list of his goods reads like a department store inventory. His wife's gowns (described, interestingly enough, as "creations") and hats were among the spoil, the best gown being valued at the equivalent of £80 or more of our money.

Ferniehurst, meanwhile, was still visiting Jedburgh with "riotts and murders"; he was forfeited, and many local leaders, including Kerr of Cessford, were riding against him, but a few years later he and his Kerrs entered into an assurance with the town, and with the Rutherfords, and in 1581 he actually became provost. To this in course of time was added the Wardenship of the Middle March—in the teeth of his rival, Cessford—and the Keepership of Liddesdale. There was no place like the Borders for making a comeback, and Thomas Kerr lived on to trouble the world and the Middle Marches in particular.

SCOTTS v. ELLIOTS

This began, typically, with a Scott being accused of stealing sheep belonging to an Elliot's dead brother. A countercharge of stealing oxen was laid, the Elliots murdered one David Scott, and Scott of Buccleuch procured the legal execution of four of the killers. With these preliminaries concluded the feud erupted into a small war in 1565, with "daily slaughter without redress between Scotts and Eyliotes, stealing on all hands, and justice almost no where."

The feud was assisted by the fact that the Marches were in an unusually disordered state. This was the year in which Mary of Scotland married Darnley and moved against her Protestant opponents, finally forcing them over the Border at the end of the Chaseabout Raid. There was commotion and fortifying along the line, and the Elliots received help from an unexpected quarter in their struggle with the Scotts: English assistance, including money. This was a variation of the classic Elizabethan gambit, which consisted of keeping the Border Scots at home so that they could not participate in Scotland's national upheavals. Encouraged, the Elliots sent a war party into Scott country, lured their opponents into the pass between the heads of Eweswater and Cheviot, and there ambushed them neatly with 400 riders. As a result the Scotts were not reluctant to patch up the feud in 1566.[12]

SELBYS *v*. GRAYS

This was not a feud in the full-scale family sense, but it illustrates how even prominent officials and civilised Border townsmen could be involved in bloody vendetta, even inside the walls of Berwick.

One George Nevill, a servant of the Gray family, had in 1597 stolen cattle from the Kerrs across the Border; the bill against him was "fyled" by Ralph Selby, nephew to William Selby, the gentleman porter of Berwick. However, when a Scottish complaint was later lodged against Ralph Selby, alleging the theft of 160 sheep, and an English avower was called for, according to custom, who should step forward but George Nevill, who swore to Ralph Selby's guilt.

The Selbys naturally saw this as pure spite; the Grays, Nevill's masters, contended that Nevill was an honest man, and that the Selbys had "long borne hatred" against them. "Hot words passed," according to John Carey, but it is not clear exactly how the fighting started.

William Selby later testified that "hearing of the unkindness", he invited Edward and Ralph Gray (Edward was no less a person than deputy Warden of the English Middle March) to a "friendly meeting" to talk things over. The Grays agreed to meet him in a churchyard, and according to Selby, Edward turned up with fifteen men, and after

---

12. But almost fifteen years later Martin Elliot of Braidley was raiding the Scotts again, and in retaliation the Scotts set upon an Elliot and cut off his hand.

they had talked alone for a little, suddenly drew his rapier. Selby, an
elderly man, drew to defend himself, but five or six of Gray's men
immediately came at him with their swords out.

"[They] drave me to the church wall, being all alone, and oppressed
with nomber, defending myself I fell, and being down receaved two
wounds" in the head and hand. The church minister emerged, and "a
shoote of women riseing, certeine of my freindes of the towne came
to my reskew." Selby admitted that Edward Grey was hurt and one of
his men killed, but not by Selby.

He concluded his account with a reminder that he had served the
Queen and her predecessors in the wars "these 48 years", and that he
was "an honest man and no brawler".

Thus William Selby: now for the Gray's version. Far from inviting
them to a friendly meeting, Selby had sent a challenge to fight. Edward
Gray, "supposing William (in respect of his years and place) of a tem-
perate disposition", suggested instead a conference in the churchyard,
and turned up with only three servants, and himself armed only with a
short walking rapier. William Selby, according to the Grays, attended
with a long rapier and dagger, and with his nephew Ralph alongside.
Other Selbys presently arrived, and while Edward Grey and William
Selby were talking, William suddenly hit him in the face, drew his
rapier, "and began the affray." Gray's three servants tried to part them,
William Selby fell down and Edward Gray ordered no one to touch
him. "So he arose unhurt ", according to the Grays, "till there came in
a company of 6 or 7 of the most notorious common fighters and evil
disposed in Berwick . . . and Ralph Selby with 10 or 12 others . . . all
prepared and plotted by the Selbys." They set on Gray and his three
men, one of whom, Bryan Horsley, was run through the back. Edward
Gray was wounded, as were several of the Selbys.

You take your choice of the two versions. John Carey seems to have
regarded the Selbys as the chief culprits. He turned out the guard in
person, ordered all Scots in the town into their houses, put armed
pickets on all street corners, and took the Selbys into custody. It may
have been just as well; William Selby claimed later that bands of Grays
were hunting his nephew to shoot him.

It was a very small affair—the Burns or the Maxwells would hardly
have noticed it, much less regarded it as a feud. But it should be remembered that these were leading Border officials, the *élite* who were

supposed to keep order and dispense justice among the wicked peasantry. It was no wonder that the Border was a disorderly place, when its leading men took their gangs behind the church to settle their arguments.

Old William Selby was shortly after this made comptroller of ordnance, and later was elected M.P. for Berwick. John Carey detested him, and touched unusually hysterical heights in describing how Selby was trying to usurp his authority and spy on his conduct; Selby, on the other hand, alleged that Carey had threatened him "with vehemencie" and had hinted at physical violence. Even allowing for Carey's paranoia, one suspects that William Selby, plausible old busybody that he seems to have been, had asked for it.

XXII

Terror, blackmail, kidnapping and "decaie"

On November 12 1597 John Carey wrote a letter to Burghley from Berwick. Or rather, he tried to write; it was not easy, for three times he was interrupted by summonses to come down and examine wounded Englishmen. They were raid victims who had been cut up in following their hot trods against Scottish forays, and their plight moved Carey to indignation.

"Pooer men, sekinge for helpe or relefe at aney manes hand, and like masterles men, feynding relefe no whear nor aney whom to moan themselves to," he wrote to Burghley. They were outside his charge, Carey added, but what could he do but try to help them? He was enraged and sick at the repeated sight of "freshe bledinge bluddey woundes and hortes", and of the ever-growing tale of death and destruction; for once he was too moved to waste time entreating London to act, and his final sentence to Burghley was fierce:

"Your honors must take better order, or the country will be laid waste and it will then be too late."

Carey, like every other responsible Border official, was thoroughly alarmed at a phenomenon that arose along the frontier in the last two decades of the century. Against all reason and probability, the Border was getting worse. By the 1590s, it was years since England and Scotland had been at war; in both realms conditions generally had become more settled, the threat of invasion from the Continent had diminished, civil strife, rebellion, and religious warfare had subsided. There was even a foreseeable prospect of the two countries being united under one monarch. With all this, it might be thought that the governments would have tried to combine effectively to deal with their Border problem. But they did not. Instead, as the century wore on, organised lawlessness along the line was allowed to increase until, by the late 1580s and 1590s there existed what can fairly be described as a reign of terror. "Decaie", a favourite word among Border writers, had set in with a vengeance.

It was a process of deterioration that grew steadily worse. Incidents like Carey's thrice-interrupted letter were commonplace; the frontier was at long last paying the price of years of maladministration, distrust, neglect, and mischief.

The decaying process is not difficult to explain. We have seen how the sixteenth-century Border came to be, how its people lived and behaved, and why. War and hardship and repeated devastation had shaped them and their country, and left the legacy of gang warfare and organised crime. But on top of this the situation had been made worse by two central governments whose weakness, stupidity and neglect had allowed frontier turbulence to develop on an unmanageable scale. Worse, they had actively encouraged it, as we have seen, for political reasons. And having helped to create the monster, they found they could not control it—not that this concerned them unduly, since only the Borderers were really suffering as a result, and neither government was going to shed many tears on their account.

The Scottish government admittedly seems to have tried harder, latterly, than England did;[1] Border affairs still mattered to Edinburgh,

---

1. Simon Musgrave did not think so; he blamed "the uncerten and fickle government of Scotland", and believed that "the grete hatred and displeasure among the [Scottish] nobilitie hath incouradgede and imboldnde the evill disposde persons".

but with the countries long at peace they were of decreasing interest to London. So the kind of joint action that was necessary was never undertaken. It should have been obvious, by 1590, that the Warden system and the Law of the Marches were a failure unless they received powerful support and co-operation from both governments. Even now, this was not forthcoming. In the end, indifference, incompetence, and mutual distrust by the two central authorities were the chief underlying causes of Border decay.

Many other causes stemmed directly from these basic ones. With the Warden system creaking into breakdown, and March justice, in William Bowes's phrase, "clean out of joint", the Borderers themselves had to find other means of settlement. So reprisal increased, and feud, and "unlawful complottes and combinacions" by English and Scots to "recover somewhat by private favour", all of which added to the unsettlement of the times. And as the defiance of law and order increased, another alarming tendency developed: men who had been wronged ceased to fight back, or to seek redress, or even to resist their despoilers, for fear of reprisal.

This symptom of terrorism had always existed along the Border to some extent, even with good Wardens, but in the later years of the century it became commonplace. Robert Carey's complaint in the Burn–Collingwood outbreak ("the country dare not kill such thieves for fear of feud") was echoed everywhere. Worse, the country dare not even complain of thieves. "There are 1000 . . . who dare not for their lives speak against a great thief, either openly or in secret," said Richard Fenwick, and then laid his finger on the nub of the problem; it was not the thieves they feared, but the officers and "great gentlemen who protect and defend those thieves". Magistrates, great men, and mean officers, he claimed, had for their own safety's sake maintained thieves and traitors to the oppression of the "comminaltye".

Fenwick was a self-promoter and his tale lost nothing in the telling, but it is well corroborated. One anonymous petition to the Queen charged leading officials with neglect and dishonesty, enlarging felons, misappropriating monies, and making "every tyrant a kinge". At best this demonstrates a lack of responsibility on the part of those who should have given a lead to the ordinary folk of the Borders. The gentry, the landowners, were too interested in self-preservation to care overmuch about those who depended on them for protection. "The

meaner sort cannot keep horse and furniture for service," wrote Robert
Carey, "the better sort are so patisht with riders that they take no care
to defend the country, and each man oversees his neighbour's wrake, so
he escapes hurt himself." Hunsdon had said much the same thing, in his
inimitable way: "The gentilmen are so afrayde of deadly feedes, as
whensoever their ys any fraye and any goods taken awaye, nott one
that will ryse to helpe his neighbour—thoughe the Scottes come by
their doares with the spoyle!"

And the Bishop of Carlisle wrote in 1593 that gentlemen were being
invaded by raiders in their own houses; most of the gentry within
twenty miles of Carlisle were in fear of their lives, and even justices of
the peace had to keep their cattle indoors.

Eure estimated in 1595 that all but a few gentlemen in Northumberland "are combined by tryste to save their goods, and let outlaws pass,
some favouring them for clan or intermarriage". Worse still, bailiffs
and officers consented to the spoil of their charges "and participated
thereof, a most horrible and unnaturalle act". Eure had a shocking
example of this on his own doorstep. His deputy, William Fenwick,
Keeper of Tynedale, was notoriously associated with Scottish reivers,
and Eure knew it. But all he did was to lecture Fenwick, and Henry
Woodrington, later a deputy of the March, on the "hateful" practice
of making "unlawful compacts for their private safety"—and later
noted that despite his warnings they had "entered assurance with the
Burns . . . and Armstrongs Bangtailes friendes". Following on which,
the Burns raided Harbottle, breaking two houses and stealing thirty cattle.

Robert Carey foresaw the Scottish raiders gaining complete mastery
of the country; Scots were able to pasture 10,000 sheep on English soil,
and leading Englishmen had Scots living in their houses "who are chief
guides for the spoil of the poor".

The anonymous petitioners were hardly exaggerating when they
described the Middle March as a land of bondage from which the
countrymen were forced to flee.[2]

_____

2. From the English Wardens' reports one might imagine that all the damage
was happening on their side, and that their Marchmen were the innocent
prey of the Scots. One should correct the balance by noting such complaints
as those filed against England by the Scottish Warden, Cessford, in August
1596. He alleges five murders, fourteen raids, a kidnapping, and a total
pillage of about 1400 beasts and £1500.

Deprived of the protection of law, neglected by his superiors, and too weak to resist his despoilers, the ordinary man's only course was the payment of blackmail. This practice is probably as old as time, but the expression itself was coined on the Borders, and meant something different from blackmail today. Its literal meaning is "black rent"—in other words, illegal rent—and its exact modern equivalent is the protection racket.

Blackmail was paid by the tenant or farmer to a "superior" who might be a powerful reiver, or even an outlaw, and in return the reiver not only left him alone, but was also obliged to protect him from other raiders and to recover his goods if they were carried off. It reached the proportions of a major industry, with the blackmailers employing collectors and enforcers (known as brokers), and even something like accountants. There was no secrecy about it; the Grahams, who were notorious blackmailers, "define it as nothing ells but a protection money or a reward pro clientalia", and regarded themselves as rather robust insurance companies. They justified themselves on at least one occasion by claiming that the payments they received were used by them to redeem stolen goods on behalf of the payers, and denied stoutly that they were in league with the thieves.

Payment was frequently made in kind. Burghley noted that blackmailed people, "being in great penurie of silver, pay rent in meal, corn, etc. Soe that this bribenge they call Blackmeale, in respecte that the cause for which yt is taken is fowle and dishonest." Young Hutcheon Graham, who ran a profitable protection racket at the end of the century at the expense of the village of Cargo, which he had taken under his protection, received four bags of malt yearly from each husbandman of the village in blackmail. From Cargo's point of view it was worth the price; they seem to have been well protected, and when Hutcheon took off on his great raid during "Ill Week" in 1603, burning and looting extensively in the English West March, Cargo escaped at the cost of victualling him and his 140 riders. He used the village as his base during the foray, and divided his spoils there.

Blackmail was levied over a wide area. There is a tradition that Border robbers collected it even in North Lancashire. In 1558 Scottish blackmailers drummed up trade in the English East March as far as Morpeth, offering protection against a supposed invasion. They visited several towns, collecting assurances and cash; those who refused to pay

were promptly despoiled and their places burned. Towards the end of
the century, however, the racket had become much more systematic,
and in 1595 Robert Carey reported that all but three or four of the
leading men in the Middle March were paying blackmail for themselves and their friends "to some Scottish thief to save them from the
rest. The poor and those unable to pay tribut to those caterpilers are
daily ridden upon and spoiled".

How little was achieved by such reports as Carey's to the central
government may be judged from the fact that three years later, in 1598,
he was repeating his complaint in almost the same words. The racket
was too firmly established to be broken up; it was part of everyday
life, recognised by lawmen as well as by the common folk, and it completed the undermining of morale on the Marches. If anyone had ever
been in doubt that crime paid on the Borders, the flourishing of blackmail, open and unchecked, was convincing proof.

The unfortunate peasants often had to pay what amounted to two
sets of rent—blackmail to the reiver and normal rent to the landlord.
Sometimes they simply could not afford it, as in the case of Rowland
Robson of Allonstead in Gilsland, who was blackmailed by Richie
Graham of Brackenhill and was also liable for rent to the Queen. His
examination before young Scrope in June 1596 gives a remarkable insight into a typical Border protection racket.

Robson testified that blackmail was being paid by more than sixty
tenants in the Lanercost area, and was being collected by Thomas ("the
Merchant") Hetherington[3] and William Hair, the latter a "special
facturr" of Richie Graham's who used "evil speeches and threatenings"
to enforce payment. Those who refused had their goods spoiled and
carried off by Graham's riders. The tenants of Burthalme all suffered
in this way with the exception of one Widow Smyth, who had agreed
to pay up—indeed, the riders appear to have been most scrupulous on
this point, for they "inquired where the widow who paid blackmail
dwelt, and then harried all the rest, except her".

Robson went to complain to Thomas Carleton, land sergeant of
Gilsland, and actually found him in the company of Richie Graham the
blackmailer; the dialogue that took place is highly significant of the

---

3. Many of the blackmailed persons were themselves Hetheringtons, no
doubt kinsmen of Thomas's.

Border attitude to blackmail, for Carleton, as a law officer, should have been duty bound to prevent it. In fact he was hand in glove with the Grahams, and all he could say, when the injured Robson demanded redress, was "that he could do him no good". Robson exclaimed that if he had known that, he would have paid the blackmail in the first place. Graham, entering the conversation, wondered why he had not done so; he seems to have been mildly surprised at Robson's obstinacy.

Robson replied that he had supposed the Queen and the Lord Warden were above Graham's "booke of blackmayle", and he intended to complain to the Queen and the Council and point out that he could not afford to pay double rent.

Robson also testified that Hair and Hetherington had been seen surveying the houses of those who refused to pay, a few days before they were pillaged, and that Hair was known to keep a register of those paying blackmail which was displayed at the parish churches of Arthuret and Canonbie.

All this evidence was forwarded to the Privy Council, with a note from Scrope adding that Richard Graham of Brackenhill was an outlaw, wanted for several murders, that other tenants were paying him blackmail of £1 a year, and being forced to serve him; that Graham further was running a coining plant in his tower, and receiving stolen goods. All of which was no doubt true, although one must remember that Scrope was at this time seeking to discredit the Grahams in every possible way.

Richard Graham had an ingenious answer to the blackmail charge. He alleged that in the time of old Lord Scrope, the previous Warden, the Lanercost tenants had been so poorly protected by their landlord, Christopher Dacre, that they had implored the Warden to send for him, Richard Graham, to defend them. Scrope passed on the invitation, and Graham draws a moving picture of his own reluctance to take on the task, which he feared might be beyond him. However, he agreed to do what he could . . . and for the remainder of old Scrope's Wardenship he claimed to have defended the Lanercost tenants faithfully, for which the Warden paid him. The arrangement seems to have ended with old Scrope's death, and the Lanercost tenants again found themselves plundered by the Scots; so, alleged Graham, they came again seeking his protection, which he gave "to the uttermost".

A nice tale, plausibly told. As to the charges that his riders had pillaged the obstinate tenants, it was unthinkable, and for the suggestion

that he kept a blackmail register which was published in Arthuret and
Canonbie . . . who, him?

The incident is only a detail in the larger indictment of the Grahams
which the Privy Council had to consider at that time, but it illustrates
how Border blackmail worked, and how difficult it must have been to
suppress, in spite of the penalties against it. By a Scottish Act of 1567,
paying blackmail was punishable by death, and twenty years later it
was decided to proceed against takers as well as payers. In England
payers were liable to a £6 fine and imprisonment, and takers to be
punished at the Warden's discretion. Only in 1601 was blackmail
made a capital offence in England.

Another curse of the time was kidnapping, which was a legacy from
the old Border wars, in which it had been recognised legitimate practice to hold prisoners for ransom. In peace-time, of course, the taking
of prisoners from the opposite realm was unlawful, but habit died
hard, and it was common for reivers to carry off not only cattle and
insight, but also people. The penalty for this was merely imprisonment
and payment of compensation, and the legislation which was passed
from time to time in an attempt to prevent kidnapped persons from
entering into bonds and assurances with their captors was generally
disregarded. In practice, prisoners were normally ransomed, sometimes
for a few shillings.

A nice example of the opportunism of the Border rider in this connection appears in a document of 1599 reporting a fray in Bewcastle—
the one which followed a six-a-side football match described in Chapter X. An appendix to the report consists of the statement of one John
Kell, an Englishman, who describes what happened to him while the
Armstrongs were turning the tables on an ambush laid by the Ridleys.
The Scots were killing and taking prisoners, says Kell, when "there
came rydinge upp unto me one Quintin Whytehede, servant to the
capten of Bewcastle, and bad me be taken with him and he should save
my lyfe, so as I yealded unto him; which so sone as he had me oute of
the company, would nedes have spoyled me of horse and sutch furniture as I had about me—for savinge wherof I must eyther promise to
pay him a ransome, or ells be carryed away into Scotland; but having
no lyking of Scotland, I agreed to pay him upon Midsomers eve next
cominge."

Kell was in something of a quandary; as an unlawfully taken

prisoner he was legally forbidden to pay the ransom he had promised, but if he failed to pay he had no doubt he would receive "ane evell turn to my utter undoing".

Kidnapping was not always committed with ransom in mind; a hostage might be lifted to use as a bargaining counter for the release of a captured reiver. The terrorists who nowadays kidnap diplomats and hi-jack aircraft to force the enlargement of prisoners could have taught nothing to Jock Graham of the Peartree, who was playing the same game in the summer of 1600.

Jock and his brother Wattie were a pair of hard men, even by Graham standards. Jock was a thorn in authority's side both in Scotland and England, having raided and received stolen goods in the Scottish West March as early as 1592, and being listed as "a notorious felon at large" in Cumberland in April 1597. In July of that year, however, he had been laid by the heels, to the delight of young Scrope, who was at that time pursuing his anti-Graham campaign with full vigour. Jock was awaiting trial at Carlisle for horse-stealing, but during the assize week brother Wattie and friends arrived at 4 a.m., broke Jock and another Graham out of the jailer's house, got them out of the city gates, where an ambush party was waiting to cover their retreat, and so escaped.

The brothers stayed out of the law's clutches for the next three years, and then Wattie, having indulged the family passion for horse-theft once too often, was captured in Westmorland by kinsmen of the sheriff, Mr Thomas Salkeld, and taken to Appleby for trial and, inevitably, hanging.

It was now for Jock to repay his brother for that rescue three years earlier. He did it in a way which struck at the Salkeld family, riding in full daylight to the sheriff's house at Corby, near Carlisle, where Salkeld's little boy, aged about six, was playing by the gate. According to Scott, Jock of the Peartree offered the lad an apple, and asked him, "Master, will you ride?" whereupon the child, who had evidently not been warned about accepting sweets from strangers, allowed himself to be taken up at the outlaw's saddlebow. Whether Scott's version is strictly accurate or not, Scrope's report is clear: the boy was carried into Scotland, and word sent that he would receive exactly the same treatment as the horse-stealing Wattie, whatever it might be. One can only hope that Peartree would not have pursued the threat to its limit; as it

was, he did not have to, for the Salkelds took fright, Wattie was released, and the child was returned.

From this, and the description of the blackmail racket, it will be
seen that the Grahams were doing their full share in the reign of terror
of the 1590s. Even taking into account Scrope's detestation of them,
which led to their characters being blackened at every turn, the roll of
their "misdemeanours", compiled in September 1600, is an appalling
one.

According to this, no fewer than sixty Grahams were outlaws,[4] for
murder, robbery, and other crimes; they had despoiled above a dozen
Cumbrian villages, sheltered felons, fought the Warden's troops,
murdered witnesses, extorted money from their enemies, and in one
specific instance burned the house of one Hutcheon Hetherington to
force him into the open so that they could cut him to pieces. Add to
this blackmail, kidnapping, and ordinary reiving, and their account was
a long one. In considering the vengeance that was to overtake the
Grahams a few years later, it is an account that is worth bearing in
mind.

★

From time to time contemporary authorities compiled actual lists of the
reasons for the increasing deterioration of the English Marches in the
last quarter of the century. A memorandum of 1579 lists them as (1)
private English feuds, (2) Scottish spoils, (3) the long peace, which led
to neglect of horses and weapons, (4) unfit keepers of strongholds,
(5) demission of property to non-Borderers.

Similarly a list of 1596 is also headed by "disorders among the English", with Scottish spoiling again placed second. Dishonest Scottish
Wardens, the practice of blackmail, and the poor state of the strongholds, are given as other causes, and it is also noted that large parts of
the English frontier were depopulated, unlike the Scottish side, and
recommended that "colonies" should be "transferred thether, from
other partes of the Kingdom, where yt laboreth of the abundance of

---

4. In Cumberland alone, 110 men were outlawed between 1592 and 1602.
Apart from the Grahams they were mostly Forsters, Hetheringtons, and
Irvines. In the same period seventy-nine Cumbrians were indicted for murder, the principal offenders again being Forsters, Hetheringtons, and Grahams,
as well as Armstrongs.

people". Another significant recommendation was that felonies committed in the English Marches should be tried farther south, where there was less chance of juries being partial or terrorised.

Landlords laying down their lands in pasture as large farms, suppression of smallholders, letting to Scots, heavy fines, and "greedy demands of farmers under the Queen" are causes listed by Burghley in his Bill to strengthen the Borders in 1596. He noted that as a result of these decays the English Borderers could no longer defend the frontier at their own expense, as they had once been expected to do.[5]

It was natural, in the climate of the times, to blame lack of religion for much of the evil along the frontier. "Want of knowledge of God, whereby the better sort forget oath and duty" was condemned by Eure. He saw churches "mostly ruined to the ground, ministers and techers comforthles to com and remaine where such heathenish people are". It was said of the Middle Marchmen that most of them could not say the Lord's Prayer—"the whole congregation goethe a whooring . . . they are fit for any religion, and old tradicion called Papistrye fitteth them best", said one account, doubtless with more zeal than accuracy, But if lack of religion was a symptom rather than a cause of decay, there is no doubt that the church suffered along with the laity—one tradition credits the Armstrongs alone with the destruction of fifty-two church buildings.[6]

But with respect it must be suggested that the ruin of churches was less immediately important to the English Marches than the shortage of horses. This became so marked in the 1590s that Eure held it to be a principal reason why retaliation against the Scots was almost impossible. The shortage was a direct result of raiding from both sides: Fenwick told

---

5. "Hard landlords", together with Scottish raids and agricultural failure, were blamed by William Bowes. He noted that in four years the Middle March's 1000 furnished horsemen were down to 100.

6. The religious backsliding of the Borderers was not a phenomenon of the 1580s and 1590s alone: it seems to have been more or less permanent, and the Scots Privy Council in 1602 were only echoing scores of earlier pronouncements when they attributed frontier disorders to the "want of preiching of the word . . . so that no small number of personis hes rune louse to all kynd of villanie and mischeif". In the area as a whole Redesdale and Tynedale were particularly irreligious, and at one time received only one church service per annum, from that courageous cleric Bernard Gilpin.

Burghley that "hundreds of your subjects would fain buy horse, but dare not, for the English thieves would steal them in a day or two".

Toleration of Scottish immigrants has already been mentioned, and there is no doubt that the discouragement this caused, and the displacement of English tenants, was an important cause of decay on the English side. As Hunsdon said, it made the work of Scots forayers much simpler. Combination by English and Scottish marauders was a long-established fact, but with the increase in Scottish immigration, and with the long peace, this criminal co-operation became more highly organised towards the end of the century. "The chief spoilers in your highness's three marches are Englishmen who join the Scots", Richard Fenwick stated bluntly. He believed that if the English thieves were dealt with, the Scots raiders would not dare to ride so far into England as they did—in 1601 they were foraying as far as Penrith, with English assistance, "without shout or cry".

"Yt would make the teares fall from your Grace's eyes to see the wretched state of the country," he added, echoing Sir Cuthbert Collingwood's heartcry of ten years earlier: "For God's sayk, remember the pitefull complaynt and lamentable estayt of this ruinose and waysted cuntre." The trouble was that no one paid much attention. At the same time, with all the outside causes which contributed to the corruption of the Borderland, one must not forget that the people who were doing the physical damage were Borderers themselves: the ruin of the land continued because so many of them liked living by spoil and gangsterism.

XXIII

"Fyre and sword upon Tuesday next"

All through the sixteenth century, however many laws were passed, officials appointed, proclamations issued, and pious intentions expressed by the authorities, it was generally recognised that the one way of coping (if only temporarily) with the Border reivers was to get in among them with brute force. Using hindsight, one can say this was a shocking admission of defeat on the part of both national governments, who had allowed the frontier to degenerate, but the mischief having been done, force was the only answer. Quite simply, it was the one thing the Marchmen respected.

This force was applied in three principal ways. There was the judicial expedition on the Scottish side, whereby the monarch or regent or another official of rank descended on the Scottish Marches with power and tried to restrain and punish the offenders: this worked, up to a point. Then there was the official reprisal carried out across the frontier, in which a Warden who could not get redress by peaceful means, got it by force and discouraged the reivers of the opposite side. Thirdly, and so mingled with the second course that the two are often indistinguishable, there was the simple method of allowing people to take their own revenge across the line.

The last course was, strictly speaking, illegal. Unlike the legitimate pursuit of hot trod, whereby a man might pursue his goods within a stated period of time, the practice of "avenging one's own cause" was forbidden by several treaties from 1367 onwards—the difference was that while recovering stolen property was legitimate, straight revenge for a wrong, on the eye-for-an-eye principle, was not.

Obviously it was often hard to draw the line between the two in practice, and neither Wardens nor their subjects were too particular.[1] Indeed, as the century wore on, and conditions grew worse, English Wardens saw private reprisal as the only effective means of obtaining real redress. Scrope in 1597 asked that "officers and oppressed people" be allowed "to take their own revenge when best may", and Robert Carey went even further. "The best way to keep them quiet is to doe one evill turne for another," he told Burghley, adding that when he had allowed his people to take the law into their own hands with the Scots, it had worked. He asked for royal permission to use his own discretion when redress was unobtainable, for "I see none other than revenge for revenge and blood for blood, as the only way to breake the necke of this evill custome—wherein the officer must be maintained by her Majesty."

---

1. Humphrey Musgrave, when English West March deputy Warden, once followed a legitimate hot trod into the Debateable Land, overtaking and skirmishing with a band of horse-thieves, but failing to recapture their booty. He thereupon destroyed the reivers' own goods and beasts, and this was held to be an unlawful reprisal.

Things had come to a sorry pass when an officer as decent and responsible as Carey was asking official backing to let his people go reiving and spoiling, but he had no choice if his Wardenry was to be
defended. Eure found himself in the same position in the Middle March,
as he explained to Burghley in March 1596 when the frequency of
Scottish raids against Tynedale had him at his wits' end.

The Elliots had come over in force and lifted sixty beasts from the
Milburns; Eure complained to Buccleuch, as Keeper of Liddesdale, and
received a promise of redress if Eure would hand over English thieves
who had recently robbed Will Elliot of Lariston. Eure investigated, and
found that the cattle taken from Lariston by the Tynedale men had
been illegally depasturing on English ground, and were therefore fair
game. He made "fair answer" accordingly, and no doubt thought that
was the end of the matter.

The next stage, however, was a raid into Tynedale by sixty riders
of the Scottish West March, who came via Liddesdale, and spoiled
Bellingham on fair day. Much of what they took was rescued by hot
trod, but they did escape with some horses and insight, and were
received in Liddesdale on their return by Will Elliot of Lariston himself. While Eure was still fuming over this, the riders of Jedburgh
Forest made a third Tynedale foray, stole twenty cattle, and kidnapped a widow named Milburn with her children and servants. At
this Tynedale "rose to the fray", but there was a shortage of riders, and
the pursuers on foot could only get close enough to see the reivers
dividing their loot at a safe distance.

This was too much for the Tynedales; while the thieves were thus
engaged they made a by-pass into the Jedforest area, and brought away
sixty head by way of reprisal. The Scots followed the trod by horse and
foot, but although the Tynedale men had only eighteen riders, their
"infantry" were strong enough to keep the pursuers at bay, and the
booty came safely to Tynedale.

Strictly speaking, they had broken the law, but no one could blame
them, least of all Eure, who ordered the loot to be divided and used to
buy horses. "I trust her Majesty will not be offended at her subjects'
act in self-defence," he wrote to Burghley. Like Carey, he had reached
the stage where he was prepared to countenance straight reprisal, even
if it was illegal. So the vicious circle continued.

Possibly encouraged by their Warden's attitude, the Tynedale folk played the same game the following year, after a small Scottish raid in which three cattle were taken. Joined by some garrison troops, the countrymen made a hot trod, but failed to recover the goods; however, "knowing of a number of cattle to be had, the soldiers without a leader ventured into Liddesdale with the country foot", and by way of reprisal lifted over 300 beasts belonging to Martin Elliot of Braidley —nice compensation at a rate of 10,000 per cent. They had to fight for them, and one of the Tynedale Dodds killed Martin's Gibb Elliot,[2] who had previously slain the Dodd's kinsman ("ytt pleased God, this Ellot, for the punishment of his sinns, was by the said Dodd now slaine, some others woonded.")

The trod-turned-raid then withdrew with their booty, having accomplished their foray almost entirely on foot. Mounted or not, Tynedale people could hold their own with anyone.

Private reprisal was one thing, but the official punitive raid by a Warden was quite another. In the late 1520s the truce made at Berwick provided that, if Wardens were unable to compose disputes peacefully, either monarch might licence official reprisals. Edward Aglionby, defining the duties of a deputy Warden in the English West March in 1592, noted that "in offence of Scotland—when the Warden doth make any rode, [the deputy] to go with a compotent number and take a boutie in Scotland; and that is called a Warden rode".

In other words, in spite of all the legal forms and strict injunctions to keep good rule, etc., the fact was that a Warden could take the law into his own hands at his own discretion, and go raiding and pillaging like any common reiver. He had to use common sense, of course, to make sure he had a good excuse (never difficult), and judge exactly how far he could go; he must not put his own country too much in the wrong, or lend the other side a stick wherewith to beat his own monarch. We have seen young Scrope retaliating against the Armstrongs after the Kinmont episode, and there is no lack of documentation about Warden raiding in the 1580s and 1590s. Forster in 1584 reports a typical incident to Walsingham:

---

2. Martin's Gibb Elliot, "a leader of that wicked race", was a reiver whose name crops up frequently in raid records. A man of some parts, he was brought up in the wars in Flanders and France, according to Eure, and on one occasion defended his own tower against a joint siege by old Scrope and John Forster.

"I caused a rode to be made, where Mr Fenwick, Mr Herone, and others killed 5 or 6 Elwetts, and brought off goods. If the King complains to her highness, I would ask you to put in your good worde. . . ."

And straight away his letter goes on to discuss meetings with the opposite Wardens, and other everyday Border business. One of the tragedies of the Border system was that neither Forster nor his opposite Warden (nor even the Elliots, probably) would have seen anything cynical or incongruous in the juxtaposition in his report of an official murder raid and the scheduling of a March meeting.

With all its faults, the Scottish government's system of judicial expeditions to quell their Borderers was as good as anything devised for dealing physically with the reivers. These large-scale descents were not uniformly successful, but they did stamp out people like Johnnie Armstrong and provided a fairly regular reminder that authority could make itself felt when it wanted to. Throughout the century these "judicial raids"[3] took place on average once a year, the monarch or deputy bringing a nucleus of regular troops to which were added local levies for a specific period. Thus when Queen Mary announced her coming to Jedburgh in 1566 to deal with an outbreak of trouble ("crewell murthere becum commoun nochte onelie among thame that hes querrell, bot kynnisfolk unnaturalie slayis utheris"), the leading men and yeomen were ordered to meet and attend her at Melrose armed and with twenty days' provisions.

The purpose of the expeditions was to hold courts and impose order as necessary; to deal with matters above the Wardens' control, to receive pledges for good behaviour, and to show the flag. In 1561, when the Borderers were "impacient of all good ordouris", various leading clansmen—Kerrs, Elliots, Scotts, Rutherfords, and Turnbulls—were summoned to the courts at Dumfries and Jedburgh to give advice to the leaders of the judicial expedition, and to receive "valentines" giving the names of wrongdoers whom they were to apprehend.

The most important part of an expedition's work was to arraign and deal with offenders, and to set to work on them with fire and sword as required. Hangings, drownings, and imprisonments were legion, and

---

3. Government missions of this kind are correctly called raids, but to avoid confusion they are referred to here as expeditions.

sometimes mass executions took place. Areas like Liddesdale, too intractable to be submitted to ordinary processes of justice, were devastated, and in some cases where the tougher clans or outlaw bands were concerned the expedition assumed the proportions of a military campaign.[4] When this happened it might be necessary to obtain English co-operation so that the Border could be sealed and the offenders prevented from slipping out of Scottish jurisdiction; occasionally the English joined with the expedition to ride against the thieves. The Earl of Moray, a notable killer of reivers, marched in concert with Sir John Forster in 1569 to harry Liddesdale, and burned every house in the valley.

Usually English co-operation was confined to a watching brief, however, as in the case of James VI's expedition against the broken men of his West March in November 1597, when he wrote to Henry Leigh, the English deputy Warden, advising him that "we have resolved to passe forward in proper person uppon them with fyre and sword upon Tuesday next, to their extermination and wreike . . . and intreat yow that yow wilbe in a redynes with some sufficient force, to remaine at the Mote of Lyddell . . . for hawlding them in at that syde, and concurrencie with us to their borning persuit and repressinge." (One does not gather, from this letter, that James was going to be over-careful about following due legal process in dealing with his disorderly subjects.[5])

Leigh readily agreed, and saw some "prettie sport" near Gretna,

---

4. Since the expeditions were to rely largely on local help they had to be timed accordingly. Many of them took place in autumn, after the harvest was in. Dr Rae, in his study of this aspect of Border administration, has pointed out that many of the expeditions took place at full moon, when conditions were suitable for night operations against the offenders.

5. James took charge personally of most of the expeditions in the last fifteen years of Elizabeth's reign, with mixed success. One writer, John Graham, accuses him of robbing and slaughtering without discrimination, treating all Borderers alike, hanging without trial or evidence, and so on. It is even suggested that the real thieves came off best—"laborious industry had more to fear at his hands than killing and thieving". Without saying quite as much, young Scrope in a letter to Cecil in 1602 suggests that His Majesty's zeal for justice might have been better directed—"He is departed well pleased: has hanged 11 poore theves, but had they bene of the great ones it had done more good." Indiscriminate slaughter was certainly a feature of James's eventual pacification policy when he came to the English throne.

where the Irvines and others were burned out—it is obvious from his
report that the Scots accompanying the King took the opportunity to
pay off private scores against the local people, which no doubt happened often enough during these official punitive excursions.

James made a habit, sensibly enough, of enlisting English advice,
assistance and arms in putting down his dissidents, and most of Elizabeth's Border officials were ready enough to help. For one thing, they
knew who the next King of England was probably going to be. Consequently we find James's correspondence with English Wardens and
officers increasing towards the end of the century, and in 1601, finding
his own officers unable to do justice, he was inviting the English to
take on the job on the Scottish side of the line. "He warrants us her
Majesty's officers to take revenge on either side of the Border," Robert
Carey reported with satisfaction, adding: "I will complain no more."

He was as good as his word. When Scottish outlaws burned a village
in his charge in the following month and took four or five prisoners,
Carey despatched Henry Woodrington, one of his deputies, into Scotland with 300 riders. They burned the houses of the chief offenders,
rescued the prisoners, and carried off sheep and cattle in reprisal. The
outlaws had taken refuge in the woods and mosses, and were beyond
Woodrington's reach, but he rounded up twenty of their best horses
so as to inhibit future raiding.

As the English were withdrawing there occurred one of those pocket
dramas so common in Border history, and reminiscent almost of the
hand-to-hand duels of the age of chivalry. One of the Scots outlaws,
Sim of Calfhill,[6] "came pricking after them" with horse and lance, and
a Ridley of Woodrington's troop turned back to meet him. The Ridleys and the Calfhill Armstrongs were at feud, the Calfhills' houses
having been burned not long before following a Ridley's murder. Now
the two men fought it out with their lances, Ridley running the Armstrong through and "leaving his spear broken in him" so that he died.

The goods taken in reprisal were divided among the folk who had

---

6. Sim Armstrong of Calfhill, one of a troublesome sept of Armstrongs, is
first mentioned in 1596 raiding the Hetheringtons; by 1597 he was so
notorious that James VI singled him out to Henry Leigh for hanging "who
haith cut the throates of so many poore people." He was named as an outlaw
in 1601.

been spoiled by the outlaws, and Carey prepared himself for further trouble. "I have power enough, and will weary them with their own weapons," he told Cecil, but he expected them "to provoke me further". They were not long about it; within a fortnight Haltwhistle was raided by Armstrongs intent on burning it to the ground—"running up and down the streets with lights in their hands". About ten houses were destroyed, but the attackers were beaten off with two dead and two badly wounded. Another blow was struck in the Armstrong-Ridley feud, a young son of old Sim Armstrong of Whithaugh being shot out of his saddle by a Ridley firing from one of the stone houses.

Balked, and swearing "bloody vows of deep revenge", the Armstrongs were obviously going to come again; Carey's subjects protested that unless something was done they would be forced to leave the district, abandoning their homes and goods. In the face of this, Carey decided to try to settle with the outlaws once and for all. As a preliminary he told Cecil of his intention to establish himself as close to the Border as possible, with his deputies and 150 horse, plus what volunteers he could raise, in an attempt to cut off raids close to their source.

All very well, said the local men; he could lie up in the Border hills in summer (it was then June), but he could never stay there in the winter. However, Carey was stubborn, and with his riders and some regular infantry he went up to the frontier and built "a pretty fort, and within it we all had cabines made to lie in." Provisions were laid in, and the watchers settled down.

The chief outlaws responded by withdrawing to the Tarras Moss beyond Liddesdale with all their goods, staying out of range of Carey and playing the waiting game in their turn. The Tarras wilderness, wrote Carey, "was of that strength, and so surrounded by bogges and marshi ground, with thicke bushes and shrubbes, that they fear no force nor power of England or Scotland.

"They sent me word that I was like the first puff of a haggis, hottest at the first, and bade me stay there as long as weather would give me leave; they would stay in Tarras-wood 'till I was weary of lying in the waste, and when I had had my time, and they no whit the worse, they would play their parts, which should keep me waking the next winter."

If Carey grinned at this typically Armstrong message his followers did not, for he tells us they shared the Armstrongs' belief that Tarras was impregnable. He was determined to prove them wrong, and on July 4 he went quietly to work. His own accounts of the operation, one in his immediate report to Cecil on July 8, the other in his memoirs written years later, differ slightly in detail, but from the two it is easy to piece together what happened. He waited for night and sent in an advance guard of 150 riders a distance of thirty miles secretly, "conveighed by a moffled man not known to any of the company". This may have been a deserter from the outlaws anxious to keep his identity secret. This force circled the Tarras, and split up to guard the three exits from the moss. The outlaws had scouts on the hills to the south, but the three ambushes were laid without discovery, and at 4 a.m. Carey attacked from the English side with 300 horse and 1000 infantry.

"Our men brake down as fast as they could into the wood. The outlaws thought themselves safe, assuringe themselves at any time to escape, but they were so strongly set upon on the English side as they were forced to leave their goodes, and to betake themselves to their passages towards Scotland."

The ambushes were sprung, the leaders of the "unrulye rout" were taken, and the rest escaped back into the moss where "our men durst not follow them, for fear of losing themselves".

Two of Sim of Whithaugh's sons were among the prisoners—there seem to have been no casualties—and Carey was able to obtain the release of English prisoners and the submission of the remaining outlaws, who gave themselves up the next day. At this he promptly released the Armstrongs he had captured. He was pleased with himself, as can be seen from the letter he wrote to Cecil from his fort headquarters, in which he calls attention to the local men who had stayed with him five weeks in the waste—"they deserve thanks, unless greater affairs cause this place not to be thought of? Pardon me if I offend, but I think myself too slightly regarded. But if thanks come yet, it is not too late."

Poor touchy Robert; three days later he was apologising to Cecil and the Council from whom he had meanwhile received a letter apparently commending the local men's service. It must have crossed with his own complaining message, and like many an embarrassed correspondent since, he finished up blaming the postal service.

However, it had been an uncommonly neat piece of work, even if Carey overestimated its lasting effect. "This March freed from the hurt of Liddesdale," he was congratulating himself two weeks later, and in his memoirs he wrote that he "was never after troubled with this kind of people." If he was not, others were, but that was not his fault; as a rider of Warden rodes he was efficient and ingenious—and, it should be noted, he was humane.

Not all official expeditions against the reivers were so successful, as James Hepburn could have testified. History knows him as that tough, unscrupulous adventurer the Earl of Bothwell, lover and husband of Mary Queen of Scots, and one of the great romantic rascals. He was also lieutenant of the Marches in Scotland, Keeper of Liddesdale and holder of the great fort of Hermitage, and in the autumn of 1566 one of the most powerful nobles in the country. His favour with the susceptible young Queen was increasing in proportion as her hatred for her deplorable husband, Darnley, deepened, and it was doubtless in high confidence that he set out to put Liddesdale in order that October, while the Queen led the main judicial expedition to Jedburgh.

His qualifications for the task were formidable, for he was recklessly brave, intelligent, and knew his Borderland. It followed that Liddesdale should have seen fine things. Unfortunately for the Earl, he ran up against the Elliots in one of their best years, when they had just successfully concluded their feud with the Scotts, and were doubtless in higher spirits than usual.

He did succeed in capturing a number of reivers, principally Elliots, and placed them in Hermitage under strong guard. Then continuing his sweep in the valley, he came on one Little Jock Elliot of the Park, a reiver of repute, and engaged him in single combat. Bothwell shot Elliot out of the saddle, and then seems to have made the mistake of approaching his fallen opponent to make sure he was settled. The result was that Elliot was suddenly all over him, Bothwell received three stab wounds, and his followers had to carry him back to Hermitage in a cart. If that was not humiliation enough, they discovered on arrival at the fortress that the Elliot prisoners had taken it over, and the stricken Earl had to bargain to get into his own castle.

It was here he was lying, recovering from the wounds to his person and his self-esteem, when the Queen came to see him on that famous ride of which her more romantic biographers have made so much. In the event she blundered into a marsh and contracted a cold from which she nearly died. All in all, it was not a happy excursion for either of them, and serves as an example of the hazards of taking on the reivers on their own ground.[7]

Either overwhelming force was needed, as in the biggest judicial expeditions when the King came with a following thousands strong, or craft and daring, as in the case of Carey's raid of 1601, and Humphrey Musgrave's kidnapping of the Laird of Mangerton. In other words, the reivers had to be fought on their own terms, and when authority could not match those terms the task was hopeless.

The three methods—judicial expedition, Warden raid, and private reprisal—were the only practical ones, but from time to time other interesting schemes were put forward for dealing physically with the Borderers.[8] Surrey, the victor of Flodden, whose knowledge of the Border was matched by his ruthlessness, had the idea of devastating a strip several miles deep immediately on the Scottish side of the frontier, on the principle that if life in the area was insupportable, there would be no one there to work mischief. Sound in logic, perhaps, but difficult of performance, as experience showed with the Debateable Land, where the natives persistently flourished in spite of efforts to establish it as a no man's land.

In purely practical terms, and setting aside all considerations of humanity and fairness, it does appear on the historical evidence that the only way in which the English could hope to keep their northern frontier reasonably quiet was to occupy Southern Scotland with an English power, wasting it systematically and keeping the Scots occupied. Something like this happened in the 1540s, and again briefly in 1570 when the large-scale invasions by the Earl of Sussex and old

---

7. Tradition has it that Bothwell's encounter with Elliot of the Park was celebrated in a popular song, the second line of which is now part of the Scottish language:

> My name is little Jock Elliot,
> And wha daur meddle wi' me?

Elliot, who is said to have died of his wounds, was one of many Jock Elliots of the Park—he was Little Jock, and there were also plain Jock, Roweis Jock, Sim's Jock, young Jock, and Scot's Hob's Jock.

8. In view of the "universall contempt and disobedience", it was suggested in the Scottish Privy Council in 1599 that 100 Scottish Highlanders should be sent to Dumfries to "daunton" the West March. As a proposal it was at least interesting, and fraught with possibilities.

Scrope prevented any Scottish raiding while they lasted. But of course such occupation was impossible on anything but a temporary basis, and even then it left unsolved the problem of how to cope with turbulence among the English Borderers.[9]

It is hardly surprising, considering the chaotic state of affairs along the frontier for most of the century, that one fertile mind in search of a solution should have cast back to the Romans, and wondered if perhaps Hadrian had the right answer. An anonymous document of 1587 submits at length to the Queen, with supporting diagrams, a plan for "an arteficiall fortyficacion, consystinge for the most parte onlye of mayne earthe, raysed with trenche and rampyour, and flauncked with bulwarkes" to be built across England's northern boundary from sea to sea, to keep the Scots out. The author was obviously more concerned with large-scale invasion than with reivers, which was natural enough in that critical year when England was menaced by the Catholic powers; however, his wall would have served the double purpose.

The scheme is elaborated in great detail, arguing the Roman precedents, and disposing of objections as to expense and maintenance. The interesting calculation is made that Hadrian's Wall must have cost about £19,000, and that an Elizabethan wall could be built for £30,000. Great "skonses" or forts were envisaged at every mile, maintained by gentlemen who would rent the ground adjoining at a penny an acre, and who would be assisted by "greate gonners". One can guess that the cost of maintaining such a bulwark would have been astronomical; what the thrifty Elizabeth thought of it we can guess, and it never seems to have got beyond the drawing-board stage. But even if it was a ridiculously impractical scheme, it is indicative of Border conditions that anyone should even go to the trouble of studying it seriously.

---

9. Those crafty veterans, Forster and old Scrope, put an interesting proposal to Walsingham in 1583. Having asked for 250 riders and 200 infantry to defend their Marches, they pointed out that such a force would not only discourage loose men from raiding in England, but would drive them to commit their depredations in Scotland. English outlaws would doubtless assist in this worthy work, and Scrope and Forster were perfectly ready to "winck at" English receivers of goods stolen on the Scottish side. An interesting example of Warden morality.

PART FOUR

*The Long
Good-night,
1503–1603*

XXIV

Flodden and after

On a summer day in 1503 the Princess Margaret, daughter of the King of England, was received at Dalkeith by her bridegroom, James, King of Scots. She was in her fifteenth year, half as old as James, which was no great age difference for those days; the splendour of her retinue, the gaiety of the court attending the handsome young king, and the spirit of good will surrounding their meeting and marriage the next day, all seemed happy portents for England and Scotland alike. No one was better pleased than the Princess's father, the astute and careful Henry VII. He had made his peace with the old enemy, France; now he was assuring the friendship of Scotland, and of the impetuous James, who had by his support for the impostor Warbeck brought England and Scotland perilously close to open war. All that was now past; the Scottish king was an intelligent man who could see no benefit in prolonging the old, useless struggle with England, and his wisdom got the better of his warlike inclinations. He was the ally of France, but since England and France were friends, there was no reason why he should not be the friend of England too.

So all was well, and Pedro de Ayala, the Spanish envoy who had laboured so hard to bring the two countries together—clinging, in his own words, to James's skirts to keep him back from renewing the English wars—could take satisfaction in a diplomatic job well done. Perhaps he, like Henry, could foresee the day when a Scottish king descended from James and Margaret would rule all Britain; it was a prospect that troubled the English monarch not at all, since he saw clearly that in such a union England would always be the senior partner. In the meantime, there were other immediate benefits; along with the marriage-treaty there were agreements for perpetual peace and an end to all troubles along the Border.

The last named was as necessary as it always was. Border violence was not yet the systematic thing it was to become, but the years of warfare had set the pattern, and reiving, arson, and murder were common along the frontier, where neither the peace-loving and thrifty Henry nor the active James could exercise full control over their turbulent tribesmen. At the turn of the century the Armstrongs were recognising no rule but their own, defying royal commands to answer for their crimes, so that seventy of them were outlawed in consequence, and orders issued "to persewe thaim to deid". Nixon, Crosier and Elliot raids were taking place as well, and in the year before his marriage King James had been busy on the Border, pacifying Eskdale— whose inhabitants were apparently also outlawed—and hanging the worst of those he could catch. But in the main his raid was more of a jolly progress; he travelled in style with his musicians, huntsmen and hosts of retainers, ran out of drink, and supplemented his mobile cellar with presents received from Northern English nobles and prelates, whom he entertained lavishly in return. (It was on this occasion that Thomas Dacre, the English West March Warden, lightened His Majesty two nights running at cards.)

Whether his presence in the Marches was responsible, or the improved climate following his marriage, the Border country in that first decade of the century was not unusually disturbed. Liddesdale was already a notorious place, but James, a man of his hands with a sense of fairness, appears to have dealt justly with it, always ready to pardon and take assurance when he could. However, he could be tough when he wanted, as in his sudden descent on the Marches in 1510, when he dealt out summary justice to sundry reivers—and fined the Lord of Liddesdale £10.

But it could never be called a peaceful Border, even with cordial relations prevailing between London and Edinburgh, and from time to time the frontier raiding strained the new-established friendship. Incidents like the murder of Kerr, Scottish Middle March Warden, at a truce day, kept the feud alive, and with the death of Henry VII in 1509 the last hope of "perpetual peace" died too.

His successor, the uxorious musical giant[1] Henry VIII, was a man of great gifts. He was also probably the worst enemy Scotland ever had.

---

1. His Majesty was 6 feet 2 inches tall, with a 42-inch chest and 35-inch waist, in his prime. Latterly his chest was 57 inches and he was 54 inches round the belly.

Whatever his virtues, his Scottish policy does nothing to contradict that judgment of Sir Walter Raleigh's, that "if all the pictures and patterns of a merciless prince were lost in the world, they might all again be painted to the life, out of the story of this king". Doubtless there were medical reasons for Henry's behaviour; it has been suggested that the arrogance, cruelty, and megalomania which appeared in him in middle life were the result of cerebral syphilis, aggravated by the head injury he received jousting in 1526. It was the worst of many such wounds, and left him unconscious for some time. Probably he never recovered from it, so that to his other disabilities may be added the fact that he was punch-drunk.

But in the first years of his reign all was reasonably well between him and James; considering the strong and fiery dispositions which they shared it is unlikely that the friendship would have lasted anyway, but it was finally broken when Henry joined the Holy League against France in 1511, leaving James in the awkward situation of being allied to two powers hostile to each other. He determined to hold to the old alliance with France, doubtless being influenced by the fact that Border strife was increasing, English and Scottish ships were clashing on the high seas, and the French King was calling for help.

Possibly the decisive factor was an outbreak of foraying in August 1513; an English raid was made in which considerable plunder was taken, and the Scottish reply was prompt. Alexander, 3rd Lord Hume, Lord Warden General of the Scottish Marches, crossed into Northumberland with a foray that has been variously estimated at 3000 to 7000 riders. They burned seven villages, rounded up a great herd of geldings, and made back for the Border laden with plunder. So much, in fact, that it slowed down Hume's retreat, and Sir William Bulmer, an English commander of resource, was able to circle ahead of him and lay an ambush in the thick broom on the plain of Milfield. Bulmer had raised the March, but his principal striking force was a company of 200 archers; all told he commanded fewer than 1000 men.

His ambush worked perfectly; more than 500 of the Scottish raiders were cut down by the sudden cloth-yard hail from the hidden bowmen, more than 400 were taken prisoner, and the entire booty, including the precious horses, was recaptured. Hume escaped for the loss of his banner, and his brother was among the prisoners.

The "Ill Raid", as it came to be called, might have been seen as an omen to add to those strange visitations and portents which were reported in Edinburgh at the same time, warning the Scots King against an English adventure. But James was not to be turned, and in late August he brought over the frontier the greatest host that Scotland ever put into the field. Its size has never been determined, but estimates vary from 60,000 to 100,000, which seem remarkably high figures. He took several strong places, and partly demolished Norham, Wark, Ford and other holds.

By rights there should have been no holding the Scots, but as so often happens with the English in time of great peril, the hour produced the man. This time it was the veteran Howard, Earl of Surrey,[2] with an army to which he added levies from the northern counties to meet the Scottish menace. History has neglected old Surrey, which is unjust, for he deserves a place among the great English captains. He never served his country better than now. Collecting the sacred banner of St Cuthbert at Durham to inspire his North Countrymen, he joined with Dacre, the West March Warden, at Newcastle, and hurried on through vile weather to Alnwick, where he despatched a challenge to King James to fight it out on the following Friday, September 9. James accepted, and Surrey pushed on to find the formidable Scottish army occupying Flodden Ridge, near Coldstream.

Outnumbered, Surrey was not to be outgeneralled. He circled the Scottish position to place himself between James and the Border and force a battle; the Scots came down to meet him, and on a rainy afternoon the "mervelouse great conflicte and terrible battaile" began, English billmen and bowmen against the Scottish pikes. The Scottish Border riders overrode the English battalion opposed to them, but James's own battle was held by Surrey's division, and although the Scottish king, fighting on foot, cut his way almost to within touching distance of Surrey's standard, the wings of his army were crumbling before the steady slashing of the English billheads[3] until the Scots'

---

2. Thomas Howard the elder (1443?-1524). Fought at Barnet (1471), Bosworth (1485), and served under Duke of Burgundy. Created Earl of Surrey (1483) and Duke of Norfolk (1513). Earl Marshal of England (1513-24).
3. Flodden is a good example of a battle won in the armourers' workshops. The Scottish pikes and spears, which had defeated the English cavalry at Bannockburn, proved no match for the English bill, with its cleaving edge,

main battle was all but hemmed in, with Dacre's March riders charging on its rear.

When the light faded over Flodden it was already England's day. James was dead on the slippery turf, England's northern frontier was safe, and Scotland had suffered the greatest military disaster in her history. More than 10,000 of her best fighting men had been killed, for the death of about 1500 English. Bannockburn had been paid for.

★

All was not lost at Flodden. Surrey apart, there were those who did quite well out of it. Hume's Borderers kept as clear of the fighting as possible, following the dictum of their chief who is reported to have remarked that the man did well that day who stood and saved himself. Thereafter they employed the night in pillaging the dead, while the reivers of Tynedale and Teviotdale, likewise keeping a firm grip on essentials, plundered the tents and baggage of the victorious English and removed their horses. "The borderours did full ill", according to one indignant English reporter, and the Bishop of Durham went even further:

". . . the borderers . . . be falser than Scottes, and have doon more harm at this tyme to our folkes than the Scottes dyd. . . . I wolde alle the orsemen in the bordours were in Fraunce with you for there schulde thay do moche goode, where as here thay doo noone, but moche harme, for, as I have wretyn byfore, thay never lyghtyd from thayr horses, but when the bataylis joynyd than felle thay to ryfelyng and robbyng aswelle on our syde as of the Scottes, and have taken moche goodes besides horses and catelle. And over that they tooke dyverse prisoners of ours, and delyveryd thaym to the Scottes, so that our folks asmoche feare the falshed of thaym as thay do the Scottes. . . ."

It must have been galling to the Bishop to realise that many Borderers were more concerned with their own welfare than with the national interest. At the same time, it is doubtful if the English would have won without their Northumbrian and Cumbrian riders and footmen, and on the Scottish side there is evidence that many of the frontier clansmen, including the Elliots, fought bravely on their country's behalf: in lives lost they probably paid more dearly than any other part of the kingdom. They were to go on paying.

---

which cut through the Scottish spearshafts. For once the English bowmen played second fiddle to the close-quarter infantry.

Surrey did not follow up his victory. He had done what he came to do—fought a brilliant defensive action and reaped an even richer dividend than he can reasonably have hoped for. But it had been a weary, under-rationed English force that he had brought to Flodden; it was soaked by the weather, running short of supplies, and almost out of beer. Against all the odds it had won, and Surrey had no intention of pressing his luck. He disbanded his army, leaving the energetic Dacre to keep the frontier by the approved method—raiding and harrying into the West and Middle Marches.[4] Soon the villages were burning along the Jed, and throughout that winter the English riders pillaged homes and rounded up cattle from Annan to the Merse. In one raid alone the Warden's brother, Christopher Dacre, lifted more than 4000 head of cattle plus horses and a great plunder in goods, and was "continewally birnyng from the breke of daye to oone of the clok after noone".

The Scottish riders retaliated and five towns in the English East March were burned, but they could not match the scale of the English depredations. In the following spring Dacre could boast to the Council that for every beast stolen by the Scots, his riders were lifting 100, and that he was burning buildings and towns at a rate of six to one by the Scots. Liddesdale, Ewesdale and Teviotdale "lies all, and every of them, waist now; noo corne sawne upon none of the said grounds", and all was so quiet on the West Border that any Englishman might ride at his pleasure from Bowness to the Hanging Stone. Annan was burned, and thirty-three villages. Never, concluded Dacre, had there been so much mischief and robbery in Scotland, and he expressed the pious hope that it would continue.

So when one reads histories which say that Scotland was spared an English invasion after Flodden, or that the country was left practically unmolested, it is as well to remember that there were parts of the country which could hardly have fared worse if Henry had brought all-out war north of the Border.

But although the greater part of the country was unscathed, and

---

4. Dacre's letters contain precise information about the extent of Scottish land under cultivation before his riders wasted it. The figures suggest that the Scottish Borderers at this time planted and sowed to a greater extent than they were able to do later in the century.

Edinburgh's hastily-built fortifications were unnecessary (for the moment), Scotland after Flodden was left in a deplorable state. Her king and the best of her leaders were dead; the new king was not yet two years old; the scene was set for another of those interminable power struggles in which factions plotted and intrigued and fought and murdered.

Briefly, the regency of the widowed Queen Margaret had no hope of lasting, and she herself ended it with her marriage to the Earl of Angus—"passion triumphing over policy", as one Victorian historian put it. In her place came the Duke of Albany from France, an honest gentleman but one who was French in all but blood. He could speak no Scots or English, and in moments of crisis was given to hurling his bonnet in the fire. He was not the man to reconcile or control contending factions.

One of these represented the ambitious King Henry, who strove to keep out Albany and the French interest. He plotted to obtain the person of the little King, but Albany forestalled him. Queen Margaret was forced to surrender her son to the Regent, and thereafter fled to the English border, where she was received by the ubiquitous Dacre, and made another contribution to history by giving birth, at Harbottle, to a girl who was later to become the mother of the ill-fated Darnley. Another power point, the turbulent Lord Hume, was extinguished by the headsman's axe, but King Henry continued his intrigues, bribing and fomenting strife, and nowhere more successfully than in the Marches. Here he was brilliantly served by Dacre, who in addition to his undercover work among the Scottish nobility, was continuing to wreak havoc by employing Scottish riders to plunder north of the Border.

"I have . . . four hundredth outlawes, and giveth them rewards that burneth and destroyeth dayly in Scotlande, all being Scottsmen whiche shuld be undre the obeysaunce of Scotlande", he wrote to Wolsey. It is no wonder that the frontier was "in grete ruyne and out of all good order" when its most powerful officer was doing his best to stir up trouble.

There was little Albany could do about it, except write pathetic notes to Wolsey in which he expressed his confidence that the Cardinal was willing to promote peace, and complained of Border inroads which he was sure "must proceed from the evil mind of those who have rule there". Albany could not believe that the King countenanced such things—that was all he knew.

Meanwhile Dacre was informing Wolsey that "the £100 of that which (he was) to spend in entertaining gentlemen of Scotland discontented with the Duke shall be well bestowed".

Dacre was also busy fortifying the frontier, rebuilding at Wark and repairing at Bewcastle, while his Scottish renegades harried north of the line, and the Berwick garrison robbed, burned and kidnapped in the Merse. Yet he could still wax indignant with the Scottish West March Warden, Lord Maxwell, over a Maxwell-Irvine raid, 400 strong, into the Debateable Land, where 700 cattle belonging to the Dacre tenants were stolen. Maxwell's reply was blunt: the cattle had been lifted "orderly according to the custom of the Borders",[5] and if Dacre wanted to press the matter they could take it up at a day of truce.

In fact, Dacre and Maxwell got on reasonably well considering the condition of the frontier, but along the line as a whole matters were not helped by Albany's policy of changing the Scots Border officials appointed during the Queen's regency; the new men seem to have been unfit for their tasks. One of them was the unfortunate Frenchman, Darcy, who was ambushed and murdered by the Humes in the East March.

So while Scotland's leaders bickered and King Henry threw oil on the flames, it was business as usual along the line. The Elliots were riding in force at this time, burning Haltwhistle and Hexham as well as other villages, in company with Fingerless Will Nixon and his kinsmen. Albany did try to pacify the Scottish tribes, and shortly before he left for France in 1517 to patch up the Scottish-French alliance, he granted a respite to the Elliots, Nixons, and other clans, but it is supposed that the Amstrongs rejected it, possibly because they were among the outlaws being subsidised by Dacre to break the peace.

But Dacre, too, was having trouble with his own English Borderers. He moved against the reivers of Redesdale, and arrested ten of the ring-

---

5. In the Debateable Land both English and Scots could pasture cattle freely during daylight, but any attempt at night pasturing or permanent occupation, such as building, was illegal, and could be resisted with force by the other side. No doubt this was the ground of Maxwell's defence.

leaders in the autumn of 1518. They were on their way into custody, under a guard eighty strong, but when the convoy came to "a strait path" a horde of Redesdale men ambushed them, killed the bailiff of Morpeth, rescued their kinsmen, and carried the principal jailer and four others over the Border into Scotland. Plainly there was no lack of enterprise among the wild men south of the line; as the Bishop of Carlisle reported to Cardinal Wolsey: "There is more thefte and extorcyon by English theffes than there is by all the Scottes of Scotland.'

Biographical note on Thomas Dacre

Thomas, Lord Dacre, Warden of the English West March from 1509 to 1525, was one of the hardiest fighters and subtlest politicians in Border history. As a stirrer-up of mischief on the Scottish side of the frontier, intriguing among factions, enlisting Scots outlaws to harry their countrymen, and promoting his monarch's policy of confusion and harm, he had few equals among English Wardens. Indeed, some have credited him with initiating the practice of Warden interference in the other side's affairs, and there is no doubt that Scotland's problems in the post-Flodden period would have been far fewer without his intervention.

As a soldier he was equally effective. The younger Surrey, under whom he served, summed Dacre up when he said: "There is noo herdyer, nor bettir knyght, but often time he doth not use the most sure order." Dacre fought like a lion at Jedburgh in 1523, but on the same night his carelessness over camp discipline cost the English force half its horses, which were run off by the Scots.

A descendant of the famous Northern family who had been Chief Foresters of Inglewood, Thomas Dacre was the son of a West March Warden and Governor of Carlisle. He was born in 1467 and succeeded his father in 1485. When he was about twenty-one he gave proof of his ardent and reckless nature when he fell in love with Elizabeth Greystoke, who was seventeen and the ward of the powerful Lord Clifford, at a castle in Westmorland. Dacre, "without leave asking, and not without peril to his person, did take her", and married her.

In 1494 he was at the siege of Norham, and in the early years of the sixteenth century he was active in all branches of Border affairs. He was on the friendliest terms with King James IV of Scotland, and while peace continued between the two countries Dacre was often engaged in negotiations with the Scots while at the same time working against them. At Flodden he fought with distinction at the head of a troop of Border horse, and is said to have been the first man to find the stripped body of the Scottish king the following day.[6] In the great English raids of 1523 he played a leading part, again distinguishing himself for his courage and recklessness.

Although he was fit enough to fight on foot at Jedburgh in 1523, Dacre was latterly much troubled by gout "so as I may not stir, if fire should bren my bed". In 1524 he asked to be relieved of the Wardenship because of "the gowte, and my leg which troubleth me sore", but when he died in the following year it was of a fall from his horse. He was on the Borders, and in the saddle, to the end.

His son, William Dacre, also served various terms as a Warden between 1527 and 1563, but was not a success in office.

XXV

The Devil, and Lord Angus

For several years an uneasy truce prevailed between Scotland and England, finally broken in 1522 by Albany who, acting in France's interest, made menacing gestures towards the English West March but could not induce his nobles to cross the Border. The memory of Flodden was still too vivid. Henry's attempts at peaceful interference in Scottish affairs having failed, he resorted to his normal policy, and sent forces under the younger Surrey (who had commanded the English vanguard at Flodden) and Dacre to devastate the Scottish Marches.

Seldom had the Border country received such a wasting as it suffered

---

6. Dacre himself said later that the Scots never forgave him for this battlefield discovery, and hated him "more than any man living".

in that spring and summer of 1523. While the elder Surrey (now Duke of Norfolk) launched the riders of Tynedale and Redesdale at the Scots Middle March ("God send them all good speed!"), his son scorched the East March and Teviotdale. Ralph Fenwick and William Heron led successful forays which yielded much spoil and many prisoners, while Dacre devastated the country round Kelso. Albany was later to complain that the English had spared nothing sacred, church, monastery, or human being of whatever sex or age, and by the end of the summer Wolsey was recording that "there is left neither house, fortress, village, tree, cattle, corn, or other succour for man".

But there were still people, as the Scottish retaliatory raids showed, and as young Surrey discovered when he came back with 6000 men to sack Jedburgh in September. The town, which he estimated to be twice the size of Berwick at that time, and well built, was "clenely distroyed, brent, and throwen downe" and its six great towers razed, but Surrey had to fight every inch of the way, and it was on this occasion that he formed his opinion that the Scots were the boldest and hottest men he had ever seen.

Dacre found them so, too, when Surrey sent him off from Jedburgh to settle accounts with Andrew ("Dand") Kerr of Ferniehurst, whom Surrey described as Dacre's "mortal enemy". Ferniehurst's tower "stode marvelous strongly" in a thick wood, and as the Kendal archers tried to bring forward the guns to assault the fortress they found themselves engaged in a bloody hand-to-hand contest among the trees; Dacre himself came to their rescue on foot with part of his force of 800 dismounted riders, "and marvelously hardly handled himself" so that the guns were eventually placed after severe fighting, the fortress was successfully assaulted, and Dand Kerr taken prisoner.

Even then Surrey and Dacre could not rest on their laurels, for as they were sitting at supper that night, a Scottish fighting patrol broke loose the 1500 horses in the English camp, causing tremendous confusion. The horses thundered through the lines, the guards loosed off more than 100 sheaves of arrows at the invisible enemy, 200 of the maddened beasts raced through the burning town, and fifty plunged to their deaths over a precipice.

Surrey estimated that in all 800 horses were lost, but evidently decided it would sound better if he did not ascribe the setback to enemy action. So he credited it to the Devil, who was seen in person no fewer than six times during the night, by Dacre and others, and it being well known that Satan always supports the Scots, the tale probably went down well with Henry VIII when he came to read Surrey's report.

The war petered out with an attempt by Albany, at the head of a mixed Scottish-French force, to take Wark Castle, but foul weather and the approach of an English force broke up the siege. The attackers, led by Dand Kerr, had lost heavily, 300 French corpses being found unburied after the final assault. It was the end of Albany's reign in Scotland, and soon afterwards he left for France for the last time. If he had brought little good to the Borderland, he had at least kept English influence in Scotland at bay, but all that ended with his departure and the rise to power of the Earl of Angus and his Douglases, who represented the pro-English element. The English envoy might still find himself cursed by the women in the streets of Edinburgh, but at the top level Anglo-Scottish relations improved, and a peace treaty was concluded.

Angus's English affections did not apparently include his wife, the Queen-dowager Margaret, who in the intervals between intrigues and corresponding with her brother, King Henry, had transferred her affections to a young lord named Henry Stewart. Eventually she divorced Angus and married Stewart, but in gaining another husband she effectively lost a son, for the little King James, who had been batted to and fro between one faction and another, was now entirely under the control of Angus and the Douglases. It was a control which the little monarch detested; he made one attempt to escape from it during an expedition of Angus's to the Borders, and in the ensuing fight one of the great Border feuds, that of Kerr and Scott, broke out (see pp. 179–82).

This feud, and others, made life difficult for Angus where the Borders were concerned. His pro-English policy called for peace along the line, but he found this hard to maintain. The Borderers resented him; for one thing, in parcelling out Scottish offices among his Douglas faction he had appropriated to himself the Wardenship of the East and Middle Marches, much to the disgust of those local leaders who regarded the posts as their own. However, like Albany, he tried hanging, obtaining pledges, and so on, without great success; the Borderers, whose view of national politics was that they should never interfere with important matters, were plundering away in fine style, and the English authorities had their hands full with the Tynedale reivers, whose depredations led to the stationing there of special garrisons.

A disquieting sign, at this time, from the authorities' point of view was the growing friendship between Liddesdale and the Tynedale riders, especially the Charltons and Dodds—"the Armstrangs and the theiffs of Ewysdaill were joined with the rebells of Tyndaill, and were comyn untoe theym and kepet all company togedders". This was bad news; what made it worse was that day forays were on the increase, and the riders were so contemptuous of law and order that they were operating in unusually large bands, and displaying banners, an abnormal thing in peace-time.

Generally Angus might enjoy no greater success on the Borders than most officials ever did, but when he moved he knew enough to move in Border style, suddenly and drastically. One of his most successful expeditions seems to have been an early one, in 1525—before the Scott–Kerr débâcle—when he made a swift descent on Liddesdale, coming "sodeinly upon the gretteste theves upon the bordours, called Armstrongges, being the gretteste maynteners of the theves of Tyndaill". His captives included two of the worst reiver leaders, the notorious Simon ("Sym the Laird") Armstrong of Whithaugh, and his brother, Davy the Lady. Angus also lifted 4000 beasts, and devastated the homes of the riders. But while supplying a check, such punitive action not only contributed nothing to lasting pacification, but made further lawlessness inevitable. The reivers had to recoup their losses somehow, and so the vicious circle of Border trouble was bound to continue.

Equally futile in a long-term sense was the Church's intervention in Border affairs. With both governments intent—for the time being—on frontier pacification, the Archbishop of Glasgow, Gavin Dunbar, about this time issued his justly-celebrated "monition of cursing" in which he excommunicated all Border thieves. It is a remarkable verbal blast, running to over 1500 words, and for sheer comprehensive power and variety it places His Grace of Glasgow immediately among the great cursers of all time, Huckleberry Finn's father and generations of military men not excepted. This splendid tirade—which is given in Appendix I—was read in all the churches of the diocese and published throughout the Border country, where it was no doubt received with admiration if not concern. Perhaps it impressed Cardinal Wolsey, but it probably did nothing to Fingerless Will and the Armstrongs, whose religious views were incendiary.[1]

In spite of Angus's raid on Liddesdale, Border plundering went briskly forward in 1525. He had barely left the Borders when 400 Scottish riders, with the Tynedale outlaws, were beating up the English side, killing, burning, and lifting "55 horss and presoners". Two weeks later they were riding in even greater strength, against the English special garrisons in Tynedale; this time they took forty prisoners and as many horse, "and brownt and killed dyvers men".

English officials complained to Scotland, and Henry's envoy noted bitterly that the Armstrongs taken by Angus were not being imprisoned, but merely kept under what amounted to house arrest, "men attending daye and night upon theym, having gret favourers". Pledges were being extracted from the Armstrongs for good behaviour, but the envoys feared that these would apply to Scotland only; he believed Angus was anxious not to displease the Borderers, which boded ill for England.

The position was made worse by the fact that the Armstrongs and their confederates in crime were enjoying the protection of the man who should have been foremost in putting them down—the Scottish West March Warden, Robert, 5th Lord Maxwell. Even at this time Maxwell was employing the Armstrongs in his family's feud with the Johnstones, and on one occasion egged them on to take part with him in an ambush on the Johnstone chief. In addition, Maxwell was hostile to Angus, and since he was too strongly placed locally to be dismissed from office, was frequently able to embarrass the Regent and hinder his Border policy.

---

1. The Bishop of Durham similarly cursed the Tynedale riders at this time, with equally little effect. The English reivers, in defiance of the interdict, held a communion service of their own, with a Scottish friar officiating, and one of the leading thieves, Hector Charlton, "resaved the parson's dewties and served them all of wyne".

XXVI

Armstrongs in action

In the circumstances, it was not surprising that the Armstrongs began to assume the proportions of a national menace to England, and foremost among them was one of the Mangerton branch, who with his own band of adventurers, operated from the Canonby district, where he had a tower upon the Esk. In the records of the time he is John of Gilnockie, brother to Thomas, Laird of Mangerton; to his fellow-Borderers he was Black Jock; but in the language of romance and the legends of outlawry he is known as Johnnie Armstrong.

There are obvious reasons why he shares with his distant relative, Kinmont Willie, the distinction of being the most famous of all Border reivers. He was the centre of a historical incident which was recorded in the folk-lore of his country. But that apart, he was a most successful scourge of the Marches. The belief persists among his countrymen that he raided only on the English side, and from what we know of Angus's Border policy and the state of frontier relations at the time, this may be true, although one may doubt whether Armstrong left his own side alone out of any patriotic sentiment. He levied blackmail throughout the English Marches, and built up a private force of formidable reputation. Indeed, its very size and splendour were to be his undoing. But beyond that, and the fact that he enjoyed the protection of Robert, 5th Lord Maxwell, Warden of the Scottish West March, we know little enough about him. He and his son Christie signed—or at least put their "hands at the pen", since Johnnie was illiterate—a bond with Maxwell at Dumfries in 1525, whereby John received the tenancy of lands about Langholm and agreed to serve Maxwell in peace and war—which probably meant leaving Maxwell's cattle alone if he turned a blind eye to their other activities.

However predatory these may have been, there do seem to have been periods in the mid-1520s when the Border was reasonably quiet. Scotland was satisfied enough with Angus's conduct to grant him £1600 for his services—he had earlier received a present of £100 from King Henry—and although he seems to have exerted pressure on the riding

clans only with political caution, this was enough to give the West
March at least the occasional outward appearance of order. But as
always appearances were deceptive; a Border official, after two months
of tranquillity, might report that the Marches had never kept better
rule, and then the peace would be abruptly shattered by an English
incursion into Roxburghshire, or by a joint Tynedale–Liddesdale
outrage like the burning of Tarset Hall, in the English Middle
March.

Attempts were made to reach agreements whereby both countries
would deny refuge to rebels and outlaws from the other side, and
Wolsey noted an arrangement under which England would give
assistance to the Scots Wardens on request, to aid in hunting down
evil-doers on the Scottish side. But such co-operation looked better on
paper than in practice; Liddesdale remained effectively outside the law,
with the old quartet of Armstrong, Elliot, Nixon and Croser causing
most of the trouble, and early in 1526 this area alone was the one place
in the Border country for which it remained impossible to obtain
redress.

Angus made another lightning raid on Liddesdale in April 1527, and
catching the thieves unprepared he killed a score of them in their
homes, and captured another two dozen. Thirteen of these were left
hanging from a convenient bridge, and the remainder taken to Edinburgh as hostages for their kinsmen's good behaviour. How much
restraining effect this had may be judged from the fact that the hostages were all executed a few months later.

Nor were the English authorities having much better luck with their
own riding families, of whom the Lisles gave particular trouble in 1527.
A number of these folk, imprisoned at Newcastle along with certain
Armstrongs, were forcibly released by a joint Anglo-Scottish foray,[1]
after which the Lisles took refuge on the Scottish side and in company
with Scottish outlaws, burned and plundered the English village of
Holmeshaugh. For a brief space the Lisle's leader, Sir William Lisle,
appeared to be at the head of a great reiver confederacy, who were
robbing and burning at will; the authorities on both sides seem to

---

1. Possibly led by Johnnie Armstrong himself. It is not absolutely clear
from Northumberland's correspondence with Wolsey in January 1528
whether the John Armstrong referred to is Gilnockie or not.

have been incapable of dealing with him, in spite of plans for joint action and appeals for co-operation which flew between London and Edinburgh. Lisle's foraying was threatening to throw the whole frontier into confusion, until the appointment late in 1527 of Henry Percy, Earl of Northumberland, as English Warden-general. He broke up a Lisle raid early in January 1528, hanging fourteen of the captured reivers at Alnwick, and followed this up within a fortnight by thwarting another foray, in which an Armstrong and a Dodd were taken and subsequently hanged. That he would now invade Liddesdale seemed inevitable, and whether because of local pressure or because Angus himself at last took a decisive hand, the leading Lisles left Scotland and submitted to Northumberland with halters round their necks. The symbols were appropriate, for Sir William and his nearest associates were hanged, and their quartered limbs publicly displayed as a warning to others.

And as though to reinforce the lesson, a Scottish foray run against Sir John Heron's flocks at Chipchase, where there was an English garrison, was repulsed with the deaths of several of the riders.

Possibly encouraged by these signs that the tide was turning against the reivers, William, Lord Dacre, the new Warden of the English West March, decided to move against the Armstrongs, who had now fortified themselves in the Debateable Land. He assembled a force of 2000 riders in secret, hoping to take Johnnie Armstrong, Sim the Laird, and their followers by surprise, but (as was to become all too usual) the English Storeys tipped off the Armstrongs in advance, and Dacre's force was driven off, badly mauled. He was soon back, however, armed now with artillery, and succeeded in destroying Johnnie Armstrong's tower at Hollows on the Esk. Which would have been highly satisfactory if Armstrong had not been engaged on the same day in plundering and destroying Netherby and mopping up a mill belonging to Dacre at Gilsland for good measure. Nor was Dacre's temper improved by the escape from Carlisle Castle of Richie Graham, who was suspected of having betrayed the first raid against the Armstrongs, and had since been lying under indictment for treason.[2] He now fled to

2. The details of Richie's escape, in March 1528, reflect no credit on security arrangements at Carlisle Castle, but they do show how well organised the reivers were. Graham had been taken to the castle loaded with chains, but once he was inside they were removed, and according to Dacre he was

Scotland, with most of his followers, while the real culprits, the Storeys, hurried over into the English Middle March, out of Dacre's reach.[3]

It was now virtually naked war between Dacre and the reivers of Liddesdale and the Debateable Land. He invaded the latter again in March 1528, and after considerable labour managed to destroy Ill Will Armstrong's tower, as well as almost all the other strong-points in the area. "I woll neithr suffer the said Armistranges to inhabit upon the Debateable grounde, nor yet suffer theim or any Scottisman of evill name or fame to com to Carlisle market", he assured Wolsey, and if it was beyond his power to carry out the first part of his threat, he could at least ensure the second, much to the disgust of the Armstrongs.

This ban illustrates one of the curious features of Border life, the curious dual personality of the reivers. The same Armstrongs, Nixons, Elliots, and the rest, who carried fire and sword into Cumberland by night, who slew and kidnapped and pillaged incessantly along the English side, were accustomed to come to Carlisle by day to buy in the market, to drink at the inns, and generally to pass the time of day with the locals round Carlisle Cross, all within a long bowshot of the port-cullis of Carlisle Castle, the seat of Border law and order and the head-quarters of the Warden.

How the ordinary citizens regarded them we can only guess; to some they would be friends, to others blood relations, just as the English riders of Bewcastle were. The strange sense of Border community, regardless of frontier and national differences, was seen nowhere more strongly than here, when the "professional" men of both sides gathered together; under the curious written and unwritten Border law there was no reason why the Elliot who had descended on Arthuret on a Thursday night with a mixed band of Charltons, Bells, and Littles, and fought hand to hand with the land-sergeant's troop, should not bid a straight-faced good day to the Warden himself on the Saturday morning if they happened to pass on English Street.

Wolsey, being a foreigner in Northern eyes, never understood the frontier spirit, and consequently regarded the free-and-easy intercourse

---

allowed to "go loose up and down the castle". At a prearranged time he made a leap through "a privy postern" which stood open to the fields, where a confederate was waiting with a led horse, and spurred off to freedom.
3. The Storeys' lands in Cumberland were subsequently occupied by the Graham family, which may be poetic justice of a kind.

of the two sides with abomination. So the Armstrongs were forbidden the market, and this disruption of their social lives further aggravated the ill will between Dacre and Liddesdale.

Through all that year of 1528 the struggle went on, raid after raid pouring over from the Scottish side, to be avenged by Warden raids on the Debateable Land. The tale of death and destruction grew steadily; in one fearful night of May the Armstrongs and Irvines cut a burning furrow along the Cumbrian frontier, through eight villages in which they destroyed more than sixty dwelling houses, apart from out-buildings; before the flames had died away another Armstrong foray crossed between Esk and Leven in the track of the first, at high noon, carried off seventy head, and killed eight people.

Christopher Dacre, the English deputy, replied with a raid on the comparatively inoffensive Routledges ("every man's prey", as one Border writer described them), and carried off their herds while the people themselves escaped into Tarras Moss, and rounded off the operation by burning the homes of Johnnie Armstrong's sons.

But while it was business as usual on the Border, important things were happening in the Scottish heartland. Young King James, now sixteen, had taken as much as he could stomach of the tutelage of Angus and the Douglas faction, which amounted to imprisonment. After a childhood spent as a shuttlecock between political parties, he was now in his adolescence determined to break free and reign in fact as well as in name. In many ways he was ill-prepared for it. His guardians had seen to it that he was poorly educated, and had succeeded in turning him into a convinced amorist—never a difficult thing to do with a Stewart. But he reached adolescence neither spoiled nor broken; quite apart from his good looks, his physical courage, his quick mind, and his ability to inspire affection, James V had an outstanding quality rare in royalty of his day—he was a genuinely nice person, at least as far as the ordinary people of his realm were concerned.

Such an eccentric could not be happy under the thumb of the Douglases, and he made more than one attempt to escape despite the comforting assurance of his guardians that they would sooner see him torn limb from limb than let him go. Finally, in the summer of 1528, he made it, slipping away to Stirling in disguise, and the country rose to him. In the course of a brief campaign the Douglases were defeated and Angus fled to England.

No doubt the reivers were glad to see Angus go, for his numerous raids[4] had caused them some annoyance, but if they thought they were blessed in the change they were mistaken. Angus might have been zealous, but he was not ruthless (as the Border understood the word) and his attempts at pacifying the Marches had been generally ineffective. James V was to show that his good nature did not extend to Border thieves; he had a fatally simple idea of how "to put gude ordoure and reule apoun thame, and to stanche thiftis and rubberis committit be theiffis and tratouris".

However, a little time was to elapse before James was ready to put his Border policy into operation, and in the interval the Armstrongs and their confederates were planning to bring to a head their struggle with Dacre, who was making life impossible in the Debateable Land. Knowing their man, they evolved a simple plan (it was a common enough stratagem in Border fighting) and the Warden fell for it.

A mixed foray of about thirty Nixons and Crosers crossed the frontier into Bewcastle one August night and carried off a small herd of cattle from Thirlwall; they also took care to kidnap a tenant of Dacre's and then set out, apparently in no great hurry, for home. The Warden promptly gave orders to raise the country, and sent a strong party in pursuit. They picked up the Scots' trail in Bewcastle, and tried to get the local garrison to join the trod, but the Bewcastle soldiers seem to have been reluctant, which in itself should have roused the suspicions of Dacre's officers. Another ominous circumstance was that when the alarm of the raid was originally raised, the Bewcastle garrison had remained oddly silent. Most sinister of all, the raiders were retiring by the very same route they had used coming in.

However, the pursuers paid no heed to these signs; they knew they had superior numbers, and the trail was hot. They pushed on hard, and came up with the reivers within a mile of the Border. The little foray was in their grasp; the Warden's men were on the point of closing for the kill—and then out of the ground round them rose up hundreds of armed riders, Armstrongs, Elliots, Nixons and the rest. Liddesdale had sprung its trap. How many of the Warden's men escaped is not certain, but at least forty were taken prisoners—thirty of them being Dacre's personal followers. Of these, eleven were cut down on the spot after

---

4. He had made at least six against the Armstrongs from 1525 to 1528.

surrendering (so much for Bishop Leslie's contention that the reivers were reluctant to kill in cold blood) and the remainder carried away into Liddesdale.

The uproar over this "fraudulent great bushement" was considerable, but it ended in a decision by both governments to appoint commissioners to look into Border affairs, and make redress for offences on both sides. It was discovered, in spite of the activities of the Scottish West March reivers, that the balance of damage on both sides was about even;[5] the obstacle to a renewal of Border peace between the two countries was Liddesdale, which the Scots authorities were forced to admit was beyond their control. The English made a counter-proposal that if peace were concluded, Liddesdale might be effectively excluded—i.e., if its inhabitants offended, the English might take revenge on them without this being regarded as a breach of the peace. It was not, perhaps, an unreasonable demand, but it points up the appalling weakness of the Scottish authorities who were in fact licensing the English to keep the peace on a particular stretch of Scottish soil.

More than that, James was admitting the right of the King of England to invade, slaughter, burn, rob, reive, despoil and destroy (these are the very words of the agreement) and to continue in this way "at his gracious pleasure" until Liddesdale had been paid off in full. There was a similar agreement permitting the King of Scots to revenge unredressed wrongs by Englishmen, but since no English area was uncontrolled in the sense that Liddesdale was, this did not mean very much.

In other words, it was to be open season against the Liddesdale riders. The Scots authorities in the meantime undertook to proceed against the reivers "and distroie them", a threat which was not taken very seriously.

What did Liddesdale think of all this? Their attitude towards the Scottish government was openly contemptuous. Late in December 1528, while the negotiations for a five-year peace were concluding, Sim (The Laird) Armstrong came across the frontier peacefully to confer with the Earl of Northumberland at Alnwick; the English Warden-General apparently hoped to make his own realistic peace with

---

5. The Liddesdale riders did not have things all their own way. Shortly after the Dacre ambush they made another raid, to the Middle March, but were sharply repulsed by Sir Ralph Fenwick.

Liddesdale, whatever international treaties might say. It was an instructive interview, if Northumberland is to be believed, with one of the leading reivers speaking his mind frankly on Border affairs; as such it is a most significant piece of frontier history.

What Sim the Laird had to say was that there would never be justice in Scotland unless the King of England ruled there; King James was no use, and his councillors were unstable. The Armstrongs were looking to England for justice, of which there was no hope in Scotland—and as evidence of the shocking state of affairs north of the Border, Armstrong pointed out, with an apparent naiveté which was the essence of subtlety, that he and his riders had devastated the land for sixty miles, destroying thirty churches, and no one dared to stop them. He was saying, in fact: It is a pretty poor government that tolerates me.

Now, one has to remember that Sim Armstrong was no ordinary robber; he was a high-powered gangster who, with Johnnie Armstrong, had raised the family to the zenith of their power. He could put 3000 men in the saddle, and more, and he had a very shrewd idea of political balances. Further, one of his reasons for coming to see Northumberland was to discuss the release of one Quentin Armstrong, recently captured by the English. It may be that he simply said what he hoped would be acceptable to the English Warden-General—and, beyond him, King Henry. He knew that his words would be widely reported in both the English and Scottish corridors of power. It may also be that Northumberland exaggerated what he said, for political purposes.

And yet, Sim the Laird's views are highly consistent with Armstrong behaviour. No Border confederacy of Scottish tribes collaborated so often and closely with England as the Armstrongs of Liddesdale and their Elliot-Croser-Nixon allies. It has been suggested that they were driven to this by the attitude of the Scottish government; that is probably true to some extent, but the main truth is more probably that it suited them. They were reivers first, Armstrongs second, and Scottish or English a long way third.

And if anything were needed to kill whatever poor shreds of patriotism existed in them, King James was now about to supply it.

XXVII

A rope for Black Jock

The Earl of Northumberland had dismissed as mere bragging the expressed intention of the Scottish government to try to do something about the Liddesdale robbers. Like Sim the Laird, he believed the Armstrongs were far too powerful for King James. But he was wrong. The young king had undertaken to "proceed to the sharpe and rygorouse pwnyssching of all transgressioune apone the bordouris", and he now went to work, beginning with a gentle approach.

He called a meeting of Border lords, despatched the Wardens to meet their English opposites, and went himself to the Border towns in the summer of 1529 to hold courts and take assurances. Patrick, Earl of Bothwell, had taken responsibility for Liddesdale, where the Armstrongs were quiet for the moment, although still refusing to submit to anyone, and other local leaders gave bonds for themselves and their followers to be of good behaviour. For a little while the frontier was calm, even in the West, and as the summer passed it seemed as though James's initial policy of patient dealing would pay off.

Then in November Liddesdale shook loose the Border once again, with a day foray of 100 riders against Birkshawes. They were pursued by the Warden-General's men under Nicholas Ridley, who seemed to have learned nothing from Dacre's misfortune the previous year, for they rode straight into an Armstrong ambush and lost more than twenty prisoners, of whom four were later murdered.

Protests from England naturally followed, and it may have been during this winter that James decided to take off the velvet glove where the Borders were concerned. In the spring of 1530 he summoned his nobles to Edinburgh and arraigned his Border lords for failure to keep order, committing outrages themselves, and protecting malefactors. He dealt with them abruptly: Hume, Maxwell, Johnstone, Buccleuch, Bothwell (who was responsible for Liddesdale), Mark Ker, Douglas of Drumlanrig, and other minor chiefs were consigned to prison in a disciplinary clean sweep which has few parallels in Border history. Adam Scott of Tushilaw, the so-called "King of the Thieves" was

executed for taking blackmail; William Cockburne of Henderland in
Peebles was convicted of high treason, robbery, and harbouring
criminals, and beheaded.

It seems that they suffered the extreme penalty in Edinburgh, although
tradition has it that they were taken by the King in the course of an
expedition to the Borders. Cockburne, without being a particularly
distinguished rascal, has one great claim to fame; it is suggested that his
death and his wife's grief inspired one of the finest of Border ballads,
"The Lament of the Border Widow". Some of it has the simplicity of
great poetry:

> There came a man, by middle day,
> He spied his sport, and went away;
> And brought the king that very night,
> Who brake my bower, and slew my knight.

Whether Cockburne was beheaded in Edinburgh or hanged over
his own gate, he received a better epitaph than he probably deserved.
But the King was to provide still further material for the ballad makers,
for with the chief Border leaders in jail he now proceeded to the one
trouble spot which had lain outside the scope of his Edinburgh assize.
With a force probably in the region of 10,000 men he descended on
Liddesdale and the Armstrongs.

The raid took place in June and July, and has been described so
memorably by various writers, in prose and poetry, that while the
main essentials are clear, the details are a matter of choice. "The Kingis
grace maid ane raid upoun the thieves, and tuik of thame to the nomber
of xxxii personis of the greitest of thame, nameit Armestrangis, Ellotis,
Littilis, Irwenis, with utheris". Among them were Johnnie Armstrong,
Ill Will Armstrong, and Thomas Armstrong of Mangerton.[1] How
they came to be taken is not precisely known; the tradition is that
Johnnie was lured unarmed into the King's presence, and this seems
quite likely. He was not the man to put his head in a noose, and nothing
but a sense of security could have led him to venture into the King's
great host.

---

1. But not Sim the Laird. He was still at large in the following year, when he
received a remission from King James for several offences. These included a
raid in company with one Clement Croser and a band of Englishmen, in
which they burned Little Newton, and the kidnapping of Sir Walter Scott of
Buccleuch.

One version has it that he was inveigled into an ambush, yet another that he came in the belief that he was covered by a proclamation that all who submitted themselves should have their lives. All the stories are fairly consistent, and the interview between the outlaw chief and the King has so much of human nature in it that it is hard to disbelieve.

They met at Carlanrig in Teviotdale, the Armstrong with perhaps about fifty riders at his back, all hoping to get their pardons. One historian says that as soon as the King saw them he ordered his troops to close in, but in Pitscottie's account there seems to be a suggestion that it was only when they came face to face that the King made up his mind how to deal with the formidable robber.

Johnnie came "reverentlie", but he and his men were so splendidly equipped and dressed, and so evidently self-confident, that His Majesty's reaction was the celebrated:

"What wants yon knave that a king should have?"

And then "he turned about his face and bade take that tyrant out of his sight." Armstrong, no doubt bewildered, pleaded for his life; he swore his loyalty, protested that he had never robbed in Scotland or despoiled a Scot, and offered to bring to the King any English subject, from a duke downwards, on any stated day, dead or alive. It was perhaps not such an idle boast as it may have sounded, but the King would have none of him. The Armstrongs must die. Whether this interchange really happened, or is just the stuff of legend, there is a startlingly genuine ring about Pitscottie's account of the reiver's final retort before he was led to the gallows:

"He seeing no hope of the King's favour towards him, said very proudly, 'I am but a fool to seek grace at a graceless face. But had I known, sir, that you would have taken my life this day, I should have lived on the Borders in spite of King Harry and you both, for I know King Harry would down-weigh my best horse with gold to know that I were condemned to die this day.'"

Whether he said it or not, that was certainly true; although Scottish historians make altogether too much of Johnnie Armstrong's supposedly patriotic activities against England, the chronicler was right when he wrote that "the Englisch people were exceeding glade when they understood that John Armestrang was execute". So might America have received the death of Al Capone.

Johnnie and his followers, without trial, were promptly "all hangit apoun growand trees", and whether they were taken by treachery or not, they had it coming to them. One of the reivers, Sandie Scott "a prowd thief", was burned alive because he had himself burned a house containing a woman and her children; it is worth remembering things like that, when considering the heroic eminence that folk-lore has given to Johnnie Armstrong and his riders.

Romantics will probably prefer to remember that "efter this hunting the king hanged Jonnie Armstrange, quhilk monie Scottis man heavilie lamented, for he was ane doubtit man, and als guid ane chieftane as evir was upon the borderis. . . . And albeit he was ane lous leivand man, yitt he never molested any Scottis man. But it is said, from the Scottis border to Newcastle of England, thair was not ane of quhatsoevir estate bot payed to this John Armestrange ane tribut to be frie of his cumber, he was so doubtit in Ingland."

The official record has a couple of grim lines only:

John Armestrange, 'alias Blak Jok' and Thomas his brother convicted of common theft, and reset of theft etc.—Hanged.

It is interesting to note that Johnnie Armstrong's goods and estates were bestowed on Robert, Lord Maxwell, who was at this time a prisoner by the King's command. But at this stage there is nothing to be proved, and it should be remembered that Maxwell had granted tenancies to Armstrong some years earlier, and received his bond in return.

XXVIII

The violent peace

The death of Johnnie Armstrong had a salutary effect, but not for long. After all, he paid only the price that reivers were accustomed to pay, in the end, and it was not long before the effect of King James's drastic lesson had worn off. There are those who have suggested that it never did, that it poisoned the Western Border, and the Armstrongs in particular, against the Scottish crown, and that James was repaid when the Liddesdale men sided with the English in the frontier fighting of the 1540s. Perhaps, but Liddesdale's motives seldom flew far above immediate gain; if James had knighted Armstrong instead of hanging him, it is doubtful if the Western clans would have been any less disloyal in the years that followed.

They were grievous years for the Borderland, for great things were happening in the world which were to have their effect in the farthest corners of the Marches. The civilised world was feeling the first pangs of the great religious rebirth which was being assisted in England by King Henry's impatience to go to bed with Anne Boleyn. A year after Johnnie died at Carlanrig, Henry broke with Rome; in the years that followed, one of his aims was to bring his Scottish nephew into line with his own religious views, a policy which the canny James resisted, informing his "derrest brothir and uncle" that he did not propose to interfere with Haly Kirk.

He had enough to occupy him in those early 'thirties, and keeping good order in his kingdom was an important part of it. He felt secure enough to release the Border leaders he had imprisoned, and for a time there was relative quiet on the frontier, but in the political climate it could not last long. Henry's machinations never ceased, and in 1532 Dacre was being instructed "to use them of Lyddersdale and other as may annoye the King of Scottis, with such entertainment as they may be the willinger to serve our purpose"—the old game of subverting the most troublesome riding families was in full swing again. Although the treaty of 1528 was not due to expire until 1533, raiding went on intermittently, backed by royal authority, with the Angus faction in England helping matters along.

And as usual Scotland had powerful traitors within. In 1531 Bothwell was secretly offering to help Henry with 7000 men and see him crowned King of Scotland in Edinburgh—which gives some idea of the strength of feeling against James among his own nobility. He was too hard a king for some of them, and he put down mischief with a strong hand—more than sixty years later the younger Scrope was to remark that it was a pity that James VI had not some of the vigour of his grandfather when it came to quelling turbulence.

Along the frontier, following inroads by Scottish raiders, with some unusually barbarous foraying by the Kerrs of Ferniehurst, a small English expedition invaded the East March, burning several villages, and in November 1532 Northumberland struck as far as Lothian, destroying every peel and house in his path. Fifteen hundred English riders descended on the Scott country, hoping to catch and kill the chief of the family, but although they ravaged the area and burned Branxholm keep, Buccleuch escaped.

In revenge he led a foray of 3000 over the Cheviots, and establishing himself in an English village, sent out smaller raiding parties of two or three hundred strong, which pillaged half a dozen Middle March towns. The countryside and garrisons rose against the intruders, but Buccleuch, who had with him both the Cessford and Ferniehurst Kerrs (their feud being forgotten for the moment) was in such strength that he was able to make an orderly withdrawal, taking a huge booty with him.

Meanwhile the fugitive Angus and his Douglases had been active in burning and killing on the Scottish side in Henry's interest—all this while the two nations continued officially at peace, with King Henry complaining that the Scots were provoking his Berwick garrison with insulting language.

Even the preparations for a renewal of the five-year truce of 1528 had little effect on the Border itself. In one month James was busy appointing commissioners for the negotiations, and the next he was writing to Henry about "silk invasion and violence" that it seemed must lead to hostilities proper. His immediate concern was a great raid by the Milburns, Dodds and Charltons into Teviotdale under the leadership of Ralph Fenwick; there is a parallel with Vietnam and Korea in our own time, for while the negotiators dickered over preliminaries at Newcastle the thatches were blazing on both sides of the frontier. Finally a year's respite was concluded, with the good offices of a French envoy, and in 1534 a peace was agreed which was to last until the death of one or other of the sovereigns.

If the peace put a temporary stop to large incursions with government backing, it hardly affected the local squabbles of the Borderers. For example, the Scotts were enlisting Dacre's assistance in their feud with the Kerrs, and Dacre himself was involved in a power struggle with the Cliffords. Both monarchs tried to stabilise their respective

Marches, and James once again clapped several of his leading Borderers into jail, while Henry was setting to work to bring his Northern administration more closely under central control—a policy which was to culminate eventually in the replacement of local Wardens by outsiders more close, in presence and spirit, to the royal power. At the same time he continued to try to bring his Scottish nephew under his thumb, by offers of marriage to the Princess Mary, and by attempts to push ahead a Scottish Reformation. But James's matrimonial interests lay all in France, and he remained maddeningly neutral on religious questions.

On the frontier itself the old (and to authority, disquieting) unholy alliance of Liddesdale and the English hotbeds of Tynedale and Redesdale, seems to have come apart—but only temporarily—in the middle 1530s, with the Northumbrians running a great foray of 400 riders in May 1536, killing, burning, and plundering "to grete quantitie" in the Armstrong heartland. But the English riders were soon to have other work on their hands.

In February 1536 the English Parliament had before it an act for the dissolution of the smaller monasteries, which were said to be nests of evil living and immoral abomination—Parliament had Henry's word for this, and no doubt recognising him as an authority, passed the act. The reaction in the country was dramatic; rumours flew that His Majesty intended further measures, such as the removal of all the Church's plate, and following the suppression of two small monasteries in Lincolnshire Henry's Commissioners found themselves confronted by armed resistance. This local outbreak was quickly extinguished, but in Yorkshire trouble broke out with a vengeance, and Henry was suddenly faced with the most dangerous crisis of his whole reign, the Catholic rebellion known as the Pilgrimage of Grace.

Norfolk, the seasoned soldier who as the younger Surrey had gained great experience fighting in the North, was sent to quell the rising, and found it simply too big to handle; 30,000 men, including those light Border horsemen whom he knew so well, provided too long odds, and he agreed to a truce. Henry was ready to conciliate, and the rising simmered down, but not without one or two last puffs of flame in the shape of minor outbreaks. At Carlisle, where some of the Border riders were active in the King's behalf, Norfolk loaded the Harraby gallows with rebels, and farther south, in Lancashire, various clerics were executed as an example to their followers.

As far as the Borders were concerned, while religion undoubtedly played a part in the rising, there were other causes of discontent, including rising rents and enclosures. Also, people like the Dodds and Charltons might not know much about religion, but they knew where their allegiance lay, and it was to their local overlord rather than to the distant King—"no prince but the Percies", in effect. The Pilgrimage had reminded Henry of just how dangerous his own North could be; plainly it was time to bring it more firmly under London's control.

The dismissal of the Wardens followed, and for a time the King himself assumed the offices. It was a nominal assumption, of course, but it prompts the thought that Henry would probably have made a good Warden in practice, if he had ever had the chance. He was brave, tough, unscrupulous, clever, and altogether the kind of ruffian whom the reivers would have recognized as a man after their own hearts. It is interesting that one of the best Elizabethan Wardens (when he troubled to appear in person on the frontier) was the redoubtable Hunsdon, who was widely reputed to be a bastard son of Henry's.

To do the actual work on the frontier, Henry appointed three deputies, two of whom were to leave their mark on Border history. One was Sir William Eure, and the other, perhaps the greatest of all Border law officers, was a shrewd and hardy Northerner named Thomas Wharton. Starting in the West, he was to serve in all three Wardenries, and was to institute the system of guards and beacons which was to make life so hazardous for the lawless bands of the frontier. He was also to be a notable intriguer with and employer of Scottish Borderers.

Following the Pilgrimage there was a comparative lull along the Borders, with the opposite Wardens co-operating well except on such ticklish matters as the return of English fugitives who had fled north after the rebellion, and whom the Scots were reluctant to deliver up to Norfolk's gallows. But King James was not looking for trouble; he assured Norfolk in September 1537 that all such fugitives were either gone abroad or were living the outlaw life in England. At the same time he assured Norfolk that Maxwell would look after the peace of Liddesdale effectively, and there was no need to employ force for the moment.

But the peace was illusory, as usual. Henry was still intent on turning Scotland into a reforming ally, despite his nephew's stubborn adherence to the old religion, and there were other causes of discontent. The Scots were writing dirty rhymes about him, "dispiteful and slanderous balladis", and Sir Thomas Wharton was instructed to draw King James's attention to this effrontery. James ordered an inquiry, and seems to have unearthed some unedifying compositions which he pronounced to be obviously the work of Englishmen or Scots fugitives in England; he wrote to the Bishop of Llandaff in this vein, assuring his lordship that no one in Scotland "evir heard, read or saw ony siclike". Plainly someone was trying to stir up trouble between him and his uncle, and he would take all measures for their suppression. In the meantime, let King Henry and his servants ignore "sic trumparyis proceeding as appearis of lycht myndis".

Henry was mollified, to the extent of thanking James and sending him a present of a lion, but if his vanity had been salved on one score it was smarting on another. Henry was now halfway through his six wives, and casting about for Number Four. His eye had lighted on a tall, dark, and handsome French lady named Marie of Lorraine, but she was reluctant; possibly she had observed the distressing frequency with which His Majesty became a widower, for she excused herself on the ground that she had a slim neck. Obviously she was not without a sense of humour, but when she capped the jest by marrying James of Scotland, whose first queen, Madeleine, had died of tuberculosis, Henry's displeasure was understandable.

How much this influenced his Scottish policy no one can say; possibly not much. There were so many things in those late 1530s contributing to discord between the kingdoms, and chief among them was the religious question; Henry's efforts to drive a wedge between James and the Scottish Catholic clergy were still proving futile, and the now-excommunicated English King could see little prospect of Scottish support, moral or otherwise, in his contest with Rome. On the Borders, although James had tightened his control—he dismissed the East and Middle March Wardens, and brought in Dand Kerr of Ferniehurst to the important Middle March, while Maxwell continued to hold sway in the West—there were still numerous causes of tension. Scotland continued to grant asylum to English religious (as opposed to criminal) refugees—Henry naturally saw no difference between the two

classes—and there was the usual raiding trouble, although the respective
Wardens were coping with it more efficiently than usual.

Indeed James was able to write to Henry in 1539 that in visiting the
Borders "for our pastyme and solace of hawking" he had seen to it that
redress for Scottish offences was promptly granted, and English malefactors handed back. At the same time he admitted that Liddesdale was
troublesome, but that he had put these "maist mysgidit" of his subjects
under efficient rule; it would be nice, he hinted, if Henry would do the
same for the marauders of Tynedale. But the English monarch had his
own notions of Border priorities. While he continued to hope that he
could bring his stubborn nephew to reason on religious matters, he
was working steadily to subvert the Scottish Border families, and
strengthening his defences along the frontier.

XXIX

The road to Solway Moss

War was obviously coming, and the last shred of Henry's patience was
worn away in 1541. By that time Anne of Cleves had come and gone—
big she had certainly been, as the corpulent Henry's taste dictated, but
the distribution did not match Marie of Lorraine's—and his brief in-
fatuation with the flighty Catherine Howard was already turning sour.
To crown it all, his Scottish nephew snubbed him. Henry had at last
got him to agree to a meeting at York, where he no doubt hoped to
talk to him like an uncle, and impress the young man with that persuasive charm which he could undoubtedly exert when he wanted to.
Fine preparations were made, Henry arrived in the city full of expectation, and then James broke the appointment.

Good manners aside, it was a diplomatic blunder of the first magni-
tude. To make it worse, while Henry was kicking his heels at York,
Liddesdale suddenly broke loose under the leadership of an English
outlaw named Anton Armstrong, ravaged Bewcastle where the barns
and Jack Musgrave's house were put to the flames, and killed seven

Fenwicks. This, following the assurance that Henry had received from Thomas Wharton that the Borders were "very qwyett", that the King of Scots "intendithe no warre", and that Wharton's espionage system was working at maximum efficiency, snapped the English king's royal temper completely. Injury had been added to his graceless nephew's insult; since diplomacy had failed, he would try force.

The circumstances now were all in Henry's favour. On the frontier Wharton and other leading English Borderers were itching to get at the Scots following the Fenwick massacre; the West March Warden saw a ready-made pretext in the Scots' occupation of the Debateable Land, which was being incited by his opposite number, Lord Maxwell. Wharton had sure information that Maxwell was looking for further trouble; spies had brought him word of a meeting at which Maxwell had told leading Armstrongs, Elliots, and Crosers: "Ye are the men I can trust: I will have some notable act done to the Inglishmen".

This was enough for Wharton. He proposed a raid on the Debateable Land, which he would carry out in such a way that the Liddesdale riders would be drawn out of their fastness to help their countrymen; Wharton would lure them skilfully over the Border, where he would have an ambush prepared—he was eager to hoist Liddesdale with its own petard.

But this scheme—good sound reiver tactics though it was—was apparently not subtle enough for higher authority. Over at Alnwick Henry's commissioners were seeking other means of dealing with Liddesdale and at the same time paving the way for a general conflict. They were discussing "by whate meanes the Tynedale and Redesdale men might beste be inducede to enterprise the slaughter of some of the Liddesdale men".

Accordingly they put pressure on the English riding clans to get busy, but the Charltons, Dodds, and Milburns were not to be persuaded. For one thing, the Liddesdale men were their professional accomplices —the differences of 1536 were now five years old and apparently forgotten—and for another, they were unwilling to provoke a deadly feud. Liddesdale was looking highly dangerous at that time: apart from Anton Armstrong's Bewcastle foray, there had been only a month or two earlier another most impressive demonstration of Liddesdale's capabilities when the Armstrongs (aided, of course, by Elliots and Crosers) had stormed Houghton Castle with scaling ladders, beaten up the garrison, and removed horses along with £40 of plate. No, Redesdale and Tynedale were regretful but firm; they were not tangling with Liddesdale at the moment. But how about West Teviotdale? There was a nice target for a foray, if the commissioners were agreeable—and the commissioners, although baulked of their principal hope, apparently were agreeable, for Redesdale and Tynedale promptly made two raids against the Teviotdale riders.

Henry's commissioners had to report regretfully on November 7 1541 that there was good order on both sides of the frontier, except for Liddesdale, Tynedale and Redesdale, "who are soo combeynede, confedderatide and knette in one that not for their officers or princes laws would they break their association". They were ready to spoil on both sides, and with at least 2000 riders between them they were "able and apt persons for warre". What made them particularly formidable, the commissioners added, was that their territories were "strate to enter and of grete strength, and within distance to relieve each other". Furthermore, they were frightened of nothing.

This was news to nobody, but its repetition must have been galling to a monarch bent on stirring up mischief between England and Scotland. However, his commissioners had not entirely failed, for the Redesdale–Tynedale forays against West Teviotdale prompted swift retaliation, the Kerrs hitting back with raids along the Coquet. Farther West, too, the action was warming up; Archie Elliot of Thirlshope led a daring Kiddesdale foray against William Carnaby's land at Halton, and sold the dummy to his pursuers by coming back along the tops between Redesdale and Tynedale—the last place that any returning reiver in his right mind would have been expected to go. As a further precaution against legitimate complaint for this raid, the leading Liddesdale raiders had entrusted it to the youngest riders, while their seniors were busy establishing alibis at Hawick.

Two, it transpired, could play at that game. John Heron and the Fenwicks, with "the beste of Redesdale and Tyndale" who had evidently been talked round at last into having a go at the Armstrongs, devised a neat scheme. They set fire to an old house belonging to Heron with the double purpose of providing a gathering signal for their own raid, and also so that they could pretend later that the Scots had done it, and then set off in force hell for leather for Liddesdale. Haste was necessary so that no Redesdale or Tynedale informers could get ahead of them to warn the Armstrongs what was coming; Heron might have "the beste" of the dalesmen riding with him, but he knew what the others could be like, and he had no desire to ride into an ambush. His speed paid off, for his raid successfully destroyed thirteen Liddesdale houses—including Archie Elliot's—and all the cattle, a great herd, were carried off.

So 1541 drew to a close, with trouble growing daily along the line, nursed by Henry's policy while at the same time his government continued to negotiate with Scotland. James, whose rudeness over the York meeting had resulted from the advice received from his clerical and Francophile advisers, was eager to placate his uncle, and had presented fulsome apologies; for the moment Henry was ready to listen until conditions should be right for the application of his final solution by force of arms.

Early in 1542 the enterprising Wharton put forward a scheme to kidnap King James while he was visiting the Borders, but Henry wisely rejected it; the price of failure was too high. Meanwhile the Scottish Borderers were stepping up their raids, and in the summer the English East March Warden, Robert Bowes, mounted a great reprisal in company with Angus and the Douglases. With 3000 riders he descended on Teviotdale, burning villages as he went. Following the classic "big raid" pattern, Bowes established his main ambush at Hadden, and sent out two principal forays, the Redesdale and Tynedale riders under Heron, and the Norham and Berwick garrisons, to scour the countryside.

They successfully rounded up herds of sheep and cattle and were preparing to rejoin the main body, when they found themselves beset by a Scottish force under George Gordon, Earl of Huntly, whose line of attack laid bare the cardinal weakness of the big raid technique, which was that the despatch of forays from a main ambush seriously divided the strength of the raiding force. Huntly's riders came between the forays and the main party, and in the crisis the English leadership failed and their forces were thrown into confusion.

The Earl of Angus, one of the few who seems to have kept his head in the disaster, has left a graphic account of what happened. "Those of Redesdale and Tynedale was the first that fled"; in fact, the Northumberland riders, putting first things first, as usual, concentrated on the cattle, to the consequent disorder of their ranks. The forays hastened to join with their main body, the trot became a gallop, and the gallop a rout, with the Scottish horsemen riding the fugitives down. Bowes and Heron was taken, but Angus cut his way out, observing bitterly afterwards that it was not that the Scots had won, but that the English had lost by their mishandling of the fight. He estimated that the invaders had lost seventy dead and captured, but later tallies put the figure as high as 1000, including many gentlemen and Border officers.

Hadden Rigg, from the English point of view, was a grossly mismanaged affair. It added fuel to Henry's rage, but his decision was already taken. On August 24, the day of the battle, his Privy Council were noting their master's intent to invade Scotland "for the distruccion of their country". The whole power of the North, an army of 20,000, was mustered under Norfolk at York, and although a valid excuse was still lacking, war was now inevitable. Both sides recognised this; the Scottish ambassadors continued to play for time by spinning out negotiations while England's musters went busily ahead.

Henry's main aim was to do as much damage in Scotland as possible; so much is obvious from the correspondence written during Norfolk's preparations. But the English general was less concerned for the moment with what he was going to do in Scotland than with the problem of actually getting his army there in working order. His main worry was a shortage of beer for the troops; on September 2 he was indenting for "vi or vii hundred tonne of bere", five days later he was noting that "I feare lak of no thyng so moche as of drynk", and this despite the brewing that was taking place at Berwick, and on September 11 he was announcing flatly that he could not hope to get his army to Edinburgh without beer. Like Napoleon, he knew what his army marched on.

By October, his force was as ready as it could be. It had sustained its first important casualty before setting out; the ailing Earl of Southampton, breathing fire against the Scots to the last, had died, in spite of (or possibly because of) Dr Buttes' pills. Still short of beer, to say nothing of food, Norfolk crossed the Border on October 21, and the war was on.

It began badly for England. Norfolk had word from Dand Nixon, a Scottish spy, that James was preparing to fight him in force; Huntly's victorious little army had been reinforced to 10,000 strong, and James himself was mustering three times that number to bar the way to Edinburgh. Norfolk advanced warily, burning and destroying everything he could touch—he probably knew that a good catalogue of devastation would console Henry for any lack of actual conquest—and Huntly's advance army scouted him up the Tweed. Roxburgh, Kelso and its abbey, and more than a dozen lesser towns were put to the fire, Hertford raided Teviotdale with 2000 riders, but provisions were running short, and after only a week in Scotland Norfolk was back in Berwick, where the beer was.

James saw his chance to retaliate, but the army he had raised would have none of it; they too were short of provisions, it was late in the year, and they felt they had done enough by seeing Norfolk off Scottish soil. Furthermore, his nobles were not over-enthusiastic for James, and so the army was disbanded.

But James was not prepared to let matters lie there. He raised another force, and while widely-publicised preparations were made for activities in the east, the new army was launched towards Cumberland. Intentionally or not, James had pulled off a fine strategic coup, for while Norfolk's strength was concentrated on the eastern March, the western frontier was wide open to invasion, and James's army under the veteran Lord Maxwell, was on its way. The Scottish King was not to march with it; he had fallen ill, and waited at Lochmaben while his forces, probably about 18,000 strong, advanced to the frontier late in November.

To Wharton, lying in Carlisle with a bare 3000 men at his call, the situation looked desperate. But Henry had chosen well; where a lesser man might have been content to try to secure the city and hold it against odds, leaving his Wardenry to its fate, Wharton fired the beacons to muster his 3000, and himself rode out in advance with 300 lances to scout the Scottish advance. He sent a little raid to burn Middleby, eight miles beyond the frontier, and learned that the Scots were in two main divisions on Langholm and Mortonkirk.

In the chill small hours of November 24 Wharton watched the spreading red glow to the north, where the invaders were burning the Grahams out of the Debateable Land. Shortly before dawn, by which time his own muster was complete, he saw the Scottish power cross the Esk; if Wharton was going to fight it would have to be now, as best he could, while the enemy were still not clear of the chief hazards on their line of march—the red-banked Esk and the great Solway Moss beyond it.

Wharton ordered in William Musgrave's "prickers", the scouting light horsemen who could hang on the Scottish flanks, darting in and out with their lances, spying and harassing; it was the kind of work that the Border riders excelled at, but never were they to excel as they did on that November dawn, as the Scottish force rolled over the Esk ford with the fire-lit sky behind them.

Wharton saw his riders chased back, wheeling and reforming to harass the Scottish flank; on the other side lay the moss, but in the very heart of the Scottish army there was an even greater danger than that posed by the skirmishing reiver horsemen or the treacherous countryside. At about this time, the Scots found themselves without a leader.

It is said that Oliver Sinclair, King James's favourite, chose this moment to announce that he had the King's commission to command the force; if so, it was dangerously late in the day. Under Maxwell, no doubt things would have been very different; as it was, dissension broke out in the Scottish headquarters, but the details are lost, like all things that come adrift in Solway Moss. Certainly the behaviour of the Scottish army admits of no other explanation than total loss of control at its head.

Wharton knew nothing of this; he was fighting the battle as he saw it, with a reiver's eye and a reiver's tactics. His steel bonnets were holding a frontier against an army, wheeling and charging, hitting and running and hitting again. And the unbelievable was happening; before the repeated slashing of the riders on its flanks, the army was beginning to crumble at the edges. "Our prickers . . . gatt theym in a shake all the waye" was Wharton's triumphant verdict later, and he could not have put it better. Musgrave's riders charged again and again, urging their ponies into the mass, and the Scottish army, trapped on the Esk ford, with the moss behind them, came apart at the seams. Vainly the Scottish leaders tried to rally the disordered rabble that had been an army; the Scots were "in a maze", according to one English account, their morale was gone, and Musgrave's riders rode through and over them. As their force disintegrated, four or five Scots were surrendering to single English riders; the rout of Solway Moss was complete.

From a Scottish point of view, it was the greatest military disgrace in the nation's history. From the side of the English Borderers, it was a wonderful triumph. A few hundred irregular light horsemen had not only stopped, but decisively beaten, a force probably ten times greater than themselves.[1] Whoever is prepared to condemn the Border riders out of hand as night-running cattle thieves and no more, would do well to remember that on one day at least they fought a great fight in their own way, and inflicted on one of Europe's great warrior races its most stinging reverse.

Wharton estimated that he had lost seven dead and one prisoner. The Scottish losses are unknown; one estimate was that they lost only twenty killed in action, but that uncounted numbers were drowned, and about 1200 taken prisoner. They lost "Earls, barons, lords, cannon and hand-guns" as well as thirty standards.

There was worse to follow. The wreck of the Scottish army, escaping northwards, found itself beset by the Scottish Borderers, eager as always to snap up plunder and prisoners, whichever side they belonged to. The Liddesdale riders slew many of the fugitives, "and for the rest took horses, boots and spurs, and any doublets worth taking". The Scottish soldiers who escaped with their lives were stripped and turned loose in their hose; some were so reduced by panic and confusion that they were prepared to surrender to women.

Wharton, with a force far too small to undertake any pursuit, was content to let the Scottish reivers put the finishing touches to his work. "To hear of the spoil and taking of prisoners that night in Scotland by the Annerdales, Eskdales, Ewesdales, Wauchopdales, and some of the Liddesdales . . . it is for goode Englishmen pleasant to hear," he concluded his report on the battle.

To King James the news of Solway Moss was, quite literally, a fatal blow. Ill and dejected, he withdrew from the Border country, wandering aimlessly from one royal residence to another, his once strong spirit utterly crushed. His two sons had died in the previous year, as had his mother, the English Princess Margaret; only a few days after Sol-

---

1. As with most battles, there is doubt about the total numbers involved. The Scottish army was probably between 15,000 and 20,000, although it has been put at somewhere just over 10,000. Wharton's force has been estimated at as little as 2000, and as high as 4000; most historians are prepared to agree vaguely that the English were outnumbered at least four to one, but this would appear to be a very conservative figure. Eustace Chapuys, Imperial Ambassador to England, emphasises the crucial point in a letter to Charles V: he puts Wharton's army at 4000, but says that the damage was done by only 700 to 800 riders.

way Moss he received the news that his Queen had given birth to a
daughter, "a vereye weyke childe, and not like to live". It was no great
comfort to him; if he could have foreseen the future career of that
"weyke childe", Mary, Queen of Scots, it would have been less comfort still. He moaned for the defeat of Oliver, "spake but few wise
words", and died raging and crying out. His body was no sooner cold
than the Scotts and Kerrs, down on the Border, were raiding the royal
flocks.

Note on the Prisoners of Solway Moss

Wharton's list of the principal prisoners and their takers is instructive.
It shows clearly the democratic spirit which governed the matters of
capture and ransom, and runs as follows:

Prisoners	Takers
Earl of Cassill	Batill Routledge: John Musgrave claimeth a part for the loan of his horse to the said Routledge
Earl of Glencairn	Willie Graham (Wat's Willie), Willie Graham of the Balie, Sir Thomas Wharton and Thos Dacre.
Lord Fleming	George Pott, Stephen James.
Lord Maxwell, Warden of the West March and admiral of Scotland	Edward Aglionby or Geo. Foster.
Lord Somervell	Richard Brisco
Lord Olivaunt	Thom Denton or James Allenson
Lord Graye	Thom Whyte, Willie Storye and George Storye.
Oliver Sinclair	Willie Bell

Sir John Forster, the celebrated Warden, fought at Solway Moss, and claimed to have captured Lord Maxwell, but this was disallowed. Wharton's list shows that the credit for the captures of Lords Maxwell and Olivaunt was still in doubt at the time of his writing, and one of the claimants to Maxwell is "George Foster". One wonders if this should read "John Forster".

Henry VIII wrote to Wharton after the battle, specially instructing him to assure the takers of prisoners that their ransoms would be duly paid, and the takers must not worry about their captives being removed to London. Foreseeing a long war, during which ransoms would not be obtainable, King Henry recommended Wharton to find out from the takers what ransoms they would be asking, "promising to do what you can, if they will be reasonable, to get them ready money". Finally, Wharton was to keep his men in service, ready to "defend and annoy".

XXX

The rough wooing

Scotland now stood in the most mortal peril she had known since the eve of Bannockburn, 230 years earlier. Her king was dead, a newborn infant ruled the kingdom, her leaders were quarrelling with each other, her army was shattered, and to the south a predatory enemy was ready to strike. If Henry had seized his chance at once and invaded with full power he might have succeeded in his life-long ambition of reducing his northern neighbour. But he saw an easier, and on the face of it, a surer way.

His little son, Edward, was five years old; Mary of Scotland was newborn. Let the children be betrothed, and later married, and England and Scotland would eventually come under one ruler—and as Henry's father had pointed out, the greater would inevitably draw the lesser. Here was the ideal solution, and Henry pursued it promptly and shrewdly. He released the Scottish nobles taken at Solway Moss, on pledges that they would further his scheme when they returned to

Scotland, where a government under the Regent Arran appeared likely to fall in with Henry's proposals. But on two points the Scots stuck fast; they would not deliver their little Queen into Henry's safe-keeping, and they would not permit him to garrison Scottish fortresses.

Henry agreed that Mary should remain in Scotland until she was ten; impatient though he was, he knew when to give a little, and with Angus and the pro-English Douglases back in Scotland, subversion going merrily ahead, and the Scottish leaders in their normal state of confused dispute, he could continue to play politics towards his desired end.

There is no need to go into the complicated history of Scotland in 1543, with its political and religious shifts and upheavals; enough to say that Henry, who in this year was embarking on matrimony for the sixth and last time, overplayed his hand—among other things he offered the little Princess Elizabeth in marriage to Arran's son, and tried to arrange secretly to have Mary shipped to England—and Scottish sentiment turned against the marriage treaty. "There is not so lytle a boy but he will hurle stones ayenst it," reported an English envoy; French influence was waxing again, and before the year was out Scotland had rejected the treaty which Henry had laboured so hard and deviously to conclude.

It was the last straw. Henry had had his bellyful of Scotland, just as they had had theirs of him; if they would not listen to reason on his terms he would convince them in the old-fashioned way. He would wreak such a horrible vengeance on them that they would be glad to submit.

The campaign he planned is perhaps the biggest blot on a royal reputation in which even sympathetic historians have discerned some blemishes. He would simply slaughter and burn indiscriminately north of the frontier, exterminating as far as possible without regard to age or sex. The work would be entrusted to a willing and capable lieutenant, Edward Seymour, Earl of Hertford. The campaigns which he and his colleagues were to wage have become known, with typical under-statement, as "the rough wooing".

But before the wooing began in earnest, and while high-level nego-tiations were proceeding and dissolving through 1543, other less public treaties were being reached at a humbler level, on the Border itself. Wharton, in the months following Solway Moss, took advantage of the Scottish government's weakness to spread his own influence among the Scottish tribes of the West and Middle Marches. By threat and bribe he revived the old English Warden policy of securing the toughest of the Scottish clans to work in England's interest; the time would come when he was able to claim that he had turned Dumfries-shire into virtually an English province, but in the meantime he managed to control the Scottish reivers' activities to an extent that even old Lord Dacre had not achieved.

He played skilfully on the feuds which, as always, were in progress along the line,[1] turning the Armstrongs on to the Kerrs and Scotts, who were themselves engaged in their perpetual vendetta. And ordinary raiding proceeded at the same time. In January 1543, shortly after Solway Moss, Henry had ordered raids into the East March; Redesdale had conducted a fire-raising foray against Ancrum, but a successful hot trod had accounted for forty of the raiders. In March Liddesdale had descended on Hexham, killing, burning, and taking prisoners, but had ridden into an English ambush on the way home and lost about a dozen men.

This was the usual small change of Border life; what Wharton was building up in addition was civil war among the Scottish tribes. He had brought the Armstrongs and Crosers to "spoil under Henry's wing", and they forayed far and wide at his orders. In September 150 Liddesdale Armstrongs plundered two villages of the Scotts', driving off 250 beasts; in October they were burning out Kerr of Ferniehurst, killing one of his men and plundering his home of corn, cattle, and goods. On the same night the Storeys, with Scottish confederates, made a fire raid on Selkirk, but were beaten off; although pursued they managed to burn corn stacks on their way home, using gunpowder, and set fire to a house of Buccleuch's.

To this Wharton added raids of his own. Those of Liddesdale who had not entered his employment were given a smart hint in September when he sent Cumbrian riders in force into the valley, burning nineteen houses, and carrying off prisoners and 250 beasts—eighty-five of

---

1. Wharton was an adept at pressurising. In September 1543 he was recommending that before any Scottish rider was enlisted officially as a trusted servant of King Henry's, he should first be given some "annoyance" to do in Scotland; not only would this give him a chance to prove himself, it would also give Wharton a lever to use against him among his fellow-Scots if necessary.

which he presented to the Elliots, as a reward for their activities on his behalf. A few weeks later he had them burning a village near Jedburgh, in which they were assisted by sixty Nixons (thirty English and thirty Scottish); there was a bloody encounter over the village's barnekin wall in which several men were killed and wounded. That same night Wharton himself was burning Bonjedworth with his Cumbrians.

Throughout the winter the toll rose, and the Armstrongs rounded off the year by pillaging two of Buccleuch's towers, burning a couple of his villages, and taking plunder and prisoners.

Wharton was a clever man; he knew that many small raids were more terrifying to a population than a few large ones, however damaging these might be. He encouraged the reivers to ride nightly in small bands, and ever worked away to bring more Scottish families into Henry's service. In February 1544 he was scheming to seduce the Middle March riding families—Davidsons, Pringles, Taits, Youngs, Turnbulls, and Rutherfords, as well as the Scottish Robsons and Halls of Teviotdale. With them he hoped to break the power of the Kerrs for good. In the East March the Dixons, Trotters and Redpaths were to be similarly enlisted against the Humes, and eventually presented with their lands.

But 1544 was to see the rough wooing developed in earnest beyond the Borders, in the Scottish heartland. Henry had contemplated a major invasion in September 1543, to lend moral support to the negotiations he had in hand, but his lieutenant on the Borders, the Duke of Suffolk, was out of sympathy with his master's Scottish policy, and, like Norfolk before him, was obsessed with the need for adequate supplies of beer. Henry dismissed him, and replaced him with Hertford, and although the September invasion was called off, the decks were now cleared for action on the grand scale.

Henry's instructions to Hertford in 1544 were precise. While the Scottish Borders were to be "tourmented and occupied as much as they can be"—Wharton could be relied on to see to that—Hertford was to raze and deface Edinburgh so that it should be a perpetual memory; if he met resistance he was to slaughter men, women, and children without exception. Holyrood was to be sacked, Leith to be utterly destroyed. No one was to be spared in St Andrews.

Hertford went to work with zeal. Landing 10,000 men from an English fleet near Leith, he captured the town, and then marched on Edinburgh with the English East March Warden, William, Lord Eure, who had joined him with 4000 Border riders. The capital, like Leith, was sacked and burned, and the country round devastated. The Scottish leaders had retired in haste, but Hertford himself has left an account of the street fighting that took place in Edinburgh, with handguns firing from the windows of the burning town, and above the din of the battle the wailing of the citizens.

Hertford then marched south, burning Dunbar and everything that lay in his way, and came to Berwick with only a few casualties.

Meanwhile along the frontier Scotland was suffering a series of hammer blows from large-scale English forays over and above the smaller raids of Wharton's renegades. Sir Ralph Eure, Warden of the English Middle March, and son of the East March Warden, stormed and burned Jedburgh. Among his troops were great numbers of Scottish Nixons and Crosers who had sworn allegiance to Henry; with the Olivers and Rutherfords of Teviotdale, they put on the red cross of St George and helped to destroy their own countrymen. Eure then turned on Kelso and served it the same way, and throughout the summer the Middle and East Marches of Scotland received the most terrible scorching even in their fearful history.

It is pointless to go into detail; enough to say that following a winter in which the Scottish riders, with English assistance, had forayed their own border night after night, almost without pause, Eure's raiders harried a great swathe of the frontier from side to side, systematically destroying everything. It is a sickening list to read through, page after page of it, and the grand totals of damage at the finish are probably conservative estimates—192 towns, towers, bastell-houses and the like destroyed, over 20,000 cattle taken, prisoners and killed by the hundred.[2] But no figures can begin to suggest the smouldering horror that was left in the Scottish Border country when the last raiders clattered away, laden with plunder, and the terrified fugitives crept out of the

---

2. These figures are for a period of less than five months, from July 2 to November 17. In the preceding winter, from September 9, 1543 to March 14 1544, English and Scottish raiders had spoiled and burned over 120 Scottish villages, carried off about 7500 beasts, slain thirty-five men and taken 400 prisoners, but these figures do not include great numbers of cattle burned to death and "menye menne also hurt". From March to July raiding was at roughly the same rate.

woods and gullies to look at the ruin of homes and fields, and search
out their relatives among the dead.

The humbler Scottish Borderers were not the only ones who helped
the English to scorch the earth. The Scots aristocracy has never been
backward to sell itself to advantage, and there were those who might
genuinely prefer the English side for religious reasons. After Henry had
successfully induced the treacherous earls of Glencairn and Lennox to
enter his service, Lennox was soon joining in a raid conducted by
Wharton and Dacre in the west. Dumfries was destroyed, the surrounding country laid waste, and much plunder carried off. Shortly
after this Wharton was made a lord.

English raids in force continued into the winter, and to Henry and
his advisers it may have seemed that the campaign of terror could not
be resisted by the Scots for long.[3] Here he made a mistake; where he
might have succeeded by diplomacy or by a proper political-military
conquest, he was ensuring his eventual failure by tactics which bred in
Scotland a determination not to give in. While the south of the country
was being reduced to a smoking desert, the temper of the people was
hardening, and to astute observers it may have been evident that
Henry had started a fight he was not going to win. What else would
have brought about the marvellous change of heart in the Douglases,
who now deserted the English cause and exhibited belated symptoms
of patriotism? One suggestion is that the English had offended Angus
by ravaging Douglas land in Scotland and desecrating tombs; perhaps
it helped, but something else surely must have been needed to cause
Angus's sudden volte-face. Not long before he had been fighting for
England at Hadden Rigg; now he was rallying, with real gallantry, a
Scottish rearguard action to save the artillery used in an abortive
attempt to retake Coldingham abbey, which was held by an English
garrison. The behaviour of men like Angus is what makes Scottish
history such an exciting and confusing succession of surprises for the
student.

But however resolute their spirit, the Scots for the moment were on

---

3. The plight of the Scottish Borderers may be judged from the fact that
even such a powerful noble as Lord Hume had been impoverished to the
extent that his castle was in danger "because he has no goods left undestroyed
to furnish the same". On October 18 1545 the Scottish Council accordingly
granted him £300.

the losing end; Ralph Eure and Brian Laiton, Wharton and Dacre were masters of the Scottish Marches in all but name, and preparing to extend their area of operations still farther northward. Their forces were increased by 3000 foreign mercenaries, terrible people of the worst sort; if it was not bad enough to be harried by English and Scottish Borderers, the inhabitants of southern Scotland were shortly to undergo the horror of spoliation by German, Italian, French, Spanish, and even Irish and Greek soldiers of fortune.

It was with confidence, then, that Ralph Eure and his colleagues carried their campaign of destruction into 1545; in the apparently supine state of the country it was easy work, and Eure had the incentive of a guarantee from his king that he could have whatever land he conquered in Teviotdale and the East March. Angus, when he heard of this, observed grimly that he personally would be prepared to witness the title deeds, with a sharp pen and in red ink. In the meantime, he intended to take care of those Scottish Borderers who were lending assistance to England.

He set out south in February 1545 to read a lesson to the Crosers, Nixons and their fellows, and especially to the Teviotdale renegades. Eure, seeing his Scottish reiver allies in danger, hurried over the Border to protect them; he led a force of 3000 riders, which seemed ample, since Angus (and Arran, who accompanied him) had a bare 300 lances, which he brought to Melrose. Eure, lying at Jedburgh, made a night foray against him, but the wily Angus and his riders were off into the hills, and stayed there, scouting Eure's force as it plundered round Melrose and then retired.

Eure, confident in his strength, mopped up the tower of Broomhouse, where an old lady and her family are said to have been burned alive, while Angus, now reinforced by Scott of Buccleuch's riders and a detachment of Fife cavalry, hung at his heels and waited. Whatever his personal defects, Angus was second to none in the rough-and-tumble of Border warfare; he was in effect conducting a large-scale hot trod in his own way, and he waited until Eure was where he wanted him, on the moor just north of Ancrum, a bare five miles from Jedburgh.

Skilfully he outflanked Eure's line of march, dismounted his riders, and waited for the English force to reach him. Using the ground, on Buccleuch's advice, he managed to conceal the full size of his little army, and Eure's mixed battalions of English and Scottish Borderers hurried on to get to grips; they were tired and heavy with plunder, and when they ran into Angus's ambush, with the setting sun and the smoke of their own gunfire hitting them full in the face, Eure realised his mistake. His charge was turned into a shambles as it met the Scottish lances, and as his force fell back in disorder he learned the bitterest lesson of all—the unwisdom of trusting Border reivers. His Scottish riders, who could read the course of a battle as well as Eure himself, tore off their red crosses and turned on their English allies; caught before the solid mass of Angus's men and with treachery in his midst, Eure could only sell his life as dearly as possible, for he did not expect quarter. He and Laiton died fighting in the press, and his followers were cut down in hundreds; at least a thousand are said to have been taken prisoner, including a London alderman named Read who had been sent to fight the Scots as punishment for failing to pay a levy demanded by King Henry; in the long run his ransom cost him more than the levy would have done.

When it was over, Arran walked among the corpses, and was shown Eure's body. He looked down at the dead man, whose prowess as a fighting soldier had been unsurpassed, and whose savagery had made him the most hated rider in the Border country. "God have mercy on him," said Arran, "for he was a fell cruel man." Then he wept for the dead. Angus asked him was he merry, and Arran replied: "My lord, I am much the merrier for you," embraced Angus, and apologised for ever mistrusting him.

Ancrum Moor was not a big battle, but it had an importance beyond its size. It received much publicity in France, and many months later an English resident there reported that, hearing the French rejoicing over some apparently new victory by the Scots against the English, he had investigated and discovered that it was just the story of Ancrum Moor being retold yet again. More important, King Francis was now ready to send help to Scotland in the shape of 3000 infantry and 500 horse under Lorges de Montgomery, but although a joint Franco-Scottish force crossed the Border it did little damage beyond beating up villages in the neighbourhood of Wark.

This was pin-pricking stuff which in no way disturbed Henry's plans for subjecting southern Scotland to another ravaging in the autumn. Hertford came north again, this time with 12,000 men, many of them the foreign mercenaries already mentioned. The destruction of 1544 was repeated, with close on 300 towns, villages, towers, and churches destroyed. Among these were the abbeys of Kelso, Dryburgh, Jedburgh and Melrose, which were no longer sacred to a reforming monarch; for the most part there was little opposition, except at Kelso, where one of the little, forgotten heroisms of Border history took place, a handful of men, including monks, holding the abbey tower to the bitter end.

Occasionally the Scots made retaliatory raids, without much success. One foray, with French help, ran into an English ambush on the East March and was cut to bits by the longbow hail; in another, Robert Maxwell, son of the old lord, was captured. But in the west the Scots were at least holding their own; in one encounter 500 English were killed or captured, and towards the year end the castles of Caerlaverock, Threave and Lochmaben were retaken. Despite the ruin of the Border country the national danger to Scotland was less critical than it had been—not that the Scottish Borderers, rebuilding their hovels for the fourth of fifth time, can have taken much satisfaction in that.

Robert Bowes, now Warden of the English Middle March (he had been released after his capture at Hadden Rigg) described to the Privy Council the havoc wrought by those two years of invasion. It was difficult, he said, to do any further injury to the Scots, as they had fled inland from the frontier "save only women, children and impotent creatures, who, nevertheless by night times and upon holydays travail as they may to manure the ground and to sow corn. . . .So wretchedlie can they live and induir the pain that no Englesheman can suffre the lyke."

Nor were the sufferings of the Borderers over yet, but in the meantime great things were happening elsewhere. In the spring of 1546 Cardinal Beaton was murdered and his body dangled from the walls of St Andrew's Castle. A notoriously lewd and evil-living prelate, his cloth and circumstances had nevertheless made him an implacable enemy of Henry's policy, and as such he had been a powerpoint in Scotland's resistance. Now he was gone, but the spirit of the nation was unchanged, and found a champion in the Queen Mother, Marie, who supplied the resolution that Arran lacked. So the fight went on, the most spectacular part of it being the siege of St Andrews, where Beaton's murderers and other opponents of the Arran regime held out, with Henry lending assistance. The siege was to drag on into the following year, by which time the garrison would include John Knox, full of fire and resolution.

On the Border in 1546 there was a comparative lull after the two years' carnage, the authorities on both sides having time occasionally to take note of the ingenuities of their own respective evildoers. Thus in May, Bowes and Wharton were at Hexham "to put down the English thieves . . . who steal cattle and put them into Scotland to make it appear as if done by the Scots; whereas the doers were really English or Scots of Liddesdale pretending to be English". No doubt they made some kind of sense of it in the end. The Scottish Council in the same month had leisure to consider what should be done about those Scottish Borderers who were serving England, and towards the end of the year an expedition was planned to restore order, but it does not appear to have got far.

Some raiding continued on a small scale, even after peace was concluded in the summer, but Bowes reported to the Council that there was "quietness and good truce kept and no incourses except by thieves in small numbers." The Scots told a slightly different tale, complaining that the English Wardens interpreted peace to mean no major invasion, but were continuing to run smaller forays. However, in the main it was a quiet year.

The year 1547 began with increased activity on the West March, where Wharton worried not only about the decaying defences of Carlisle—where fourteen yards of the city wall fell down—and the lack of bows, arrows, and fletchers in his Wardenry, but also because Dumfriesshire was showing signs of getting out of hand. Arran had recaptured Langholm Tower, which the Armstrongs had handed over to the English two years earlier, and the Maxwells and Johnstones were raiding in Cumberland again; after a year in which there had been no major English invasion, Wharton felt it necessary to send Sir Thomas Carleton in to remind the natives of the benefits of English overlordship (see Chapter XV).

While preparation for this expedition was going forward, Henry VIII was setting out on an infinitely more important journey. The gigantic body and brain which had dominated the British scene for so long were running down at last: diseased and worn out, his will and his treasury drained by a war which he could not win, the old wild bull of England died on a January night, raging to the last, it is said, of monks,

monks, monks. No doubt there was rejoicing along the frontier where he had caused so much misery, and in St Peter's at which he had struck such lasting blows, but no one can have been better pleased than a leathery old Border fighter who was waiting in the Tower to have his head cut off. Norfolk, survivor of Flodden and the frontier campaigns, had heard his doom pronounced by Parliament for treasonable practices; all that was needed to bring him to the block was the royal assent, but Henry considerately passed away at the eleventh hour, and the old warrior survived once again, and lived to see his eightieth birthday seven years later.

Henry's death, and the accession of his nine-year-old son Edward VI, had little immediate effect on the Border. In the west Wharton continued to extend English power north of the line and to recruit Scots to his service. "The old laird of Mangerton," he wrote, "his son, and of the Liddesdales and others, once or twice a week are with me, and show themselves ever willing to serve the King's majesty . . . they are continually doing displeasure to the enemy."

The Armstrongs were indeed serving him well. One of them, young Archie of Mangerton, took the Laird of Johnstone prisoner by a typical ruse concocted by Wharton. The Warden, with Robert Maxwell already in his hands, had been anxious to capture the Johnstone chief as well, and succeeded in luring him out of Lochwood Tower by sending forty riders to burn Wamfray, the hold of Johnstone's brother. The laird sallied out to avenge the attack, and rode into an ambush laid by the Captain of Langholm and his garrison. He was apparently prepared for this, and although the garrison men fought stoutly, he captured several of them and pursued the Captain and his remaining followers vigorously. The cunning Wharton, however, had a second ambush waiting, led by his son Henry, John Musgrave, and Archie Armstrong; it was 300 strong, and the Johnstones were hopelessly outnumbered.

About 140 of them were captured, many were wounded and eight killed. Johnstone himself fought hard, and three lances were broken on him; one of them struck him painfully in the buttock and he was captured.[4]

So the Armstrongs were earning their English pay, and Carleton

---

4. Lochwood was subsequently captured by Carleton and the Armstrongs (see Chapter XV).

employed them extensively in subduing Dumfriesshire. Lists taken at
this time show as many as 7000 Scots in assurance with England;[5] certainly by September 28 Wharton could count on 1900 Scottish Borderers; by October 5 the number had risen to 2400, and by October 12
it was 2700. And he found them plenty of work to do; in one week's
raiding his son, with the assured Scots and the English garrisons at
Langholm and Milk, had taken goods worth 1000 marks; Wharton
lamented that the English Borderers had been less active, or "the same
had been much more". However, daily raids were being made, the
Scottish renegades being allowed to keep whatever plunder they won.

At the same time Wharton was imposing some kind of law and
order on the Scottish West March, hearing complaints between Scottish and English at Carlisle "with which they seem to be well pleased
and obedient". He gave justice against thieves (presumably these being
irregular operators who did not enjoy his licence for their crimes), and
was able to report in October that "the countrymen of Liddesdale and
other parts stand in better order and obedience to the King than this
twenty years before. They say themselves they were never in such order,
for where great offenders have been, they may travel without trouble."

What this meant was that they were behaving from Wharton's point
of view; what they did to their fellow-Scottish Borderers was another
matter. But most of them were probably ready enough to submit to
the English Warden, as the dominant power in the area; his writ ran
as far as Clydesdale, and he was besieged with offers of service from
even the most "active offenders".[6] The Johnstones had come in, following their chief's capture, and were, in Wharton's opinion, "a great band
of proper men, and do good service." Earlier the Irvines had offered to

---

5. It is impossible to say how many Scots did swear loyalty to England, but
if the lists referred to above are anything like accurate, it may have been as
high as one in three for the West March. One list gives 300 Liddesdale Armstrongs bound to England, along with seventy-four Elliots and thirty-two
Nixons; another mentions 619 Armstrongs and "others under them", eighty
Elliots and others, and sixty Nixons and allies.

6. The oath administered to the Scottish renegades required them to serve
the King of England, Edward VI, renounce the Bishop of Rome, do all in
their power to advance the king's marriage to the Queen of Scotland, take
part with all who served the king against his enemies, not assist the said
enemies, and obey the Lord Protector, lord lieutenants, and Wardens.

bring 200 riders to the English service, and to compel everyone between Dumfries and the Border to follow suit (except Maxwells and
Johnstones) if Wharton would finance them.

XXXI

Wharton and Maxwell

It is worth taking a slightly closer look at one aspect of Wharton's work
at this time, because it shows how closely diplomacy, intrigue, pressure,
and violent action could be blended in the life of a Border official.
Wharton's relations with the Maxwell family, and particularly with the
remarkable John Maxwell, later Lord Herries, are illuminating both of
Border custom and character.

The keys to the Scottish West March were its fortresses—castles like
Lochmaben, Lochwood, Caerlaverock and Threave. Who held them
held the Western frontier, and it was of the first importance to England,
when she began to extend her dominion north after Solway Moss, to
secure as many of these strongholds as possible. The best of them were
in the hands of the Maxwells, whose chief, old Lord Maxwell, had been
taken at the Solway battle.

Accordingly, Henry VIII put the pressure on him. With the other
Scottish prisoners he was obliged to promise to further English policy,
promoting the marriage, and so on, but he balked at giving up his
castles. Short of that, he was ready to work in Henry's interest when he
returned to Scotland.

However, after a deal of negotiating, temporising, intriguing, and
blackmailing, the English did get Caerlaverock, Threave and Lochmaben, only to lose them again very quickly in the winter of 1545.

By 1547 the position had changed: old Lord Maxwell was dead, and
his eldest son, Robert, had been for over a year a prisoner in English
hands. It was now for John Maxwell, Robert's younger brother, to
conduct the affairs of the clan.

It is difficult to know what to make of Johnny Maxwell from this distance. He has been represented as a flawless Scottish patriot, as a black-hearted traitor, and as an accomplished double agent. In the 1540s he was, admittedly, in a difficult position, between the devil of English pressure and the deep sea of Scottish loyalty. Most Scottish Borderers were in the same position, noble and humble alike.[1] But he was a key man in the West, and as such singled out by Wharton for extra-special attention, particularly in the vital matter of those Maxwell-controlled fortresses which were so necessary to English security. Johnny Maxwell had to steer the difficult course of keeping in with both sides, and looking after his own interests. He brought to the task a nimble intellect—he needed it, for Wharton was as cagey a customer as Maxwell himself.

John Maxwell and his brother had been in receipt of English pensions of 200 crowns each up to July 1546; from that time on, John was acting as Warden of the Scottish West March, his brother being in English hands. At the same time John was under oath to serve the English interest, was being paid for it, and was forever conferring with Wharton at Carlisle. He was greatly concerned about the safety of his own and other Maxwell lands; Wharton, on the other hand, was trying to get hold of Lochmaben and Caerlaverock. The fencing and negotiating was intense; Wharton on his side had certain Maxwell hostages as bargaining counters, which he was later to use with deadly effect.

Through the late months of 1547 John Maxwell managed to temporise, hedge, and generally stave Wharton off. The Warden became both suspicious and impatient; near the turn of the year he was writing to Somerset about the possibility of the Maxwells handing over Lochmaben, and observing "their deeds follow not their words", and that "the Master of Maxwell (John) does not proceed in such a substantial sort in His Majesty's affairs as I should wish".

Finally, early in February 1548 Wharton spoke out plainly to Maxwell at Carlisle. "I entered with him on the present state of these two realms . . . the want of liberty his brother had, his own oath to serve His Majesty, and the great presents which he received . . . and advised

---

1. Writing of certain Maxwell adherents on November 15 1547, Wharton summed up the position: "I find them all untrue to this realm, but the scourage has lately so hung over them and does, that they have no hole to leap into from the intended godly purpose and his majesty's service."

him to frankly offer to me . . . the houses aforesaid"; that is, Loch-maben and Caerlaverock. Johnny still hedged; he would speak to his friends, and let Wharton know. The Warden persisted, and Johnny was understood to hint that if his captive brother consented, something might be arranged.

Wharton reported on this to Somerset, rather doubtfully; he was obviously not entirely sure that Maxwell could be trusted, in spite of oaths and payments. However, he had other work on hand, in the shape of an expedition against the Douglases; a few months earlier he had been employing Johnny Maxwell against them (Somerset hoped that a Maxwell-Douglas feud would be in England's interest, and told Wharton he should help Maxwell and wink at his doings against the Douglases).

Now Wharton was setting out to deal with the Douglases himself, with a force of assured Scots under the traitor Lennox and his own Cumbrians; his one anxiety appears to have been how his force should support itself in "a wasted country, where small relief is to be had". Had he known it, that was to be the least of his worries.

On February 20 1548 he crossed the frontier and struck deep into Nithsdale, through the territory of his supposed ally, Johnny Maxwell, who rode with him. Wharton had 3000 men, including one of his own sons, Henry Wharton, whom he sent ahead, apparently with Maxwell and "with all the true horsemen" in a foray to burn and waste the area around Durrisdeer. Wharton himself followed on with the main body, in the approved style, towards Drumlanrig.

The Douglases, under that proven expert Angus, were ready and waiting for them. The first hint that Wharton got of trouble was when a messenger came flying back to tell him that Angus had wiped up his advance foray, Maxwell and many assured Scots having changed sides; hard on the messenger's heels came Angus himself, and Whar-ton's Anglo-Scottish infantry found themselves hard-pressed. Whar-ton's other son, Thomas, wrote a panic-stricken letter to Somerset describing what happened.

". . . when the assured Scots with my father perceived the enemy coming, they took or laid hands upon any Englishman in my lord's company. I cannot tell whether my father or what others are taken or slain, but few or none came away."

It had not been quite so disastrous as Thomas Wharton's letter, with its final appeal for help for "this poor country now destitute, not only of all the gentlemen, but most of the true men within the wardenry, and also of good horses", made out. It had been a stinging reverse, but Wharton was back in Carlisle a week later, grinding his teeth over the perfidy of Johnny Maxwell "who shows himself an enemy, against his oath. The world wonders here of his and the other Maxwell's' false-hoods." Plainly the Warden had no doubt who was the author of his ambush and overthrow.

To fuel his rage came a letter from Johnny himself on March 1, beginning with the delightful phrase "Though all has not proceeded as you looked for when in this country . . .", and continuing with a complaint that while he, Johnny, had taken oath to advance the royal marriage and had given Wharton pledges, he had been poorly repaid by having his lands despoiled by the English. "Your people took from mine goods, etc. worth £1000. I came to Carlisle for redress but could not get £10". Furthermore, he would rather be hanged from Loch-maben Castle walls than give it up, it being his brother's possession, "and you know what has to be done"—a pregnant phrase.

There is more in this vein, Johnny protesting that he will advance the marriage "as much as any poor man in the realm", but not if Wharton is going to allow his possessions to be spoiled. Lastly, if the English would return what they had taken from the Maxwells, Johnny would release the recently-taken English prisoners.

Considering how closely Maxwell had been negotiating with Eng-land, the letter seemed merely to confirm his treachery— "bragging his treasons", as Wharton put it. The Warden's reaction was savage. He condemned ten Scottish hostages to be hanged, and several were executed at once, among them being one John Maxwell who was next in succession to Johnny and his brother for the Maxwell chieftainship. Also hanged was Sir Herbert Maxwell, vicar of Caerlaverock, "who had the greatest wit and invention of them all".

Wharton spared the others for ten days, "to prevent more dis-pleasure among the blood of Maxwell"—a remarkable reason in the circumstances. He also wrote to Somerset to assure him that his defeat by the Douglases had not been as bad as it was made out, and that he trusted he would yet cause the Johnstones and others "to be a scourge to the Maxwells".

Indeed, Wharton was probably telling the truth about his Nithsdale foray. One account of it suggested that he knew in advance he would be ambushed, but believed his band was strong enough to come through;[2] in the event, he seems to have fought a cool retreat and mauled the Scots considerably. But the Douglases kept his temperature up subsequently by sending him a message in which Angus observed blandly that while he and his brother George Douglas had been able to please King Henry and other English leaders, it seemed they couldn't please Wharton at all, "and if he will not be satisfied, we will learn him his A.B.C. again."

The effect on Wharton may be imagined. He sent back a reply: "When I was a boy I learned my A.B.C., and if George Douglas and I be in school together, I shall learn him to spell and read two of the first lines."

Thereafter he wrote to Somerset assuring him that in Scotland ballads were being made about Johnny Maxwell's falsehoods, and that Maxwell himself was now being rewarded for his treachery by being given Lord Herries' daughter in marriage, with her considerable inheritance. Johnny was now about thirty-five; the Herries heiress was fourteen. Wharton closed his letter with a promise that his two sons were ready to take on any two sons of Scotland who would take Maxwell's part.

It can be argued that Johnny Maxwell was treacherous; it can also be argued that Wharton, dealing as he did in intrigue and seducing Scots from their national allegiance, deserved to be betrayed. From the length and strength of his correspondence on the subject one concludes that when he died, the word "Maxwell" must have been engraved on his heart.[3]

---

2. A report from Sir Thomas Holcroft on April 16 says 400 English were taken prisoner, with their horses, but that Wharton "handlyte the thyng verey honerably and wytylye". He knew he was being betrayed, but considered his force strong enough; however "some gentylmen of honest houses dyd not so well that day as they myght." Holcroft does not identify the laggards, but does insist that Jack Musgrave and the Bewcastle men served well, and so did the Liddesdale Armstrongs, "or hyt had bene wrong with the Warden".

3. Johnny Maxwell eventually received the Herries title. He had several spells as West March Warden, was a faithful supporter of Mary Queen of Scots, and fought for her at Langside. He also saw the inside of jail, like most of his fellow-nobles, and was at one time accused of being in league with

XXXII

England's grip broken

While Wharton was having his grey hairs increased by the Maxwells, great events were taking place on the other coast. Francis I of France had died soon after King Henry, and under his successor, Henry II, France began to take a much more active interest in Scottish affairs— political union between the two states was not ruled out, and in the meantime the French exerted themselves to increase their influence north of the Border. The great Strozzi brought a fleet of galleys to assist Arran in the siege of St Andrews, and in July 1547 the garrison capitulated, John Knox being among those of the defenders who were carried off to France to become galley-slaves.

This was a blow to English policy: plainly she must exert herself. Henry's death had left the country to his son, Edward VI, a bright child, but already doomed with tuberculosis; the government of the realm lay in the hands of Edward Seymour, that Earl of Hertford who had wreaked such mischief in Scotland and was now advanced to the title of Duke of Somerset and Protector. Somerset, while he might

---

wreckers and pirates. In 1565 the Scottish Privy Council investigated his association with the English twenty years before, with remarkable results. It was alleged that he had sold himself to the enemy and had induced others to do the same; the Council noted that after the Battle of Pinkie he had indeed assured with England, but they decided that "he had not offended by so doing". He had accompanied with rebels at Dumfries, but had not aided them. Further allegations were made that "throw him and by his grediness" Scots had been forayed by the English, that he had received 6000 marks to assist England, and had been bribed to sell state secrets. Much of which may have been true, but the Council cleared him absolutely. Late in life he turned Protestant, and died of apoplexy in Edinburgh when he was seventy, on his way to a house "to see the boys bicker". A contemporary described him as one who blustered "full of the Rancour of a Rancke Scotte". No doubt Lord Wharton would have agreed.

behave like Attila the Hun on the Borders, was nevertheless a remarkable man; almost two centuries before his time he foresaw the union of England and Scotland as independent partners, ruled by one monarch, with all the benefits of such alliance accruing to each. If this dream was to be realised, however, French influence in Scotland must be broken and the Scots reminded of where their best interests lay.

Somerset, like all English rulers, knew only one way of demonstrating this: he invaded with fire and sword in September 1547. His army of 18,000 men advanced briskly up the East March, with an accompanying fleet on its right flank, and the two forces converged on Edinburgh, Somerset mopping up one or two strongpoints on the way, including the Hume stronghold of Dunglass. (Of its capitulating garrison the chronicler Patten was moved to remark: "I never saw such a bunch of beggars come out of one house together in my life").

Arran had not been idle in the face of this invasion. The fiery cross had gone out, and summoned an army estimated at almost 30,000; the contending forces met at Pinkie near Edinburgh, on September 10, "Black Saturday". Border riders under Hume opened the ball on the Friday, but were driven off with heavy losses, including Hume himself. Some negotiating followed, in the course of which the Earl of Huntly challenged Somerset to a personal duel (refused), and on the Saturday the ubiquitous Angus led the Scottish vanguard against the enemy, abandoning what had been an advantageous position.

The Scots paid for it, for although they broke the English horse they found themselves enfiladed by the fire of Somerset's gunners and the cannon of his fleet. The English cavalry rallied, and the Scottish army was driven from the field in bloody rout.

The loss on the Scottish side was immense, with about 10,000 dead and 1500 prisoners who included Huntly. Even allowing for the misconduct of the battle by the Scottish generals, and the decisive English artillery advantage, the size of the defeat suggests not only that Somerset's excellently-manned and equipped force fought extremely well, but that the Scots fought extremely badly.

To Somerset it now seemed that all was plain sailing. He had defeated the Scots decisively and was master of her entire Lowlands. He could look on himself as an occupying power, and accordingly he behaved rather more moderately than in his previous invasions. He did not burn Edinburgh, and the destruction of Leith took place against his wishes. He was more concerned to secure and rebuild strongpoints for his garrisons[1]—so enthusiastic was he, in fact, that at Roxburgh he worked himself as a labourer helping to refortify the castle. At the same time he received submission from leading Scots of the Middle and East Marches, principally the Kerrs.

Meanwhile Wharton, aided by the renegade Lennox, was beating up the West March during the winter of 1547–8. Not all his forays were as unsuccessful as the Nithsdale *débâcle* against the Douglases; he and Lennox, with a force which included Armstrongs, Beatties and Littles, as well as broken men, sacked and burned Annan two days before Pinkie, despite a spirited resistance by a garrison of 100 who held the castle and chapel until artillery had reduced it to a ruin. As a result those Borderers in the area who had not already submitted now made their peace with the English Warden.

England's grip on southern Scotland was now stronger than it had been since Wallace's time, and was extended throughout the winter. It was time for Stage Two of Somerset's operation: the proposal of peace and union, with Scottish independence assured, English claims north of the Border to be renounced, and the countries to be ruled by the children of Edward and Mary. Even the national names could be forgotten, and replaced by "Britons".

For that age, it was a remarkably generous proposal, although to a sensitive Scot, even today, it will doubtless seem unacceptable on emotional (and possibly practical) grounds. But one wonders what a Scottish national referendum would have shown, had such a thing been possible in 1548? Southern Scots (and Northern English) who had survived the hell of the 1540s, who were perforce living like animals in the ruin of their countryside, who did not know what it was to sleep secure at night, or plant and reap a crop in security, or bear a child with a fair chance of seeing it grow, might have thought Somerset's offer fair. It is easy to turn it down at a safe distance, but from among the wasted hovels of Teviotdale the view was probably rather different.

But of course there were no referenda: there never are. And possibly

---

1. In November 1547 the English commander, Lord Grey of Wilton, received an offer from one Patrick Kincaid to betray Edinburgh Castle by opening the gates to the English. A reward of 1000 crowns was asked, but although Grey thought the scheme feasible it was not followed up.

Scotland was right to reject Somerset. Certainly the French party were in no doubt; they knew where their advantage lay. At any rate, after Pinkie the last hope for Somerset's plan vanished, and with the nobility faithful to their French paymasters and the clergy firmly opposed to the English heresy, it was finally buried. "Reason," says one historian, "was no match for pride, prejudice, and vested interests."[2]

So the war went on, the little Queen Mary was shipped off to France, French help was forthcoming to carry on the struggle, and the Borderland continued to suffer and survive. Not all of them suffered, of course; for the bold and active there was a good living to be won by plunder, and Wharton was telling no more than the truth when he wrote to Somerset in March 1548 that some Borderers on both sides "desire continual war for their private gain". He certainly did his best to oblige them, and so now did Somerset himself. If Scotland would not come to terms, she must take the consequences. In April Haddington was taken, Musselburgh, Dalkeith and Dunbar were given to the flames, and the country around wasted.

But the drive was now going out of England's effort. With French help Scotland held, the English garrison at Haddington barely managed to hang on by the skin of its teeth, and an invasion by Shrewsbury with 15,000 men was more notable for the atrocities it committed than for any strengthening of England's hold. Teviotdale and Liddesdale were singled out for special attention, and were mercilessly ravaged by German mercenaries under Lord Grey.

The injection of French assistance, notably a force of 6000 under Sieur d'Esse, roused southern Scotland to one last desperate effort. One by one the English garrisons began to fall. Hume Castle succumbed to a night raid; Fast Castle was taken by a daring ruse, the attackers gaining entrance disguised as victuallers, and in the Middle March d'Esse recaptured the hold of Ferniehurst. Under his protection the Scots even began raiding again in strength south of the line, wasting the country round Ford.

England's grip was prised loose only with difficulty, and the fighting that took place across the Border country in 1548–9 was perhaps the cruellest that even the Marches had seen. The Scots, paying back the

---

2. A. F. Pollard, *The Reformation under Edward VI* (Cambridge Modern History, 1907), p. 487.

ravages of years, were pitiless, and one hears even of their buying English prisoners from the French in order to slaughter them. The English gave back atrocity for atrocity, and when Hume Castle failed to fall to a counter-attack the English besiegers wreaked their disappointment in Teviotdale and beyond. Now was the time when assured Scots began to turn on their former employers, with a consequent deepening of hatred on both sides; Wharton reported to Somerset in June 1548 that French money was beginning to draw away many of the Scots that were under oath to England, so that "many of the greatest thieves have had at one time in their purses both of His Majesty's and of the French king's". At the same time, wrote Wharton, "there are more riots and misdemeanours within these two months than in three or four years before". The English occupation was breaking up in blood and fire, and in the last resort the slow liberation of the Scottish Border was a fitting climax to the hideous destruction it had endured in the previous years.

England's expulsion was hastened by her own domestic difficulties. Peasant rebellion in the south, religious dissension, and renewed war with France combined to drain her energy from the northern Border, and early in 1549 the dreadful war came to an end. England's garrisons were withdrawn, and assurances given that she would never attack Scotland again.

But of course the damage was done, finally and irrevocably. Whatever treaties were drawn, the Border had been taught once again the harsh lesson it had been learning for 250 years—that might was right, that wolves survived where sheep went under, that security existed only in the sword and the tower. If King Henry's war had never taken place things might not have been very different in the second half of the century; one can only speculate. But it is certain that any hope of a lasting peace on the Marches vanished finally in the smoke that drifted up from Liddesdale, Teviotdale, the valleys of the Annan and the Nith, and across the plains of the Merse. King Henry had lit the fire in which the steel of the frontier received its final tempering.

XXXIII

The Debateable Land

A few minutes' drive north of Carlisle on the main road one comes to a fine new motorway bridge across the River Esk. It is, nevertheless, called the Metalbridge; beneath it the Esk runs wide through red sandbanks towards the Solway, and on one's right hand, looking north-east beyond the river, the meadows and hedges stretch away into the distance towards the dimly-seen Border hills.

That meadow country, so green and even and quiet, looks like typically British farm-land, which it is. It is hard to imagine that once upon a time it could have laid claim to being the toughest quarter in Britain. In a sense it belongs in the same class as the Khyber Pass, the Badman's Territory, the Barbary Coast, or even Harlem, Soho and the Gorbals. It has no name of its own nowadays, but once it was called the Debateable Land.

There is a good deal of misunderstanding about the name, just as there was about the area itself. Some people wrongly apply it to the whole Border country, and there were in fact other little pockets on the frontier, far away on the East and Middle Marches, which were known as "threap" or disputed territory—a natural enough thing on a Border as troubled as this one. But only one area was known as *the* Debateable Land, and it is the country which stretches away in a narrow strip north-eastward from the Metalbridge.

This is the very hub of the Border country. Just a mile or so from the bridge to the north is the place where Wharton's lances shattered a great Scottish army in the rout of Solway Moss; running into the Esk close by the bridge is the little River Line, and it was in the crook of these two rivers that the Scots van was caught before it was hurled back across the Esk into the moss beyond. Through these fields Buccleuch led his night-riders to Carlisle to rescue Kinmont Willie; going the other way, the great English Warden raids advanced to harry the West March; barely two miles on from the bridge is Gretna (probably the best-known name in the whole Borderland because of its smithy for runaway marriages), and there the Debateable Land reaches its western limit, at the little River Sark which is itself the Border line.

But the length of the Debateable Land stretches away from Metalbridge and Gretna for another dozen or so miles, almost to the little town of Langholm on the north, and the mouth of Liddesdale. Between the two, and farther north still lies the Tarras Moss, where the riders hid their families and cattle when the law, Scottish or English, came riding in force to ferret them out.

So it is not a big stretch of country, perhaps about four miles wide at most, and over twelve long. But what it lacked in size it made up in quality.

It was called the Debateable Land as long ago as the fifteenth century, because its ownership was disputed between England and Scotland; it was a constant menace and nuisance to them both. The most peaceful kind of dispute was about fishing rights, but that was just the tip of the iceberg. Investigation and inquiries were frequently made to try to settle the fate of the Debateable ground, without much success, and in the unsettled times it became more and more of a thorn in the flesh of both kingdoms.

The trouble was that since neither side would admit its ownership by the other, so neither side could hold the other responsible for the activities of people living there. Naturally, there were those on the Border quick to see the advantage of residence, and it became a resort for the worst elements on the frontier—which was saying something. "A most strong ground for offenders to be relieved in" Wharton called it. And even when well-disposed and peaceful Borderers used the area, for temporarily pasturing their cattle, trouble could easily break out if anyone was foolish enough to put down "stob or stake"—that is, build even a small hut, or do anything that hinted at permanent occupation. This was enough to lead to bloodshed, and with a large and volatile outlaw community on hand as well, there was never any lack of violent activity.

One way of dealing with the area was simply to devastate it, and so make it totally unfit for human habitation. This was done frequently, with as much effect as weeding a garden. The kind of people who were ready to make the Debateable Land their home were not the kind to be permanently discouraged by Warden raids, and as quickly as they were driven out they came back in, and continued to rob and burn as they pleased in both realms. As we have seen, Lord Dacre did his best to keep the Armstrongs out of the area in 1528, and paid dearly for his efforts.

The Armstrongs, who underwent something of a population explosion in the sixteenth century, spilled over into the Debateable Land in large numbers from the surrounding valleys, and were among its most important inhabitants. (For once they were not accompanied by the Nixons, Crosers, and Elliots, who never settled there in a family sense, but only in occasional individual cases). However, they were less of a threat to peace and good order latterly than that other great family of the Debateable Land, the Grahams—"that viperous generation" who so obsessed the younger Scrope during his Wardenship.

The Grahams appeared in numbers in the southern Debateable Land, by the Esk, early in the sixteenth century, settling on both sides of the river. Burghley's list says that Long Will Graham headed the clan, and "planted" eight sons in the area, whose families and inter-relations are painfully set out by Burghley and his secretary. Previously the area had been inhabited by the Storeys, who fled to the Middle March to escape the wrath of Lord Dacre in the 1520s, they having betrayed one of his raids against the Scots (see pp. 227-8).

With the Armstrongs and Grahams in the area, as well as large numbers of unattached Border riff-raff and fugitives, it became necessary to solve the Debateable question, and action was taken as soon as the war of the 1540s had ended. England proposed a simple solution by claiming the whole area; the Scots countered with a proposal for division "so that ilk realme might ken their awin part and puniss the inhabitantis thereof" provided that Canonbie should be entirely in Scotland.

As a preliminary to actual division it was agreed that anyone should be free to rob, burn, plunder, and kill within the Debateable Land without being held guilty of any crime; this, it was felt, would discourage the inhabitants if anything could. To drive the point home Lord Maxwell, the Scottish Warden, devastated the area in 1551, and left no buildings standing. There was still a school of thought that held this was the best solution, and that the area should be evacuated and permanently laid waste, but possibly because it was such excellent land, and devastation had never worked satisfactorily in the past, the proposal for division went ahead. In 1552, with the French Ambassador on hand to see fair play, the commissioners of both sides met to cut the

Debateable Land in two. Douglas of Drumlanrig was among those on the Scottish side, with Wharton in the forefront for England.

Fighting did not actually break out at the meeting, but it may have been a near thing. Both sides had schoolboy ideas of what constituted equal halves, and finally it was left to the French Ambassador to split the difference; he gave the Scots the lion's share, but Wharton was not disposed to argue, and the new frontier was marked by a trench and bank dug on a straight east–west line, and called to this day the Scots Dike. Stones were set up bearing the English and Scottish arms, the Scottish Lord High Treasurer, among a tremendous catalogue of expenses, splashed £1 4s. on "ane greitt cord of gold and silk to hing the greite seill of the confirmation, upoun the treaty", and there was general satisfaction all round, in which the locals joined with renewed outbreaks of raiding.

But although the Debateable Land continued to be known by its old name, and remained virtually as evil and as great a resort of thieves as ever, the respective Wardens at least now knew the extent of their responsibilities, and it was officially possible to proceed against malefactors under Border law. The division of 1552 was a slight gain for the commissioners engaged in negotiating to restore some semblance of order after the disastrous war of the 1540s. It was at least a sign that co-operation had returned to the administration of the Marches.

XXXIV

The women's touch

In the peculiar history of the Anglo-Scottish Border, the decade of the 1550s is a watershed. The last great war between the two countries was over; the half-century ahead, although it was occasionally to be disturbed by large armed invasions, was officially "peace-time". At least, it was peace-time in a political sense, but not in a social one. Those next fifty years were to see the phenomenon of Border reiving flourishing more strongly than ever without warlike excuse and without military direction. The Border raider, trained and shaped by warfare, was now to develop his potential to the full within a peace-time social framework.

Those middle years of the century were crucial for both England and Scotland. The Reformation reached a critical stage and the political balance was importantly altered. It is an interesting coincidence that at this period the scene was, for the first time, dominated by women—indeed, the British Isles has never had such a concentration of feminine power at the heart of its affairs: Marie of Scotland, widow of James V; Mary of England and her sister, the great Elizabeth; and Marie's daughter, the ill-starred Mary Queen of Scots. John Knox commented memorably on this situation. But the great events of the '50s had less direct and immediate effect on the Borderland than those of Henry's reign, when the frontier had been an important theatre of political action. Now the pressures had shifted elsewhere, and from a Border viewpoint the decade can look almost like a breathing space—rather laboured breathing, perhaps, but a comparatively quiet time after the holocaust of the '40s.

After the peace of 1550 the authorities on both sides moved to set their frontiers in order. War had ceased, but the local officials were under no illusions as to what would follow. Frontier administration and co-operation between the Wardens, which had fallen into ruin during the war, had to be built up again. Scotland's Marches, which had not seen a judicial expedition from the central power in almost ten years, now received five in the space of eighteen months, in which an attempt was made to quell the lawless elements of the Debateable Land and Liddesdale. On the other side England, having withdrawn from her Scottish garrisons, began to strengthen her frontier defences; forts and strongholds were surveyed, and additional bodies of troops brought in. The Earl of Warwick was appointed Warden-General, and created Duke of Northumberland; he made a point of examining defences personally and giving justice, and most important of all, he brought in Wharton to be his deputy-general, with Sir Thomas Dacre, Lord Eure, Sir Richard Musgrave, and Lord Coniers in subordinate posts. If it had weaknesses, it was still a vastly experienced team, with Wharton the driving force.

The rules that he now laid down for frontier security have been described in Chapter XII. They were tantamount to a great police operation, with provision for watches, garrisons, and prompt alarms; on paper they were extremely good, and if they did not work perfectly in practice it was not for want of zeal on Wharton's part. He knew what he was up against, and was determined to overlook nothing: in 1552 Berwick was even being told to get its streets properly paved, because they were "so foul that on alarm the soldiers cannot pass through to repair to the walls".

On the Scottish side it was rather harder to make provision for Border security, even in theory. There was a wilder element to deal with, and it included those who held the Warden offices. In 1550 Robert, Lord Maxwell, had celebrated the return of peace by coming over the frontier to assault the Grahams, and had been checked by Dacre. In the Middle March, where during the war the Kerrs had been running with the English, the Kerr–Scott feud was being revived; Buccleuch was cut down by the Kerrs in Edinburgh in October 1552, and Arran, who on one of his Border expeditions had knighted the Lairds of Cessford and Ferniehurst, found himself having to move against them and their allies, the Humes. An ugly situation was avoided by despatching both Kerrs and Humes to the continental wars of the French king, where they were out of harm's way.

At a lower level, the Border was in the kind of highly troubled state inevitable in the aftermath of a long war. The Scottish Council noted the mischief caused by the increasing number of broken men and outlaws, who were finding sanctuary in the Debateable Land and were the principal breakers of the peace. Redesdale and Tynedale were getting into their stride again, harrying daily north of the line; when Johnny Maxwell took over the West March Wardenship from his brother in 1552, he found the job so difficult on account of the feuds in which he was involved that he had to give it up a year later. Even £500 a year would not induce him to take it on again without proper support and powers; his successor, Douglas of Drumlanrig, gave up office after a year.

This rapid turnover of Wardens, which so inhibited proper control on the Scottish side, also troubled the Middle March, although in the East there was more stability with Lord Hume occupying the Warden post for several years. And on the English side, although superficially the Wardens appeared to have better control, it was being noted in 1552 that the "disunion among the inhabitants (of Northumberland) impairs the strength of the frontiers, for they will not help each other, and procure displeasure towards each other by the Scots. They refuse forage and victuals to the soldiers at reasonable prices, saying they had rather the Scots should have or burn it. . . ."

It had not taken long for the frontier to forget the traditional Anglo-Scottish hatred, when it paid them to do so. Within two years of the war's end they were back in the old routine of cross-frontier alliances against authority—these, of course, having been kept alive, even during the hostilities, by those Scots who had for much of the time been in England's service.

Thus many of the good intentions of the central authorities, who did try to improve conditions on the frontier, were nullified by the character and behaviour of the Borderers, and by the authorities' failure to understand Border conditions. Despite good relations between the governments, the Scottish Council were complaining in August 1553 that the English reivers were riding in Scotland night and day, sometimes foraying as deep as twenty miles over the line, and "tendying alway, be al the craft thai can, to provoke the leigis of this realme to do siclyke".

Even truce days were not exempt, for in that same month the Captain of Wark was accused of coming with 180 men across the frontier at Reddenburn, two hours before a Warden meeting, and killing two Scots.

On paper, it can look like a productive and progressive period of Border history, with many meetings of commissioners, revision of Border laws, and overhaul of administrative machinery. But it really amounted to no more than freshly marking the touch-lines of the field for the same old game.

Meanwhile disturbing things were taking place in London, Edinburgh, and Paris. French aid had helped Scotland to keep England at bay, but in the 1550s France was bidding fair to take Scotland over. Marie, James V's widow, became Regent, and French influence was paramount. Many in Scotland viewed these developments with alarm, particularly the adherents of the new Protestantism. In England the reformers faced an even greater menace, for with the death of Edward VI in 1553 the throne had passed to the rigidly Catholic Mary, who in 1554 married the arch-enemy of Protestantism, Philip of Spain. This meant that England was drawn to the Spanish side in France's struggle

with Spain; it was natural that a French-dominated Scotland should be
in the opposite camp if Queen Regent Marie could so contrive it.

Thus England and Scotland found themselves drawn into a conflict
which neither wanted, but which was forced upon them by their
continental allies. The Scottish nobles were especially unwilling, and
the Queen Regent had to force the issue by provocative acts along the
Border. This was not difficult, for after the fine flourish of commissioners' meetings, treaties, and frontier discussion had spent itself,
conditions on the Marches had deteriorated rapidly in the middle
years of the decade. The number of forays and crimes rapidly out-
stripped the ability of the Warden courts to deal with them, and at one
time in 1556 there were at least 1000 bills of complaint unredressed in a
single March.[1] The Liddesdale men were rapidly getting the better of the
authorities, and an expedition by Douglas of Drumlanrig and Patrick,
Lord Bothwell to put down the Armstrongs was easily repulsed.

So local conditions were ripe, as they normally were in peace-time,
for exploitation into war. In 1557 Henri D'Oysel, the French lieutenant
in Scotland, whose word under Marie was law in the land, refortified
Eyemouth in defiance of the peace treaty with England; the Berwick
garrison tried to knock it down again, and so the fighting started. In
August a Scottish force was in the English East March, harrying along
the Till and menacing Ford Castle, but Henry Percy raised the country
against them, and the Scots retreated. Percy promptly retaliated, by a
quick foray into the Merse, where he burned more than a dozen villages and brought off 4000 head of stock, as well as horses and prisoners.

Within a week the Scots were back, in force this time, with Huntly
at their head and a strong body of French under D'Oysel. To meet
them England hurriedly summoned all the strength she could; Thomas
Percy, 7th Earl of Northumberland,[2] his younger brother Henry Percy,

---

1. Wharton, in a brief note of "attemptates" drawn up in May 1557, and
covering an unspecified period (probably about three years) lists a total of
922 Scottish raids in the East and Middle Marches, with thirty-two killings,
two burnings, twenty-two receipts of fugitives, "and the rest robberies to
the total value of £10,228 16s 8d".

2. The Northumberland title had now returned to the Percies, who had lost
the earldom in 1537 for rebellion. In the interval John Dudley, Earl of
Warwick, had been made Duke of Northumberland, but had gone to the
block in 1553 for his leadership of the Lady Jane Grey conspiracy.

and Wharton from the west mustered horse and foot in the East March, and while Wharton concentrated on making Berwick secure the Percies turned on the Scottish army.

It was too big to be fully attacked, but Henry Percy and his riders did what they could, Border fashion, and were driven off for their pains with the loss of 100 men. The Scots, however, were more interested in loot than conquest, and withdrew after destroying several villages; thereafter the two armies, neither of which had any desire to fight, lay on the Border and scouted each other.

This policy of inactivity suited the English and the Protestant Scots, but it was not good enough for Queen Regent Marie and her French party, who wanted war. Accordingly Her Majesty came in person with a new army, commanded by the former Earl of Arran, who since Marie had succeeded him as the head of affairs had been operating modestly under the title of Duke of Chatelherault. The army marched by way of Kelso, advancing on the Border with ferocious caution. Short of the line it stopped, and the Scots nobles announced that they would on no account cross the frontier; if Queen Marie wanted to fight the English, that was her affair and France's, but the Scots were having none of it.

Remonstrations followed, and the gallant Sieur D'Oysel announced that since the Scots were reluctant he and his men would champion Her Majesty's cause and uphold the honour of France. Accordingly he set off with his artillery to besiege Wark as a preliminary to invasion, no doubt with the good wishes of the Scottish nobles following him. When he had gone, however, their indignation against D'Oysel seems to have increased, for they sent messages recalling him; at the same time, to convince the disconsolate Marie that they meant business, they disbanded the army.

The English Borderers had observed all this with interest, and what might have been predicted happened. D'Oysel's artillery train, labouring back from Wark, was ambushed and was fighting a successful rearguard action when the Wark garrison joined in, and the invaders fled for their lives across the Tweed.

The English possibly thought they had had a lucky escape, since the Scottish army had been so powerful, and the defences of the East March were by no means secure. So Northumberland took no chances; D'Oysel's French, simmering with indignation, were still at Eyemouth, and there were French garrisons menacingly close to the frontier. The English policy was to watch the line, and keep the Scots and French occupied by raiding. One ambitious foray under Henry Percy almost turned into a full-scale battle, for the Northumbrians were engaged by a powerful force of Kerrs, and were only saved from rout by the personal bravery of Sir John Forster, who laid about him with such effect that, although he was badly wounded and had a horse killed under him, the English rallied and won the day.

Reading of this, and the inroads which were made on both sides during the following year of 1558, an outsider might suppose that both countries were prosecuting the war with vigour. This was not so; neither Scottish nor English had the least interest in fighting on behalf of France or Spain, and the raiding of 1558 was simply normal Border foraying, with the official state of hostilities merely making it possible to plunder under government licence, so to speak. So while little Mary Queen of Scots was marrying the Dauphin (and secretly selling her country to France) it was coincidence that at about the same time Scots and English were slaughtering each other heartily in the Merse.

The occasion for this was a powerful raid by Henry Percy, with Berwick garrison men and Border riders, about 3000 in all. They rounded up many cattle, burned a few places, including Duns, and were heading home when a Scottish force of about the same size caught up with them at Swinton. There was a stern fight which the English riders eventually decided, breaking the ranks of the Scottish horse, and with Percy playing a leading role in the English victory.

The Percy brothers were busy that summer, for shortly after Swinton they repulsed a large Scottish foray on the Till, although without doing it much damage, and followed up by themselves crossing the Border and burning Ednam. Henry Percy was less fortunate against another Scottish raid under Bothwell towards Fenton, the English riders being routed by the steady fire of the Scottish reivers and over 100 captured.

Official skirmishing there was also, on no great scale, for neither side wished to provoke the other unduly. The war was dying for lack of enthusiasm; England had other things to occupy her, and Scotland was heartily sick of the French, who were greedy and disturbing guests, and whose presence was regarded as a check to the increasing popularity of Protestantism. John Knox, long free from his servitude at the oar of a French galley, was back in Scotland in 1559 after a spell of preaching in the Borders, and with that tremendous human dynamo behind it the Scottish Reformation was nearing accomplishment. The story has been told elsewhere; sufficient to say here that as the decade closed two important deaths occurred which dealt the final quietus to Catholic (and French) hopes in Britain.

England had been suffering from what appears to have been an influenza epidemic, and among its victims was Queen Mary. A miserable, syphilitic creature, cursed by a deplorable father and an even more abominable husband, she remains the only woman in history to be remembered by the crowningly insulting nickname "Bloody". Poor soul, she earned it. She was succeeded in November 1558 by her sister Elizabeth, a formidably-educated, clever, thoroughly resourceful and canny young woman of twenty-five, who had already learned much of politics and even more of life. Like so many of the best British monarchs, she had had her eyes opened early to the dirtier sides of human nature, and had learned the lesson of survival.

Among the troubles she inherited with her crown was a Scottish Border which was, in the oft-repeated phrase, tickly. It had to be secured, but even more important, the possibility of Franco-Scottish invasion must be checked within Scotland itself. Elizabeth's cousin, Mary Queen of Scots, was now Queen of France also, and had an arguable claim to the throne of England; it was time for England to rescue Scotland from its now unwelcome French alliance, and at the same time remove any threat to Elizabeth from north of the Border.

Thus in early 1560 there came the unusual sight of a friendly English fleet off Leith, and a friendly English army joining the Protestant Scots against the occupying French, whose situation was now hopeless. They fought as best they could, but with the second important death—that of the Scottish Queen Regent Marie, in the summer—France gave up the struggle. Under the treaty of Edinburgh French influence in Scotland died, Protestantism was triumphant, and Elizabeth's forces could be withdrawn. For the first time in almost a generation, the Scots were more or less free of foreign troops.

However, although conditions should now have been right for Anglo-Scots relations to develop harmoniously, no one was over-optimistic about the Border country. The religious struggle was not finally settled in the reformers' favour, and both sides were conscious that as far as the

Borderers had any religion at all they inclined to the old faith. And the end of the war did not mean the end of frontier violence, which could be expected to continue in the peace-time raiding tradition.

So it was not surprising that England should continue to strengthen her northern defences, both to be ready to help the Protestants in Scotland if necessary, and to keep the March riders at bay. Berwick's fortifications were improved, the garrison increased and better paid—a typical piece of Elizabethan parsimony had been seen in 1559, when a pay rise of three pence a day for the soldiers was rejected—and the place turned into a sort of Elizabethan Aldershot. All this was the more necessary because Border administration was at a low ebb. For the past four years the Scottish central power had not made a judicial expedition to the frontier, the Wardens on both sides left much to be desired, blackmail was flourishing, and there was little local justice to be had.

For this the Wardens were principally to blame. William Dacre and Maxwell, who faced each other in the West, were indifferent officers, and did not get on; in the East Lord Grey was more successful for England than Hume was for Scotland; in the Middle Marches Walter Kerr of Cessford conformed more or less to the standard pattern of his clan, which is to say that he was as much bandit as peace officer, and opposite him in England there had just been appointed one of the most controversial figures in frontier history, the experienced old rascal John Forster. He was to set a record for Warden service, and to be a central character in events until almost the end of Elizabeth's reign.

These were not the men to control the wilder elements of the Marches, although admittedly their job was not an easy one in the aftermath of the years of warfare. And however disordered the frontier was, looked at from a distance it may have seemed comparatively settled; at least Elizabeth thought so when she referred to "a better peace betwixt the realms than ever was heard of in any time".

XXXV

Queen on the Marches

Given stability within Scotland in the next few years Elizabeth's statement might have come true, but stability was not what Scotland was going to get. The principal disturbing influence was an unusually tall and attractive auburn-haired girl who landed at Leith towards the end of summer in 1561. Vivacious, gay, and eighteen, in our own time she would probably have been a highly successful fashion model and jet setter. Unfortunately she was the Queen of Scotland, and John Knox groaned at the sight of her. Her own high spirits may have been equally damped, for she came to a Scotland which was wet and woeful after the cheerful French court which she had left.

The tragedy of Mary Queen of Scots is too well known to need much repetition, except where it touches on Border history, which it sometimes did. She has been represented as a heroine, hardly used by fate; on the other hand one historian has referred to her as the original gangster's moll. It is a question of point of view, usually highly coloured by sentiment. No doubt she had a difficult task, for which her upbringing had ill prepared her—one would sympathise with anyone born to rule Scotland. But whatever gifts she brought to it, statecraft and judgement were hardly among them. Her perception and handling of affairs was on a par with her taste in men, which was deplorable. Her first husband, Francis II of France, had died in 1560; of her next two one was to be blown up and thereafter strangled, and the other to die in a dungeon.

Her main misfortune, of course, and Scotland's, was that as a Roman Catholic monarch with at least pretensions to the English as well as the Scottish throne, she was to be a focus for Catholics throughout Britain, and a menace to her cousin Elizabeth. It would have taken a cleverer woman than Mary Stewart to avoid the pitfalls before her.

However, she was ready to please at the beginning, and shortly after her return to Scotland she was trying to smooth matters with England by dealing with her Borders, which were "impacient of all good ordouris". Justice courts were arranged for Dumfries and Jedburgh, and her bastard half-brother James Stewart led a successful expedition which, employing men from eleven counties, armed and provisioned for three weeks, descended on the reivers of the Middle March, capturing and hanging between twenty and thirty of the most notorious offenders. Their strong places were destroyed, more than forty leading prisoners were taken to Edinburgh, and the local leaders summoned and instructed to keep good order. James Stewart also met Forster and Grey, the English Wardens, to discuss measures for the future.

It was a promising start, and in the following summer Lord James followed it up with a descent on Hawick in which twenty-eight reivers were summarily executed by drowning in the Teviot; others were hanged or jailed. If this did not put the wild men of the West and Middle Marches out of business, it checked them temporarily, and just briefly in the next two years it began to look as though central authority might be beginning to get on top of the Border problem. The Wardens were co-operating well, and in 1563 commissioners of both sides were meeting at Carlisle and Dumfries under command to proceed "not as parties for one or other kingdom", according to Ridpath, "but with perfect indifference".

There was a wealth of Border experience on the 1563 commission, including John Maxwell from the Scottish West March, John Forster, and the new English West March Warden, Henry, Lord Scrope of Bolton. He had served as Marshal of the Field in the English army which had helped the Scots against the French in 1560; if he had not the intimate local knowledge of men like Forster and Maxwell, he had intelligence, energy, and honesty, and was to become one of the best Wardens in Border history.

The commissioners' job was really to bring Border law and custom up to date, as well as redressing grievances, and the treaty they made operated for the next twenty-five years, while the reiving system was approaching its zenith. Its most important details have been touched on in Chapter XIX, and it seems to have been comprehensive enough. In practice, like most Border treaties, it was less useful than it might appear in theory.

For the moment all went well on the frontier, principally because both queens were anxious to do nothing to offend each other. Mary was still hoping to be named next in succession to the English throne, and Elizabeth, well aware of papist threats at home and abroad, was intent on avoiding trouble with Scotland. The Scottish Privy Council records of 1564 testify to the good order that was being kept along the line; the most serious complaint before the councillors seems to have been that Walter Kerr, in the Middle March, was not receiving the assistance of local leaders as he should, and the Council accordingly issued instructions to gentlemen and clan chiefs "to serve the Warden and attend him on truce days". A similar reminder was also necessary to the leading men in the West March.

It was the quiet before the storm again. Late in 1564 the Elliot–Scott feud broke out, and after the normal preliminaries of murder, complaint to the authorities, and a few executions (three men were beheaded in Edinburgh by torchlight), the vendetta blazed up violently in 1565. The Elliots, under the expert leadership of Martin Elliot of Braidley, raided the Scott country, burning and plundering, and the Scotts demanded the right to make legal reprisal. Before they got the chance, the Elliots were back again, with their Croser and Nixon allies and various loose riders from the Debateable Land; they came in a band 300 strong, devastating and killing over a wide area of Buccleuch's territory.

The Scotts struck back at Liddesdale, killing several Crosers and Elliots and driving off many cattle. The Elliots, finding themselves considerably outnumbered, looked for help to England, and offered to deliver up to Elizabeth the castle of Hermitage in return for protection. Scrope, who received the offer, wisely rejected it, along with the Elliot's suggestion that they should become subjects of the English crown. He probably foresaw that such an interference in Scottish affairs would have shaken loose the whole Border, and almost certainly led to open war. But the English Wardens could not resist the temptation to assist mischief on the Scottish side so far as it was safe to do so, and when Maxwell, on Queen Mary's instructions, asked their help in quieting the Scottish West March, they refused and sat tight. "The longer such conditions continue . . . the better quiet we shall be," observed Forster; and to keep the pot boiling money was smuggled across to the Elliots to assist them in their struggle with the Scotts, with hints of more to follow.

To the Elliots this was manna from heaven. They were in the best of all possible worlds, for they were finding the English Wardens most accommodating in the matter of providing sanctuary in England when the Scott pressure built up, and the Elliots were forced to slip over the Border. They repeatedly offered to become English, and to bring the Armstrongs with them, but Forster and Scrope were too canny for that; why should they go to such lengths when the Elliots were doing England's work anyway, keeping the Scottish Marches in constant turmoil?

The Elliots would probably not have got away with it for so long if they had not been assisted by conditions inside Scotland. In the summer of 1565, while the Elliots were winning the most spectacular battle of the feud by bushwhacking the Scotts in a mountain pass, Queen Mary was marrying that "fair, jolly young man", the worthless Henry Stewart, Lord Darnley. In his own right he had a claim to the English succession through his descent from Margaret Tudor, and the matrimonial alliance of two such rivals was more than Elizabeth could stomach. She gave her support to the Scottish Protestant nobles who opposed the marriage, and who rose in rebellion under that Lord James Stewart who had so successfully suppressed the wilder Scottish Borderers in 1561, and was now Earl of Moray.

In the crisis Mary showed up well. She rallied her supporters, reassured the Protestants, and showed the Stewart bravery and charm at its best. It worked, not least in the Borders, where the majority of the most powerful tribes came out in her favour—the Humes in the East March, the Kerrs of both Ferniehurst and Cessford, and Maxwell in the West. Moray and his associates found their rebellion dying stillborn; there did not seem to be much hope of sufficient help from England to enable them to win. Meanwhile that staunch supporter of Mary's, James Hepburn, Earl of Bothwell, was down on the Borders trying to talk the Elliots out of their Scott feud and English friendship, into siding with the Queen.

It was an unusual and delightful situation for the Elliots. Both sides were wooing them; there was English money to be had (although Elizabeth, typically, was inclined to cut in half the amount of Elliot subsidy proposed by her Wardens); on the other hand, they could do a deal with the Scottish authorities. One gathers that they did quite well out of both sides.

In any event, Mary had sufficient strength to chase Moray's rebels over the frontier, and they took refuge in Carlisle, where their retreat had been covered by 300 soldiers specially detached from the Berwick garrison. The unfortunate Moray thereafter presented himself to Elizabeth, his sponsor, and was dismissed with offensive language.

All this turmoil on the Borders had the inevitable side-effect. The Liddesdale riders and broken men took advantage of the situation to raid far and wide, especially in the English East March, and the Warden, Francis Russell, Lord Bedford, protested against the lack of control exercised by Kerr of Cessford over his tribesmen. Since Bedford had been acting on secret instructions from Elizabeth to create mischief in the Scottish East March, it was a case of the biter bit.

However, Bedford followed up his protest with a large reprisal raid into the Merse, 800 of his men attacking Chirnside and Edington and carrying off prisoners and loot, with some slaughter. The excuse was that he had been arresting Scottish thieves, had been ambushed, and had had to stage a rescue in force. At about this time Bedford was complaining that Bothwell and his "rank riders" were spoiling the victualling train by which the Berwick garrison was supplied.

Thus in a few short months the Borders had slipped back into their customary chaotic state, thanks largely to the policies of the central governments. Liddesdale was riding again harder than ever, the Middle Marches were disordered, Maxwells and Johnstones were at feud, and "Scottish rebels, withdrawn to England, resort to Scotland as though they were true lieges, seducing good subjects". The pattern had been re-established with a vengeance.

Events at the heart of Scottish affairs ensured that trouble would continue. Mary had discovered that her husband's handsome exterior covered a repulsive nature; he was jealous of her precedence and of any attention she bestowed on other men, particularly her secretary, an Italian musician named David Rizzio, whose Latin elegance and increasing influence with the Queen both rendered him detestable. On a March night of 1566 Darnley and his associates broke in on the Queen at Holyrood, dragged the shrieking Rizzio from her side, and splashed his blood over her threshold in a murder as callous and spiteful as may be found even in Scottish history. The wonder is that Mary, who was pregnant at the time, survived and kept her reason. Not only that; she bided her time until opportunity served to revenge her on the assassins.

Moray, a fugitive in England after his abortive rebellion, came back to Scotland and a pardon; his return was to be significant for the Borderers, for he was eventually to repeat the raids with which he had tried to tame them in Mary's early days. In the summer following Rizzio's death, however, it was the Queen herself, and that rising star of the frontier, the Earl of Bothwell, who were to undertake the pacification of the Marches, with near-fatal consequences.

Mary's child was born in June, and on the surface she was reconciled with her husband. At the same time she appears—this is a point on which historians will argue forever—to have fallen in love with Bothwell, the man "sold to all wickedness" who was her lieutenant of the Border country, and as some will have it, her evil genius. However, it was with Darnley that she announced her intention of proceeding to the Marches in that summer to give justice at Jedburgh; "crewell murthere" had "becum commoun nocht onelie among thame that hes quarrell, bot kynnisfolk unnaturalie slayis utheris", and she instructed her leading men to attend her at Melrose with twenty days' provisions for a campaign against the thieves.

Nothing came of it, and when the Queen did visit the Borders in autumn, it was with Bothwell and Moray in her train. This expedition has been partly described in Chapter XXIII; during it Bothwell, it will be remembered, suffered from a surfeit of Elliots and was lucky to escape with his life. The Queen toured in the Middle and East Marches, behaving graciously, and meeting not only her own Wardens but also English officers, including Forster. However, her gentle touch left the frontier as bad as ever.

Mary's reign was now approaching its end. Early in 1567 Darnley was murdered by explosion at Kirk o' Field, Bothwell's wrecking crew applying the finishing touch by strangling the unfortunate victim. As to Mary's complicity in the crime, which her defenders usually deny, it can only be said that when a woman marries her husband's murderer, people will talk. But this she did, only three months later, and so ensured her own overthrow.

Whatever was the truth of Mary's relations with Bothwell, whether she went willingly to the altar with him or not, and whatever may be said against his character, which is plenty, one thing is evident—for sheer hard nerve he would be a difficult man to beat. He had stood trial for Darnley's killing, with a troop of his Border riders close by to see that justice miscarried; once acquitted, he carried Mary off and married her, gambling his life for a kingdom. It was too much for some of the

Scottish nobles, and for some of the Border chieftains. The Humes, Kerrs and Scotts came down against Bothwell; his hopes of raising a Border force collapsed, and with Hume's riders on their tail Bothwell and the Queen found their situation desperate. Mary surrendered, to be imprisoned in Lochleven, Bothwell made good his escape, and Mary was forced to abdicate in favour of her son, the little Prince James, with Moray as Regent.

Borderers had been important actors in the drama of Mary's decline and fall, and as usual when the Marchmen were drawn into mainstream politics, conditions along the frontier deteriorated. In the few months from Darnley's death to the abdication there was panic and alarm on the English side. Troops were mustered, not only to intervene against the Bothwell faction if need be, but to protect the English Marches from the inroads of Scottish riders who exploited the political unrest to the full. It was a stormy summer; Biggar, a prosperous little town which had hitherto been immune from raiding, was attacked and despoiled by the Liddesdale reivers, who also struck deep into England; frontier administration broke down, and when the Scottish Privy Council ordered the leading chieftains to appear in Edinburgh the summons was ignored. By early summer the depredations all along the line were so bad that the Council compared the situation to open war.

To this situation the new Regent, Moray, applied himself with his customary energy. One of his first acts as ruler was to summon the Humes to answer for the East March, but for the tougher districts he employed the only effective weapons, rope and steel. The autumn found him suddenly at Hawick, where about forty leading thieves were surprised and either executed or imprisoned. It served for the moment; Moray had a possible civil war to worry about, for the imprisoned Queen's party were still strong and active. They received a considerable fillip with Mary's escape from Lochleven in the spring of 1568; she gathered an army and staked her last claim to Scotland when she encountered Moray's forces at Langside, not far from the present field of Hampden Park, Glasgow, which is nowadays given over to battles of an equally desperate but generally less bloody sort.

It was a brief, decisive fight. The Borderers, as usual, were present and, as usual, were on both sides. Hume fought like a lion for Moray, being wounded several times, and on one occasion being dragged to his feet again by Walter Kerr of Cessford, who was also on the Regent's side. The Ferniehurst Kerrs, on the other hand, fought for Mary, along with the Johnstones and that well-known West March veteran, Johnny Maxwell of Herries. Not for the first time, he found himself on the wrong side, for Mary's forces were thrashed out of sight in a little over half an hour, and the Queen was in flight again.

The West March seemed the safest place, and there she rode with a small band of supporters, including Herries. But Scotland was too hot to hold her, and in the hope that royal blood might be thicker than water, she determined to fly to England. On May 16 she sailed from Dundrennan across the Solway and landed well south of the Border area, at Workington in Cumberland. The following day she rode inland to Cockermouth, on the fringe of Lakeland, where the English deputy Warden of the West March, Richard Lowther, met her and escorted her to Carlisle.

Mary was still only 25, and would live until middle age, but she would never be free again. The long captivity which would end on the scaffold at Fotheringay when the little dog scampered out from beneath the red skirt on the headless body, began at Carlisle Castle. They treated her kindly; that part of the castle where she lived has since been destroyed by fire, but they still play football on the broad meadows of the Bitts Park and the Sheepmount beneath its walls, where she watched a game four centuries ago. She was too dangerous a figure to keep so close to the frontier for long, even in the strongest hold in the Marches, and presently she was moved south to Bolton Castle, the home of Scrope, the West March Warden. She never saw the Border again, but it felt her influence for years to come.

XXXVI

The Countess and the reivers

Everywhere that Mary went, trouble was sure to follow. She might be a prisoner, banished from her own land, but she was a focus for violence and intrigue. As a direct result of her arrival in England the Border suffered, in the two years after Langside, two major rebellions on the English side, and consequent disorder in the Scottish Marches. Running through these events was the thread of one of the strangest, most romantic stories of the frontier, in which some of the leading nobles in England found themselves rubbing shoulders with legendary outlaws whose names are now remembered only in ballads.

Following Langside, Moray moved south-west to deal with Mary's supporters on the frontier. He drove through the West March with 6000 riders and supporting infantry, mopping up strongpoints of resistance, hanging thieves, and obtaining pledges of good behaviour. It served for the moment, but the frontier was in a nervous state, with Mary's supporters continuing to harry in England in the hope of provoking war.

On the English side also there was considerable sympathy for the banished queen among those adherents of the old religion who were particularly strong in the North. Thomas Percy, seventh Earl of Northumberland, was especially solicitous, and during her captivity in Carlisle he tried unsuccessfully to have her delivered into his custody.

We are told that he was a jovial easy-going man of forty, devoted to such sports as hawking, and reputedly as popular as only a Percy could be. There is evidence, however, that his tenants did not share the enthusiasm for "Simple Tom" that is commonly shown by romantic historians, whose admiration for the Earl is surpassed only by their ecstasies over his wife, Lady Anne, who has become one of the more idealised Border heroines. Apparently she was beautiful and spirited, and undoubtedly she was devoted to her dim-witted husband.

However, Northumberland, although an easily-led and not over-talented man, had been a reasonably good Warden of the East and Middle Marches, and he was a figure to reckon with in the North. London looked with suspicion on such power-points so far from central control, particularly when they were Papists; Northumberland's father had been out in the Pilgrimage of Grace, and the son's attachment to Mary Queen of Scots set the alarms sounding at Elizabeth's court. It is suggested, not without cause, that Cecil was waiting for a chance to trap Northumberland, whom he detested, and had been provoking him for years in the hope of goading him into revolt: Northumberland was soon to provide the opportunity himself.

Meanwhile raiding from the Scottish side continued, in spite of

Moray's efforts, and in the summer of '68 Elizabeth introduced to the
Border scene a new figure who was to play a leading part on the
frontier for most of her reign. Possibly because she thought he was the
man for the job, but more probably because she wanted someone on
the frontier whom she could trust, she appointed to the Wardenship
of the East March, and Captaincy of Berwick, a rugged, short-tempered
gentleman named Henry Carey.

History knows him by his title of Hunsdon, and for all his inex-
perience of the Border, and the peculiarity of his qualifications, it has
to be said that he was a good Warden—while he was there, for the difficulty throughout his career was to induce him to stay at his post on the
Border. His previous employments had included being Master of the
Queen's Hawks, and Captain of the Gentlemen Pensioners; more important, he was a cousin of Queen Elizabeth's, being the nephew of
Anne Boleyn, but the relationship was quite probably closer than that,
for it was widely believed that Hunsdon was Henry VIII's bastard
son.

He certainly behaved like one, for his notion of Border justice was
that the only good reiver was a dead one—a point of view which has
much to be said for it. Possibly the fact that he suffered from gall-stones
made him irritable, for he started in office as he meant to continue, by
hanging Scottish thieves. And soon he was to prove on a more important scale that Elizabeth's trust in him had not been misplaced.

At first he found a valuable ally to Border justice in Moray, who was
soon voicing golden opinions of him to the English Queen. Moray was
finding the Scottish Borderers a handful throughout 1569, especially
in the West, where the "innumerabil slauchteris, fyre raisingis, herschipps
and detestabil enormities" by the people of Liddesdale were so bad that
the inhabitants of the Scottish East and Middle Marches, in a memorandum to the Privy Council, declared themselves enemies "to all
thieves of Liddesdale, Annandale, Ewesdale, Eskdale and especially to
all Armstrongs, Elliots, Nixons, Crosers, Littles, Batesons, Thomsons,
Irvines, Bells, Johnstones, Glendennings, Routledges, Hendersons, and
Scotts of Ewesdale".

This comprehensive list was signed by Hume, Buccleuch, principal
Kerrs, and others; its effect was to send the named clans, with "their
wives, bairns, etc.", to Coventry. However, Moray believed in more
straightforward methods. He led two expeditions to the West March

during the year, the first having the help of John Forster. This was in March, when Moray, with Hume, Ferniehurst, Cessford and Buccleuch, took 4000 horse and foot into Liddesdale, devastating the whole valley and destroying Mangerton.

It reads like a most effective suppression, for it was followed by the taking of assurances on a large scale. But just how intractable the Armstrongs and their allies were may be judged from the fact that soon after this raid, it was being noted that the whole Border was under control—with the exception of Liddesdale.

Moray was experienced enough to know that there could be no such thing as permanent suppression; he must simply hit Liddesdale and keep on hitting it. Consequently he was back again in October, and put such fear into the inhabitants (for the time being, at least) that "thair wes sic obedience . . . as the lyk wes never done to na king in na mans dayes befoir". Reading the signs, about 100 Armstrongs, Johnstones, Elliots and Grahams gave pledges. These were recorded in vast numbers at Hawick on October 20 1569; they included pledges by various people for their kinsmen, and even for their entire tribe. Some were simply to be of good behaviour, but many agreed to enter themselves to be warded until such time as "good order could be taken with them" —in the meantime they were warded at their own expense. Doubtless this zeal for self-reformation was encouraged by the fact that the Scottish Privy Council had decided that any Middle March people who rode into England thieving should, on the third offence, be hanged forthwith.

In between these raids, Moray was busily occupied elsewhere in Scotland against Mary's supporters, but the Border remained his principal anxiety. There lay Mary's strength, aided and abetted by the Catholic element on the English side, and throughout the summer the rumours spread south of the line of a new rising aimed at the release of the captive Scottish queen, who had been moved again, to Tutbury.

The Earl of Northumberland, and his associate the fiery ne'er-do-well Charles Neville, Earl of Westmorland, were at the heart of the plot, aided and abetted by "Crookback" Leonard Dacre of Naworth, a former deputy Warden of the West March. Not that Dacre cared much for Queen Mary, but he was deeply concerned about the Dacre inheritance, which was then in contention: Dacre's nephew, the heir, had been killed in falling from a vaulting-horse in May, 1569, and the crown had bestowed the estates and title on the Howards, to Leonard Dacre's intense displeasure.

Three more unsuitable leaders of an insurrection it would have been hard to find—Northumberland irresolute and ill-organised, Westmorland reckless, and Dacre unscrupulous and treacherous—a "cankred suttil traitor", as the Queen called him. Word of their intentions leaked south, and Elizabeth summoned the two earls to answer the suspicions against them. This startled the plotters into premature action. Their consciences were guilty enough, for they had been in correspondence with Spain, and hoped for troops under the Duke of Alva to support them; their rebellion even had the blessing of the Pope. Elizabeth's summons convinced Westmorland, at least, that the time had come to strike, and although Northumberland had finally to be persuaded at gunpoint, the banner of revolt was broken out in November, and the Rising of the Northern Earls was under way.

With the Border in its "tickle" state, the strength of its loyalists doubtful, and Moray's ability to prevent Scottish participation uncertain, the situation posed a frightening menace which Elizabeth must crush before it could spread. The riders of Redesdale and Tynedale came out for Northumberland; would Cumberland and the Scottish side rise as well? The rebels were in arms at Brancepeth, and in sign of their intentions they rode on Durham, where they sang Mass in the cathedral, tore the Bible to pieces, and consigned the prayer books to the flames. The Earl of Sussex, the royal lieutenant in the North, was trying to raise forces farther south, and making heavy weather of it; Alnwick and Warkworth fell into the rebels' hands, and now Northumberland turned southward, evidently with the intention of rescuing Queen Mary, who was hurriedly moved to Coventry. The insurgents marched into Yorkshire through a string of small towns, contemplated an attack on York, and finally retreated to attack Barnard Castle, which they took after a pointless siege of almost two weeks. Hartlepool was also occupied, since it was hoped that Alva's troops would arrive there.

Meanwhile, the English West March was on a knife-edge: the Forsters and Hetheringtons were ready to join the rebellion, and a plot was afoot to murder the Bishop of Carlisle and take the castle. His Lordship reported in alarm that there were fifty Hetheringtons in Carlisle town with sixty Scotch fighting men as well. Although Northumberland's insurgents in the east had retreated, it was still a highly dangerous situation all along the line, and disaster might easily have followed had not Moray held the Scottish side in check, preventing help from reaching the rebels. The salutary effect of his Liddesdale expeditions was still strong enough to restrain the wilder elements.

Even so, the rising might have become general in the North of England if Elizabeth had not been so well served by one of her Northern Wardens. John Forster has had a bad press from history; he was, no doubt, a venal old scoundrel with a taste for racketeering and turning a blind eye to Scottish reivers when it suited him, but given a fight in front of him there was no better man in the pinch. While the rebellion hung in the balance he held his ground for Elizabeth, and it is doubtful if anyone could have done it better.

Raising his March riders, and with some of the Berwick garrison, he rode on Warkworth and Alnwick, dislodging the rebels, blocked the passes to prevent further recruits joining Northumberland, and then occupied Newcastle. Here he was joined by Harry Percy, who (typical Borderer) was in arms on the Queen's behalf against his brother, Northumberland. Together they rode on the rebels in North Durham, harassing them, and with word coming north that the Queen's armies were mustering in the south, Northumberland's revolt began to dissolve. Sussex, who had managed to scratch together only 500 men at York, was on the move, with Hunsdon commanding his cavalry,[1] but the crisis was already past.

The "bankrupt earls", as a contemporary called them, could now think only of flight. They had learned too late that tenants who had been enclosed and oppressed were not over-anxious to risk their necks even for Percies and Nevilles. With a few hundred horsemen they made for Hexham, and there the rebel army finally dwindled to a handful—the two earls, Northumberland's Countess, Lady Anne, her attendants and about forty followers.

Leonard Dacre had long since deserted the rebellion and sought to make his peace with Elizabeth, but it was to Naworth that the fugitives rode, with Forster on their trail. Leonard showed them the door without hesitation—he was about to join Scrope in the West March to

---

1. Hunsdon was caustic about this army; if it had not been for the Northern troops, he believed, "this lusty Southern army would not have returned laden with such spoil, nor put their noses over Doncaster bridge; but others beat the bush, and they have the birds".

assist in mopping up his former rebel associates—but his brother, Edward Dacre, helped them on their way. It was a bad year for brotherly love in the Borderland.

There was nowhere left for the rebel earls now but Scotland, and the only safe place in Scotland was Liddesdale, the traditional haven of fugitives and the last outpost against authority and law. The Earls may have thought twice about putting themselves and the Countess at the mercy of the Armstrongs, but they were worn out and helpless, and there was no alternative but surrender to Elizabeth.

So they pushed on through the Debateable Land, evading Scrope's patrols, and came in the dead of winter to Liddesdale, where they were received by two of the most notorious bad men of the district, Black Ormiston, who appears to have acted as a guide, and Jock of the Side. Of Ormiston not much is known, and most of it is bad: "an outlaw of Scotland, that was a principal murtherer of the king of Scots" (i.e. Darnley), he was apparently a Teviotdale man and had ridden with Bothwell. In some letters he is identified as the Laird of Ormiston or "Wormistoun", who eventually met a violent end in 1571; on the other hand, there was a "Black Ormiston" still alive as late as 1587, when he is mentioned in a letter to Walsingham as being "clean exempted" by the Scottish Parliament. So his end may be something of a mystery.

Jock of the Side is even more difficult to pin down. The name is famous in Border legend as that of the reiver whom Hobbie Noble rescued from Newcastle Jail, and was well known even outside the Marches:

> He is weil kend, John of the Syde,
> A greater thief did never ride.

But there were many Armstrongs of the Side, and trying to identify one particular John is a chancy business. Scott does not hesitate to say that the John of the Side in the ballad is the man who received the Earls, and that he was a nephew of the Laird of Mangerton's; perhaps he was. And he may be the same John of the Side who is listed as an outlaw of Liddesdale on April 18 1601, more than thirty years after the rebellion of the Earls, but since there would be at least one John Armstrong of the Side in every generation it is impossible to be certain.

Even in Liddesdale, the fugitives were still in considerable danger.

Sussex knew where they were, and although he regarded the Scottish Borderers as "very unwilling to deny aid to banished men . . . it [being] against their custom to deliver such as fled out of England, for that they many times in like manner receive succour in England", he was confident of getting the rebel Earls betrayed. "Their whole trust is upon three or four mischievous thieves and men full of treason . . . they shall be had by corruption, though the Queen pay dear for it."

Moray, anxious not to offend Elizabeth, wished to catch the rebels and hand them over,[2] but lifting them by force would have been dangerous, and would have given grave offence to Mary's adherents; instead, Moray offered the Liddesdale outlaws "rewards of large profit" for the fugitives, and Sussex suggested that a pardon for Ormiston for the Darnley murder would be an added inducement.

To the rewards Moray added naked threats. On the day following the Earls' arrival in Liddesdale, Martin Elliot of Braidley, who was under pledge to Moray, brought a force of riders to confront Ormiston, and told him that while he would be sorry to enter into deadly feud with him, the Earls must be out of Scotland within twenty-four hours, or else. Ormiston, either from fear or greed or both, did not hesitate; he and the Armstrongs decided that their English guests must move on into the Debateable Land, so Northumberland and Westmorland were forced to take the road again, Westmorland disguising himself by changing clothes and sword with Jock of the Side.

The Countess and her ladies were left behind; she was exhausted, and the Liddesdale men had spirited away the party's horses, so she stayed in Jock's house, "a cottage not to be compared to any dog kennel in England".

It is possible to be sorry for the fugitives, who had fallen among thieves with a vengeance, but it should be remembered that their condition was no worse than most Borderers endured permanently. It is also worth considering the myth of Border honour and hospitality in the light of what happened to Northumberland and Westmorland.

They were conducted to the stronghold of Hector Armstrong of Harlaw, who managed to separate Northumberland from his com-

---

2. On December 8 the Scottish Privy Council had decided that fugitives from the rebel army who tried to cross into Scotland must be resisted. Obviously many did cross over, and on the 18th the Council noted that the rebels were "tending to entir with displayit banneris".

panions on Christmas Eve and promptly shopped him to Moray's men.[3] Westmorland tried a rescue with the assistance of some Scottish riders and English Forsters, but was beaten off, and Northumberland remained a prisoner until he was handed over to Hunsdon two years later, in return for a cash payment, and beheaded at York. His brother Harry Percy succeeded him.

Meanwhile the Countess, left in Jock of the Side's hovel, had been robbed by Ormiston, but was soon afterwards rescued by a raid of the Ferniehurst Kerrs. Border historians delight in this episode, and make much of the fact that Ferniehurst sank his enmity with the Percies and saved the Countess out of pure chivalry. This is not impossible, but it is also true that he had fought for Mary at Langside, and like the Scotts and Humes, was in political sympathy with the rebellion of the Earls.

But while Westmorland and Northumberland's Countess had escaped, their humbler supporters on the others side of the Border were less fortunate. Black Ormiston and Jock of the Side were less fearsome than Elizabeth's officers; Sussex had promised six or seven hundred executions among the common folk as "a great example", and indeed hundreds did go to the gallows, not only in Tynedale and Redesdale but elsewhere, with little attention to forms of law. In addition there was much plundering and confiscation of land. (John Forster picked up £4000 in loot, in addition to grants of £500 a year from a grateful government.) However, the fact that the rebellion had collapsed so easily probably spared the English Borderers from a worse vengeance still.

One head that would have fallen, if John Knox had had his way, would have been that of Mary Queen of Scots, whose release had been a prime motive of the revolt. At least, it has been suggested that when Knox wrote to Cecil on January 2 1570, urging him to "strike at the root", he was hinting that Mary should be brought to the block. Whatever the true interpretation, it was certainly a doom-laden letter, even to the characteristic signature—"John Knox, with his one foot in the grave".

---

3. Harlaw's treachery became a byword on the Border, where "taking Hector's cloak" came to mean betraying a friend. Apparently he was indebted to Northumberland, who had saved him from a hot trod some years before. It is suggested that, following the betrayal, he fell from prosperity into poverty, and in view of the odium he attracted this is not unlikely.

The sound and brief fury of the Earls' revolt had barely died away before the Marches were ablaze again. It is possible to trace the origin of the new outbreak to a window in Linlithgow, where one Hamilton of Bothwellhaugh was lying in wait for the Regent Moray to ride by: a string of drying washing concealed the assassin, and through it he shot the unsuspecting Regent. Moray, wounded in the stomach, managed to stagger to his feet and reach his lodging, but died within a few hours.

This was on January 23 1570, and one may judge the strength and stature of Moray by the fact that the Border began to shake loose on the following day. He had been, when all is said, as capable a guardian of the Scottish Marches as any before him; tough, ruthless, and sudden, but reasonably fair and well respected. With his fall, a weight was off the riders of the frontier, and his death was greeted with delight by those Border lords who, although they had aided him in suppressing Liddesdale a few months earlier, were pro-Marian and bitterly resentful of Moray's assistance to England in the capture of Northumberland.

"The Regent is as cold as my bridle bit," exclaimed Buccleuch, and Westmorland, who had taken refuge with him following Northumberland's seizure, was so overjoyed that he hurled his bonnet in the fire.[4] By way of celebration they set off immediately, with the ever-ready Kerr of Ferniehurst, to raid in England, pausing *en route* to put Hector of Harlaw's roof to the flames. With them rode various English rebels who, like Westmorland, had flown from Elizabeth's vengeance.

The purpose of this raid, and the many which followed, was to take up where the Earls had been forced to leave off; if war could be provoked between England and Scotland, it might serve Queen Mary's end. Further, there was a willing agent on the English side, in the bristling shape of Leonard Dacre, whose hopes of regaining his family's inheritance had vanished with the Earls' defeat. He was ready to take the field again, backed this time by 3000 lances, most of them the hardiest broken men, outlaws, and loose riders of the Western frontier.

For the second time in as many months Queen Elizabeth found her northern Border on the point of explosion, for it was plain that with Moray's curbing hand removed there would this time be nothing to

4. This curious method of displaying emotion has been mentioned before, in the case of the Duke of Albany.

stop the Scottish reivers riding to Dacre's assistance, with Hume, Ferniehurst and Buccleuch in the van, to say nothing of Westmorland and his English fugitives. Suddenly the danger seemed even greater than it had done in the previous November. Scrope, foreseeing the Maxwells and Irvines breaking loose in the West, wrote from Carlisle at midnight on February 8: "This city stands in peril"; there was little dependable power in the north to send against the new insurrection.

There was, however, the resolute Hunsdon, and the ubiquitous Forster. Hunsdon, who a few weeks earlier had been damning the Berwick garrison as fitter for the almshouse than for soldiering, now added them to a force of Borderers which he scraped together, and with Forster's Middle March riders came west to Hexham. It was going to be touch and go, for he was conscious that Dacre's force at Naworth outnumbered him, the bale-fires were burning along the frontier, and the Scottish riders were mustering in force to come to Dacre's assistance. "Every hill was full of horse and foot, crying and shouting as if they had been mad." Hunsdon's orders were to take Naworth, that "hot and well-furnished" place, and arrest Dacre, but with his 1500-strong force outnumbered at least two to one, and Dacre strong in artillery while he had none, Hunsdon decided to avoid battle and make for Carlisle, where he could join forces with Scrope. Accordingly he set out from Hexham by night, and if Dacre had been wise he would have let him go, and waited for the Scottish reinforcements that were on their way.

But Dacre was spoiling for a fight. Scrope, in a desperate effort to get messages through to Hunsdon, had been sending out couriers in threes, and Dacre's scouts had intercepted some of them. Now the rebels came south from Naworth, shadowing the Queen's force for four miles, and when Hunsdon came to cross the Gelt river just below Brampton, he found Dacre's red bull banner waiting for him. It is one of the loveliest beauty spots in Cumberland, where the Hell Beck joins the Gelt, a place of gorgeous woodland and deep red rocky river gullies; on the heath close by Dacre gave Hunsdon "the proudest charge upon my shot that ever I saw."

It was a little battle, as battles go; how decisive it was Hunsdon himself probably guessed, for he estimated that if his men had broken and Dacre been victorious, Carlisle itself would have fallen to the combined force of rebels and Scots who were even then on their way. And with

Carlisle gone, nothing could have stopped the Border catching light from end to end. As it was, Hunsdon's small army was one of those horse-shoe nails of history which did not come loose; it sustained the shock of Dacre's attack, and Hunsdon, placing Forster with 500 horse to cover his rear, led his own riders in a neck-or-nothing charge on the rebel army. In a vicious hand-to-hand struggle which resolved itself in a series of mêlées up and down the river, Dacre's force was broken, and he himself was the first to flee. One of Hunsdon's men grappled with him, "and if he had not been rescued by certain Scots, he had been taken". He fled to Scotland, leaving between three and four hundred of his followers dead, more than 200 prisoners, and his red bull standard in Hunsdon's hand ("which I trust the law of arms will allow me to bear").

Hunsdon and Forster rode on to Carlisle, and looking north as he approached the city the Queen's cousin had cause to thank God that Dacre had chosen to fight when he did, for in the distance he could actually see the "great company" of Scottish riders coming down too late to support the revolt: in another three hours Dacre would have had 1500 Scots under Ferniehurst and Buccleuch to back him.

"If we had tarried," reflected Hunsdon, "he had been past dealing with." Scrope agreed: in his opinion it had taken a combination of God, Forster and Hunsdon to overthrow Dacre, and the Queen's relief and delight were apparent in the thanks she sent to Forster, and the terms of her address to Hunsdon—"my Harry". It had been a near thing, but in the event Dacre's Raid had failed. The English Borderland had seen its last battle.

XXXVII

The last armies

The rebellions were finished, but the rebels were not. Dacre and Westmorland, with various of their followers, were still at large in Scotland, which was experiencing the birth pangs of yet another civil war following Moray's assassination. The English Marches, which had been torn apart by first Northumberland's and then Dacre's insurrection, were suffering constant inroads not only from the pro-Marian Scots who hoped to start another war, but from the non-political reivers and broken men who were quick to seize the advantage of the general confusion. With Hunsdon, Forster and Scrope chiefly occupied in fighting rebels, conditions were ideal for the professional forayers, who "took up whole townships" and kidnapped 140 persons in the English Middle March alone.

Once the rebellions had been crushed, however, England had time to look beyond the frontier again. It was not, from Elizabeth's point of view, a pretty sight. There were her rebels, being harboured in Scotland; there were the Scots Border lords, like Buccleuch, who had aided them. Both were tempting targets for vengeance, and at the same time there was the general reiver fraternity, which would be none the worse for a sharp lesson. The competent Earl of Sussex was the very man to kill three birds with one stone.

Accordingly he mounted a triple assault on the Scottish Border country, delivered by himself and Hunsdon from the East, Forster from the Middle March, and Scrope from the West. It was a well-planned, deftly executed, and (from the point of view of devastation) extremely successful operation.

It was timed for mid-April, Sussex and Hunsdon driving in at Teviotdale shortly before dawn from Wark while Forster came over the frontier to meet them at Crailing. Hunsdon described how they burned a two-mile strip along their line of march "levying neyther castell, towne nor tower unburnt tyll we came to Jedworth (Jedburgh)." That town itself made no resistance, and was spared, along with the possessions of the Kerrs of Cessford, who had also been hostile to Mary's cause.

But the Ferniehurst Kerrs and the Scotts of Buccleuch took a hammering. Hawick was burned, and the country around subjected to systematic destruction. Hume Castle was besieged, and after an artillery duel it surrendered, on instructions from Hume himself, who was in the vicinity. The garrison was allowed to go free, with the exception of two English rebels who were later hanged. Fast Castle also surrendered, and both were garrisoned with English troops.

Altogether about fifty castles and towers were destroyed, including Branxholm and Ferniehurst, either by blowing them up or razing them with pick and crowbar. More than 300 towns and villages were burned. But although the invaders went about their work with cold-blooded efficiency, there seems to have been some attempt to distinguish between the property of known hostiles and innocent folk who had given no offence either by harbouring English rebels or raiding southward. It was not a killing expedition, like those of Henry's time; in fact, it was a gigantic Warden "rode" and not an invasion of war.

Scrope, at the other end of the frontier, had the hardest part, not only because he was going into the toughest region but also because he was operating independently of the main force. Unlike the Sussex–Forster raid which met only pockets of resistance, his entailed some fighting, for after mopping up villages between Carlisle and Dumfries he was attacked by Maxwells and Johnstones whom he drove off. He did considerably less damage than the main raid, and did not go near Liddesdale at all, confining himself to southern Dumfriesshire. Later in the year Sussex himself came across to Carlisle and carried the work of destruction farther inland up the Nith Valley, bringing back considerable loot.

As a discouragement to Mary's supporters in southern Scotland, and as a last stroke against the English rebels, the raids were entirely successful; as far as settling the local troubles of the frontier were concerned, they provided no more than a temporary check. But in retrospect they can be looked on as closing an era in Border history, for they were the last occasion on which anything that could be called an army was let loose on the Marches. By the time war came again to the Border country, there were no longer any Marches to be fought over, for the old Border had passed away.

Indeed, when Sussex's last trooper had ridden back to England in 1570, the frontier of Wardens and March law, of hot trod and the reiver system, had little more than thirty years to run. The man who was going to end it all was already four years old. In the year following Sussex's raids he attended his first Parliament in Stirling, as James the Sixth of Scotland, and gave proof of that characteristic folly-wisdom for which he is celebrated by noticing a defect in the roof of the building and observing gravely to his counsellors that Parliament had a hole in it. His entire country had holes in it, for that matter, which he would spend a lifetime trying to mend, not without success, but that is another story.

*

Thus far we have traced the history of the Border people in the six-teenth century on a straight year-to-year basis. After 1570, however, the treatment has to be varied slightly. For one thing it is possible in those closing years of the century to view the Borders apart from the mainstreams of English and Scottish history. They were still to be much influenced by the politics of both countries, but not as directly and drastically as hitherto. Conditions, as far as the ordinary peasants and riders were concerned, did not change much throughout Elizabeth's reign; there was no more war, and in the last thirty years the reiver system reached its peak and flourished more or less unaltered by external history.

That system has been described at length in the central portion of this book, and most of the illustrative examples have been taken from the 1570-1603 period, because the records of that time are fuller and more easily available than earlier ones. So to continue the story chronologically in detail would mean repeating a good deal of what has already been covered. Instead, I shall try to sketch the final thirty-odd years briefly, taking in the main Border events which have not been mentioned so far. These include the Raid of the Reidswire, the Russell shooting, and the Kinmont Raid.

From a historian's point of view these were the "good" years, which is another reason why I have already drawn on them so heavily in describing what the Border was like. They were the years of Kinmont Willie and the Bold Buccleuch; of Auld Wat of Harden and the Scropes; of Robert Carey and the Carleton brothers. It was almost as though the Borderers saw the end coming—as it did with Elizabeth's death—and tried their best to make the old days die hard. With two devious, anxious, and often incompetent governments keeping the frontier troubled by their policies, the reivers were able to say a long and resounding farewell. One can think of the 1570-1603 period as being one of fairly continuous local trouble along the line, with occa-sional quiet periods and other times when the raids and trods mounted into what was virtually a constant reign of terror. It grew steadily worse as time went on. This then, was the background against which the last acts of the Border drama were played out.

The 'seventies were comparatively quiet years. There was a civil war in Scotland following Moray's death, with the party of the exiled Queen Mary fighting it out against the faction controlling her infant son. It lasted about two years, and although it was mostly fought farther north, the resultant unsettlement provided the Borderers with good opportunities for local mischief: this was the period, for example, when the Ferniehurst Kerrs were having it out with Jedburgh, and the Fenwicks were reviving a thirty-year-old feud with the Crosers, invading Liddesdale by night and slaying several of their foes in bed. At the end of the war, however, and for most of the rest of the decade, the Regent Morton, who was friendly to England, was active in keeping the Scottish Marches under control, and succeeded not too badly: the Scottish Privy Council, while noting "what harme and inconvenient occurris" on the Border in 1576, mildly put this down to "ignorance of the laws and lovabill custumes thairof". They were more concerned with outlaws and broken men than with the Border tribes as a whole, and in 1577 the broken men were "quieted" with an expedition to the West March.

The outstanding frontier incident of the 'seventies, such as it was, occurred halfway through the decade, and since it has been popularly remembered in legend and ballad, and caused some stir at the time, it is worth a brief mention here.

XXXVIII

Reidswire and Windygyle

Not far from where the main road crosses the Border at Carter Bar, in one of the loneliest stretches on the whole frontier line, lies the Reidswire. It is nothing to see, and its sole importance is that there, it is said, Englishman and Scotsman fought each other for the last time as national enemies. It is a statement that has to be hedged around with a good many qualifications, but it is true enough to say that the "unhappy accident" known as the Raid of the Reidswire might have started the last Anglo-Scottish war.

It was a good example of what could go wrong at a day of truce, and characteristically, it is still impossible to apportion the blame. Since John Forster was present, there is a tendency to look no further for the guilty party, but this may be unfair.

A Warden meeting took place at Reidswire on July 7 1575 with Forster leading for England and Sir John Carmichael, Keeper of Liddesdale, heading the Scots. Whether there was bad blood between them beforehand it is impossible to say; in the event, the behaviour of both seems to have been less than diplomatic. There is an outside possibility that the drinking which took place during the meeting contributed to the quarrel.

The first bills that came before them were quietly disposed of, and then came one against a notorious English thief, named in one account as Farnstein. The bill was "fyled", Carmichael demanded delivery of the offender, and Forster either alleged that Farnstein had fled out of reach, or made some excuse for non-delivery. Carmichael insisted, and depending on which account you believe, was either righteously indignant or downright offensive. He certainly seems to have cast doubts on Forster's integrity, and hinted that the English Warden was prepared to place his own interests before justice. (All of which was true; Forster was neck-deep in deals and arrangements with law-breakers, but it is not certain that he had any axe to grind in the case under discussion.)

His reply to Carmichael is described as "haughty"; probably he pulled rank on the Scot, who as Keeper of Liddesdale did not count as a full Warden, and after reflections on each others' families had been made, their respective followers took up the cat-calling, and suddenly the shooting started. As was usual at any Warden meeting, there were plenty on either side who were at feud, and glad of the chance to indulge it, so it is difficult to guess who actually started the fray, but it is worth noting that the first casualties were Scots, which lends colour to the story that the Tynedale bowmen fired the opening shots.

Forster and Carmichael tried to restore order, without success; the Scots were driven back, but being reinforced by some Jedburgh men (one version says they were coming peacefully to attend their Warden) they rallied, and in the ensuing scuffle, several Englishmen were killed, including the English deputy, Sir George Heron. Forster, Cuthbert Collingwood, and Lord Francis Russell, who was Forster's son-in-law, were among those taken prisoner, and were held for some time in Scotland. The Scots also carried off some spoil.

This was the Raid of Reidswire, and although it is often referred to as though it were a notable event in Border history, it was really comparatively unimportant. Relations were strained, but neither side wanted war, and the English authorities were obviously doubtful whether Forster had been in the right or not: they knew their man. The English prisoners were well treated and compensated, Carmichael was handed over to England as a pledge and briefly detained, and the lawless elements on the frontier took advantage of the international tension to step up their raiding activities. But except for the fact that a Warden was taken prisoner in peace-time, it was not a sensational affair, and hardly justifies the treatment it has received from popular Border historians.

★

The moderate 'seventies were followed by the bloody 'eighties, which were fateful years for the world at large. In this decade Mary Queen of Scots was executed, and if James had not been a realist, with an eye to the English throne, a horror of violence, and a less than filial affection for the mother he had never known, war could easily have followed. Towards the end of the decade came the great Armada scare, which caused some commotion at the West end of the frontier, where the Maxwells were active. Frontier control was generally poor, and raiding was never-ending during the 'eighties. Border "decaie" had set in, and after Morton's fall in 1580 England was looking to her frontier and arranging musters of men along the line. But although international strife did not break out, the feuders and forayers throve in the unquiet time, and the Borderland became more of a jungle with each passing year.

In 1585, the year in which England and Scotland reached a permanent alliance for offence and defence, a noteworthy piece of Border mischief took place somewhere in the desolate wasteland at the eastern end of the Middle Marches. Here is the hilltop called Windygyle, with its enormous cairn of stones; not far away is another huge cairn, called "Lord Russell's Cairn", although it is probably only mistaken tradition that connects it with him. But somewhere close by, in the midsummer of 1585, he was shot dead at a Warden meeting.

In some ways the incident was not unlike the Raid of Reidswire ten years earlier. It, too, is an unsolved mystery; it, too, began as a peaceful truce day, and two of the principal actors, Russell himself and his father-in-law, John Forster, were again present. Forster, indeed, is the principal authority for what happened, but since he told two different stories it is difficult to judge which, if either, is entirely true. Even Walsingham, as capable a sifter of evidence as ever lived, seems to have been in two minds as to the motive behind the killing.

Forster's original story says that the meeting took place quietly, with himself and the Scottish Warden, Sir Thomas Kerr of Ferniehurst (the former scourge of Jedburgh) calling their bills in the normal manner. Russell had come to the meeting, Forster says, "against my will"; it seemed that Russell had some private business there of his own. There was some "lyttle pyckery" among "the rascalles of Scotlande and Englande", but nothing serious enough to disturb the Wardens, and presently Russell got up, leaving Forster and Ferniehurst, and went over to talk to someone among his own men. Suddenly a shot was fired, and Russell fell mortally wounded.

Forster and Kerr at once "stoode together and made a quietnes", and Forster emphasises that Kerr was as willing as he in restoring order. Business was suspended, pledges exchanged, and the matter left there for the moment, but Forster insists that the most careful inquiry did not reveal who had fired the shot.

Overnight he came to a different conclusion, and incorporated it in a second letter. In this he says that at the beginning of the truce day, when he expected to find Ferniehurst accompanied by his usual retinue, he found him instead in order of battle—the Scottish force being concealed by some fold of the ground until Forster got to close range. It was then too late to withdraw, so the meeting went ahead until the shot was fired.

Forster's second letter insists that what he had originally supposed to be an accident was, in fact, "a pretended matter beforehand". To support this, he alleges that the Scots suddenly broke out a charge, in which Russell was shot, and that the Scots pursued the chase four miles into England, taking prisoners and horses.

Ferniehurst's version, given before King James, says that the trouble was started by an English boy stealing a pair of spurs from a Scot. William Fenwick, the English deputy Warden, says the boy was brought before the Wardens, and Forster ordered him to be hanged. There was then quiet until a Scottish drum sounded, the Scots charged, and Russell was killed.

Ferniehurst was quickly cast as the villain of the piece, and a more suitable candidate, in view of his record, it would have been hard to find. But there are great holes in the English story. If the Scots were in battle array, how was only one Englishman killed? If there was a plot to murder Russell, would Ferniehurst have come extravagantly equipped for war? Possibly; if he knew Russell was to be killed, he may have decided it would be as well to have a strong force on hand to prevent retaliation. And it seems that Ferniehurst did have a grudge against Russell, who had intercepted coded letters of his and sent them to London. Forster maintained that this was at the bottom of the affair, and that Ferniehurst, as well as King James's current favourite, James Stewart, Earl of Arran, were the prime movers. Forster also denied that the incident of the stolen spurs had caused the trouble; it had passed off quietly enough. At this rate, concluded the indignant Forster, the choice seemed to be either to have one's throat cut or have no Warden meetings at all.

The alleged complicity of Arran—which the English government probably played up for all it was worth—took the matter into the realm of high politics, and King James "shed tears over it like a newly beaten child". Arran's downfall followed, and although Ferniehurst was never clearly shown to have been responsible for Russell's death, there was great correspondence over his part in the affair, with demands for his delivery from the English and much temporising by the Scots. He was removed from the Wardenship, and in November 1585 Sir Cuthbert Collingwood noted that the Scots "intendes to prosecut Farnherst". In that month Ferniehurst fled, and Lord Hume was sent to arrest him, but the following February came the news that he had died in Aberdeen. Forster's comment was typical: "Pharnihyrst is dead, whereof I am sorie that he and some betters had not beine hanged."

The Russell murder remains another Border mystery: possibly it was a genuine accident, more probably it was a revenge killing, by Ferniehurst's agents (several Kerrs were outlawed for failing to come to trial for the murder) or persons unknown. If it was a premeditated murder, it was most efficiently done, and somebody got clean away with it. The unlucky Russell had the posthumous consolation of the memorial cairn associated with his name; he remains one of the few Borderers to have a local landmark named after him.

XXXIX

The stirring world of Robert Carey

In the 'nineties Border history entered its final phase. Old John Forster finally gave up the Middle March, after the longest, and surely the most adventurous, term of service ever completed by a Border officer. Incredibly, he was in his nineties when he retired; he had been a well-grown lad in the year of Flodden, had fought at Solway Moss and been knighted at Pinkie, had helped to hold the frontier in two rebellions, and had ruled one of the toughest stretches of territory ever assigned to any lawman anywhere. He had been pretty crooked, in his way, but they never made the charges stick; not long after Russell's death a massive list of faults was laid to Forster's door—favouring the Scots, executing the wrong people, releasing murderers, conniving with the Elliots, neglecting his March while securing his own property, and so on. If half of it was true, Forster was one of the biggest villains on the frontier; probably rather more than half of it was. At any rate, it was enough to get him suspended, pending an inquiry by Hunsdon.

This other veteran, noting Forster's denials, backed him to the hilt. Cuthbert Collingwood and other enemies were trying to discredit Forster out of pure malice, said Hunsdon, and the old warden ought to be restored to his post. He was "the fittest man for the tyme". Possibly this was Hunsdon's honest opinion, or perhaps he was prepared to look beyond the evidence, and see only the figure of that Forster who had been foremost in a score of Border fights, and had ridden with him on the knife-edge journey which ended in the blood-stained waters of the Gelt.

In any event, old Sir John was restored to his Wardenry and held on until 1595, when partly because of renewed charges of dishonesty and incompetence, partly because he was now ninety-four and a prey to "imbecility and weakness", he was supserseded, and went to spend his declining years at Bamborough. But if he was finished with the Borders, they were not finished with him; if he had favoured Scots in his day, there were still some who regarded him with deadly hostility, and on a night of October 1597 a band of thirty riders came over the line to Bamborough with intent to settle his account at last. Forster was in his own room, but by chance Lady Forster saw the raiders coming up the stairs, and with great presence of mind "gott the chamber door put to and bolted." So Forster escaped yet again, and lived on to see the seventeenth century. It was on the afternoon of January 13 1602 that the old warrior died, aged probably 101. For better or worse, no man so typified the old Border; if one could write his biography, it would be the history of a century on the frontier.

Robert Carey, whose judgement is as trustworthy as any, had this to say of Forster: "[He] had been an active and valiant man, and had done great good service . . . [but] grew old, at length to that weakness by reason of his age, that the borderers, knowing it, grew insolent, and by reason of their many excursions and open roads, the inhabitants of the March were much weakened and impoverished." This is a fairer judgement on Forster, by a contemporary, than he normally receives from historians.

When Forster was dismissed from the Middle March in late 1595, he was succeeded as Warden by the third Lord Eure, the new generation of the great Warden family which we have seen in action during Henry VIII's wars. According to Robert Carey, Eure came with 100 horse "to the great joy and comfort . . . of the March, and to the terror and fear of the malefactors, expecting their utter ruin".

But, Carey noted, "it oft falls out that seldom comes a better," and Eure proved the point. He was a feeble Warden, he did not understand the frontier or its people (which Forster had done, perhaps all too well), and he had evidently none of Forster's capacity for wheeling and dealing. Carey, looking back, was probably human enough not to be too unhappy about Eure's poor showing; he concedes that Eure tried hard, but was too trusting. "For all his 100 horse . . . hee had not been long there, but the theeves were free of their fear, and the poor inhabitants in worse case than ever."

During Eure's office, the Middle March deteriorated steadily. He had taken the office "terryfied . . . knowing my infinite wants", and it was one long bitter struggle in which he felt his authority undermined by his subordinates (which it doubtless was) and spent as much time defending his character and complaining, as he did looking after his March. Eventually his pleas for release were listened to, and Robert Carey himself, not without misgivings, took over.

Later generations of adventure story writers, who had never heard of

Robert Carey, found it necessary to invent him. For he was the living image of the gallant young Elizabethan, a figure straight out of the *Boy's Own Paper* or the romances of Rafael Sabatini. Dashing, brave, intelligent, clean-cut, and saved from priggishness by an honesty that borders on *naïveté*, Carey is simply as nice a person as one comes across in Border history.

Admittedly much of what we know of his character rests on his own account, that slim volume of memoirs which he left behind and which gives such an invaluable eye-witness account of frontier life. It is just a brief glimpse, but fortunately he concentrated on his active service against the reivers, and the picture of the man and his times has a genuine ring.

Carey was the seventh (or possibly the tenth) and youngest son of Lord Hunsdon. Robert's service as a Border official lasted only a few years, but in that time he served in all three Marches, first as deputy in the West, and later as Warden in the East (1596–8) and Middle Marches (1598–1603). In these posts he was energetic, ingenious and, by the standards of the time, successful.

He admits himself that he was no scholar. Born about 1560, he was abroad by the time he was seventeen, on an embassy to the Low Countries with Sir Thomas Leyton. He was in Scotland with Walsingham in 1583, when that shrewd minister was weighing up King James of Scotland, and James seems to have been favourably impressed with Carey, for he asked Elizabeth to send him back again—a request which was granted and then countermanded. However, his early contact with James was eventually to prove useful to Carey, although it did not achieve him the advancement he hoped for.

His education was progressing in a more practical way, with service on the Sluys expedition and as a volunteer against the Spanish Armada. He held a command in Normandy in 1591, was at the siege of Rouen, and was knighted by the Earl of Essex. He had seen something of the Borders already, having once walked from London to Berwick to win a £2000 bet, and when Thomas Scrope succeeded as West Warden in 1593, Carey accepted the post as deputy, with six men and horses, and half Scrope's fee of 1000 marks per annum. It was the life for Carey: "I lived with great content," he says, "for we had a stirring world, and few days passed but I was on horseback, either to prevent mischief or take malefactors." He gives an immediate example.

Private word reached him at Carlislie that two Scots had killed a churchman in Scotland "and were by one of the Grahams relieved. This Graham dwelt within five miles of Carlisle; he had a pretty house, and close by it a strong tower for his own defence in time of need".

Here was a situation tailor-made for a young Border officer eager to prove himself. Robert lost no time; he took horse from Carlisle at two in the morning, with twenty-five riders, including that wily veteran Thomas Carleton, and set out in the hope of surprising the house. But his quarry was too quick for him, and before the house could be surrounded "the two Scottes were gotten into the strong tower, and I mought see a boy riding from the house as fast as his horse would carry him".

This puzzled the inexperienced Carey, he admits, but Thomas Carleton knew the signs. "He told me that if I did not prevent it, both myself and all my company would be either slain or taken prisoner. It was strange to me to hear this language. He then said to me: 'Do you see that boy that rideth away so fast? He will be in Scotland inside this half hour, and he has gone to let them know that you are here, and to what end you have come, and the small number you have with you, and that if they make haste, on a sodaine they may surprize us, and do with us what they please.'"

One may guess—but only guess—that Carleton said this with some satisfaction. He knew his frontier inside out; Carey was raw, and impetuous, and an aristocrat, and probably, in Carleton's view, less fitted to be deputy Warden than Carleton himself. It is a situation which every young officer knows—and every sergeant-major.

Carey reacted as young officers usually do. "Hereupon," he writes, "we took advice what was best to be done." They sent messengers to Carlisle to raise reinforcements, and presently more than 300 foot men arrived, who were directed to climb the tower, remove the roof, and so break in. At this the Scots in the tower offered to parley, "and yielded themselves my prisoners", but at the same time 400 riders appeared from Scotland, and Carey found himself in the middle of a potentially explosive situation.

The Scottish riders halted and "stood at gaze. Then I had more to do than ever, for all our borderers came crying with full mouths: 'Sir, give us leave to set upon them, for these are they that have killed our fathers, our brothers, our uncles, and our cousins, and are come thinking to surprize you, upon weak graffe nagges, such as they could get on a sodaine, and God hath put them into our hands, that we may take revenge on them for much blood that they have spilt of ours.' "

Carey kept his head. "I . . . bethought myself, if I should give them their wills there would be few or none of them that would escape unkilled (there was so many deadly feuds among them)." So he told the Carlisle men that he could not turn them loose against the Scottish riders—"the blood that would be spilt that day would lie heavy on my conscience"—but he would tell the Scots to withdraw, and if they refused, then the Carlisle men could attack if they pleased.

His followers were ill pleased, but agreed to wait, and Carey sent his messenger to the Scots. There was a nervous moment as the two sides looked at each other, and then the Scottish riders wheeled without a word and rode off. "Thus by God's grace I escaped a great danger," Carey concludes, "and by means there was a great many men's lives saved that day." He had, in fact, behaved like a good Warden officer.

Shortly after this incident he married Elizabeth Trevannion, "more for her worth than her wealth. Neither did she marry me for any great wealth. Besides, the Queen was mightily offended with me for marrying, and most of my friends." But Hunsdon gave his blessing, and Carey brought his bride to Carlisle, where they lived in the castle.

However, he remained out of favour with the Queen, and his account of what followed shows how cautiously even her more prominent subjects had to deal with that fickle and dangerous monarch. Robert's brother, John, marshal of Berwick, wanted a trusty messenger to ride to King James in Scotland on secret business; very well, sniffed Elizabeth to Hunsdon, "I hear your fine son, that has lately married so worthily, is hereabouts: send him."

Hunsdon said he was sure Robert would be glad to obey the Queen.

"No," said Elizabeth, "do you bid him go, for I'll have nothing to do with him."

This was passed on to Robert Carey, who was most reluctant to venture into Scotland on a secret mission without express orders; like most Elizabethans he had a well-developed defence mechanism where court intrigue was concerned. "I had need to be wary what I do," he observed. "It were ill trusting her."

Hunsdon, laughing, told this to the Queen; he knew her better than his son did, and whatever Elizabeth may have felt she kept to herself. 'If the gentleman is so mistrustful," she replied, "let the secretary make a safe conduct and I will sign it." So Carey went to Scotland with official licence, delivered the secret business to King James, and received a reply to the Queen. James apparently wanted it to be verbal, which alarmed the cautious Carey.

"Sir," he told the King, "between subject and subject a message may be delivered without any danger; between two great monarchs I dare not trust my memory . . . but must desire you be pleased to write your mind to her."

James did so, and Carey returned to Hampton Court with it. "Dirty as I was, I came into the presence, where I found the lords and ladies dancing." He insisted on seeing the Queen personally, and in private. It was a "stormy and terrible" interview, with Elizabeth venting her displeasure at full pitch. Robert took it quietly, and then dared to suggest that the question of his marriage was all the Queen's fault; if she had been kinder to him he would never have left court in the first place. Presumably he knew what he was doing, and framed his defence suitably; he admits, "I was never off my knees till I had kissed her hand and obtained my pardon," which suggests that he was courtier enough to know how to get round Good Queen Bess when he wanted to.

In the end "she was not displeased with my excuse, and before we parted we grew good friends". It was a friendship that was to last to Elizabeth's dying day.

In July of 1596 old Hunsdon died, and Robert took charge of the English East March. This brought him into opposition with a young man who, although of a far wilder and more bloodthirsty nature than Carey's, was not unlike him in many ways. Robert Kerr of Cessford, son of the Scottish Middle March Warden, was in his early twenties, a fierce, fearless, and proud Border callant who, although he normally acted as Warden in his father's place, was as practised a reiver as any on the frontier. "Ambitious, proud, bloody in revenge, poor, and easily framed to any purpose" was how a contemporary described him. It went without saying that he and Carey would collide.

XL

"Fyrebrande"

By modern standards Robert Kerr was a juvenile delinquent, and if anyone wants to defend him they can argue that it was no wonder he grew up a ruffian, since he was learning the trade of raid, robbery and fighting for a living at an age when modern children are preparing for their first school examinations. His first "voyage on horseback" was made in 1585, when he was fifteen (but possibly even younger) at the raid of Stirling. Two years later he was a leader, with the Bold Buccleuch and Lord Johnstone, of a 2000-strong foray against the Collingwoods, a raid which so displeased King James that he forbade Kerr's marriage to Maitland of Lethington's daughter. However, Kerr did marry her, and was jailed the following day for his pains.

Thereafter he continued as he had begun. Before he was of age he was in flight to England after conspiring in the murder of one of the Ancrum Kerrs; his possessions were forfeited, but he was pardoned in 1591, although his feud with Ancrum lasted another sixteen years. Possibly on the theory that so much talent should not be wasted, he was made Deputy Keeper of Liddesdale in 1593 (a post which Forster noted he held only briefly), and about the same time he began to act as his father's assistant in the Middle March. He did not allow this to hamper his personal activities, such as feuds with various English and Scottish families; in 1595 he was at Wooller with eight riders, killing three men; not long after he was over the line looking for Storeys to murder, but being disappointed he spent the day visiting local fairs and ale houses, with only two companions, and generally being sociable in his enemies' territory. John Carey, Robert's nervous brother, wondered what the country was coming to.

During the next year Kerr's riders were frequently foraying in England, and possibly in consequence he began to lose control of his Wardenry, and failed to satisfy his English counterparts. His record for the year includes several murders, much theft, his elevation to the Privy

Council, and a feud with the Turnbulls—not bad for a man of twenty-five. But by '97 he was to be credited with sixteen killings, and his depredations, along with the Bold Buccleuch's, were reckoned to have cost the English Marches over £60,000. And this, it must be remembered, was a Warden of the Marches of several years' standing.

Sir Robert Carey arrived on the English East March in the middle of all this. He must have known what kind of a man Kerr was—a dangerous, quick-tempered killer and clever with it—but he tried friendly overtures, writing to Kerr to propose a meeting, at which they would confer privately for the peace of the Border.

Kerr welcomed the messenger jovially, filled him with drink, and while the messenger was sleeping it off at Kerr's house, slipped over the Border, murdered an Englishman with whom he had a quarrel, and then went home to bed. In the morning, the messenger having sobered up, Kerr gave him a reply to Carey, who rejoiced at receiving it, for it was "a kinde letter". He rejoiced less later in the day, when he learned what Kerr had done during the night; his earlier opinion of the Laird of Cessford ("a brave active young man") was modified, and we find his correspondence sprinkled with expressions like "unworthye officer", "wicked man" and so on.

It was a bad start, and things got worse. This was one of the worst years on the Border, with nightly raiding; Cessford was if anything a greater thorn in the side of England than Buccleuch, and Carey was stretched to the limit in defending his March.[1] Reluctantly, he found himself frequently hanging reivers, "a course which hath been seldom used, but I had no way to keep the country quiet but to do so." It helped to check the inroads a little, but with Kerr rampant across the frontier there was no way of stemming the trouble at source. Carey admits: "All this time wee were but in jest as it were, but now beganne the great quarrell between us."

This arose over Carey's hanging of Geordie Burn, a notorious reiver whose life was "neere and deare" to Kerr; the details are to be found in the biographical sketch of Burn on pp. 103-5. Kerr was

---

1. In a long list of Cessford's crimes, the most offensive was his raid thirty miles into England in the autumn of 1596, when he attacked Swinburn Castle, capturing Roger Woodrington, and "sownding his trumpett upon the topp of the house".

furious and "full of grief and disdaine", uttering threats of "cruell revenge". He came down to the line with 100 riders to lay an ambush, and sent small troops of his reivers over to make raids, hoping to provoke hot trods which he would be able to waylay. The raids carried off cattle, but the English were too wise to pursue. Kerr's reaction was characteristic; when the stolen beasts were brought to him he ordered his men to drive them back again—"as it was not goods but blood he desired". His raiders, incidentally, did injure two or three men, "but as they were men of no account they left them unkilled". To be worth having in a Border feud, a scalp had to be a good one.

Carey waited, expecting the worst, but for all his rage Kerr did little damage. There was an alarm when Carey heard that the chief riders were to attend a football match at Kelso—always a likely occasion for plotting mischief—and an English ambush was laid accordingly. Having posted it, Carey was riding home alone when he suddenly remembered that his tithe-collectors were due to rendezvous that night in the alehouse at Norham. Kerr could not wish for a better target, and Carey hastily sent word for the collectors to leave the inn and seek refuge in the castle. Grumbling, they obeyed, and sure enough, they were hardly settled when Kerr's riders swept into the town, battered down the inn doors, and demanded to know where Carey's tithe-men were hidden. Finding them gone, Kerr smelled an ambush, and wasted no time in withdrawing.

But the threat remained, and for months the English officials had Kerr constantly on their nerves. One moment he was reported to be secretly making rope ladders in his own tower for an assault on Berwick, the next that he was going to strike at the Middle March. There was enough evidence to demand his delivery into English hands, and no other visible way of clipping his wings; William Bowes was insistent that he and Buccleuch—"the twoo fyrebrandes"—must be turned out of office and imprisoned.

Of the two Kerr was considered the greater menace—which is one way of saying that he has a fair claim to the all-time top position in the dishonourable league of Border bad men—but Buccleuch was even more in the spotlight for the moment since he had only a few months earlier broken Kinmont Willie out of Carlisle Castle. Border affairs were in such a fearful mess at the end of 1596 that commissioners were appointed to meet early in 1597, and after much argument various bills were settled and a treaty drawn up. A meeting took place at Norham for the exchange of pledges,[2] and while the commissioners parleyed Carey and Kerr watched each other at a distance of half a mile. The pledges themselves, however, did not turn up ("frivolous delays," complained Carey), and it took another three months and two meetings before the business was completed.

Even then it was a near thing. William Bowes arrived at Norham on the morning of October 8, with Lord Hume appearing for the Scots; Kerr and Buccleuch rolled up during the afternoon. Buccleuch's pledges had not arrived, so to the surprise of the English he offered himself, and crossed the river into English custody. Cessford presented his pledges for East Teviotdale, "but not without a stratagem to serve his turn."

According to John Carey, while Kerr, Bowes, Hume and others were all clustered together, one of Kerr's riders let off a pistol, and then reeled in his saddle, roaring that he had been shot while his associates cried, "Treason! treason!" Fighting promptly broke out, but in the dusk the shots went astray, and the day was saved by Hume, who placed himself in front of Bowes and said that if the Englishman was shot it would be through his (Hume's) body.

The meeting, not unnaturally, broke up, and the English side, who claimed that Kerr had now failed three times to deliver his pledges, demanded that he should be given up in person. After prolonged correspondence, negotiation, and, of course, further raiding, it was agreed that Kerr should be handed over, and Lord Hume, by royal command, brought him to Berwick in February 1598.

It was a considerable relief to the English Marches, and to no one more than Carey, when the great "Border bloodsucker" was delivered into England. No one, perhaps, had ever disturbed the frontier so grievously for so long, but at the end of the long duel Carey, in a sense, had won. However, there was a surprise in store for him; in a way it was an honour, for it reflected the esteem it which he was held. When Kerr was handed over he was asked into whose custody he wished to be de-

---

2. As has been explained earlier, the pledges were the malefactors or substitutes who were to be handed over to the opposite Wardens and detained until amends had been made for their crimes. Carey adds that if these pledges were not delivered, the Wardens responsible were to surrender themselves—as happened in this case.

livered; "contrary to all men's expectations" he named his old enemy, Robert Carey.

Surprised, but obviously not displeased, Carey "brought him to my own house . . . lodged him as well as I could, and tooke order for his diet". He warned Kerr, however, to expect no favours, "yet, heering so much goodness of him, that he never broke his word, if he should give me his hand and credit to be a true prisoner, hee would have no guard sett upon him". Kerr thanked him, but kept to his room for four days, and then asked Carey to come and talk to him. Face to face, they threw charge and counter-charge at each other, bringing up all the old wrongs, until each had said his piece. At the end, they were friends, Kerr promised never to trouble Carey again, and after that "I tooke him abroad with mee at the least thrice a weeke, a-hunting, and every day wee grew better friends."

Theirs was one of the few Border stories that had a happy ending, for when Kerr returned to Scotland, says Carey, "I found him as good as his word . . . and so wee continued very kinde and good friendes."

Carey was either an unusually generous man in his estimate of character, or else when he came to write his memoirs he was in that mellow state which tends to minimise past faults. No doubt he and Cessford remained "good friendes", but only a few years after their reconciliation Carey was complaining to Cecil about "Kerr's malice" and the possibility that the Scot might even kidnap him.

Carey had been made full Warden of the East March in the winter of 1597, at his own charges; it was an expensive business. "I often did solicit Mr Secretary for some allowance to support me in my place, but could get no direct answer." Elizabeth ran her Marches, like everything else, on a shoe-string, and finally Carey, greatly daring, left his Wardenry (which was quiet at the time) and went to London to plead his case. He wheedled Elizabeth round ("I tooke her by the arme") and charmed her to such an extent that he got £500 for the time he had served, "where wise men thought that I wrought my own wracke".

In March of 1598 Carey was succeeded as East March Warden by Lord Willoughby, "a military nobleman of a very bright character" who rejoiced in the unlikely name of Peregrine Bertie. Willoughby had won celebrity as a commander in France and the Low Countries.

He was a comparatively young man, but his health deteriorated, and he died in office after only three years.

Carey, on giving up the East Wardenry, was transferred to the notorious Middle March, a daunting prospect. It had been bad under Forster, and had run quite out of his control latterly; it had totally defeated Eure. But Carey, being what he was, determined to tackle the job in his own way. They offered him 100 horse; he said he would take forty, his own men. He "cleansed" his under-officers, appointed Harry Woodrington and William Fenwick to be his deputies— "gentlemen's sons of the country, and younger brothers of good rank". He cleaned up the "inbred thieves" within his March—"by them most mischief was done, for the Scotch riders were always guided by some of them in all the spoils they made"—and reckoned that in his first season he had executed sixteen or seventeen of the most notorious offenders. He found the Scottish East March, and much of their Middle March, reasonably peaceable, but the Western end of his Wardenry "kept me a great while incumbered".

How he eventually dealt with that, by harrying the Armstrongs out of their retreat in Tarras Moss, we have already read in Chapter XXIII. But before that he had all he wanted of that "stirring world" which he had so enjoyed as a young man. The Middle March frontier, in those closing years, provided one damned thing after another, and although Carey's memoirs make fairly light of it, the records (including his own correspondence) tell a different story of raid, reprisal and violence. By and large he handled it well (or as well as any man could have done), and it is necessary to select only one incident by way of illustration. The affair of the Redesdale hunting in the summer of 1598, soon after Carey had taken over, also shows how the kind of slack government of Forster and Eure had encouraged transgression, and could have bred a serious frontier incident.

The Scots, taking advantage of Forster's laxity, had been accustomed to hunt, fell timber, and generally make free on the English side of the line. On August 2 1598, according to Carey, 200 of them "armed with calyvers and horsemens peeces" came across the frontier, and Carey despatched his deputies, Woodrington and Fenwick, who set upon the intruders and chased them back over the Border. In the pursuit "private men slew their enemies who were in deadly feud with them", four or five Scots died, and about fifteen were captured.

The Scots version, naturally, was rather different. They contended they had been only about sixty strong, and armed merely for sport. Moreover, they knew of no objection to their hunting.

Carey, in his memoirs, blames his predecessors in the Wardenry for this, but admits that "Eure had no time to attend to such small matters", and that he himself had had little time to begin with either—"the Armstrongs kept me so at work". But he contends that he had written to Ferniehurst,[3] his opposite, several times saying that if the Scots wished to hunt in England they had only to ask permission in advance, and it would be granted.

On the occasion of the Redesdale hunting, however, they had not asked leave, and he had sent off his deputies with orders to intercept them, but to do as little harm as possible. It looks as though Woodrington and Fenwick were over-zealous, and perhaps they took the chance to pay off private scores.

In the event King James complained, the two deputies were briefly confined, and according to Carey "there was no more of the business". Which was not strictly true, for the Scottish reivers hammered his March immoderately in the ensuing months, but at least the international peace was not endangered.

*

While these stirring events were taking place in the Middle March throughout the 1590s, the West Marches were maintaining their reputation as the roughest quarter of the frontier. Old Henry Scrope died early in the decade, and after a brief interregnum in which Richard Lowther held sway, the post went to Scrope's son Thomas. Not unnaturally, the Lowthers resented him, and his term of office was to be bedevilled by hostility towards him within his own March, even some of his closest officers betraying him on occasion. He was perhaps the unluckiest of Wardens, even including Eure; he came to a turbulent region at a bad time—on the other side of the line the Maxwells and Johnstones were turning the Scottish West March into a shambles as their feud reached the climax of Dryfe Sands, and the Earl of Bothwell was a constant disturbing element—but in justice it has to be said that young Scrope was not big enough to fill his father's boots.

---

3. This according to his memoirs, but it must surely have been to Cessford that he wrote.

He was brave, not unintelligent, energetic, and had behind him all the prestige of a distinguished frontier family—one ancestor had fought at Flodden, and Henry Scrope had been universally respected, even on the Scottish side.[4] Against this, young Scrope had several defects of character, He was devious, volatile, and over-ready with excuses; he wrote an excellent letter, but had an unerring aim for just missing the point. It is perhaps unfair to suggest that he was neurotic and had persecution mania: many Wardens did, and considering what they were up against it is hardly surprising. But be it because of his experiences as Warden, or because of imperfections of character, he certainly developed obsessions—about the Grahams, about Buccleuch, about his own subordinates—which impaired his judgement. He had a weakness for gambling, shared by his wife Philadelphia (Robert Carey's sister, and, incidentally, a most diabolical speller, even by Elizabethan standards), and by their son. On one occasion Scrope even tried to borrow £300 from Robert Cecil to clear his gaming debts.

James VI found him irresponsible and thoughtless, and Scrope's own brother wrote on one occasion that he feared the Warden "by this course that he takes . . . will be a man of noe longe life". But the Bishop of Durham probably summed him up best when he wrote that Scrope was "verily a right honorable person, of a depe witt, of a noble and liberall inclinacion, but so secret and sole in his intencions, as some doe holde him overjelous". Conditions in the March, his lordship felt, had forced the Warden "to more warynesse and less credulitie, yea lesse affabilitie, than his owne disposicion dothe leade him unto."

Altogether, he lacked the broad understanding and stable temper essential to a good Warden, and he was punished for it. He held his office to the end of Elizabeth's reign, and given luck might have left a record no worse than many of his contemporaries. But history had a grievous shock in store for Lord Scrope which was to make him a laughing-stock in the folk-memory of the frontier. All that posterity remembers of his career is the one blustery night in April 1596 when the sky fell in on him.

---

4. King James observed that his death was "na plesant newis unto ws (saulffing Goddis pleasour)".

XLI

Lances to Carlisle

In the early spring of 1596 a day of truce was held near Kershopefoot, on the Border, between the deputy Warden of the English West March and the deputy Keeper of Liddesdale. It was a routine meeting, the presence of only the deputies signifying that the matters for redress were "ordinarie", but it was well attended, with upwards of 200 riders on the English side alone.

Among those accompanying the Scottish deputy, Scott of Haining, was a powerful Borderer well into middle age, a man of obvious consequence and, from the authorities' point of view, some notoriety. This was Armstrong of Kinmont, whose career has already been briefly sketched. He was a large-scale reiver, thoroughly seasoned in the local mischief, had his own tower and followers, and had been the subject of dishonourable mention in official correspondence during the past thirteen years. He is prominently mentioned in Musgrave's list of Border riders, where he appears as William of Kinmont, living at Morton Rigg on the frontier line; the world remembers him simply as Kinmont Willie.

Whether he took an active part in the day of truce on March 17 1596 is unknown. In view of what followed, and of his notorious record, it is quite likely that he did; it seems obvious that some spark flew between him and those on the English side who "had quarrell" against him, either at the meeting or shortly afterwards. But what the cause of it was cannot even be guessed, and what happened when the meeting broke up is not satisfactorily established.

A Scottish account says the truce ended without incident, and the various parties turned homeward. Armstrong of Kinmont, with a handful of riders, parted from Scott of Haining, the Scottish deputy, and made his way along the north bank of the Liddell Water; it was unfortunate that the main band of English riders, making for Carlisle, naturally followed the same course, on the south side of the river. This should not have mattered; under the law of the Marches, specially framed for just such an occasion, every man attending the truce was held to be inviolate to his enemies until next day's sunrise, so that Kinmont, even with a small army of hostile riders keeping step with him on the opposite bank, was theoretically as safe as if he had been in Edinburgh Castle.

But according to the account, on that late afternoon, the law went by the board. The Englishmen, "seeing him ryding on his waye, and lyming for na harme, as that day fell, they brake a chace of more than 200 men out of the English trayne". They crossed the river, and Kinmont put his head down and his heels in and rode for his life. For three or four miles he held his lead, but with a horde of the finest irregular light horsemen in Europe on his tail his capture was foregone. They ran him down and carried him across the Border, and so began the most celebrated "incident" in the long history of the Anglo-Scottish frontier, a cold-war episode which was to cause diplomatic activity in both capitals, lead to the best-publicised of all Border raids, and provide material for one of the most widely-known examples of ballad poetry (see Appendix II).

But why the English riders took him is the first mystery of the Kinmont Willie story. Another version of the capture says that certain Englishmen who had crossed the Border in pursuit of outlaws encountered Kinmont, who hindered them, so that they were compelled to pursue and arrest him. It sounds unconvincing, especially since Scrope does not mention it later among the various official excuses for the arrest.

What Scrope did say was that the captors had made an attestation, "which if true, it is held that Kynmont did thereby breake th'assurance that daye taken, and for his offences ought to be delivered to the officer against whom he had offended". But that phrase "which if true", coming from Scrope, perhaps suggests that the Warden did not seriously believe that Kinmont had broken assurance on the truce day. How had he broken it? Scrope never said. It is inconceivable that if Kinmont had openly offended, by violating the truce, the great correspondence which followed his arrest would not have made some mention of the actual details. In the absence of such evidence, the story of breaking the assurance is not to be accepted.

Nor, incidentally, is the suggestion in the ballad—which is a bombastic piece of Scottish propaganda at its worst—that the English took him with the intention "on Haribee to hang him up". In the weeks following his capture the English authorities never looked like hanging him. They kept him a prisoner in Carlisle Castle, not very severely; indeed, Scrope seems to have placed him on some kind of limited parole.

It looks, at this distance, as though the arrest was technically (and possibly morally) quite illegal, and resulted from a rashness committed on the spur of the moment by English riders. What they did, on a truce day, was well outside the limits of the Border code, and quite unnecessarily stupid. It is only speculation, but if there was discord at the Kershopefoot meeting, and if Kinmont flaunted his immunity across the Liddell Water with those words and gestures which are such an eloquent currency in the West Marches to this day, it is not difficult to understand Cumbrian tempers being lost and the honour of the Border being lost with them. The sight of the notorious Kinmont Willie, virtually alone and in their grasp, but for the inconvenient truce convention, may have been too great a temptation.[1]

Whether the English deputy, Salkeld, encouraged the outrage, or merely winked at it, or (as seems probable) knew nothing about it until the mischief was done, is unimportant. To the Scots he remains "the fause Salkeld", and he was technically guilty on that March evening of failing to repair immediately the wrong his followers had done. But in the absence of his Warden (Scrope was away from Carlisle at his country home) he may be excused for not releasing Kinmont with an apology. When the great reiver was brought to Carlisle, Salkeld lodged him in the castle. He may have assumed that the captors had good reason for what they had done, and that until it was all cleared up, Kinmont was none the worse for being in custody.

The first shot in the correspondence which was to grow in volume and acrimony for several months, was fired by the Keeper of Liddesdale, young Scott of Buccleuch. At this time, although just turned thirty, he had been in charge of Liddesdale for almost two years and was recognised as one of the most daring and energetic leaders on the frontier. His influence was great, his gallantry and courage proverbial, and his general conduct deplorable. He remains the beau idéal of a Border chieftain; he was also a murderous, plundering ruffian, but as

---

1. Breaking assurance was not unique, as we have seen—Reidswire and Russell's murder, for example, and Robert Kerr's death at the hands of Lilburn, Starhead, and Heron—so the Kinmont episode is not the hideous exception it is sometimes made out to be.

we know, within the loose limits of Border morality these things were not incompatible. He and Scrope did not get on; they were of the kind that would grate on each other from the start, and there was "no justice" between them. And now, Buccleuch was the last man to accept meekly the kind of affront to his official and personal dignity which he chose to see in Kinmont's seizure.

The Border ballad writer makes the most of this. "Now Christ's curse on my head, but avenged of Lord Scrope I'll be," Buccleuch is supposed to have said, and there follow several verses of rhodomontade in which he is credited with regrets that, there being no war with England, he is prevented from burning Carlisle Castle, erasing it from sight, slockening it with English blood, and the like. In fact, what Buccleuch did was to write to Salkeld, properly demanding that the wrong be set right at once.

Receiving no satisfaction, he readdressed his demand to Scrope, with no better result. One version says that Scrope replied that he could do nothing; the thing was done, and that was that—further, Kinmont was such a notorious villain that Scrope dare not enlarge him, having got him, without permission from the Queen and Council. Scrope certainly did take a line rather close to this in making his explanations later to his masters in London, who, it is worth noting, do not seem to have been satisfied that Kinmont's arrest was lawful. However, Scrope told Burghley that "I had th'opinion of some of good accompte and longe experience in Border causes, who thought Kinmonte to be a lawfull prisoner," which was a thin reason for a Warden to give, and then went on to add that even if the arrest had been illegal, he had still made an offer to Buccleuch that all their differences (including Kinmont) should be laid before King James and the English ambassador, and thereafter Scrope would make any amends necessary.

If he did reply to Buccleuch in these terms, lumping in Kinmont with all other causes of dispute, it is not surprising if Buccleuch was dissatisfied, since he would regard Kinmont's arrest as all-important, and not to be confused with smaller controversies. Scrope also put forward his allegation of Kinmont's breaking truce,[2] without elaboration, and

2. The report in which this is contained is annotated by Burghley as "18 Martij", but this was surely a mistake on his part. Kinmont was arrested on the 17th, and it seems clear from the wording of Scrope's report that it was not written the following day, but at some later date.

added the untenable argument that "another reason for detaining him is his notorious enmity to this office, and the many outrages lately done by his followers".

Now this was nonsense, and Scrope must have known it; whatever Kinmont had done, he could not be justly held on such a vague and general ground. There was little more to be said for another of Scrope's arguments, which was that it was none of Buccleuch's business anyway. Kinmont, said Scrope, "appertains not to Buccleuch, but dwells out of his office, and was taken beyond the limits of his charge."

This was perfectly true, but it could be argued that since the breach was of a truce at which Buccleuch's deputy had officiated, this made it Buccleuch's affair. Also, since the Scottish West March, in which the breach had occurred, did not have a Warden for the time being (several gentlemen declined the job), it was reasonable for Buccleuch to take the matter on himself.

Scrope's apparent last word on the subject was that he intended to detain Kinmont, "thinking it good to do so till good security be given for better behaviour of him and his in time coming, and recompense of damages lately done to the people here."

Behind the bland phrases it is easy to see that there was now a question of face involved. Whatever the initial rights and wrongs of the matter, Scrope was not going to bow down to demands from Buccleuch; Kinmont was just the pretext for Scrope to cock a snook at his rival; he was no doubt justified in supposing that Buccleuch had seized on the affair "as a mere pretext to defer justice", and was paying the Scot back in his own coin. The personal jealousy and dislike between the two men made it impossible for either to back down; how great that dislike was, Scrope makes clear in his letters to Burghley.

"A bad man he has been to this office," he complains, and describes how Buccleuch has ridden at the head of 200 men in day forays, slaying the Queen's subjects and driving off herds of cattle. And again, he recounts some of Buccleuch's offences "before he was an officer", relating his tale of slaying, stealing and kidnapping with some relish. He had every reason to detest Buccleuch, whose "pryde of himself" and "skorne" towards Scrope were especially irksome, but he was letting his own pride and scorn run away with him, by picking a poor case and sticking to it unreasonably. One suspects Scrope knew he was at least technically in the wrong, but the temptation to twist Buccleuch's tail was too strong for him. He may have asked himself what could Buccleuch do, except grin and bear it. He did not know his man.

Having written to both deputy and Warden without success, Buccleuch next tried the English ambassador, Robert Bowes, who "wrote furiouslie to the Lord Scrope", advising him to redress the matter before it went any further, but apparently without effect. "Nothing was done or anserit till a purpose nevertheless; neither upon the kingis his masters awin instance towards the warden, by the ambassador of England first, and afterwards to the Queen of Englande by his majesties selfe."

So there it was; every diplomatic means had been tried and failed. Kinmont Willie lay behind the red walls of Carlisle Castle, and presumably would stay there until Scrope saw fit to let him go, or was prodded into it by London. Probably, with any other man but Walter Scott of Buccleuch, the matter would have had to rest there, while he swallowed his anger. But Buccleuch was a fiery and impatient spirit smarting under Scrope's bland refusal. Justice for Kinmont was of secondary importance; Buccleuch's personal credit and honour were now at stake, and if Armstrong could not be released by peaceful means, Buccleuch would break him loose.

It was an awesome task. Buccleuch, for all his dash and daring, was no fool. If ever he gave way to raging in the ballad vein, he did not let it cloud his judgement where Carlisle Castle was concerned. Two hundred years later the Duke of Cumberland might dismiss it as an old hen-coop incapable of resisting artillery, but in Elizabeth's time, in spite of cheese-paring maintenance, it was one of the strongest places in the length of Britain. It is not a showy castle of pinnacles and romantically-crenellated battlements; its great square red keep squats like a piece of living rock behind plain, massive walls which in the sixteenth century extended from it to girdle the city. From outside the old town on the north side one looks up a steep slope to the battlements towering overhead; beyond them the inner hold has walls that are yards thick in places. It is a fort not to be taken except with an army; it is a working castle, built to hold enemies out and keep prisoners in, and to take any kind of punishment a besieger can throw at it.

If Buccleuch was to get into it and take Kinmont out, his one hope lay in stealth and speed, supported by meticulous planning and intelligence work. He had the wit to plan and to lead, he had the ideal men to follow; he had, among an appalling array of obstacles, one important advantage, and that was that an armed raid was the last thing the defenders of Carlisle Castle would expect. All he needed in addition was a foul Cumberland night and a great deal of luck.

He now set to work like the professional he was. It was not difficult to gather intelligence from Carlisle; most of the Scots of the West Border knew it well, and it was a simple matter for Buccleuch to despatch agents to survey the castle's defences, and to glean exact information about Kinmont's place of confinement. His "persons of trust" also examined a postern gate which had been picked as the point of entry for the assault. But more than this was necessary; Buccleuch knew from the start that he would need English help, but he also knew where to go for it. (This is a point which the ballad, and popular legend, entirely overlooks: that the rescue of Kinmont Willie was in fact a combined Scottish–English operation. To a large extent it was what is technically called an inside job.)

Considering the cross-pattern of alliances, marriages, and blood kinships which spanned the frontier, this is not remarkable. Buccleuch was later to be quoted as admitting, of the Carlisle raid, that "I could nought have done in that matter without the great friendship of the Grahams of Eske," and there were others in England, associates of the Grahams, but much closer to Scrope, who were ready to help Buccleuch if only to spite their own Warden.

Thus on a day some weeks after Kinmont's capture three Grahams, Richard of Brackenhill, Will's Jock, and one Andrew, rode to keep a rendezvous with the Carleton brothers, Thomas and Lancelot, and presently went with them to Archerbeck, on the Scottish side, where they met Buccleuch and his principal lieutenants, Gilbert Elliot and the redoubtable old ruffian, Walter Scott ("Auld Wat") of Harden. What was remarkable about this meeting was that both the Carletons were English West March officers and men of influence in North Cumberland. Thomas had been Scrope's deputy and constable of Carlisle and held the post of land sergeant of Gilsland; he was a Border officer of experience and (when he wanted to use it) of considerable ability; we have seen him already at Robert Carey's elbow in the siege of a tower in the Debateable Land.

Unfortunately Thomas was also as crooked as a corkscrew. He was related to the Grahams by marriage, and through them was actually a not-too-distant kinsman of Kinmont Willie himself. He was neck deep in Border politics and intrigues, on friendly terms with the Liddesdale Armstrongs, and widely believed to be an accomplice in their raids into his office at Gilsland. He also appears to have had a stake in a blackmail racket with Richard Graham of Brackenhill (who was now with him at the Buccleuch meeting). Altogether, he was a highly suspect officer, very thick with Richard Lowther who had been disappointed of the West March Wardenry by Scrope some years before, and Scrope had ample grounds for supposing that, deputy and constable though he might be, Carleton was a man whom he would be foolish to trust. Accordingly, he had fired him from these posts, and incurred his undying enmity.

Lance Carleton was as bad a character as his brother, if anything rather more subtle, and with an insolent, devil-may-care swagger which Scrope found particularly provoking. These were the two who now met with Buccleuch to plot Kinmont Willie's escape. In doing so they would fulfil their obligations to a kinsman and at the same time deal Scrope a crippling blow.

This we know from the details of the plotting later revealed by Andrew Graham, one of the conspirators, and also by one William Graham, known as Richie's Will, and a most unctuous stool-pigeon. "Englishmen duelland" in England "was counsels and causes" of the raid, he wrote to Scrope, adding that "the discharging of Thomas Carleton of his office has helped your lordship receive this schame". The Grahams had "done what they could to brake the country" after Thomas was dismissed.

One has to take Border evidence cautiously, but there seems no reason to suppose that Richie's Will, when he blabbed the plot to Scrope afterwards, was not telling the truth. He was supported by the testimony of Andrew Graham and Thomas Armstrong, who were at the meeting with the Carletons, and later gave evidence (not, admittedly, always consistently) before the Carlisle justices on how the scheme was hatched.[3]

_____

3. Richie's Will was evidently in some terror about turning informer; his letter to Scrope, unsigned, concludes with a request to "your lordship to read this and ryve it (tear it up), or els I thinke your lordship falce to me." His fears were well grounded: Andrew Graham was subsequently threatened

The meeting at Archerbeck, at which Buccleuch, the Carletons, and the Grahams spent four hours discussing how to break Kinmont out, was business-like. Thomas Carleton pointed out that "unless you make some way with the watch, you cannot prevail". It was argued that some of the Castle guard were already in the plot, and that it might be dangerous to admit any more to the enterprise. Thomas undertook to make sure that those involved could be relied on, and Lance observed genially that "if it come to pass, it will make an end of Lord Scrope".

They parted, and Buccleuch, confident that the Carlisle end of his operation would function smoothly, could concentrate on mustering his striking force.

The day chosen for the raid was Sunday April 13, and on the Saturday Buccleuch was at the horse races at Langholm. There several Grahams were seen talking to him (Scrope's witnesses were specific), and some of them dined with him that day. One of them, young Hutcheon Graham, was later credited with having first moved Buccleuch to attempt the raid, and it was alleged that Buccleuch had ensured the Grahams' co-operation by causing some stolen beasts of theirs to be returned. In any event, he made his final arrangements with them at the Langholm races, with Willie Kang Irvine acting as go-between and general fixer.

It was vital for Buccleuch to have Graham co-operation. Not only did they have a special tie-up with the Carletons, who were essential to the English end of the affair, they also controlled—so far as anyone could—the country between the Debateable Land and Carlisle, through which Buccleuch must run his raid in complete secrecy. Without the Grahams his operation would have died still-born.

By Saturday night all was ready. Ladders and implements for the break-in had been cached at Morton—Kinmont Willie's place—only ten miles from Carlisle. There were, by Buccleuch's account, eighty riders in his party, which seems more probable than the 200 quoted by Scott from the Shawfield manuscript, or Scrope's estimated 500. (Eure says there were not more than forty riders.) Stealth was imperative, and

---

with death for himself and his family by Richard Graham of Brackenhill unless he denied "all that which he had affeirmed agaynst the Carltones and himself", and a brother of the deponent Thomas Armstrong was murdered by Brackenhill's men, assisted by Carleton's followers and the notorious Jock ("Stowlugs") Armstrong.

even eighty horsemen, expert reivers though they were, would be hard put to it to pass unseen and unheard.[4]

Besides, if all went well, eighty would be enough; if it went ill 800 would have been too few. Buccleuch had picked the best: his own Scotts, the Elliots, and the inevitable Armstrongs, among them Kinmont's four sons, and such redoubtable individuals as Auld Wat of Harden and Willie Kang, Willie ("Redcloak") Bell and his brothers, and Christie Armstrong of Barngleish.

Buccleuch disposed them in classic fashion (he would have made a superb commando leader three-and-a-half centuries later) with a screen of scouts in advance—probably Armstrongs—a supporting body of riders behind, then the assault group with the ladders and crowbars, and finally himself with the main body. They went forward slowly and in silence, the strangest foray that was ever run in the Border country: there was to be no spoiling, no burning, no killing, nothing but the lifting of one man from the strongest hold in the Marches. They were not to know, as they slipped through the dusk, the hooves silent on the moss and turf, without a glint or a clink of arms, that they were riding on the last great good-night, that the old days were passing behind them, that within a few short years the man who led them would be clearing the reiving bands from the frontier, that soon there would never be moonlight again. Theirs was the last great riding, and the best; eighty lances against the Corbie's Nest.

They crossed the Esk at nightfall, probably not far from the point where the Metalbridge now spans the red sandbanks, and pushed silently into the southern moss. They must have gone slowly, probably with frequent halts, for they took the best part of the night to cover the half-dozen miles that took them through the King moor to Stanwix Bank, the high line of bluffs that rears above the Eden on the north bank, away from Carlisle city. It was two hours short of dawn when they came within sight of their quarry.

This northern approach to Carlisle is unusual, in that the Stanwix Bank makes the city invisible until one is within a quarter of a mile of it; it is likely that Buccleuch's force crossed the Eden some distance below the modern bridge ("beneath Carleill brig," says the account),

---

4. In addition to his raiding party, Buccleuch laid two ambushes on the Border to cover his retreat if he was pursued. One consisted of Irvines under the Goodman of Bonshaw, and the other of Johnstones under their chief.

and landed on the meadow beside the river Caldew which runs on the west side of the town.[5] "It happened to fall to be very dark in the hind-night, and a little mistie"; the Eden was running high, and it was raining heavily. The weather was on the raiders' side.

They could hear the sentries on the wall far overhead; with the noise of the storm there was a good chance of escaping detection. But at this point it is difficult to be sure exactly what happened next; perhaps the ladders were too short, and they had to resort to "opening the wall a little, hard by the postern". Considering what that wall is like to-day, it seems unlikely that anyone could open it, even "a little", in less than several days; Scrope says that the postern was "undermyned speedily and quietly," but he is an unreliable witness here; he may have been reluctant at first to concede what quite possibly happened, that the postern was opened from inside. Or perhaps it was simply battered down; which ever way it was, suddenly they were inside, scattering the few guards who were at hand (two of the watch were left for dead, according to Scrope), and making for Kinmont's prison.

Where this was is uncertain. It obviously was not in the keep, with its series of dungeons; even to break into the Licking-Stone Cell, which is by no means the most inaccessible, could hardly have been accomplished by a hit-and-run raid. It is probable that he was confined in some building outside the main fortress—the domestic buildings of Carlisle Castle are west of the Keep, within the castle wall, and the Shawfield account says plainly that he was in a "hous", that Buccleuch had learned this through a woman spy,[6] and that 'ther lacked not persones enough thaire that knew all the rewmes thaire". This is consistent with Scrope's hint that Kinmont was on parole. It is quite clear

---

5. The Shawfield document, quoted by Scott in his "Border Minstrelsy", says they came "to the Sacray". The land north of old Carlisle towards the Eden is called the Soceries or Sauceries.

6. Kinmont Willie probably knew his rescuers were coming, and when. According to Scrope, one of the Grahams brought Buccleuch's ring to the imprisoned reiver, "for a token for his deliverance by him", and if Richie's Will's letter means what it seems to mean, it is even possible that Kinmont's wife visited him in the castle. The letter says: "There was never a turne done fornenttes the lowsing of Kinmont, but thur men [the Grahams] was all counsell to it and causit Kynmontes wyfe, quha is Androwes sister, make it all with Kinmont within the howse."

that he was not chained, and that the tradition of his being carried, fetters and all, down a ladder, is a fiction.

The first of the raiders "brought him furth, and so be the posterne gat away". It is not unlikely, supposing exact information beforehand, a few helpers among the garrison, and precise directions to each raider as to his part in the break-in, that it was just as simple as that. The essence of the plan was speed; Buccleuch had to be in and out again before the alarm was spread, and it seems that he managed it. There may have been a sudden brief brawl (one of Kinmont's keepers is said to have been wounded), and then the prisoner was being hustled through the postern to a waiting horse.

Outside, Buccleuch had taken no chances. His main force was waiting between the postern and the nearest of the city's gates (the Irish Gate,[7] on the west side), so that in the event of a sally from the gate he would be able to screen his break-in party. It was not necessary. They had the prisoner out at speed, Buccleuch's trumpet sounded the retreat, and then the whole force was falling back to the river. One account talks of an attempt made to bar the passage on the north bank, but nothing came of it, and as dawn broke they were galloping north, "and came back to Scottis ground at about two hours after sunrysing".

It had, in the event, been quite easy; expert marauders had carried out a perfectly planned break without a slip; there had been no bad luck. This, it seems most reasonable to suppose, is how they took Kinmont Willie Armstrong from Carlisle Castle. Official accounts and legends have embroidered the comparatively simple story, for various reasons; the very fact that it had been a smooth, swift and entirely efficient strike made it, paradoxically, equally unsatisfactory to the chroniclers and publicists of both sides.

Scottish myth-makers have enlarged it as a glorious commando raid in the face of tremendous odds. So it was, up to a point; but the fact that it was made possible by informers, traitors and fifth columnists is

---

7. Carlisle has three gates—the Scotch, or Rickergate (supposedly named after Richard III, who lived in Carlisle in his Warden days) to the north, the Irish or Caldewgate to the West, and the main English or Botchergate to the south. The three main central streets are still on the original Roman Y-plan, and their names are significant of what mattered most in the city's history— English Street, Scotch Street, Castle Street.

overlooked because it detracts from the gallantry of Buccleuch's raiders. They have tended to magnify a professional job into a chivalric feat of arms, which is to do Buccleuch less than justice. Much is made of the fact that no door but that of Kinmont's prison was "so much as knockt at", that no other prisoners were released (it is even suggested that some were sent back), and that no advantage was taken of the opportunity to loot and despoil. It is true that Buccleuch was determined to do absolutely nothing but release Kinmont, and keep his hands clear of any other possible charge; at the same time, his raiders were limited not only by his orders but by circumstance. The opportunity to loot and despoil did not exist, and to suggest that the raiders "war maisters of the castell" is wishful thinking. For a few minutes they controlled that small part of it that was necessary, but it was a case of hit-and-run. They were not there to take the castle, but to break out a prisoner.

However, exaggeration and poetic embellishments are excusable; Lord Scrope, when he came to write his accounts of the affair, had other motives for making it appear that the raid was on a rather grander scale than it actually was.

It is possible to be sorry for him. In a few minutes his world had tumbled. The splendid fortress under his charge had been burgled of its prize prisoner, without great difficulty. His arch-enemy had scored an incredible victory. Scrope had been hit, quite literally, where he lived; his garrison had been caught flat-footed; he had been made to look a complete fool. What, he must have asked himself, would the Queen say?

It was even difficult to find excuses. All he could do was admit his garrison's incompetence, as when he wrote to the Privy Council on the following day. There had been 500 men in the raiding party, he wrote, under Auld Wat of Harden, and they had undermined the postern and been in and out again before resistance could be made.

"The watch, as yt shoulde seeme, by reason of the stormye night, were either on sleepe or gotten under some covert to defende themselves from the violence of the wether, be meanes whereof the Scottes atcheived theire enterprise with lesse difficultie."

An appalling admission, and probably true. Still, Scrope can hardly have hoped that London would accept it as an adequate explanation. He goes on:

"The wardinge place of Kinmonte . . . and the assurance he had given that he woulde not breake awaye, I supposed to have bin of sufficient suretie, and litle looked that any durst have attempted to enforce in the tyme of peace any of her Majestys castells."

For the rest, some of his servants had told him that they had heard Buccleuch's name called out during the raid. Scrope closed by promising revenge, unless he was countermanded: "yt shall cost me both life and lyvinge, rather than such an indignitie to her highnes, and contempt to me selfe, shalbe tollerated."

At the same time he was writing to Burghley, giving him the inside information about treachery on his own side. The Lowthers were ready "to do villeny unto me" and he was "induced vehementlye to suspect that their heades have bin in the devise of this attempt, and am also perswaded that Thomas Carlton hath lent his hand hereunto; for yt is whispered in myne eare, that some of his servants, well acquainted with all the corners of this castell, were guydes in the execution thereof."

Scrope's intelligence service was obviously more efficient than his security forces; it was a pity they had not been as active before the event as they were to be after it. Indeed, an intriguing feature of the Kinmont affair is that Scrope went in apparently total ignorance of the projected raid beforehand; although it was obviously a well-shared secret, neither he nor Salkeld nor any of his loyal subordinates seem to have had even a whiff of it. It is at once a tribute to the Carletons' judgement and caution, and an indication of how out of touch Scrope was with the undercurrents of his March.

In a postscript to his letter to Burghley, Scrope added that he now had sure information that Buccleuch had been involved, and had indeed been the fifth man into the castle. He had actually been heard to cry out: "Stand to yt, for I have vowed to God and my prince that I will featch out of England Kinmont dead or quicke."

Possibly Burghley may have been prepared to believe that Border reivers were in the habit of delivering patriotic speeches which implicated their monarch, at the critical moment of their forays; probably he was not. The interesting point is that hereafter in his correspondence Scrope shifts the emphasis on to Buccleuch, the Carletons, the Grahams, *et al.* His own incompetence is naturally forgotten, and he rather represents himself as the hapless victim of Buccleuch's villainy and even bad sportsmanship.

The Grahams came in for a major share of his reproaches. The Privy Council, having digested Scrope's reports, were apparently not fully satisfied about Graham complicity, and Scrope was indignant to the point of offering his resignation. In August he was citing the evidence of the Langholm horse races as proof of the complicity, and referring to the "awfullness of the Grahams".

For the next year the unfortunate English Warden was pursuing evidence of the Kinmont raid, maligning Buccleuch, developing a positive mania about the Grahams (a long and, from Scrope's point of view, painful story which there is not room to include here), and managing to convince himself that the breaking of the castle had been a cad's trick for which no respectable Warden could in decency be held responsible. And in spite of the Queen's wrath, and the diplomatic activity which followed on the raid, Scrope does not appear to have been in any danger of losing his office; he continued in it until Elizabeth's death seven years later. But it is doubtful if he ever forgot Black Sunday April 13 1596.

His own government gave him little cause to. The rage and indignation which Kinmont's rescue occasioned was loud and memorable, and it resounded nowhere so powerfully as in the vicinity of Ambassador Bowes in Edinburgh. Queen Elizabeth wanted Buccleuch's head, metaphorically at least; he was not only a castle-breaking scoundrel ("God's curse", in Her Majesty's own choice phrase), but suspect of Popish plotting, and must be jailed forthwith, and proper redress given. Bowes, a shrewd and capable man who understood, if he could not approve, the Carlisle raid, found himself in a position of some delicacy, and asked London for "timely and perfect directions". He got them: Buccleuch must be handed over.

Bowes presented himself accordingly to King James, who one suspects was enjoying himself hugely. He was, however, disposed to be conciliatory to his dear sister of England, and his response to Bowes shows him at the top of his diplomatic form. In earnest and amiable vagueness no prince ever surpassed James. He had not given Buccleuch permission, no indeed, and who said he had? Personally, he thought Kinmont's release should have been procured by "a secret passage, through some window, or by some such like practice". But he assured the ambassador that he would give Elizabeth "good contentment".

He wrote to her, and the response he received would have curdled the blood of anyone closer to Elizabeth than Edinburgh.[8] But James, in spite of his soft approach, was not to be budged just yet; he approved Buccleuch's behaviour, and he knew that his countrymen did too.

Meanwhile, Buccleuch had stated his defence before the Council. It was plain, and calculated to win him sympathy. He had not tried to take the castle; he had behaved moderately, although he admitted the necessity of wounding a couple of Englishmen; he had been responsible in the first place for sending Kinmont to the day of truce; he had done nothing but secure the release of a man unjustly held.

It might have been sufficient, but in the wake of the Kinmont raid Border turbulence was stepping up, the opposing Wardens' relations deteriorated, and in the turmoil Buccleuch seemed to be doing more to harm than help. While Scrope was conducting reprisal raids into the Scottish West March,[9] Buccleuch was causing much havoc on the English side, both by "procurement" of forays, as the English saw it, with Auld Wat of Harden and others riding vigorously, and by raiding personally. Scrope was warning London in August that Buccleuch was "ready with 3000 men to invade us" but had retired on seeing the English beacons. His own government warded him briefly at St Andrews, but in the following year he was hammering Tynedale, and both he and Robert Kerr of Cessford were the subject of continual English complaints. Eure, in the Middle March, saw only one way of dealing with him; in a fit of enthusiasm he offered to bring in the heads of both Buccleuch and Cessford, remarking that he would need only

8. "Shall any castle or habytacle of mine be assayled by a night largin, and shall not my confederate send the offender to his due punisher? I am as evill treated by my named friend as by my knowen foe", etc.

9. Some account of these raids has been given in Chapter XVIII. One of them, far from satisfying Scrope's thirst for revenge, must have raised his blood pressure still higher. It was conducted by Thomas Musgrave in July, to an unspecified target in Scotland, but the houses when he got there were empty, and in returning home "over carelessly" he allowed his band to scatter, and was himself ambushed in Bewcastle. He rode for refuge—with what one can only describe as unwarranted optimism—to the house of Richard Graham of Brackenhill, but they barred the door against him ("such good service do the Grahams to her Majesty!" fulminated Scrope) and he was captured by the Scots. At least one version states that his captor was Kinmont Willie which, if true, was the crowning irony. However, Musgrave was shortly afterwards released on bond.

a small assistance—the joint forces of all the Wardenries, plus the Berwick garrison. It may not have occurred to him to ask for the navy as well.

But plainly Buccleuch could not be allowed to continue at large, although the enormity of the Carlisle raid was fading as the months passed. He and Scrope even had a meeting, the English Warden showing himself rather huffy. At last, in the autumn of 1597, Buccleuch eventually handed himself over to England, and while he was there he seems to have given no trouble, and won good opinions from his warders. At least, when he was sent back to Scotland the following February, in exchange for his son, aged ten, who was entered to England as a hostage, even John Carey was moved to remark that "the gentleman hathe behaved him selfe verie well and honorably, and left . . . hope of his behaviour heereafter". When he was not riding Buccleuch was no doubt a likeable enough man, and his son must have had some of his father's personality, for Carey thought the little boy "a propper and towarde childe".

After he came home Buccleuch seems to have been a different man. Robert Carey found that he ran "a dyrect course" and was zealous for justice; Scrope found him "busy to be familiar", but could not bring himself to be friends with the man who had broken his castle. More than three years after the raid Buccleuch journeyed to London, remarking to Robert Carey that he hoped to kiss the Queen's hand; it is just possible that he did, although the story of their meeting is not supported by sound evidence. Tradition has it that Elizabeth asked him how he had dared to break into her fortress, and is supposed to have received the answer: "What is there that a man will not dare?", at which Her Majesty is said to have observed that with 10,000 such men King James could have shaken any throne in Europe.

It would be nice to believe it was true. Walter Scott of Buccleuch, young, swaggering, and dare-devil, was certainly Elizabeth's kind of man.

The Kinmont raid was a small affair, in itself, but it remains the brightest of Border legends. Obviously it will never be known fully what went on in the background, and much of the surface evidence is incomplete. If it was less romantic than the popular legend suggests, it is still a little gem within the strictly professional limits of guerrilla warfare or international crime, depending on how it is viewed. Its importance is less what it was, than what people think it was; if it casts a better, more chivalrous light on the Border reivers than they generally deserved, it still shows them at their best. When men put their lives in the hazard for a single friend, with no thought of gain and only the spice of mischief to set against the risk of death, it is not altogether unworthy.

XLII

The Carleton Brothers

Shocking knaves though they were, one has to admire the Carletons. They emerged from the Kinmont affair with nothing but stains on their characters, and yet try as Scrope might (and for the next few months he pursued them like a man possessed) he never managed to pin anything on them. Indeed, the Carletons, who seem to have had a hot line of their own to the corridors of power,[1] by a policy of stout denial and counter-charge almost managed to convey the impression that Scrope was pursuing them out of demented malice. They were not unskilled in public relation; Thomas was a good, clear writer, and Lance had undoubted persuasive gifts.

Some of these were certainly applied to possible witnesses who might have testified against them, and one Armstrong was murdered in revenge for evidence given by a kinsman. But in the gentler arts of personal abuse and public vilification the brothers held their own against the infuriated Warden, who was equally unsuccessful in his efforts to have the Grahams punished for their complicity.

Thereafter Scrope could find nothing too bad to say about Carletons, Grahams, and Lowthers, since he regarded Richard, the head of the last-named, as hand-in-glove with the Carletons to disgrace him. He was not far wrong, and in view of the Carletons' record it is surprising that Scrope never managed to bring about their downfall; he tried

---

1. Scrope refers to Lancelot Carleton in one letter as being the Earl of Essex's man.

hard enough, alleging against them crimes and defaults that had nothing to do with the Kinmont raid, but which were probably well
justified.

This verbal feuding would seem trivial enough, but it gives an added
insight into the politics which surrounded a March Warden; one begins
to see the kind of difficulties that even a good officer might encounter
through personal enmities and local jealousies inside his own March.
The Scrope-Carleton controversy was not unique; similar power
struggles took place all over the Marches, but because of the publicity
attracted by the Kinmont affair, and the energy with which Scrope
committed to paper every scrap of gossip or suspicion that might discredit the Carletons, we have a fuller dossier than usual on this Warden-
subordinate relationship.

It is well to consider what Scrope was up against. These were not
run-of-the-mill men, who could be broken or turned out at the
Warden's pleasure. The Carletons were an old and influential family,
built into the fabric of Cumberland. Old Sir Thomas had done notable
service in Henry VIII's time, and the later generation, led by Thomas
and Lance, were tough, unscrupulous, worldly-wise, and numerous.[2]
North-east Cumberland seems to have been aswarm with them, all
villains (in Scrope's view) out to disgrace him, and to disturb the peace
by assisting Scots, plotting with malcontent Cumbrian gentry, and the
like. Even allowing for the fact that Scrope became obsessed by them,
and remembering his own defects of character, the Carletons emerge as

2. There are so many Carletons, and their Christian names are so often
repeated in the generations, that it is often difficult to tell one from the
others. For example, Thomas Carletons abound, and the record of Lancelot's brother contains many references which might be construed as applying to some other member of the family. A common mistake with regard to
this Thomas Carleton is to suppose that he was Kinmont Willie's son-in-law;
this arises from a clumsy construction in Musgrave's list, where the meaning
of the word "his" is ambiguous. In fact, as Carleton himself stated in a letter
to Burghley, the relationship was rather more distant. Carleton married the
daughter of one George Graham (also known as Thomas Gorthe Graham)
of Esk; this George Graham was married to Kinmont Willie's sister—thus
making Kinmont Willie a kind of uncle-in-law by marriage to Carleton.
The complexities of any Border relationship are heart-breaking, but those of
the Grahams, despite the heroic endeavours of Burghley and his clerk to
reduce them to some sort of order, are fit only for the computer.

dangerous bad men. Not that that makes them untypical Border peace officers. They did the job, they made something on the side; this was the way the frontier was.

In the winter following the Kinmont raid, Thomas Carleton, as land sergeant of Gilsland, arrested one Christopher Bell, a notorious murderer (eleven victims), thief, and March traitor, and handed him over to Lord Eure in the neighbouring Wardenry, where he was duly executed. Scrope chose to take deep offence at this; he had been left out of the business, and the Carletons were far too much at home in Eure's Wardenry for his liking. As he saw it, they had no business there. The Warden's paranoia was in full flower, and there followed other charges, that Thomas was aiding and abetting Auld Wat of Harden to ride in Gilsland (200 riders in a day foray), Richard Lowther was shielding the family and helping them evade justice, they were harbouring thieves, and at this rate Scrope could see nothing for it but to declare Thomas an outlaw.

Lancelot stepped in smoothly to his brother's defence. Christopher Bell had been a proclaimed outlaw, and as a result of Thomas's action (which by implication was presented as being his simple duty) the Bells, Elliots and Armstrongs were combining to murder him, reviving a feud over Thomas's killing of an Armstrong two years earlier, in the course of duty. A hundred Liddesdale riders had lately tried to kill Thomas in his house, the Bells were accusing the Carletons falsely of March treason, and had procured the death of one of them through a Warden court sentence. The Carletons, Lance concluded, were just trying to do their job, and this was the thanks they got.

While the Privy Council were considering this, Scrope was burning up the paper in reply. Christopher Bell was a notorious offender, was he? Then why had Thomas Carleton been favouring him for years, and receiving benefits from him? It was only when Bell had entered into assurances with Scrope, to answer for his offences, that Carleton had suddenly moved against him, setting on him in his home, tricking him into a confession, and having him executed in Eure's Wardenry. Scrope had been kept in the dark the whole time, and the implication was that Carleton had arrested Bell simply out of malice to the West March Warden.

As for the talk of a Bell–Armstrong–Elliot combination to murder

Thomas Carleton, Scrope laughed it to scorn. If anyone was in league
with Elliots and Armstrongs it was Thomas himself. Far from associat-
ing with the Liddesdale reivers, the Bells were actually among their
principal victims. In conclusion, Lance Carleton was a liar, and the
Carleton condemned by the Warden court had been a horse-thief.

Scrope's temper was not improved, during the thrashing out of these
cross-allegations, by Lancelot's personal defiance of himself in the
presence of Warden officers and justices at Carlisle. Lance was evidently
at his impudent best, "defying the world, and standing before his lordship, did give a great and lightlie girtt with his thume upon his fynger"
—all of which was solemnly recorded, attested, and forwarded to
London.

Before a few months had passed, Scrope was laying before Burghley
further proofs of Thomas Carleton's iniquity and of his alliance with
those Armstrongs and Elliots whom he had pretended were trying to
kill him. In July, 600 Scottish riders, guided by Carleton's people, ran a
day foray into Gilsland, stealing 200 beasts from the Bells and taking
prisoners. Scrope assembled a trod, but the Liddesdale forayers escaped,
so the pursuers turned instead on Kinmont Willie's herds at Morton
Rigg (without any excuse, apparently) and stole 300 of them. Scrope's
attitude appears to have been that if he could not recover the Bells'
stolen beasts, Kinmont's would do instead, and he would award them
to the Bells by way of compensation. But as the herd was being driven
to Gilsland, a band of Grahams appeared on the scene and lifted the lot.

This was bad enough, from Scrope's point of view, but to increase
his wrath he discovered that his trod, in lifting Kinmont's cattle, had
also taken prisoner Kinmont himself, but had let him go again. Secretly,
this may not have disturbed him too much; it is doubtful if he wished
to entertain Kinmont as a prisoner a second time. However, he soon
had more pressing business to attend to, for two days later the Scots hit
Gilsland again, lifting nearly 300 beasts and prisoners, and when
Scrope gave orders for a reprisal the Carletons terrorised the Warden's
riders into abandoning it.

To support Scrope's charges, the Bells of Gilsland weighed in with a
letter to the Privy Council. Two of them, Thomas and James Bell,
alleged that Thomas Carleton was arranging for Liddesdale raids into
Bell territory because they, Thomas and James, had once arrested two
Carleton adherents on Scrope's behalf. One of these arrested men had

been an Armstrong, and as a result the Armstrongs "after their bruteish manner", had declared a deadly feud on all of the Bell surname. What with this, and Carleton's hatred and malice towards them, they feared that they and their fellow-Bells of Gilsland (500 all told) would be "cleane rooted out". Already eighty of them had been beggared and sixty kidnapped.

Burghley asked Carleton to answer this complaint, and Thomas scoffed it out of court. One, he had never heard of James Bell. Two, Thomas Bell did not speak for the whole surname of Bells. Three, the Gilsland raids had actually been guided not by Carletons (as Scrope had suggested), but by Thomas Bell's own brother: Carleton could bring other Bells to prove it. Four, the Bells who had arrested the two Carleton adherents were not Thomas and James Bell, but two others of the clan. Five, it was nonsense to suggest that eighty Bells had been beggared and sixty kidnapped, since there were not fifty Bells in Gilsland, let alone 500. Six, Thomas Bell and his associates were liars, "which God forgeve them". And there the matter rested.

If considerable space has been devoted to this Scrope–Bell–Carleton controversy, it is simply to show the kind of complexity that affairs of this kind could assume, and the difficulty of sorting out truth from falsehood. Undoubtedly the Carletons were out to create havoc among the Bells, and undoubtedly they were using Liddesdale to do it, but among all the welter of evidence it would have been hard for Scrope or anyone else to prove these things conclusively.

Nor was Scrope's conduct in the business beyond reproach. It will be recalled that it all began because Thomas Carleton arrested a Bell and handed him to Eure for execution, and that Scrope had reacted with violent complaint. But that was not all he had done—in addition he had decided to teach Eure a practical lesson, and had sent his riders into the Middle March to drive off fifty sheep. A trod had taken place, and Scrope's riders and Eure's subjects had come to blows, several of them being wounded. That aspect of the matter seems to have blown over, but it demonstrates what a state the English Marches had fallen into, when Wardens on the same side were virtually at feud. It is not surprising that in such conditions professional law-breakers—and the Carletons—flourished like the green bay tree.

Scrope continued to ply the Privy Council with further tales of the Carletons' villainy: Thomas was again bringing in raiders, he and

Lance were the "two chief spoilers of the country", and were "living in a manner as outlaws"—which was patently ridiculous. There followed another charge—not from Scrope—that Garret Carleton, Thomas's son, had killed one of Scrope's servants, a Milburn. And so the controversy dragged on, and Scrope must have despaired of ever bringing the Carletons to book.

However, when Nemesis caught up with Thomas Carleton it was, strangely enough, when he was in the appearance of doing his duty, and Scrope had nothing to do with it. A notorious Scottish reiver, David Elliot, known as "Carlyne", had been the leader of a band of Scots who had killed an Englishman, William Ogle, in the English Middle March, doubtless in the way of feud. The Ogles, a powerful clan with various vendettas on the Scottish side, bided their time until word reached them that Elliot had taken refuge in Gilsland, where Thomas Carleton held sway as land-sergeant. No doubt he had an illicit understanding with the Elliot, and was holing him up; the record simply says the Elliot was "resayt within Thomas Carleton's charge".

The Ogles were business-like; they found out exactly where David Elliot was hiding, and on July 4 1598 they gathered a band thirteen strong, rode to the house, and without ceremony killed him. They took care to do no harm to anyone else; having despatched their man they rode off quietly homeward. Word of their raid had reached Thomas Carleton, however, and he overtook them with a posse of six riders, and in a great fury "voud to have the lives of some of them" for killing a man who was in his charge and under his protection. The Ogles tried to placate him, asked only that he leave them alone, and no doubt pointed out that they had done nothing but settle their score with a notoriously evil ruffian.

Carleton would have none of it; in his rage he charged them with his lance, unhorsing one of them, and fired his pistol at another, missing narrowly. With the land-sergeant going berserk among them, one of the Ogles shot him neatly through the head, and Thomas fell dead from his saddle.[3]

At this his friends charged home, and if anything testifies to the

3. Thomas Carleton was evidently a man of high courage who did not count odds. On one occasion, with only four followers, he attacked a band of sixteen Armstrongs who were driving stolen cattle, killing one and capturing two.

Ogles' peaceful intentions it is the fact that, although they apparently outnumbered the posse two to one, they fled to the safety of an old tower, where they took refuge, turning their horses loose. Parleying took place, and eventually the Ogles agreed to give themselves up, provided they were unharmed; however, when they had handed over their weapons there was a scuffle, and one of the Ogles was badly wounded. Seven of them were taken to jail in Carlisle, but they do not appear to have been punished for Carleton's killing.

With Thomas's death the power of the Carletons was much diminished. This is seen in Lancelot's failure to inherit his brother's office of land-sergeant at Gilsland; Lance was bailiff of Brampton, and his local influence made him a logical successor,[4] but with Scrope determined to oppose the Carletons at every turn the job went to John Musgrave. The Carletons had no use for the Musgraves at the best of times, and Lancelot subsequently tried to frame John, and also produced for Cecil a remarkable report of the state of the West March, in which he warned of dangers to the peace, and managed to get in several side-swipes at the Musgraves. At the same time he included a subtly understated and dispassionate condemnation of Scrope; the best thing that could happen to the March, said Lance, would be to appoint "an assured man of worth and quality" as Warden.

The Carletons were probably contemplating more direct action against Scrope, however; in November, only a few days after Lancelot's report, Robert Carey got wind of a plot to murder the West March Warden, either by surprising him at Rose Castle, or if he was not well guarded, catching him unawares either in his home or as he went abroad. Carey suspected the Carletons and Grahams, and was worried that Scrope's personal indifference to danger would prevent his taking proper precautions.

Nothing came of the plot, and Lancelot's principal activities seem to have been limited to maligning the Musgraves, and causing a public scandal by his "impudent, malicious and railing speeches" against the

4. Both his brother and his father had held the land-sergeantship at Gilsland. If Thomas Carleton is to be believed, it was no sinecure. The Gilsland area was continually being forayed; one land sergeant, George Skelton, was killed by the Elliots inside his area, and another, Thomas Carleton senior, was lured into a trod by the Liddesdale Armstrongs, ambushed and captured, and many of his followers badly wounded.

local authorities. However, he may well have been behind an attempt made on the life of John Musgrave at Brampton, where the Grahams set upon the land-sergeant and his followers with dags and guns, and tried unsuccessfully to burn him alive in a house.

Eventually the Musgraves' patience gave way. One of the charges levelled against them in Lancelot's report had been that Thomas Musgrave, captain of Bewcastle,[5] had offered to betray his charge to the Scots; Thomas denied it, and challenged Lance to trial by combat. Carleton accepted, and the fight was fixed for April 8 1602 at Canonbie, in the old Debateable Land, "before England and Scotland"—for obviously the event would be the biggest attraction for years.

The most exact rules for the duel were drawn up—swords to be "one yard and half a quarter of length", two Scotch daggers to be carried, plus steel bonnet, jack, plate sleeves, and so on, and nobody to attend on the fighters except two boys under sixteen who would hold their horses. Neither man was taking any chances. But after all that, we cannot know whether the combat actually took place, or what the outcome was. However, it appears that both men survived—Scrope has an apparent reference to Thomas Musgrave in a letter later in the year, and there is definite proof that Lancelot was not only alive, but with his talent for mischief unimpaired, only three months after the date set for the duel.

In July of 1602 he was writing to Lord Thomas Howard; it is the last letter of his of which we have record, and it is interesting to see that Lancelot Carleton was a scoundrel to the last. In it, he unblushingly offers his services to the Crown to arrange the murder of the Earl of Tyrone, in Ireland. Irish politics, one would have thought, might have been outside Lancelot's province, but it seems that he had once known

---

5. Brother of John Musgrave the land sergeant, and author of the famous and often-quoted list of Border riders, which he sent as a letter to Burghley in 1583. The Musgrave brothers, as we have seen, were most active Borderers, frequently engaged in feuds and killings with the Scottish side. If all that was alleged against Thomas was true, there was not much to choose between him and the Carletons; he too was accused of favouring Scots, admitting thieves, and conspiring with reivers and outlaws. He is supposed to have given his illegitimate daughter in marriage to Sim Armstrong of Whithaugh, and to have been under the rule of a "very unhonest and unworthy woman, by whom he hath had dyvers children; she is hateful to God and man".

a man in Scotland who detested Tyrone, and would have been glad to deliver his person, or his head, for "hope of proffit, for that he was marsanarye".

However, Lancelot had fortunately heard of someone else who would be glad to give Tyrone "his due deserts, if the Queen greatly desires it: choosing to lay the same open to your lordship, whom I am bound to serve on my knees, if I had no feet to stand on". This new assassin was "of wonderful resolution, but both perilous and marsenary"—Lancelot affects a touching delicacy where anything "mercenary" is concerned; he also makes a poker-faced reference to the "corrupt nature of the people" who would be involved in the plot. However, he tells Howard, there it is; let London say the word and Lance will take the matter in hand.

Whether the government seriously considered accepting the offer from this Cumbrian fore-runner of Murder, Inc., does not emerge,[6] although there is a further reference to it in the same year, from Scrope of all people. Apparently Carleton had mentioned the offer to him; Scrope writes wryly to Cecil remarking that if the government think the matter is "fit to deal in", he will find out how much Lancelot wants for arranging the murder.

Scrope may have had his shortcomings, but his Border experience had taught him all about "marsanarye" and "corrupt natures".

---

6. Tyrone eventually died in Rome in 1616.

PART FIVE

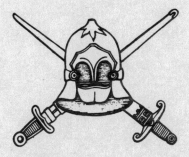

The Middle Shires

We have thot good to discontinue
the divided name of England and Scotland
out of our royal style, and do intend
and resolve to take and assume to us . . .
the name and style of
King of Great Britain . . .

—*Proclamation of King James VI and I*

XLIII

Carey's ride

On a wild March morning in 1603 Robert Carey rode north across the eastern frontier, urging on a spent horse as fast as it could carry him. If any of the frontier riders saw him they must have had difficulty in recognising the courtly English Warden; his clothing was plastered with mud, his face blood-stained from a head wound received when his horse had fallen and kicked him, his whole appearance that of a man near the limit of his strength. But he was stopping for nobody, for he was riding against time to be first in Edinburgh with the most momentous news the British Isles had heard in half a century.

He was, if the Borderers had only known it, a most significant and symbolic figure, for the news he carried was going to change the frontier country as nothing—not invasion, nor war, nor treaty—had ever changed it before. Carey's ride marked the beginning of the end.

Two days earlier he had been in London, where he had arrived to find Queen Elizabeth "ill disposed". She was seventy years old, and a cold taken in January had been aggravated by her insistence on going abroad on a bitter winter day. Her throat was badly affected, she suffered recurring nightmares and fever, and when Carey saw her "she tooke mee by the hand, and wrung it hard, and said: 'No, Robin, I am not well,' and then discoursed with mee of her indisposition, and that her heart had been sad and heavy for ten or twelve days . . . she fetched not so few as forty or fifty great sighs."

The only other time Carey could remember her sighing was when Mary Queen of Scots was executed. He was concerned, and tried to cheer her up, but she only seemed worse and would not go to bed. When Cecil insisted that she must, she growled back, with a flash of the old Queen Bess, "Little man, the word must is not to be used to princes." But her energy was seeping away; to the experienced Carey it looked like approaching death, and his natural anxiety was accompanied by a deeper, more personal alarm.

"I could not but think," he confesses frankly, "in what a wretched state I should be left, most of my livelihood depending on her life. And hereupon I bethought myself with what favour I was ever received by the King of Scottes."

It was understandable, if not entirely admirable, that he should so bethink. James was the man who counted now. Carey has been sniffed at by later writers for considering his own interests when his Queen lay dying; it does not occur to them that he was behaving exactly like the rest of humanity. Possibly he was cold-blooded, but there was nothing he could do for Elizabeth, and at least he was honest enough to confess to some qualms of conscience. They did not trouble him for long. "I assured myself it was neither unjust nor unhonest for me to do for myself," and he wrote to James reporting on the Queen's condition, and assuring him that he would be the first with the news when she died. He arranged for post horses north, gave instructions that he was to be called in the event of any crisis, and waited.

Elizabeth died slowly. Her voice went, and when they eventually put her to bed, prayed over her, and asked her to name James as her successor, she could only do so by sign; Carey, who was a keen watcher among those at her bedside, was satisfied that she understood what she was doing.

At last she was left alone with her ladies, among them Carey's sister, Philadelphia, the wife of Lord Scrope. Early in the morning of Thursday March 24 she died, and soon after dawn Carey was in the saddle, riding north for dear life. He was in Doncaster by night, and on Friday in Northumberland, instructing his deputies to keep the Border quiet and proclaim James King of England while he galloped on into Scotland. His fall and injury made him go slower, but on the Saturday evening he was clattering into Edinburgh, having covered close on 400 miles in sixty hours—an impressive ride, considering the state of Elizabethan roads, the weather, and his accident. No doubt zeal for loyalty to the new monarch spurred him on.

The King had gone to bed, but Carey was admitted to the royal chamber, where he knelt by the bed and saluted its occupant as King of England. It must have been the happiest moment of James's life, but he seems to have behaved admirably, talking at length about the Queen's sickness and death, and showing a proper solemnity when Carey produced proof of the news he brought. Before the Queen died her coronation ring had been cut from her hand, because it had become too tight to slip off; Carey writes:

"I had brought him a blue ring by a fair lady. He took it, and looked upon it, and said, 'It is enough: I know by this you are a true messenger.'"

It must have been a weary, well-pleased Robert Carey who took himself to bed that night. He had been first with the good news, and the King had promised him honour and reward. As a foretaste he was made a gentleman of the bedchamber, and presently he was honoured by being allowed to assist at the royal toilet.

"Now was I to begin a new world," he wrote, but there was disappointment in store. "I only relied on God and the King. The won never left me, the other . . . deceived my expectation." Carey's haste to be first had caused resentment in London, and he lost his bedchamber post when the King went south. His money was cut down, and he was forced to sell his possessions at Norham for £6000. However, he later received some posts and honours, the most important perhaps being Master of the Household to Prince Charles, the future Charles I. In this capacity, at least, Carey and his wife did something to shape the course of British history, for it was through Lady Carey's resistance that the little prince, then aged four, was spared the operation of having the string under his tongue cut, which James I supposed would have assisted his speech. The Careys also prevented the little prince from having his weakly legs "cased in iron boots".

Perhaps Charles remembered their kindness, for when he came to the throne one of his first acts was to create Robert Carey Earl of Monmouth. So the eager young Warden of the frontier lived into an honourable and happy old age; at sixty-three, when he was in Spain, he noted that he "had such a stomake to my meat as in my younger days I never had the like". He died in the spring of 1639, aged nearly eighty; doubtless had he lived a few years longer he would have been in the saddle again in the Civil War, reliving those happy days when "we had a stirring world".

His old friend and enemy, Robert Kerr, outlived him by ten years. He, too, was eighty when he died, and he too was a belted earl.[1]

---

1. One wonders if a tiny seed of the Kerr-Carey rivalry survived into their middle years. After Kerr was made Earl of Roxburgh in 1616, it was recorded that he was "discontented at not obtaining the place of Chamberlain to the Prince".

XLIV

Breaking the Border

"The heich and michtie Prince James the Sext" of Scotland, "with all the rairest gifts of mynd and bodie", was now King of all Britain. As such he was the living embodiment of that dream of union which had possessed Edward I and Henry VIII—and that would have made the pair of them turn in their graves, no doubt. But whatever they had thought of him, they would have approved the zeal with which he set about his unifying task, and seconded the policy by which he sought to make an end of the Borderland.

It is fatally easy, in considering the last chapter of British frontier history, to cast James as the revolting villain who tortured the old Marches into submission. He and the officers appointed by him to pacify the Borderland certainly used a heavy hand, and it makes an ugly story. Against that, one has to take a wide view of the task that James set himself to do: he was determined to make one country where there had been two before, to bury the old quarrels, and to keep the peace. He was not disposed to be over-gentle or over-patient in realising his aim, and knowing the Borders as we do by now, we cannot entirely blame him.

This is not an attempt to whitewash James, even less to defend the men who worked his Border policy. But one should not permit popular and romantic (and possibly inaccurate) concepts to cloud the case. It used to be fashionable to regard James as a slobbering, goggling, pedantic pederast, stuffed with ill-digested scholarship, vain and cowardly and dishonest, and to relate what happened on the Borders after 1603 to these supposedly unroyal characteristics, and to see Border policy as the inevitable result of having such a creature on the throne.

This is emotional nonsense. If James were truly the compound of all the vices that have been attributed to him (and it is no part of this book to argue the point) the fact still remains that at the end of the day he left the old, wild bloody Border a fit place for ordinary folk to live. If the Border riders were harshly dealt with, it is not irrelevant to point out that they had dealt fairly harshly in their time. Undoubtedly injustice and atrocity took place in settling the frontier, but the victims are not to be accounted any nobler just because of that.

It is also wrong to suggest that James was ignorant of Border conditions. He knew a great deal about them, from first-hand experience—certainly more than any occupant of the English throne since Richard III. He may be charged with cruelty, indifference, and dishonesty in his attitude to Border affairs, but not with ignorance or stupidity. And having said this much, it is best simply to see what happened along the frontier from the moment when Elizabeth died.

On his ride north, Robert Carey had instructed his deputies to keep the frontier quiet. Possibly he knew what was coming. In the first days following the Queen's death the Border resounded with that remarkable outbreak known as "Ill Week", in which the riders broke loose all along the frontier, looting, burning, reiving, and driving deep into England in search of plunder. The West March riders, over 200 strong, by-passed Carlisle and forayed as far as Penrith; on the East Marches, Carey wrote later, there was "unruliness" at the news from London; Hutcheon Graham, blackmailer and wild spark of the English West March, took off on a predatory sweep through North Cumberland. He and his riders roared along the meadows south of the Eden at Carlisle, to the scandal of the Bishop, who watched them from the safety of the battlements; having provisioned himself at the terrified village of Cargo, Hutcheon spoiled several places, burning and looting before returning to Cargo, where the gang divided the spoils. Hutcheon, as leader, took one-eighth.

It is suggested that the "Ill Week" outbreak arose from a belief on the Borders that when a monarch died the laws of the land were automatically suspended until the new king was proclaimed. Although this is a tradition not confined to Britain, it is doubtful if anyone on the Borders took it seriously, which is not to say that they did not regard the Queen's death, and the consequent distraction of attention which it caused, as a heaven-sent chance to cut loose in search of plunder. If so, the Grahams especially were to pay dearly for it; the Bishop did not forget young Hutcheon's bravado.

Meanwhile the new king, entertaining notions not entirely dissimilar to those of his Border subjects, was coming south to claim his inheritance. On April 6 he was at Berwick, being received with salutes of guns and other expressions of enthusiasm, including an eloquent sermon from Toby Matthew, Bishop of Durham, and a purse of £2000 presented by the English authorities. Thus spiritually and materially sustained, His Majesty journeyed on, having despatched a strong force of horse westward along the frontier to deal with the wild riders whose forays were marring the solemnity of his entry into his new kingdom. In the West the Laird of Johnstone, with 100 riders, repressed "certein lewd people", reivers were chased back to their holds, several of which were destroyed, and various offenders were locked up at Carlisle.

The King, entering into the spirit of the thing, hanged cutpurses on the way south, including "two gentlemen". But for the most part it was junketing all the way to London.

Amid all the excitement of entering into his new kingdom, James did not lose sight of the vital point, which was the cementing together of England and Scotland, and the obliteration of all barriers between them. These included the actual Border line; His Majesty always having "special regard to the Marchis and Bordouris", it was his intent that "the verie hart of the cuntrey sall not be left in ane uncertaintie". Accordingly, like Hertford before him, he studied to abolish even the names of England and Scotland (North and South Britain seemed a better idea), and pointed out that what had previously been the extremities of the old kingdoms were now the centre of the new realm. The laws and usages of the late borders and marches were "vanished and delete". The Border no longer existed; where the old Marches had been would be henceforth The Middle Shires.

As a first step, those guilty of foul and insolent outrages in the area must submit themselves to his justice and mercy, or be excluded from it permanently.

It was a noble concept, no doubt, but James was wrong in supposing it would meet with universal approval. Giovanni Scaramelli, the astute Venetian Secretary in London, concluded that the Scots and English would never be able to pull together; he noted, however, that those four Scots who were now added to the English Privy Council were quickly bought over by the English. Previously they had been receiving Spanish subsidies.

Scaramelli's diplomatic experience doubtless rendered him cynical, but he was right when he remarked that the Scots would never abandon their name or national identity. Nor was this the only bar to James's perfect union; the English began to ask themselves, as they listened to the new monarch's rolling speech, and observed the mob of needy moochers who followed in his wake, if perhaps they had not exchanged Scottish frontier depredations for a more extensive system of plunder in the heart of their kingdom. A Scotsman on the make is proverbial, but when he comes in large numbers, under the protection of royal authority, it is a daunting sight.

However, when James set his not inconsiderable intelligence to a problem, he pursued it; it might take time to make the lion and the unicorn lie down together, but in the meantime the obvious symbol of division could be removed. He embarked on the pacification of the Borderland.

It was to take him about seven years, all told, but the back of the business was broken in the first four, from 1603 to 1607. The means employed were theoretically simple: the Borders should be disarmed, the old Warden system and March laws consigned to oblivion, the riding families subjected to the same law and discipline as the rest of the kingdom. The last part was the tricky one—a whole way of life had to be swept away and replaced by a new one, and the people convinced that living by robbery and extortion would no longer be tolerated. It sounds reasonable to modern ears; to a community who had existed by plunder and organised banditry for as long as folk-memory could go back, it was less simple. But this was the new order, and those who resisted would have to go—either to the gallows or to exile.

They did not go easily. They were not accustomed to the rule of law, and their way of resisting those who enforced it had always been to fight and to run and to come and fight again. It had worked for generations, but with the gathering of the two governments into one authority the reivers had lost the great, the vital advantage by which they had existed: they could no longer play off one side against the other. It has been said earlier that a true co-operation between England and Scotland, working whole-heartedly together, could have pacified the Borders; this was what was now to happen, in effect.

In that first year of 1603 Lord Hume was made lieutenant of the three Scottish Marches, with Sir William Cranston as his deputy. A similar appointment for the English side was given to George Clifford, Earl of Cumberland. In November a detachment of the new Armed Guard was sent to Dumfries, and in the same year the first of a long, dreadful crop of executions of principal offenders took place. Thirty-two Elliots, Armstrongs, Johnstones, and Batys, with others, went to the gallows, fifteen more were banished, and 140 outlawed. The purging process had begun.

Among those who have been credited with pacifying the Borders was the arch-reiver himself, Walter Scott of Buccleuch. He did at least afford his old associates a better future than the rope or the emigrant ship, by employing them as mercenary soldiers overseas. In 1603 about 2000 Scots under the "Lord Bluch" crossed to the Low Countries to help the States in their war against Spain, and as might have been expected, they rendered distinguished service. The Spanish Ambassador in London was moved to complain, but was told that King James was "not altogether displeased that this rabble should be taken out of the kingdom"—furthermore, if the King of Spain himself wanted levies he was most welcome to them in Scotland.

Those who went with Buccleuch may well have been the lucky ones. On the frontier itself pacification began to take an ugly turn, for it had not escaped the gentry employed in restoring order to the Marches that there was considerable profit to be gained from the operation. For the first time it was going to be safe to hold land on the Borders, and if some of the better-endowed riding clans—the Grahams of Esk, for example—could be dispossessed of their territory, the pickings would be rich. Excuses were easy to find.

Early in 1605 a Commission of ten (five English, five Scots) was appointed for the whole Borders, with headquarters at Carlisle, which was seen as the obvious capital for the Middle Shires. To carry out the Commission's orders, and to enforce discipline, Cranston on the Scottish side and the veteran Henry Leigh were appointed to command the horse garrison—they were, in effect, chiefs of police. Their rule was ruthless; Cranston scoured the Scottish Marches, arresting on old charges as often as not, and giving short shrift; doubtful cases, in which there might be room for clemency, were officially reported, but invariably the instruction came back to hang.

The instructions issued earlier and during this period indicate the kind of rule that was to be imposed; it must be emphasised that not all the recommendations were implemented, but enough of them were carried out to turn the Borderland into a police state which was most barbarously administered.

It was recommended that all iron gates on towers should be removed and turned into ploughshares, that the riding families should be dispersed, arms forbidden, and that no one should own a horse worth more than £30 Scots—in other words, only work horses were to be permitted, and they must have no saddles except "soddes". None of which could be seriously objected to, since this was no more than depriving the reivers of the means to rob; but there was more to follow.

The Privy Council records contain long proposals for the tracking down of fugitives, their capture and punishment, and such prohibitions as that forbidding "broken men" to be absent from home for more than forty-eight hours without licence. Sleuth hounds were to be kept in the Border towns for the pursuit of offenders; there should be "sworne men" (informers) and "rypers" (searchers) in every parish, to search out and give up suspect persons, or those who had "no sufficient trade"; among the broken clans only the eldest was to inherit, and others in the family were to be transported where the council should think fit. It was also thought advisable to reduce the number of ale houses.

This discipline was not accepted gladly. In Dumfries the townsfolk tried to massacre Cranston and his troopers; three or four mounts were shot down, and Cranston—not for the only time in his Border experience—had to cut his way out. Dumfriesshire continued to the end to be the last outpost of turbulence, the final refuge of thieves and outlaws, but in the face of an authority whose policy was one of wholesale hanging there was no great amount of armed resistance. On the whole, the Borderers submitted more quietly than might have been expected, but not on that account were they spared.

XLV

Malefactors of the name of Graham

The chief sufferers along the whole line were the Grahams of Esk. They had been a thorn in the side of two kingdoms for as long as anyone could remember, and they paid for it terribly. Yet they would certainly have suffered less if they had not been the owners of some of the most fertile land in all the Marches, on which Lord Cumberland had cast his eye. It was enough; submission would not suffice in the Grahams' case—they would have to go.

There followed one of the most comprehensive and cruel examples of race persecution in British history. It is not easy to defend the Grahams, who were as wicked a crew as any in the Borderland, but none of their crimes could have justified the spite with which they were murdered, dispossessed, and banished by their persecutors, in the name of law and order, and with the full approval of the King, whose aversion to them seems to have been acute. One of his proclamations announces that the Grahams had confessed themselves to be "no meet persons to live in those countries, and have humbly besought us that they might be removed to some other parts". Their lands would be inhabited by "others of good and honest conversation". Cumberland was just full of good and honest conversers ready to take over.

Attached to the proclamation are the names of almost 100 Esk and Leven Grahams and their families. The Border Commission had special instructions to deal with "the malefactors of the name of Graham", and after their lands had been confiscated 150 of them were listed on April 17 1605 for transportation. In May it was announced that they would be sent to serve in the British garrisons in the Low Countries, and in that same month twenty-eight condemned Borderers who had been held in prison at Carlisle broke jail. Leigh and Cranston were ordered to hunt them down forthwith, burn their homes and expel their families. Cranston burned every house at Stakeheugh in June, and seven "principal Grahams" were posted as fugitives.

Of the 150 Grahams who had submitted and were awaiting transportation, it was decided to send about 100 to Flushing, and the remainder to Brill. Of the 100, only seventy-two were shipped out, the remainder having escaped or died, but it proved easier to send them to the Low Countries than to keep them there. Within the year an estimated fifty-eight out of the seventy-two had stolen back, through Newcastle and the Forth. Some were arrested and condemned, but others made their way home to Eskdale—"if some order be not taken", observed Sir Wilfrid Lawson, one of the commissioners, "they will all be shortly at home again".

Cranston and Leigh were busily engaged in hunting the fugitives, as well as the twenty-eight condemned escapees from Carlisle; special detachments of the horse garrison were stationed in the Graham country for this purpose, and to catch fresh recruits for the Low Countries. By November Leigh was claiming that he had cleared English ground of Grahams, but that they were being received in Scotland, and despite claims by the Scottish Commissioners, that on their side they "made no bones to kill such fugitives and felons as resist", the hunted Grahams were later reported to be hiding up among the Carlisles, Johnstones and other families of the Scottish West March.

Not only that, they were riding abroad in troops armed with lances and pistols, in defiance of the disarming laws. "They had rather die at home with shame than serve his majesty abroad with profit," the commissioners reported. Few seem to have been caught that winter, despite the searchers' efforts; one excursion against them, disguised as an ordinary fox hunt (presumably in case the fugitives got wind of it) resulted in the capture of ten Grahams, which was a poor bag to send overseas.

However, some of the most notorious of the family were in custody, including young Hutcheon Graham and the celebrated Jock of the Peartree. The latter had escaped from the Low Countries but had been caught in London; young Hutcheon had submitted and been placed in Carlisle Castle in October. Like other fugitives against whom the authorities wished to discover a capital charge, he was not only indicted for his raids in "Ill Week", and for previous offences of murder and blackmail, but actually found himself charged with his part in the Kinmont Raid, ten years before.

This gives some idea of the lengths the authorities were prepared to go to against the Grahams. Several were hanged for "Ill Week" activities, although these were supposed to have been generally pardoned—

indeed, seventy-eight of them had presented a petition, admitting and repenting their crimes of "fire, sword, robbery and murder" in that week, and praying to be banished as an "evil colony". They would hardly have confessed so much if they had expected to hang for it.[1]

Another commonly revived charge about this time appears to have been the murder of Sir John Carmichael, the West March Warden, in 1600. Sandie Armstrong had swung for it in the spring of 1605, and now the notorious Willie Kang was also indicted, as were some Grahams.

The year 1606 opened with the hanging of five Borderers at Carlisle and seventeen at Newcastle, and the English commissioners hit on the shrewd idea of throwing into Carlisle Castle even entirely innocent members of the Graham clan, on the theory that "their restraint will not a little bridle their friends who are out". But the work of pacification was getting no easier; there does not appear to have been such perfect co-operation between the English and Scottish commissioners, or between Leigh and Cranston, as King James' notions of union demanded. On March 27 Cranston was reporting that he was having to take bonds of assurance from outlaws because he had no jails to put them in, and that his company of horse was having to be split up because he could not be everywhere at once; in May it was being alleged that he was not giving up prisoners who were wanted in England.

Cranston possibly had his hands overfull; quite apart from chasing Grahams and other ill-doers, there is a brief report of his having been in a fight outside an alehouse at the Esk sandbeds. And neither he nor his colleagues can have been greatly encouraged by a message in January 1606 from James at Whitehall, in which His Majesty expressed dissatisfaction with the methods of his frontier administrators, which he found to be "savouring altogidder of barbarisme". Such means should not be necessary, His Majesty thought, since now malefactors had all means of escape removed.

If there was barbarism in Border administration His Majesty was chiefly to blame. The officials who reported in April 1606 that severity

---

1. John Graham, in his *Condition of the Border at the Union*, argues forcibly that this petition was a put-up job by Sir Wilfrid Lawson. Certainly it is impossible to believe that the Grahams presented it voluntarily; it has the ring of a concocted confession, which they may well have been pressured into signing in the hope of being more leniently dealt with.

was better than lenity on the frontier, because "any forbearance has bred greater insolence", were simply expressing the royal philosophy. There is repeated proof of this, but one example will serve. It is an exoneration granted to Cranston by His Majesty in that same year— December 1606—and it is not the only one so granted. Its terms show clearly how James expected his Middle Shires to be pacified, and the kind of licence he was prepared to give to his officers. In its way, it is one of the most terrible documents in the whole catalogue of papers relating to the frontier.

It says that Sir William Cranston is exonerated for executing outlaws without trial, because the necessity of the service did not permit "those prolixe formes accustumed in the civil parts of the kingdom"; there might be too many dangerous prisoners, and it would have taken time to convey them to jail. So he had to make a "quick dispatche" of many notorious thieves and villains without trial. The cure may have been grievous, but Cranston's intentions were "dewtifullie groundit".

Now "Jeddart justice", which means hanging first and trying later, is a Border proverb. No one would dispute that most of the Border reivers had it coming to them. Nor is there reason to suppose that Cranston was anything but a good officer who probably did not abuse the awful trust reposed in him. But the document is not unique for the time; there were plenty of James's officials who were not of Cranston's quality, and the thought of what must have been done in the name of justice in those years makes the blood run cold. Even for James, who was pursuing a worthy end, the means were unspeakable. At the least, it was an odd way of impressing the supposedly lewd, turbulent, and lawless Borderers with the purity of the new justice, and the benefits of the rule of law.

Nor was it particularly successful at first, despite the optimistic reports being put out by officials early in 1606. The Grahams, with Leigh and Cranston harrying them, were said to be hoping for pardon, and in February Leigh reported them quiet. In March the whole frontier was "reasonably well quieted", with "oppin ryding and robreis" described as only a detestable memory, and nothing but minor crime in the Eastern Borders. But with the spring Redesdale came to life again; its inhabitants, and those of Tynedale, had complained of the severity which which they had been treated by Sir William Selby, who was working for Leigh in the east, and now word came that Redesdale was a hotbed of murderers, thieves, and outlaws living openly, "with twenty outcries for things stolen every Sabbath day".

Plainly King James had some cause for complaint, and a general shake-up of Border administration began. Plans were made for streamlining the commission, which was to be reduced to only two members from each side, with the Earl of Dunbar in charge. It was some months before the new system came into operation; in the meantime Leigh was superseded, having been pronounced "infirm", and his charge of the horse garrison transferred to John Musgrave.

Leigh, for all his energy, had perhaps been under something of a cloud—at least he had found it necessary to defend himself the previous autumn in the matter of people escaping from custody in Carlisle. One of his offices had been that of Keeper of Carlisle Castle, and following the mass break-out from the jail in May 1605 he had pointed out that while the castle was his responsibility, it was no fault of his if people escaped from the prison. And although he had spared no efforts to persecute the Grahams—a duty which he found lucrative through escheats—the problem of how to catch and dispose of them remained unsolved.

Indeed, they were showing they could still sting. Rob Graham of Meddop was rescued from Cranston in April, and one of Leigh's last acts in office was to scramble out of a Graham ambush by the skin of his teeth. He and a single companion were riding from Dumfries when they were bush-whacked by Rob's Fergie Graham, one of the fugitives. Leigh's colleague was shot in the ribs, they lost a horse and both their cloaks, and narrowly escaped with the two of them riding one mount. Rob's Fergie, it was reported, "is said to be since dead".

Plainly something had to be done about the Grahams, and quickly, and since neither licensed murder nor banishment to the Low Countries had worked, it was decided to transplant them to Ireland. Sir Ralph Sidley, a landowner of Roscommon, agreed to settle "the Greames, and other inhabitants of Leven, Esk and Sark" on his farms, on short leases unless His Majesty decided they should be extended permanently. He also undertook to provide them with a minister to teach them their duty to God. The Border Commission, who no doubt privately thought that Sidley ought to have his head examined, went to work with enthusiasm. The gentlemen of Cumberland and Westmorland were invited to subscribe to the cost of the settlement, and it is testimony to the general desire to get rid of the Grahams that £300 was raised, in contributions ranging from £5 down to 2s 6d. Not everyone approached was ready to subscribe (notably a certain Sir John Dalston), but pressure was obviously brought to bear: there is a sinister little note from the Privy Council to the commissioners, dated November 1606, saying that the King desires to know the names of those who refuse to contribute to £200 yet to be levied for transporting the Grahams. That was probably a broad enough hint.

Collecting the Grahams themselves was rather harder. The commissioners had been writing eagerly about who should be transported, with special reference to Jock of the Peartree and Jock's Richie Graham, who were safe for the moment in Carlisle Castle. In June of 1606 it had been reported that there were not above thirty Grahams in Esk fit to be transported; by September there were only three, two of them over eighty. Death, banishment and outlawry had reduced one of the biggest Border clans to a pitiful remnant; those families who could be induced to come in were herded to Workington by the sheriff and the horse garrison—it had been hard enough trying to get conductors for the Low Countries migration, when the rate of 4s a day had proved insufficient attraction, and had had to be raised to 6s—but even the troops were unable to prevent many of the poor souls escaping at the last minute. Of those who went there is no accurate estimate; fifty families are mentioned, and 124 names, but pregnant women and infants were held back to be transported the following year, presumably to spare them the hardship of winter in their new home, which was largely wasteland.

The Grahams did not take to Roscommon. They had a "prosperous voyage" to Dublin late in September 1606, and were met there by two gentlemen of their own name, Irish residents, who promised to help them to settle. Sidley was optimistic; he believed the Grahams were "a witty and understanding people"—which was one way of putting it—"and withal very civil, compared with most of their nation". But the scheme was a flop from the start. If the whole of the Graham clan had been transported, and if they could have settled as a balanced community, they might have flourished and been of great benefit to Ireland and themselves; but the best and most able-bodied of them had either died, or escaped, or been outlawed and exiled already. The Roscommon plantation were those who could be coerced, and it follows these were not the pick of the clan. But even if they had been willing, able colonists, the difficulties they faced were formidable.

The land, when they reached it, proved to have gone to waste, and lacked wood and water. They compared it with the fertile Borderland they had left, and detested it. Then the rents were too dear, labourers were few and demanded double wages, and the Grahams could not understand their language. Worst of all, they had no money, for the cash subscribed towards the cost of the settlement had never reached them, and they could get no satisfaction out of Sidley, who had evidently pocketed it. "We ... cannot get a penny to buy meat and drink withal," wrote Richard Graham of Meddop. With one voice they clamoured to be allowed home again, and in November came the first reports of desertion: the Bishop of Carlisle informed the Council that two had returned, one of whom was caught, and that others were reported landing in Scotland.

In a matter of months the plantation was disintegrating, and within two years there were said to be only about half a dozen families of Graham left in Roscommon. The rest had scattered, some of them settling with one of their Irish kinsmen, Sir George Grame, and some of the youngest males being sent into the army, but these were complained of "as being so turbulent and busy, that one of them is able to dispose a whole garrison to become so ... their minds are so much at their homes, from whence they come without hope of return, that they will not like the poor soldier's life and fare".

This rings true, and the disillusioned Sidley had more to add. The Grahams, he now concluded, were idle people, not only unwilling to settle themselves to any labour or industry, but also addicted to spend both the time or anything they had or might get, in drinking and on horses and dogs. It also appears that their dislike and distrust of the Irish was returned, the more enterprising of the natives suspecting that the Grahams might be more than a match for them at fighting and rustling.

Undoubtedly many succeeded in returning to the Border country about this time, but four years after the initial settlement, the scattered Grahams in Ireland were still a problem, and thought was given to the possibility of moving them to Ulster. But the Lord Deputy of Ireland had learned about the Grahams by this time, and his conclusion echoed what any West March Warden could have told the authorities in the first place:

"They are now dispersed, and when they shall be placed upon any land together, the next country will find them ill neighbours, for they are a fractious and naughty people."

As late as 1614 a proclamation was issued forbidding any Grahams to return from Ireland or the Low Countries; there were still those who were willing to run the risk of coming home.[2] But the policy of banishment had worked, for the time being; the largest riding clan of the Western Border had been dispersed and broken. It had been barbarously done, even allowing for the standards of the time, and the fact that the Grahams had been a lawless and troublesome people. Perhaps, recalling the hatred they had incurred over the years in Cumberland— among enemies like the Musgraves, for example, and their allies—their persecution can be seen as the last act in the last Border feud, played according to the old deadly rules.

Which is not to say that the Grahams lost in the end. There is a footnote to the story of their struggle to stay in their homeland, and it shows how little even great rulers and all-powerful goverments may achieve at the last against ordinary folk who will not give in. It is said to be an invariable rule that in any city in the English-speaking world the Smiths outnumber any other surname. In the Carlisle telephone book after the Second World War the most common name was Graham.

---

2. Many of them bided their time, and probably some came home under assumed names. It is interesting that one unusual name in Western Scotland and Northern England is Maharg (as distinct from McHarg), which is Graham spelled backwards.

XLVI

The thieves dauntoned

If any Englishman steal in Scotland, or any Scotsman
steal in England, any goods or cattels amounting to
12d, he shall be punished by death.

BORDER COMMISSIONERS, 1605

While the Grahams were being transported and scattered across Ireland,
the final chapter was being written on the frontier. The slow process of
hanging and pursuing and beating the other riding families into submission was gradually coming to an end. They were not giving up
without a struggle either, and by the end of 1606, the year the Grahams
were shipped out of Workington, the list of declared outlaws had risen
to 300—Armstrongs, Elliots,[1] Johnstones, Kerrs, Irvines, and Nixons
for the most part, with some well-remembered names among them—
Jock of the Side, Hob Elliot of the Park, Hob Croser, and Jock ("Halfe
Lugs") Elliot.

Apart from such fugitives, who seemed determined in their obstinacy
to try to keep the old ways alive, there were those in authority striving
manfully to maintain the worst traditions of the Border officers.
Thomas Musgrave, captain of Bewcastle, was still apparently milking
his office for what it was worth in November 1606. Complaints were
made of his "partiality" to evil-doers on the Scottish side, his alleged
relationship through his bastard daughter to the "bloodie and theevish
clan of Whithaugh in Liddesdale" was again recalled, and it was remarked that he "readily undertakes apprehension, but slenderly
performs."

But others were already bowing to the inevitable. In the following
year various "ringleaderis" were earmarked for confinement outside
the Borders, and one of the great bastions of mischief began to crumble
with the announcement that 100 outlaws of Tynedale and Redesdale

---

1. Many Elliots were also transported. One of the family's historians calculated that there were nearly 3000 of them in Ireland at the beginning of the
present century.

were to be enlisted for service in Ireland. (One feels sympathy for any Irish community which may have suffered from a coincidence of Charltons and Milburns on the one hand, and Grahams on the other.)

For those who continued to resist, even the fastnesses of the frontier were providing fewer and fewer hiding places. Scott of Buccleuch, home from the wars, was briefly active in hunting down and destroying his former fellow-reivers on the government's behalf, hanging and drowning without trial, and burning towers and houses as he thought fit, for which, like Cranston, he was granted full immunity.[2] It is a curious example of the romantic prejudice of Border myth-makers that Buccleuch, the arch-brigand who turned on his own kind at the finish, should still be presented almost as a fairy-tale hero. The legend spun round the Kinmont Raid is remembered, and the cruel, brutal, treacherous reality is forgotten. In 1608 he was commended for his Border services. He died in 1611, aged forty-six.

Occasional entries in the records of the time indicate how some of the last thieves died. Christopher Armstrong, alias Barnegleish, was killed late in September 1606, apparently while his house was being searched by twenty of the horse garrison under John Musgrave; three reivers, Anton's Edward's Tom Armstrong, Jock ("Stowlugs") Armstrong, and Chris Irvine, were captured by Lord William Howard (known as Belted Will), after an all-night chase from Naworth to the Yorkshire border. Howard wrote to Wilfrid Lawson, expressing particular satisfaction at Stowlugs' capture, and adding: "If you find matter sufficient to hang the other two, hold up your finger and they shall be delivered." All three were hanged within the month.

The *coup de grâce* to the reiver system, and to large numbers of the riders themselves, was now delivered by the Border Commission, which had been reconstituted under the Earl of Dunbar in 1606. In the next few years the old Border finally died. In July 1609 a mass hanging of thieves taken by Cranston was held at Dumfries, with Dunbar presiding, and the Chancellor Dunfermline was able to report, with classical allusions no doubt designed to please his scholarly royal master, that the Earl "has purgit the Borders of all the chiefest malefactors, robbers and brigands . . . as Hercules sometimes is written to have

2. Sir James Douglas of Drumlanrig received a similar remission for fire-raising and hanging without trial.

purged Augeas the King of Elides his escuries". The leading Armstrongs, Johnstones and others had been "cut off", and the ways
through the frontier region were as free and peaceable as Phoebus
made his way to the oracle at Delphi.

The Middle Shires, Dunfermline concluded, were now "as quiet as
any part in any civil kingdom in Christeanity".

One seems to have heard the same thing before, from Border officials
in the old days after one of the breaks in the reiving storm, when they
were trying to convince themselves and their masters that things were
getting better. But this time it was true. There were later outbreaks of
thieving and disorder, of cattle lifting and extortion, but the system of
the frontier had been destroyed. The days of the riding families were
dead; the life of plunder and banditry by a great community was over;
the whole fabric of rustling and racketeering, of feud and organised
mass foray, of beacon fire and blackmail, of Warden court and hot
trod, of local Border law and native custom, had vanished. It was not
before time.

In the context of history, it had ended almost overnight, in one
murderous decade at the start of the seventeenth century. And then
there was no more Borderland, in the old wild, independent, turbulent
sense of the word. As one looks through the records of Privy Council
and State Papers, it can be seen finally fading away round about 1611,
when a report of courts on the frontier lists the names of thirty-eight
who are to hang, at Jedburgh and Dumfries, of others cautioned, and of
about sixty still fugitive. Elliots, Nixons, Armstrongs, Irvines,
Johnstones, and even Grahams are among those marked for death,
warning and banishment—"Thom, Jok and Lancie Armestrangis . . .
sall pass furth of the kingdomes of Scotland and England, and sall
not returne . . ."

It was the last good-night, indeed. In the same year Cranston could
finally turn in his commission and resign from the Border horse garrison. He had been ennobled in 1609; as the instrument of government
he had probably done more directly to change the face of the Border
than anyone else. He had been policeman and executioner, and he had
done the job well. Perhaps it troubled his conscience a little, or it may
just have been to clear his feet that he had received two further indemnities for the hangings, fire-raisings, besiegings and "sindrie
slauchteris" committed in the line of duty. The King was sure that in

all this Sir William "hes done na wilfull injurie nor manifest wrong". Possibly not—but who was there to care if he had?

Ironically, Cranston found it easier to collect moral indemnities than his salary: he was still suing for arrears of pay to the horse garrison in 1610. Government Border policy, like the reiving brotherhood, died game.

The last little kicks of the frontier are felt occasionally through the state documents thereafter. In 1610 "privy thefts" were still taking place daily in the West, and in 1611 the Elliots took a last swipe at the Robsons in Tynedale, but by 1612 there is record of the charging of customs duty on horses, cattle, and other beasts passing peacefully across the line. Nothing better illustrates the changing times, testifying to a settled pattern of life which was now only occasionally disturbed by the activities of a handful of wilder spirits. They force their way into the records just here and there—in 1616 it was primly noted that the Middle Shires were "not free of the mischief of thefte", and in 1618 appears a list of what have been called "the last of the Border blackguards". In fact they were not quite, but the list of thirty-two names is in the old tradition, beginning with "Fergie Bell, callit the Crow", and then the usual roll-call of Elliot, Scott, Johnstone, Graham, Hall, Turnbull, Rutherford, Beattie, Tait, and the inevitable Armstrong.

But this is police court stuff, the petty crime that any community has. One gathers the tone of it from the official complaint of 1618, which spoke of the "greit and unnecessar number" of ale houses in the Middle Shires as being "ane of the cheiff causes that procures the disordoures and insolencies so frequentlie occurring in the same . . . disordourit and idill persons . . . spend the tyme thair in dyceing, cairting and uthir exerceissis, and do consult upon the meannis to prosecute their wicked pretensis. . . ."

Such wickedness; His Majesty forthwith ordered that innkeepers of good character should be found who would prohibit gaming "nor no excessive drinking, bot in moderate sorte and at seassonable houres".

If that was the worst the authorities had to worry about it is no wonder that the horse garrison, who had been putting in their time confiscating illegal arms and horses worth more than £30, were finally discharged in 1621. At which "nichtlie stoulthis" broke out in the old Scottish West March—someone stole a sack of corn from Eckie Irvine's wife, and two depraved scoundrels wearing pistols and hagbuts went hunting hares in the snow.

One final flicker there was about this time, when armed Maxwells besieged the tower of Kirkconnell so closely "as not ane persone within dar sett out thair headis." But the main complaint seems to have been that they carried pistols.

The Border Commission lapsed after James I's death in 1625, but was revived ten years later as a result of lawlessness which seems to have been on the increase in Charles I's time. But although this may seem superficially to resemble the conditions of the previous century, it is not part of this story, for it had nothing to do with the Border reiver system.[3] About thirty executions took place in 1637, and with the outbreak of the Civil War the Scottish Privy Council were obliged to note that "for want of joint commissions and justitiarie" the peace was being broken and the subjects infested by depredations, thefts, etc. This was ordinary crime, by a new generation of Border bad men, the sons and grandsons of the last Border reivers. To show how history repeats itself—and for old time's sake—the list of their names, as recorded in the Privy Council minutes of 1642, is as follows:

> John Johnstone of Gretna
> John Armstrong, called "of the Side"
> Symmie Armstrong, alias Caffield
> Hob Elliot
> Will Croser
> John Croser, the "Fryday thief"
> Jock Elliot, called "a God's name"
> Willie's Richie Irvine
> William of Kinmont
> Edie Graham
> Walter Scott, called "Wat of the Bus"

Justice courts to be held at Jedburgh and Dumfries.

---

3. In the middle of the seventeenth century a new kind of Border malefactor arose, called the "moss trooper". This term, so commonly misapplied to the reivers of the sixteenth century, simply signifies a brigand. The earliest mention I can find of it is 1646, in the Scottish Privy Council records, when official action against the "mosse trouppers" is discussed, and they were numerous after the Civil War, particularly in the period 1661–4.

XLVII

After the riding

And that is the story of the Border reivers. It goes without saying that it is not complete; for every exploit and adventure and piece of skull-duggery recorded, I have had to leave out ten. It is equally inevitable that it must contain its inaccuracies, but I trust these are trifling ones—it is no excuse, of course, but better men than I have had to admit defeat when it came to picking out one Laird's Jock from another, or unravelling assorted Kerrs and Grahams; even the ubiquitous Earls of Arran, Angus and Surrey pale by comparison. But I believe it is a faithful picture of the Border people in their time; if it does not do them justice the fault is mine, not theirs.

There may be lessons to be learned from them, wicked and yet not unattractive ruffians that they were. As long as there are frontiers there will be people something like them—I dare say one could relate some of the Warden's problems to what happens along the Suez Canal and the Jordan today, where governments are unable to control their irregular people.

Comparisons have been made between the Border reivers and the Indian North-West frontier—which is not a bad parallel—and the cattle rustlers of the American West. There are certainly strong resemblances there, provided one remembers to separate Western myth from Western reality. One of the canons of the Western code, in its Hollywood translation, is that good triumphs and the villain bites the dust. If anyone believes that, the story of the Border reivers should convince him otherwise. Its moral is clear: there is little justice to be had. The good man survives, if he is lucky, but the villain becomes the first Lord Roxburgh.

*

The Borderland today is a very peaceful place, where the greatest turbulence is to be found along the main highways which run through the lovely landscape where road once had a different meaning. They carry a traffic as lethal as anything that passed this way four centuries ago. But that is different; that is civilisation.

Names like Warden and land-sergeant are long forgotten; even
reiver is barely a folk-memory. The norm at the rural police courts is
driving without due care and attention, bicycles without lights, and
every now and then an affray—although they are still hot against
poaching at Longtown.

Berwick sleeps by the cold sea, and Carlisle lies red and peaceful under
the rain, the voice that breathed o'er Eden encourages the cricketers who
play their knock-out matches on the green meadow beneath Stanwix
where Buccleuch's raiders came on the night that every Borderer remembers. In Alnwick old John Forster's descendants go quietly about
their business. The Cheviots lie as lone and empty under the sky as
they did four centuries since. There is peace in King James's Middle
Shires.

In Liddesdale, Hermitage stands roofless, like a hollow tree that will
not fall. The valley is still suffering from authority; an all-wise government has taken away its railway, thus demonstrating how much progress can mean in real terms in the twentieth century. Even Scrope and
Wharton never completely immobilised the Liddesdales, but a later
generation of civil servants has succeeded beyond the capacity of
simple soldiers.

Farther east the Scott Country remains mercifully unspoiled—as yet
—by industrial planners who understand neither the country nor its
people. Hawick and Jedburgh and Kelso bustle and look well, and worry
about depopulation and the future. Their rugby teams try to butcher
each other with a primitive energy that belongs to this land, and the
names are still the same. This is so all along the Border line; the roots
go very deep, although the people of the Marches have travelled farther
than most since the old days. When mankind first set foot on the moon
it was an Armstrong who rode the greatest foray of all.

Carey, Hunsdon, Cessford, Ferniehurst, Eure, Carmichael—it is as
though they had never been. The work they did is long forgotten.
Kinmont Willie, Black Ormiston, Hobbie Noble, Fingerless Will,
Nebless Clem, Willie Kang, Bangtail, Fire the Braes, Hutcheon
Graham—their names live a little in the legends and ballads, but only a
little. Anyone who has read the facts about them and cares to sit in
judgement is welcome to do so. We have seen how they and their
country came to be, what shaped them, what they suffered, what they
did, and how they survived. That, after all, is what matters, since it is

what life is about; their people and their families are along the Border line today. The Grahams live in the Debateable Land, the Scotts in Teviotdale, the Humes on the Merse, the Fenwicks and Forsters on the Middle March. There are fewer Musgraves and Dacres than there once were, but the Charltons play football for England, a Nixon sits in the White House (with Scotts, Cliffords and Percies high in U.S. government), and not very long ago Albert Armstrong had a stall in Carlisle Market. Poor Lord Dacre, there was nothing he could do about it.

But there is very little to remind the visitor to these quiet fields, humdrum little towns and villages, lonely hills and lovely valleys, that this was once a fierce and bloody frontier. Strife and raid and burning and murder seem so out of place and remote, that it is hard to imagine that they were the daily business of the people of the Border. Only now and then, if your romantic imagination is sharp enough, there can come a little drift from the past—in the Cheviot wind, or under the vast stones of Carlisle Keep, or among the sad trees by Liddell Water, or most vivid of all, perhaps, in a little fellside village at night, when there is a hunter's moon and a strong wind, and the black cloud shadows hurry across the tops, and beasts stamp in the dark, and an inn door down in the village opens and slams with a blink of light, and the rough Norse voices sound and laugh and die away.

But this is just sentimental imagination. The old Border is buried a long time ago, and there is hardly a trace now to mark where the steel bonnets passed by. They would have had no quarrel with that.

AFTERWORD

"They're Still a Pretty Hard Lot"

A CONVERSATION WITH
GEORGE MACDONALD FRASER

A cold bright afternoon in Pleasantville, New York, a few days before Christmas 2000. Across the Atlantic, on the Isle of Man, a similarly undemonstrative winter's day—fair sample of what was shaping up as the mildest Manx winter in years—progressing now into early evening.

Exchanging notes on the weather allowed us to settle into our talk. But it also, I must admit, gave me a moment to concentrate solely on the wonderful *sound* of George MacDonald Fraser's soft-spoken voice, with its light but striking accent.

So while "Just talk; I'll listen" may thus have been on the tip of my tongue, I did manage to remind myself that the occasion called for something more. In the works, after all, was our COMMON READER EDITION of *The Steel Bonnets*, scheduled for publication in 2001, exactly thirty years after the book's original appearance. After noting the milestone, I drew attention to those early years of his writing career. *Flashman* in 1969; *Royal Flash* and the first collection of McAuslan stories, *The General Danced at Dawn,* in 1970; *Flash for Freedom!* and *The Steel Bonnets* in '71: in three years, four widely-admired volumes of fiction, plus one exhaustive four-hundred-page work of straight history. The last, at least in retrospect, seemed a puzzling work to have embarked on, in the circumstances. Just how had it come to be researched and written? And why then?

"It was a labor of love," Mr. Fraser explained. His interest in Border history had been stimulated by growing up in Carlisle, where that history seems present "in the stonework" even to this day. To play as a child on the ruins of the Roman wall, or to be constantly in the presence of the old Castle or Cathedral—indeed "it's difficult not to be drawn into" the ancient stories and legends while "treading the same ground" the great heroes and villains trod. (And for the record, years later and far from Carlisle Mr. Fraser underwent a similar sort of experience: "it may be fanciful," but just in wandering around Bent's Fort in southeastern Colorado, the big trading post known as "The Castle on the Plains," he felt he learned more about the old American "mountain men" than all his reading could ever teach him.)

When, therefore, Mr. Fraser's agent had asked "Can you do a nonfiction?"—straightforward answer to my query about the book's timing—the writer's abiding fascination with the Border instantly supplied him with the project's subject. As for the practical side of things: Mr. Fraser and his wife travelled over to Dublin, where the indulgent authorities of Trinity College library gave them free rein of the collections. "That's the Irish"; a more congenial arrangement for research would be difficult to find.

Hearing him recall those days, I could readily imagine the enthusiasm and excitement he brought to the task of sifting through a rich body of material which no one had exhaustively dealt with before; enthusiasm, excitement, and probably a bit of panic as well, for after twenty-two years on newspapers in Britain and Canada Mr. Fraser had, at the time, just set out his shingle as a full-time writer, and the realization that he would have to write for a living concentrated his mind, as the saying goes, wonderfully.

The result, as I hope you've already discovered, is a detailed and gripping story, praised by historians and championed by its many readers. *The Steel Bonnets* has never been out of print in Britain since 1971, has sold well around the world, and has even prompted the formation of family societies devoted to maintaining, in some form or other, various clans' awareness of their Border heritage.

Through the years these societies, as well as unaffiliated enthusiasts of Border history, have no doubt been prompted by *The Steel Bonnets* to seek the writer out. But if our talk is any indication, then what seems to have been Mr. Fraser's most memorable such encounter was with the actor Buddy Ebsen, who turns out to have been an especially keen student of not only the Border but—"Don't ask me why"—Mary Queen of Scots as well. (Might it have been that a biography of her "was the only thing to read on location" during the making of a film— or, I didn't dare suggest, an episode of *The Beverly Hillbillies?*) As Mr.

Fraser bemusedly recalls it, he and Mr. Ebsen toured the Border country, in weather harsh enough to have caused the lanky actor to be "shivering slightly." When their travels brought them to a Border tower built in 1492, the writer couldn't helping noting the coincidence—to be with an American at a site whose antiquity allowed one to juxtapose Columbus's voyage to the long chronicle of Border troubles.

And speaking of Americans: it was the face of another prominent Yank which Mr. Fraser, as he points out in his Introduction here, thought could hardly have fitted better under a steel bonnet. Nixons figure dramatically in the history of the Border, and when *The Steel Bonnets* was originally published one of their number was President of the United States. (Having been at school with a couple of the clan, Mr. Fraser found the storied toughness and combativeness of the Nixons of old to be very much alive in their descendants: "They're still a pretty hard lot.") Think back, then, to 1971: Richard Milhous Nixon in the White House, America in Vietnam; wouldn't it be hard not to have found contemporary resonance in Mr. Fraser's chronicling of the ineffectual efforts of distant central governments to stamp out "the custom of the country" and subdue a native populace whose intimate familiarity with their baffling and treacherous landscape gave them incalulable advantage as guerrilla fighters?

According to Mr. Fraser, parallels between the Border and Vietnam were indeed there to be drawn, whether or not they were at the time, and perhaps the basic parallel was this: when the chips are down, men will do what they must to survive, will step outside the bounds when there simply is no choice. "The King's law," George Washington had said, "runs with the King's muskets," and perhaps the fighting in the Border lands and in Vietnam demonstrated that "when the chips are down, laws and constitutions don't mean much." This clear-eyed, realistic perspective will, I think, be familiar to readers of any of George MacDonald Fraser's books.

Given the success of *The Steel Bonnets* and the pleasure the author took in writing it, I brought our conversation to a close by asking whether he had ever been tempted to return to nonfiction historical writing. The answer, not surprisingly, was that he found he could get closer to the truth of the past in fiction. His readers would of course cite the Flashman novels or—two favorites of mine—*The Candlemass*

Road and *Black Ajax*—in support of this belief; the writer himself looks to Raymond Chandler's books, which, he maintains, convey what California was like in the Thirties more tellingly than does any social history.

A final word. Readers who have enjoyed *The Steel Bonnets* should know that Mr. Fraser was drawn back to the Border many years later, publishing *The Candlemass Road* in 1993. It is a robust fiction based firmly on Border fact, and is now also available in A COMMON READER EDITION.

—Thomas Meagher
Editorial Director
THE AKADINE PRESS

Appendices,
Bibliography,
Glossary and
Index

APPENDIX I

The Archbishop of Glasgow's "Monition of Cursing" against the Border reivers

Gude folks, heir at my Archibischop of Glasgwis letters under his round sele, direct to me or any uther chapellane, makand mensioun, with greit regrait, how hevy he beris the pietous, lamentabill, and dolorous complaint that pass our all realme and commis to his eris, be oppin voce and fame, how our souverane lordis trew liegis, men, wiffis and barnys, bocht and redemit be the precious blude of our Salviour Jhesu Crist, and levand in his lawis, are saikleslie (innocently) part murdrist, part slayne, brynt, heryit, spulzeit (spoiled) and reft, oppinly on day licht and under silens of the nicht, and thair takis (farms) and landis laid waist, and thair self banyst therfra, als wele kirklandis as utheris, be commoun tratouris, revaris, thciffis, duelland in the south part of this realme, sic as Tevidale, Esdale, Liddisdale, Ewisdale, Nedisdale (Nithsdale), and Annanderdaill; quhilkis hes bene diverse ways persewit and punist be the temperale swerd and our Soverane Lordis auctorite, and dredis nocht the samyn.

And thairfoir my said Lord Archibischop of Glasgw hes thocht expedient to strike thame with the terribill swerd of halykirk, quhilk thai may nocht lang endur and resist; and has chargeit me, or any uther chapellane, to denounce, declair and proclame thaim oppinly and generalie cursit, at this market-croce, and all utheris public places.

Hairfor throw the auctorite of Almichty God, the Fader of hevin, his Son, our Saviour, Jhesu Crist, and of the Halygaist; throw the auctorite of the Blissit Virgin Sanct Mary, Sanct Michael, Sanct Gabriell, and all the angellis; Sanct John the Baptist, and all the haly patriarkis and prophets; Sanct Peter, Sanct Paull, Sanct Andro, and all haly appostillis; Sanct Stephin, Sanct Laurence, and all haly mertheris (martyrs); Sanct Gile, Sanct Martyn, and all haly confessouris; Sanct Anne, Sanct Katherin, and all haly virginis and matronis; and of all the sanctis and haly company of hevin; be the auctorite of our Haly Fader the Paip and his cardinalis, aned of my said Lord Archibischop of Glasgw, be the avise and assistance of my lordis, archibischop, bischopis, abbotis, priouris, and utheris prelatis and ministeris of halykirk,

I denounce, proclamis, and declaris all and sindry the committaris of the said saikles murthris, slauchteris, brinying, heirchippes, reiffis, thiftis and spulezeis, oppinly apon day licht and under silence of nicht, alswele within temporale landis as kirklandis; togither with thair part takaris (partakers), assistaris, supplearis, wittandlie resettaris (knowing receivers) of thair personis, the gudes reft and stollen be thaim, art or part thereof, and their counsalouris and defendouris, of thair evil dedis generalie CURSIT, waryit (execrated), aggregeite, and reaggregeite, with the GREIT CURSING.

I curse thair heid and all the haris of thair heid; I curse thair face, thair ene, thair mouth, thair neise, thair toung, thair teith, thair crag, thair schulderis, thair breist, thair hert, thair stomok, thair bak, thair wame, thair armes, thair leggis, thair handis, thair feit, and everilk part of thair body, frae the top of thair heid to the soill of thair feit, befoir and behind, within and without.

I curse thaim gangand (going), and I curse thaim rydand (riding); I curse thaim standand, and I curse thaim sittand; I curse thaim etand, I curse thaim drinkand; I curse thaim walkand, I curse thaim sleepand; I curse thaim rysand, I curse thaim lyand; I curse thaim at hame, I curse thaim fra hame; I curse thaim within the house, I curse thaim without the house; I curse thair wiffis, thair barnis, and thair servandis participand with thaim in thair deides. I wary thair cornys, thair catales, thair woll, thair scheip, thair horse, thair swyne, thair geise (geese), thair hennys, and all thair quyk gude (livestock). I wary thair hallis, thair chalmeris (rooms), thair kechingis, thair stanillis, thair barnys, thair biris (cowsheds), thair bernyardis, thair cailyardis (cabbage-patches), thair plewis, thair harrowis, and the gudis and housis that is necessair for thair sustentatioun and weilfair.

All the malesouns and waresouns (curses) that ever gat warldlie creatur sen the begynnyng of the warlde to this hour mot licht apon thaim. The maledictioun of God, that lichtit apon Lucifer and all his fallowis, that strak thaim frae the hie hevin to the deip hell, mot licht apon thaim. The fire and the swerd that stoppit Adam far the yettis (gates) of Paradise, mot stop thaim frae the gloir of Hevin, quhill (until) thai forbere and mak amendis. The malesoun that lichtit on cursit Cayein, quhen he slew his bruther just Abell saiklessly, mot licht on thaim for the saikles slauchter that thai commit dailie. The maledictioun that lichtit apon all the warlde, man and beist, and all that ever tuk life, quhen all was drownit be the flude of Noye, except Noye and his ark, mot licht apon thame and droune thame, man and beist, and mak this realm cummirless (free) of thame for thair wicket synnys. The thunnour and fireflauchtis (lightning) that set doun as rane apon the cities of Zodoma and Gomora, with all the landis about, and brynt thame for thair vile sunnys, mot rane apon thame, and birne thaim for oppin synnis. The malesoun and confusion that lichtit on the Gigantis for thair oppressioun and pride, biggand (building) the tour of Babiloun, mot confound thaim and all thair werkis, for thair oppin reiffs and oppressioun. All the plagis that fell apon Pharao and his pepill of Egipt, thair landis, corne, and cataill, mot fall apon thaim, thair takkis, rowmys (places) and stedingis, cornys and beistis. The watter of Tweid and utheris watteris quhair thai ride mot droun thaim, as the Reid Sey drownit King Pharao and his pepil of Egipt, persewing Godis pepill of Israell. The erd (earth) mot oppin, riffe and cleiff (cleave), and swelly (swallow) thaim quyk to hell, as it swellyit cursit Dathan and Abiron, that ganestude (withstood) Moeses and the command of God. The wyld fyre that byrnt Thore and his fallowis to the nowmer of twa hundredth and fyty, and utheris 14,000 and 700 at anys, usurpand aganis Moyses and Aaron, servandis of God, not suddanely birne and consume thaim dailie ganestandand the comandis of God and halykirk. The malediction that lichtit suddanely upon fair Absolon, rydant contrair his fader, King David, servand of God, throw the wod, quhen the branchis of ane tre fred (parted) him of his horse and hangit him be the hair, mot licht apon thaim, rydand again trew Scottis men, andhang thaim siclike that all the warld may se. The maledicitioun that licht-it apon Olifernus, lieutenant to Nabogodonoser, makand weair (war) and heirchippis apon trew cristin (Christian) men, the malediction that lichtit apon Judas, Pylot, Herod and the Jowis that chucifyit (crucified) Our Lord, and all the plagis and trublis that lichtit on the citte of Jherusalem thairfor, and upon Symon Magus for his symony, bludy Nero, cursit Ditius Mak-censius, Olibruis, Julianus Apostita and the laiff (rest) of the cruell tirrannis that slew and murthirit Critis haly servandis, mot licht apon thame for thair cruel tiranny and murthirdome of cristin pepill.

And all the vengeance that evir was takin sen the warlde began for oppin synnys, and all the plagis and pestilence that ever fell on man or beist, mot fall on thaim for thair oppin reiff, saiklesse slauchter and schedding of inno-cent blude. I dissever and pairtis thaim fra the kirk of God, and deliveris thaim quyk to the devill of hell, as the Apostill Sanct Paull deliverit Corin-thion. I interdite the places thay cum in fra divine service, ministracioun of the sacramentis of halykirk, except the sacrament of baptissing allanerlie (only); and forbiddis all kirkmen to schriffe (shrive) or absolve thaim of thaire synnys, quhill they be first absolyeit of this cursing.

I forbid all cristin man or woman till have ony company with thaime, etand, drynkand, spekand, prayand, lyand, gangand, standand, or in any uther deid doand, under the paine of deidly syn. I discharge all bandis, actis, contractis, athis (oaths) and obligatiounis made to thaim be ony persounis, outher of lawte (either of loyalty), kyndenes or manrent (personal fealty), salang as thai susteine this cursing, sua that na man be bundin (bound) to thaim, and that thai be bundin till all men. I tak fra thame and cryis doune all the gude dedis that ever thai did or sall do, quhill thai ryse frae this cursing. I declare thaim partles (excluded) of all matynys, messis, evinsangis, dirigeis or utheris prayeris, on buke or beid; of all pilgrimagis and almouse dedis done or to be done in halykirk or be cristin pepill, enduring this cursing.

And, finally, I condemn thaim perpetualie to the deip pit of hell, the remain with Lucifer and all his fallowis, and thair bodeis to the gallowis of the Burrow Mure, first to be hangit, syne revin and ruggit (then ripped and torn) with doggis, swyne, and utheris wyld beists, abhominable to all the warld. And their candillis gangis frae your sicht, as mot their saulis gang fra the visage of God, and thai rgude faim fra the warld, quhill thai forbeir thair oppin synnys foirsaidis and ryse frae this terribill cursing, and mak satisfaction and pennance."

APPENDIX II

The ballad of Kinmont Willie

O have ye na heard o' the fause Sakelde?
  O have ye na heard o' the keen lord Scroope?
How they hae ta'en bauld Kinmont Willie,
  On Haribee to hang him up?

Had Willie had but twenty men,
  But twenty as stout as he,
Fause Sakelde had never the Kinmont ta'en,
  Wi' eight score in his cumpanie

They band his legs beneath the steed,
  They tied his hands behind his back!
They guarded him, fivesome on each side,
  And they brought him ower the Liddel-rack.

They led him thro' the Liddel-rack,
  And also thro' the Carlisle sands;
They brought him to Carlisle castell,
  To be at my lord Scroope's commands.

"My hands are tied, but my tongue is free,
  And whae will dare this deed avow?
Or answer by the Border law?
  Or answer to the bauld Buccleuch?"

"Now haud thy tongue, thou rank reiver!
  There's never a Scot shall set thee free:
Before ye cross my castle yate,
  I trow ye shall take farewell o' me."

"Fear na ye that, my lord," quo' Willie;
   "By the faith o' my body, lord Scroope," he said,
"I never yet lodged in a hostelrie,
   But I paid my lawing[1] before I gaed."

Now word is gane to the bauld keeper,
   In Branksome Ha', where that he lay,
That lord Scroope has ta'en the Kinmont Willie,
   Between the hours of night and day.

He has ta'en the table wi' his hand,
   He garr'd the red wine spring on hie—
"Now Christ's curse on my head," he said,
   "But avenged of lord Scroope I'll be!

"O is my basnet[2] a widow's curch?[3]
   Or my lance a wand of the willow-tree?
Or my arm a ladye's lilye hand,
   That an English lord should lightly[4] me?

"And have they ta'en him, Kinmont Willie,
   Against the truce of border tide?
And forgotten that the bauld Buccleuch
   Is keeper here on the Scottish side?

"And have they e'en ta'en him, Kinmont Willie,
   Withouten either dread or fear?
And forgotten that the bauld Buccleuch
   Can back a steed, or shake a spear?

"O were there war between the lands,
   As well I wot that there is none,
I would slight Carlisle castell high,
   Though it were builded of marble stone.

"I would set that castell in a lowe,[5]
   And sloken it with English blood!
There's never a man in Cumberland,
   Should ken where Carlisle castell stood.

"But since nae war's between the lands,
   And there is peace, and peace should be;

---

[1] lawing—reckoning. [2] basnet—helmet; [3] curch—coif; [4] lightly—set light by; [5] lowe—flame;

I'll neither harm English lad or lass,
　　And yet the Kinmont freed shall be!"

He has call'd him forty marchmen bauld,
　　I trow they were of his ain name,
Except sir Gilbert Elliot, call'd
　　The laird of Stobs, I mean the same.

He has call'd him forty matchmen bauld,
　　Were kinsmen to the bauld Buccleuch;
With spur on heel, and splent on spauld,[1]
　　And gleuves of green, and feathers blue.

There were five and five before them a',
　　Wi' hunting-horns and bugles bright;
And five and five came wi' Buccleuch,
　　Like warden's men, array'd for fight.

And five and five, like a mason gang,
　　That carried the ladders lang and hie;
And five and five, like broken men;
　　And so they reach'd the Woodhouselee.

And as we cross'd the Bateable land,
　　When to the English side we held,
The first o' men that we met wi',
　　Whae sould it be but fause Sakelde?

"Where be ye gaun, ye hunters keen?"
　　Quo' fause Sakelde; "come tell to me!"—
"We go to hunt an English stag,
　　Has trespass'd on the Scots countrie."

"Where be ye gaun, ye marshal men?"
　　Quo' fause Sakelde; "come tell me true!"—
"We go to catch a rank reiver,
　　Has broken faith with the bauld Buccleuch."

"Where are ye gaun, ye mason lads,
　　Wi' a' your ladders, lang and hie?"—
"We gang to herry a corbie's nest,
　　That wons not far frae Woodhouselee."—

---

[1] splent on spauld—armour on shoulder.

"Where be ye gaun, ye broken men?"
    Quo' fause Sakelde; "come tell to me!"—
Now Dickie of Dryhope led that band,
    And the nevir a word of lear[1] had he.

"Why trespass ye on the English side?
    Row-footed outlaws, stand!" quo' he;
The nevir a word had Dickie to say,
    Sae he thrust the lance through his fause bodie.

Then on we held for Carlisle toun,
    And at Staneshaw-bank the Eden we cross'd;
The water was great and mickle of spait,[2]
    But the nevir a horse nor man we lost.

And when we reached the Staneshaw-bank,
    The wind was rising loud and hie;
And there the laird garr'd leave our steeds,
    For fear that they should stamp and nie.

And when we left the Staneshaw-bank,
    The wind began full loud to blaw;
But 'twas wind and weet, and fire and sleet,
    When we came beneath the castle wa'.

We crept on knees, and held our breath,
    Till we placed the ladders against the wa';
And sae ready was Buccleuch himsell
    To mount the first before us a'.

He has ta'en the watchman by the throat,
    He flung him down upon the lead—
"Had there not been peace between our lands,
    Upon the other side thou hadst gaed!—

"Now sound out, trumpets!" quo' Buccleuch;
    "Let's waken lord Scroope right merrilie!"—
Then loud the warden's trumpet blew—
    "*O wha dare meddle wi' me?*"

Then speedilie to wark we gaed,
    And raised the slogan ane and a',

---

[1] lear—lore; [2] spait—flood.

And cut a hole through a sheet of lead,
   And so we wan to the castle ha'.

They thought king James and a' his men
   Had won the house wi' bow and spear;
It was but twenty Scots and ten,
   That put a thousand in sic a stear![1]

Wi' coulters, and wi' forehammers,
   We garr'd the bars bang merrilie,
Until we came to the inner prison,
   Where Willie o' Kinmont he did lie.

And when we cam to the lower prison,
   Where Willie o' Kinmont he did lie—
"O sleep ye, wake ye, Kinmont Willie,
   Upon the morn that thou's to die?"

"O I sleep saft, and I wake aft;
   It's lang since sleeping was fley'd[2] frae me!
Gie my service back to my wife and bairns,
   And a' gude fellows that speir[3] for me."

Then Red Rowan has heute him up,
   The starkest man in Teviotdale—
"Abide, abide now, Red Rowan,
   Till of my lord Scroope I take farewell.

"Farewell, farewell, my gude lord Scroope!
   My gude lord Scroope, farewell!" he cried—
"I'll pay you for my lodging maill,[4]
   When first we meet on the border side."—

Then shoulder high, with shout and cry,
   We bore him down the ladder lang;
At every stride Red Rowan made,
   I wot the Kinmont's airns play'd clang!

"O mony a time," quo' Kinmont Willie,
   "I have ridden horse baith wild and wud;
But a rougher beast than Red Rowan
   I ween my legs have ne'er bestrode.

---

[1] stear—stir; [2] fleyd—frightened; [3] speir—inquire. [4] maill—rent:

"And mony a time," quo' Kinmont Willie,
    "I've prick'd a horse out oure the furs;[1]
But since the day I back'd a steed,
    I never wore sic cumbrous spurs!"—

We scarce had won the Staneshaw-bank,
    When a' the Carlisle bells were rung,
And a thousand men on horse and foot,
    Cam wi' the keen lord Scroope along.

Baccleuch has turn'd to Eden Water,
    Even where it flowed frae bank to brim,
And he has plunged in wi' a' his band,
    And safely swam them through the stream.

He turn'd him on the other side,
    And at lord Scroope his glove flung he—
"If ye like na my visit in merry England,
    In fair Scotland come visit me!"

All sore astonish'd stood lord Scroope,
    He stood as still as rock of stane;
He scarcely dared to trew his eyes,
    When through the water he had gane.

"He is either himsell a devil frae hell,
    Or else his mother a witch maun be;
I wadna have ridden that wan water
    For a' the gowd in Christentie."

---

[1] furs—furrows.

BIBLIOGRAPHY

The following are the sources from which I have taken the material for this book. I have not indicated references consistently in the text, because I feel most readers would rather not be confronted by forests of little numbers and initials. The opinions and judgements in the book are my own, and the authorities given here should not be held responsible.

Some of the books listed below may be of particular interest to readers who would like to go further into Border affairs, so here is a brief selection:

Robert Carey's *Memoirs* is hard to come by, but is invaluable as a first-hand account of a Border Warden of the Marches at work in the 1590s.

James Logan Mack's *The Border Line* is a step-by-step journey along the Anglo-Scottish boundary, and the perfect guide for anyone who has both the historical interest and the energy.

D. L. W. Tough's *Last Years of a Frontier* is an excellent study of the Elizabethan Border, particularly on the social side, but with much information on Border law and Warden activity.

Dr T. I. Rae's *The Administration of the Scottish Frontier, 1513–1603* is a splendidly researched study of Warden work and Border government machinery, local and national, on the Scottish side.

Robert Bruce Armstrong's *Liddesdale*, of which only the first volume is in print (a second one being in manuscript), is a scholarly account of Liddesdale and its environs up to 1530, with much information on local customs, social conditions, laws, etc.

Ridpath's *Border History* traces the whole story of the frontier, but is more concerned with the subject from a national standpoint, although there is much local material that I have not found elsewhere.

Lastly among the individual authorities, although he should really be first, there is Sir Walter Scott, whose *Border Antiquities* and *Border Minstrelsy* are mines of information on every aspect of Border life.

But for anyone who wants to see the Border reivers almost at first hand, there can be no substitute for the *Calendar of Border Papers*, which contains the letters and reports of the English Wardens of the Marches in Elizabeth's time. They are the basis of my book, and like everyone who writes about Border history I owe an incalculable debt to Joseph Bain, their editor.

Calendar of Border Papers, 2 vols, 1560–1603.

Calendar of State Papers relating to Scotland, vols i–xii, 1547–97.

Calendar of State Papers relating to Scotland (Scottish series), vols i, ii, 1509–1603.

Calendar of State Papers (Domestic series), 1547–1610, and Addenda, 1580–1625.

Calendar of State Papers, Ireland, 1606–10.

Calendar of State Papers, Venetian, 1603–5.

The Hamilton Papers, 1532–90.

Henry VIII, Letters and Papers, Foreign and Domestic, 1509–46.

James VI, Letters and State Papers, Abbotsford Club, 1838.

Register of the Privy Council of Scotland, 1545–1642.

Historical Manuscripts Commission publications

MSS. of Lord Muncaster, H.M.C. Tenth Report, Appendix, Part IV.

MSS. of the Duke of Buccleuch at Drumlanrig, H.M.C. 15th Report, Part VIII.

MSS. of the Marquis of Salisbury at Hatfield House, Parts XI, XII and XVI.

Hope Johnstone MSS.

Transactions of the Society of the Antiquaries of Scotland, 1792, vol. i.

Municipal records of Carlisle, Cumberland and Westmorland A.A.S. transactions, extra series, vol. iv.

Armstrong, R. B. *The History of Liddesdale,* Vol. I (Edinburgh, 1883).

Balfour, James. *Practicks, or a System of the more ancient law of Scotland* (Edinburgh, 1754).

Bates, C. J. *History of Northumberland* (London, 1895).

Black, J. B. *The Reign of Elizabeth, 1558–1603* (Oxford University Press, 1962, 1965).

Borland, R. *Border Raids and Reivers* (Glasgow, 1910).

Bowden, Peter J. *The Wool Trade in Tudor and Stuart England* (London, 1962).

Bruce, J. Collingwood. *Handbook to the Roman Wall* (Newcastle, 1947).

Cambridge Modern History, Vol. II, *The Reformation* (Cambridge University Press, 1903).

Carey, Robert. *Memoirs* (London, 1747).

The Complete Peerage.

Dickinson, W. C., G. Donaldson, and I. A. Milne. *Source Book of Scottish History.* 2 vols. (London, 1958).

Elliot, G. F. S. *The Border Elliots and the Family of Minto* (Edinburgh, 1897).

Flinn, M. W. *Economic and Social History of Britain, 1066–1939* (London, 1962; St. Martin's Press, 1962).

Fordun, John. *Chronicle of the Scottish Nation.* Ed. William F. Skene (Edinburgh, 1872).

Fraser, William. *The Scotts of Buccleuch,* Vol. I (Edinburgh, 1878).

Froissart, Jean. *Chronicles.* Trans. Berners, ed. G. and W. Anderson (London, 1963, Southern Illinois University Press, 1964).

Graham, John. *Condition of the Border at the Union* (London, 1907).

Hadrian's Wall (Ministry of Public Buildings and Works publication, H.M.S.O., 1962).

Hardie, R. P. *Roads of Medieval Lauderdale* (Edinburgh, 1942).

Harrower, Kate. Presidential address, Medical Women's Federation, on the medical history of the Tudors (1956).

Hasbach, W. *History of the English Agricultural Labourer* (London, 1920, Kelley, 1908).

Hume Brown, P. *History of Scotland*. 2 vols. (Cambridge, 1911).

Jenkins, Elizabeth. *Elizabeth the Great* (London, 1965; Coward, 1959; Putnam, 1969).

Johnstone, C. L. *History of the Johnstones* (London, 1909; Supplement, Glasgow, 1925).

McDowall, William. *History of Dumfries* (Edinburgh, 1867).

McIntire, Walter T. *Lakeland and the Borders of Long Ago* (Carlisle, 1949).

Mack, James Logan. *The Border Line* (Edinburgh, 1926).

Mackenzie, Agnes Muir. *The Scotland of Queen Mary* (London, 1936).

Mackie, J. D. *The Earlier Tudors, 1485–1558* (Oxford University Press, 1952).

Mackie, R. L. *Short History of Scotland* (Edinburgh, 1930; Praeger, 1963).

Macmillan, Donald. *Short History of the Scottish People* (London, 1915).

Maxwell-Irving, A. M. T. *The Irvings of Bonshaw* (1968).

Murray, Sir Thomas. *The Laws and Acts of Parliament . . . of Scotland* (Edinburgh, 1681).

Neale, J. E. *Queen Elizabeth I* (London, 1967; St. Martin's Press, 1959).

New Cambridge Modern History, Vol. I *The Renaissance* (Cambridge University Press, 1957).

Nicolson, J., and R. Burn. *History and Antiquities of Westmorland and Cumberland* (London, 1777).

Nicolson, William. *Leges Marchiarum* (London, 1747).

Oman, C. W. C. "The Development of the Art of War, 1517–58", and "The Elizabethan Army" (in *Social England*), Vol. III ed. H. D. Traill and J. S. Mann (London, 1901).

Ordnance Survey of Great Britain. 7th series, 63, 64, 68–71, 75–7.

Pease, Howard. *The Lord Wardens of the Marches of England and Scotland* (London, 1913).

Rae, Thomas I. *The Administration of the Scottish Frontier, 1513–1603* (Edinburgh, 1966; Aldine, 1966).

Rennie, James Alan. *The Scottish People* (London, 1960).

Ridpath, George. *The Border History of England and Scotland* (Berwick, 1858).

Rowse, A. L. *The England of Elizabeth* (London, 1964; Macmillan, 1961).

Speed, John. *History of Great Britain* (London, 1629).

Scot, W. *Metrical history of the honourable families of the name of Scot and Elliot . . .* (Edinburgh, 1892).

Scott, Walter. *The Border Antiquities of England and Scotland*. 2 vols. (London, 1814). *Minstrelsy of the Scottish Border*. 3 vols. (London, 1869; Singing Tree, 1967).

Topping, George, and John Potter. *Memories of Old Carlisle*. (Carlisle, 1922).

Tough, D. L. W. *The Last Years of a Frontier*. (Oxford, 1928).

Trevelyan, G. M. *English Social History*. (London, 1946; Tartan McKay, 1965).

GLOSSARY

In quoting from the letters and reports of Wardens, and from State papers, I have not presumed to tamper with the splendours of sixteenth-century spelling, except in one or two extreme cases where it was absolutely necessary. Here and there I have inserted a translation in parentheses, and it may be that the following glossary of terms will be useful.

bewray: betray.
broken men: men without a responsible head or chief, but not necessarily outlaws.
bruiking: possessing.
cairting: playing at cards.
Captain: the guardian of an area, but not apparently obliged to "follow the fray except it come to him".
champian: level open country.
cleared, cleane: innocent.
Constable: the commander of tenants on castle lands who might be called on to serve either in the castle or in the field.
fyled, fouled: found guilty, case proved.
gar: make.
heirschip: harrying, plundering.
insight: household goods.
Land-sergeant: the principal officer of an area, such as Gilsland. His duties, like those of most subordinate Border officers, are far from clear, but he appears to have been able to act independently in guarding his charge.
nolt, nowt: cattle.
patisht: in agreement or covenant with.
plump watch: guard of a troop or party.
pricker: scout, light horseman.
pullyn: poultry.
rode: raid.
shifting, shyfting: making do, providing.
siclyk: suchlike.
speir: inquire.
valentine: royal warrant for arrest.
wight: robust, vigorous.

INDEX